The Global Economy
Today, Tomorrow, and the Transition

Edited by
Howard F. Didsbury, Jr.

WORLD FUTURE SOCIETY
Bethesda, MD • U.S.A.

Editor: Howard F. Didsbury, Jr.

Editorial Review Board:
James J. Crider, Howard F. Didsbury, Jr. (chairman), Charles H. Little, Andrew A. Spekke and George J. Viksnins

Staff Editors: Edward Cornish, Daniel Fields

Production Manager: Jefferson Cornish

Editorial Coordinator: Sarah Warner

Editorial Consultants:
Cecelia Faith Kelly, Patty McNally, Frances Segraves

Layout and Production Assistant: Judy Dillon

Published by:
World Future Society
4916 St. Elmo Avenue
Bethesda, Maryland 20814-5089 • U.S.A.

Copyright © 1985 World Future Society
All rights reserved
No part of this book may be reproduced by any means, nor transmitted, nor translated into machine language without the written permission of the copyright holder.

Library of Congress Catalog Number: 85-062031

International Standard Book Number: 0-930242-28-9

Printed in the United States of America

Contents

Introduction vi

The World Economy: European Overviews

How Do We Manage the Global Society?
Jan Tinbergen 3

Global Problems in an Interdependent World
József Bognár 16

The Problem of Unemployment

Global Unemployment: Challenge to Futurists
Bertram Gross and Kusum Singh 35

Social Values, Political Goals, and Economic Systems:
The Issues of Employment in European Societies
Jacques F. Lesourne 60

The Prospect of Work in the Western Context
David Macarov 76

The Search for Appropriate Development Models

The Japanese Development Model
E. Wayne Nafziger 111

The Family Farm: A Success Story with Global Implications
Orville Freeman 135

The Economic Impact of the Emerging Global
Information Economy on Lesser Developed Nations
Kenneth B. Taylor 147

Debt and World Trade

Latin American Debt:
Lessons and Pending Issues
Eduardo Wiesner 167

The United States as the World's Largest Debtor:
Implications for the International Trade Environment
Richard L. Drobnick 175

Asian-Pacific Economic Developments

Japan and Asian-Pacific Economic Integration
Hiroshi Kitamura 193

Decision of the Central Committee
of the Communist Party of China
and Reform of the Economic Structure 211

Formulas for Productivity Growth

Productivity Standard for a Healthier Global Economy
Christos N. Athanasopoulos 239

The Global Economy Requires Greater U.S. Productivity
Charles W. McMillion 251

Oil: Past and Future

Economic Growth Before and After
the Oil Crisis and the
Possibility of Deindustrialization
Yoshihiro Kogane 267

1995: The Turning Point in Oil Prices
Hamid Gholamnezhad 296

Conventional Economic Assumptions Questioned

Post-Economic Policies for Post-Industrial Societies
Hazel Henderson 317

Bioeconomics: A Realistic Appraisal of Future Prospects
William H. Miernyk 334

The Crisis of Industrial Overcapacity: Avoiding Another
Great Depression
Frederick C. Thayer 353

Note

This volume was prepared in conjunction with a special conference of the World Future Society, "The Global Economy: Today, Tomorrow, and the Transition," held in Washington, D.C., August 8-9, 1985. The general chairman of the conference was Kenneth W. Hunter. He was assisted by Scott Foote, staff coordinator.

Many people have generously contributed to the success of this volume. A special word of thanks is due Professor Jan Tinbergen, who offered invaluable advice and assistance.

The papers presented here were selected from a large number submitted to the Editorial Review Committee. A number of distinguished papers whose subject matter did not lie within the limits of the volume could not be included.

Footnotes and other academic paraphernalia have been minimized to avoid disrupting the flow of the authors' ideas and insights.

Introduction

From the end of World War II until approximately 1973, the United States experienced sustained economic growth. Its economy had few, if any, serious competitors. But now the mass media, study and research groups, presidential commissions, and congressional hearings bear witness to a new phenomenon—an interrelated, international global economy powered by a spirit of intense competition.

National and international theories are being reexamined. "National" varieties of capitalism and emerging varieties of "national" communism suggest that orthodox rigidity is incompatible with the real world. Orthodox economic thinking, while innocuous in the classroom, is useless in today's complex world.

The Roman poet-philosopher Lucretius said, "When confronted with ignorance, theories abound." This observation seems applicable today. Kondratieff cycles, periods of technological innovation and ultimate market saturation, and the role of defense expenditures as a means of avoiding market saturation or a means of providing socially acceptable waste are being studied anew. Fresh thinking is needed for this new age of a global economy.

Policies aimed at assuring sustainable growth are the goals of the West. Less-developed countries are in search of conditions favorable to their development.

The papers included in this volume focus on a variety of global economic challenges. They have been separated into eight sections in an effort to assist the reader.

1. *The World Economy: European Overviews*

Western and European perspectives are presented. Jan Tinbergen poses important questions on "How Do We Manage the Global Society?" and Jozsef Bognar examines "Global Problems in an Interdependent World."

2. *The Problem of Unemployment*

Bertram Gross and Kusum Singh, in "Global Unemployment: Challenge to Futurists," note: "The specter of more and more jobless people haunts the modern world.... Global joblessness by the year 2000—with all the accompanying poverty, disease and social breakdown—could easily victimize a billion people." The authors call for a constructive approach in meeting this challenge based upon a moral vision "that weaves the highest human values together with the strands of specific macro- and micro-policies." They write approvingly of the draft pastoral letter on the American economy recently issued by the American Catholic bishops.

A European viewpoint is presented by Jacques F. Lesourne in his "Social Values, Political Goals and Economic Systems: The Issue of Employment in European Societies." "Around 2020, when economic historians consider the rise of unemployment in European societies of the 1980s," he observes, "there is little doubt that they will be as amazed about the inadequacy of our analysis, the inconsistency of our projections or the inefficiency of our policies as we are when we study the reactions of our grandparents to the economic situation of the 1930s." His paper includes a number of scenarios, all of which assume modest world economic growth.

David Macarov's "The Prospect of Work in the Western Context" confronts the problem of unemployment (and work in general) from a stimulating and provocative perspective:

> "New technology will bring about an even more rapid increase in per-person productivity than has been known in the past, resulting in more goods and services, as well as shorter hours and more unemployment. Needing more jobs but less work, society will attempt to maintain the present emphasis on human labor as its central value and structural base by dividing jobs into smaller and smaller components; by condoning, if not encouraging, the maintenance of useless jobs and the growth of unproductive work time; and by engaging in various job-creation and job-sharing schemes."

Finally, Macarov believes that, after what may prove to be a period of great strains and tensions, it will be recognized "that human labor need play only a minor role in a healthy economy."

3. The Search for Appropriate Development Models

In "The Japanese Development Model," E. Wayne Nafziger advances a provocative thesis. "The Japanese development model (JDM) from 1868, following the restoration of the Meiji emperor, through the late 1930s is different," he notes, "from the JDM after the 1945-1947 U.S. occupational land, educational, labor union, antitrust, and political reforms." From the Meiji period to the late 30s the JDM has "application to low-income and lower-middle-income countries from noncommunist sub-Saharan Africa and south and southeast Asia. These countries are in earlier stages of industrialization . . . and have an average real income perhaps comparable to 1868 Japan. I argue that the appropriate JDM for these countries is from 1868 through the late 1930s, rather than the period after 1945."

For Orville Freeman, the family farm is the key to sound development. "The family farm is a practical manifestation . . . of how high technology and human freedom can be melded—indeed, must be melded—for optimum results." Freeman believes that "agriculture today is at the forefront of technological advance." The improvement of agriculture would "reverse the massive migration of impoverished people from the countryside to horrible, putrid city slums that is taking place all over the world." Freeman concludes his observations by offering "five keys to understanding the full meaning and impact of agriculture."

4. *Debt and World Trade*

Eduardo Wiesner offers a succinct account of the factors underlying the debt crisis in his article "Latin American Debt: Lessons and Pending Issues." He feels that "the traditional absorption approach should be complemented to take into account the difficulties of developing countries in absorbing external savings efficiently." He then comments on the role of risk in the debt problem. He concludes by noting key issues facing policymakers in Latin American countries.

Latin American debt is not the only cause for great concern. Richard L. Drobnick's "The United States as the World's Largest Debtor: Implications for the International Trade Environment" raises important issues. "In the space of three years, the United States reversed its 70-year-long tradition as a net capital exporter to become a net capital importer. Although its unprecedented $100 billion per year current-account deficits are making it technically possible for LDCs to service their renegotiated debts, these deficits are leading to the decimation of both low- and high-technology industry in the United States. Demands for 'fair' or 'reciprocal' trade relations are becoming popular and increasingly acceptable to a broad section of the American business community." The author cautions, "The adoption of such policies would accelerate what might already be an irreversible trend towards the formal creation of preferential trading blocks."

5. *Asian-Pacific Economic Developments*

"The Asian-Pacific region has recently been building up one of the most integrated high-growth systems of increasingly interdependent nations. That system has been characterized by an increasing share of regional trade taking the form of intra-industry specialization, which opens up the possibility of developing a well-balanced, self-contained, and stable grouping of highly efficient economies in the area." So writes Hiroshi Kitamura in "Japan and Asian-Pacific Economic Integration." He feels, "The formation of... [a] regional network of intra-industry specialization provides a unique chance for transforming Japan's traditional 'self-sufficient' industrial structure into a more balanced and mature shape. This, in turn, will possibly lead to the development of a ... self-contained economic community of nations in the Asian-Pacific region." Such a development should "be regarded as supplementary to and supportive of a genuine global solution to world trade problems."

Readers interested in the current "Chinese economic revolution" should find the full text of the "Decision of the Central Committee of the Communist Party of China on Reform of the Economic Structure" highly informative.

6. *Formulas for Productivity Growth*

"'Productivity standard,' simply put," Christos N. Athanasopoulos points out in "Productivity Standard for a Healthier Global Economy," "means tying wage and salary rates to productivity gains, but neither at the departmental or functional level (as piece rates for blue-collar workers only) nor at the national level (with uniform rates and terms across whole diverse industries, as labor-management contracts are drawn up now). Ideally, the productivity standard should be applied at the company level. It can also be applied at the divisional or as far down as the plant level." "The crucial point," Athanasopoulos insists, "is that wage increases do not outpace productivity gains."

To meet global economic competition effectively, Charles W. McMillion believes the United States must do three things: "establish a reasonable and stable currency exchange rate system," "dismantle unfair and nonproductive foreign trade practices," and "dramatically increase economic productivity." In addition, the author's "The Global Economy Requires Greater U.S. Productivity" stresses the importance of an effective partnership on the part of government with business and labor.

7. *Oil: Past and Future*

Yoshihiro Kogane's "Economic Growth Before and After the Oil Crisis and the Possibility of Deindustrialization" is rich in facts and ideas about the economies of the United States, Europe and Japan. Kogane presents a broad historical survey encompassing growth rates and an analysis of the four cycles in the past 20 years of industrialization. He foresees a crisis period in a fifth cycle in the 1990s. He suggests three options for coping with this crisis.

"1995: The Turning Point in Oil Prices" sets forth Hamid Gholamnezhad's model to predict oil prices in 1995. The model considers both quantitative and qualitative factors affecting oil prices. The method used is called the analytic heirarchy process— a method with demonstrated effectiveness for this type of problem. The author feels that by using an appropriate model and good judgment, one can arrive at viable answers in a very short time.

8. *Conventional Economic Assumptions Questioned*

Whereas the previous authors seem to share similar economic assumptions with respect to global economic problems, the three authors in this final section do not. Each offers a critique of these assumptions on the one hand and suggestions for alternative policies on the other.

Hazel Henderson, in "Post-Economic Policies for Post-Industrial Societies" writes: "Our current models and theories of economics, being based on equilibrium assumptions, cannot deal adequately with the forces at work in the transformation to post-industrial societies. In particular, they have no capacity to cope with the phenomenon of irreversibility. Furthermore, they consider technology to be a parameter rather than the central dynamic of industrial societies. Because all policy decisions made by our government and financial institutions rely on the recommendations of economists using macroeconomic theory, it is critically important that these theories be applicable to our times. There is ample evidence they are not." Many reasons are given as to why present economic theory is unsuitable for the management of post-industrial societies.

William H. Miernyk's "Bioeconomics: A Realistic Appraisal of Future Prospects" presents a comparison betweeen conventional economics and bioeconomics. The former concludes that free-market pricing will ensure optimal allocations of resources and energy, as well as an equitable distribution of output. It ignores energy and resource constraints on economic growth by accepting the principle of unlimited substitutability. Bioeconomist Miernyk considers the economic process to be cumulative and irreversible. Because of entropy, supplies of energy and resources will steadily diminish. Strict conservation is imperative. Market forces will not result in the optimal allocation of resources under conditions of absolutely diminishing returns. They will have to be supplanted by noncoercive, strategic planning. This will work in a democratic society only if unstable competitive forces are replaced by an ve process.

...st to the current talk concerning the need for ...u productivity, Frederick C. Thayer's analysis in "The crisis of Industrial Overcapacity: Avoiding Another Great Depression" finds excessive industrial capacity and output and agricultural overproduction to be the causes of economic crises. "Economic history clearly indicates that, under conditions of unrestricted competition and free trade, overcapacity and/or overproduction are inevitable, and are the recurring cause of 'panics' or depressions." He adds:

> "All contemporary global economic problems are byproducts of unrestricted competition and trade that, if not completely 'free,' is much too free to permit stability. On these matters, all widely-known economic theories, including Marxism, are equally wrong, if not in precisely the same manner. Obviously, a new approach must move beyond all such theories while allowing for redistribution and alternative approaches to finding jobs, principally by a considerable shift in emphasis from the unnecessary overproduction of private goods to the necessary production of such public goods as social infrastructure. Any such solution will have to cut across both national and ideological boundaries."

Howard F. Didsbury, Jr.

The World Economy:
European Overviews

How Do We Manage the Global Society?

By
Jan Tinbergen

1. Forty years of socioeconomic development

Some 40 years ago, World War II came to an end. A period of intense suffering finished, in which millions and millions of victims had been made, leaving impoverished survivors—many of them disabled—amidst ruins. Once again, humankind was given an opportunity to use its capabilities for better purposes—for well-being and happiness instead of death, sorrow, and want. Perhaps the last opportunity.

The main subject to be discussed in this essay is how human society has to be designed in order that, indeed, prosperity is our future and new disasters can be avoided. It seems appropriate to remind the reader of what, in the 40 years that have elapsed, has been attained and what has not been attained.

A large part of physical damage was reconstructed, production of goods and services for peaceful ends resumed, and, in large parts of the world, prosperity increased, even though population grew at an unprecedented rate. New technologies helped to increase productivity and both world production and world trade expanded.

Not everywhere, however, and not constantly. In the underdeveloped continents, where population increase was largest, large groups did not share in the increase in prosperity. The number of undernourished rose. Inequality between real incomes in the world's countries increased, even though the interdependence of national economies also became stronger.

In addition, some of the new technologies, and the expansion of some productive activities, introduced new difficulties. The

---

Jan Tinbergen is professor emeritus at the University of Leiden, The Hague, Netherlands. He shared the Nobel Prize in economics in 1969.

human environment—the atmosphere, water, and soil—deteriorated: Desertification, erosion, pollution, and acid rain increasingly threatened health and food production. Prosperity did not increase as much as was initially believed and planned for.

Another unfavorable feature was a new type of economic depresssion, consisting of stagnant production and employment but rising prices (inflation). Economists and politicians needed a reorientation in order to understand this unusual combination, and it took years before finally some recovery from this "stagflation" started in 1983, in only part of the countries affected.

Perhaps the most dangerous new development of all, finally, was an ever-increasing armament race, mainly between the two superpowers (the United States and the Soviet Union) and their alliances, NATO and Warsaw Pact (WP). Technological development in this activity introduced nuclear weapons—and with them a more serious threat to the world at large than ever before.

Toward the end of World War II, the then independent nations had understood that, in order to avoid new armed conflicts, more international cooperation was necessary. They established the United Nations as a successor to the prewar League of Nations, and this time the United States became a member. A process of decolonization transformed most of the colonies into sovereign new nations, which all wanted to become members of the United Nations. The number of member countries now surpasses 150, the majority of which are economically underdeveloped. A number of them are very small and may be nonviable.

The UN General Assembly held not only its regular annual meetings but also a series of Special Sessions, in which subjects of particular importance were discussed. Among these subjects were population growth, new forms of international economic cooperation, food production, human environment and disarmament. A considerable quantity of relevant information resulted from these activities. The effect on political decision-making was far less positive, however; most of the resolutions passed by the General Assembly did not result in relevant changes in the policies of the large industrial nations.

The Assembly and the Secretariat of the UN are not the only of what is known as the "family of UN institutions." This family consists of a large number of other institutions, including some that are older than the UN, such as the International Labor Organization (ILO), and some that have been reorganized, institutions such as the international Food and Agricultural Organization (FAO).

Among the important new institutions established around the war years are the "Bretton Woods" organizations: the World Bank

Group (as it is now called) and the International Monetary Fund (IMF). These two financial institutions provide their member countries with loans—the World Bank Group for long-term objectives (development investments) and the IMF for short-term objectives (to equilibrate the balance of payments). These institutions were able, as a consequence of their organizations and their management, to contribute positively to their aims in a significant way. The IMF may have imposed too heavy conditions on some of its borrowing members; this is an open question. The number of votes of less-developed countries, however, is too low in both institutions.

Unfortunately, the present American administration has not been cooperative in providing the funds needed by the International Development Association (IDA), the "cheap window" of the World Bank Group. Here is a task for Japan and the EEC to compensate for this American shortsightedness, likely to damage the United States itself in the long run.

Among the younger UN institutions, two are the UN Conference on Trade and Development (UNCTAD) and the UN Industrial Development Organization (UNIDO). Both have had limited success so far, for the same reason as the General Assembly.

An attempt to create, as a complement to the Bretton Woods institutions, an International Trade Organization (ITO), was unsuccessful, and this lack of success was only partly compensated for by the establishment of the General Agreement on Tariffs and Trade (GATT). A number of "rounds" of reduction of trade impediments obtained must be judged positively, although the developing countries profited less from them than the developed countries.

This brief sketch of 40 years of socioeconomic development must be completed with some remarks on the most important task of the United Nations, that of peacekeeping, with which mainly the UN Security Council is charged. This task can only be taken care of in cases of conflicts between countries less powerful than the main powers. Conflicts among the main powers cannot be solved, because these powers can veto the Council's decisions. In particular, the most important threat to world security, the armament race between NATO and the Warsaw Pact, is dealt with mainly by these two organizations—or even only the United States and the Soviet Union.

It is against the background of these 40 years of experiences that we propose to discuss the necessary reorientation of international cooperation.

2. How to learn from errors and from new ideas

Looking back, we cannot doubt that in the past 40 years many mistakes have been made, whose avoidance might have made the world's present situation and prospects better. In order to plan for the future, we have two main sources of inspiration: We must try to learn from these mistakes, and we must try to develop new ideas by rethinking the doctrines adhered to over the past 40 years.

Errors have been made by single persons, by groups, and by institutions. In order to give some structure to our argument, it may be useful to make such distinctions. We may also try to distinguish between different types of mistakes. Thus, the interests of the individuals or groups considered may have been damaged, for instance, by acting too traditionally, or too slowly, or too shortsightedly. Another type of mistake, in contrast, may be that their interests have been served too strongly, damaging others' interests too much. Finally, the essence of an error may be that some institutions, although badly needed, have not been created.

In an attempt to trace the most important errors made, let us start considering the activities of others than the UN family of institutions. These "others" may be the member countries of the UN, or political parties, or powerful enterprises. Among the member countries, there are many "soft states" in Myrdal's sense (Myrdal, 1970). Soft states do not optimally deal with their own nation's interests.

We already mentioned one mistake: that too-small nations have been created by too large a desire to be sovereign. Still another mistake is that, maybe as a reaction to softness, too-militarized governments seize power. Too much emphasis on sovereignty is a generally committed error by practically all national governments—and in particular by the superpowers. The misunderstanding at the basis of the preference for sovereignty is the belief that sovereignty implies being able to determine the nation's lot, i.e., to maximize the country's welfare. This is not correct, because other countries are able, as a consequence of the high degree of interdependence, also to influence that welfare.

The attitude of many social groups and political parties has blocked various attempts at a more intensive and more equitable international cooperation. In developed countries, both employers and employees, and consequently their associations and unions, in industries unable to compete on the world market made the mistake of exerting pressure on governments to protect them by trade impediments or subventions. Similarly, British parties have opposed joining the European Economic Community. French peasant organizations opposed the entry of Spain and Portugal into the EEC. So did fishery organizations.

In the business world, a number of multinationals did not always behave in the interest of the countries in which they operate. This induced several institutions to design codes for good behavior. The baby-food question is one example. Of course, there are many other instances in which multinationals have made positive contributions.

Looking now at the errors committed by the UN family of institutions, a distinction may be made between an erroneous setup of some of these institutions, that is, their charter, and a wrong use of the possibilities offered by that charter. The 40-year experience has made it abundantly clear that the system of one vote for each member does not work. The other extreme, where only financial contributions determine the number of votes, is not optimal either. Parliamentary history of democratic countries may be consulted to arrive at some guideline. Initially, these countries also had voting rights only for the wealthy. They now have voting rights for all adults who have had some minimum of schooling. International institutions may follow a similar process, although adapted to the much larger differences in schooling existing among nations.

Experience also teaches that the effectiveness of many institutions also suffers from a lack of competence or terms of reference and, in addition, a lack of power to implement their decisions. This power may be undermined in particular by a veto power of some, or all, members. It means that only unanimous decisions can be implemented.

Erroneous use of an institution's charter is a more subjective concept, in need of some criterion to evaluate the voting behavior of member states. Taking world welfare as such a criterion, it may be stated that in numerous cases the rich countries' votes neglected the interests of a majority of the world's population. This is less important, however, than a nonimplementation of resolutions adopted by UN institutions. The attitude assumed by the developed world vis-a-vis the New International Economic Order is the more recent and most important example. A concrete case in this category is the attitude of the present American government with regard to the replenishment of IDA, where an amount of $9 billion was offered instead of the $16 billion needed (on the basis of a careful analysis).

As observed, future policies should be inspired not only by drawing lessons from errors but also by innovating ideas or developing new insights. One of the most important concepts for the solution of our problem is the concept of the optimum level of decision-making. It applies to decision-making in hierarchical structures, such as big enterprises, public authorities, and—in particular in communist countries—political party organizations. For our problem, public authorities in a large country are the closest example since the hierarchy considered has both a geographic and a spatial dimension. The lowest-level public authorities may be municipal and the highest may be national. Between these extremes, we may have districts, provinces, and states; the names vary among countries, but an authority one level higher is responsible for an area subdivided into smaller areas at the level considered. For the solution of different problems, decisions may be taken at different levels; closer investigation shows that the interests of the nation's total population will be taken care of in the best way if the necessary decisions are taken at one particular level. This will be called the optimum level and will be discussed in the next section.

Another example of new ideas, already formulated, is that sovereignty of a nation is not as attractive an idea as is often believed.

Finally, new ideas have been developed as a consequence of new scientific discoveries or theories. The rapid development of chemisty and biology has led to phenomena of pollution and the necessity to reflect on ways and means to reduce it. The development of physics brought the discovery of nuclear energy which had an enormous impact on industrial as well as military possibilities.

Summing up, in the future world society another type of management is possible, and the changes in management may be based on our desire to avoid a number of mistakes made and to profit from new ideas about the optimal way to manage world society. In other words, we may find ways and means to reform and improve the effectiveness of the family of United Nations institutions.

3. Optimal management

Instead of the disorderly, entangled present forms of international cooperation, in some respects fairly effective and in other respects ineffective and uncoordinated, we are in serious need of a systematic vision in order to design a more coherent view on how to solve the many problems we face. Such a vision can only be arrived at if we try to develop a "helicopter view"—an expression used to indicate what is needed to manage a large enterprise. Surely world society is not an enterprise: its aims are different; but in several aspects, political leadership can learn from able businessmen. It will not be the first time that a society (usually a national society) is tested by comparing it with a great firm, even though we know perfectly well that society must have other tasks than pure business ventures. So management science certainly enables us to better understand how to organize our thinking and deciding.

The helicopter view now needed implies our viewing the world as a whole; that is, to understand that the world's nations and their alliances are so interdependent that another approach simply is unrealistic. What we need is a set of institutions that together may be called a world social order. This means, in essence, that thinking in terms of separate sovereign entities (superpowers or the alliances with which they have surrounded themselves—NATO and the Warsaw Pact) falls short of what is needed. Even the superpowers' lot cannot be determined soley by their own decisions; rather, it will be codetermined by what other powers are going to do. For smaller nations, this applies even more, of course.

If this view is correct (and we think it is), one very important conclusion is already apparent: we must tackle the problem at the world level from the start—and not by negotiations among representatives of sovereign powers, but among representatives of the various aspects of world aims.

Since for any policy or any social order, decisions have to be based on the aims pursued, identifying the aims in more concrete language is necessary first. Before we can maximize the welfare of the world population, we must first define that welfare. This definition may be the total of welfare of all citizens. The welfare of each citizen depends on the citizen's consumption of all consumer goods and on the satisfaction derived from his or her occupation. In addition, the availability of public goods or infrastructure must be considered. The way in which these elements contribute to total welfare may also depend on the inequality aversion in the reference groups the citizens belong to. Although scientific attempts to estimate the welfare of nations have been available (cf. D.W. Jorgenson, 1983, and B.M.S. van Praag, 1971) for quite some time, intuitive or simplified (cf. I.B. Kravis et al., 1982) methods will have to be used.

The maximum of total welfare will have to be aimed at under a number of restrictions humankind is subjected to. These are restrictions imposed by nature, such as climatic conditions, but also the laws of nature that production processes are depending on and a number of psychological features of human beings. Conditions of a political nature must not be accepted, however, since it is these that we want to change in our common interest.

The means to be used in order to attain the aims are the set of institutions or the world social order mentioned, and here an important concept is the optimum level of decision-making about the instruments to be used for implementing the decisions and the intensity with which to use the instruments. We will now specify this optimum level, mentioned in the previous section. Any decision taken by some authority affects both the population for which that authority is responsible (internal effects) and the population for which that authority is not responsible (external effects). The optimal level must be as low as possible, so as to allow as much participation or democracy as possible. It must also be high enough to have negligible external effects, since the decision-making authority will not take into account—or not sufficiently—the interests of populations for which it is not responsible.

In order to clarify the concepts defined, some specific examples of the institutions of the world order will now be discussed. A distinction between concrete and abstract institutions will be helpful.

Examples of concrete institutions are government departments and the school system. Among other things, government departments order a number of needed public goods, such as the infrastructure of transportation and energy and water supply. The Treasury organizes the collection of financial means to pay for the public goods ordered. The school system, from the lowest to the highest levels, has to provide for the formal education of the labor force and also has to satisfy the social demand for schooling.

Other concrete institutions are private and public production units where the goods and services, including public goods, are produced and distributed, often subdivided into primary, secondary, and tertiary sectors.

The most important abstract institution is that of markets, where, in perfect or imperfect competition, production units sell their products, and other units (as well as family households) buy investment or consumption goods and supply factors of production.

The examples mentioned can all be found within national societies. Our main interest, however, is directed at discussing to what extent similar institutions serving more than one nation are needed.

This is desirable in particular for small countries and implies that these should conclude treaties by which they integrate themselves into larger units. The already most advanced examples are the European Communities (EC) and the Andean Common Market. The European Communities are a combination of the

European Coal and Steel Community, the European Atomic Energy Community (Euratom), and the European Economic Community. The ten member-countries (in 1985) do have a number of common institutions, including a parliament, the Council of Ministers (which might be called the Executive), and the Commission. Decisions of the Council are prepared by initiatives of the Commission. The Commission is assisted by the Administration (Secretariat).

Conflicts between member-countries and the Commission can be submitted to the European Court. Financial control of the Administration is the competence of the European Audit Office. The structure briefly described implies that the member-countries have transferred a number of elements of their sovereignty to the European Administration, including, in particular, agricultural and trade policies. More transfers are in preparation, for instance in the field of transportation. A European Investment Bank finances some types of investments. Pressure is exerted by important international enterprises to accelerate integration and to come to a common industrial policy.

Although similar integration is to the advantage of groups of smaller countries in each others' neighborhood—as, for instance, in the Caribbean—this is not always adhered to by these countries. They are insufficiently aware of the threats to their material well-being as a consequence of remaining very small sovereign units; as observed, they overestimate sovereignty.

On the basis of the criterion set out—negligibility of external effects—some important institutions of today's world must operate at the world level. This applies—to begin with a not-too-controversial example—to some environmental institutions, especially those for atmospheric and oceanic purity. Pollution of both the atmosphere and the ocean tends to spread over the earth as a whole and can only be controlled under a worldwide authority. This kind of cooperation should be started as soon as possible.

The same argument applies, however, to a very controversial subject, security. As long as the sovereignty of more than one authority in the field of security is maintained, the world's security cannot be guaranteed. Security can exist only if one world authority is in charge. In different terminology, peaceful coexistence requires an institution in charge of world security. In still other words, peaceful coexistence requires a world police force able to implement security decisions taken by a world security council with well-defined voting rules and without a veto. Whoever considers such a structure impossible or undesirable blocks the future of mankind. Of all the lessons to be learned, this abstention from sovereignty for some fields of activity is by far the most important one. It requires a considerable quantity of independent thinking and a nondogmatic mentality. The main argument in favor of such a partial transfer of sovereignty to the world level is the self-interest of the superpowers. Smaller nations are able to understand this more easily; but everywhere nationalist intuition will object. Yet it is the basic condition for survival.

4. How to implement the optimal world order?

Once agreement on a number of main features of the optimal world order has been reached, a complicated process of implementation must be designed. In this section, an attempt will be made to identify some components of this process. Starting from the definition of a social order as a set of institutions, each characterized by a number of aims and means, we can make a distinction between institutions that can be obtained by reforming existing institutions and institutions that must be newly created.

It stands to reason that the most urgent reforms are those of important institutions for the material existence of humanity. As such important institutions, the Bretton Woods institutions, the World Bank Group, and the IMF must be considered. Two essential proposals, submitted on various occasions, concern (a) the distribution of voting rights and (b) the expansion of the financial means to be made available.

In both institutions, the voting rights of the member nations depend on their financial contributions, with an upper limit. For the Bretton Woods institutions, logical steps might be to let the number of votes depend on the size of each country's population and to reserve a number of seats for experts from developing countries in the fields covered by the Bank Group and the IMF. Thus, the presidents of the investment banks of the largest countries in Asia, Africa, and Latin America might conceivably be members ex officio of the Executive Boards.

With regard to the financial means, concrete proposals are available for the IDA and the IMF and, to begin with, these could be implemented.

The other UN institutions are also faced with a problem of voting rights, from the General Assembly to UNESCO. If, as a perspective, the UN family of institutions has to develop into some form of World Management, it is unsatisfactory that very large and very small nations each have one vote. It is more natural for the number of votes to depend on the number of inhabitants. At the same time, this might constitute an encouragement for small nations to integrate into larger units, if, for small countries, votes increase more than proportionately with population.

There are numerous other reforms to be considered, but the present essay constitutes an attempt to concentrate on the more important among them. It is particularly in the field of trade policy that the 40-year history led to some less satisfactory developments. The Havana conference devoted to this field proposed the creation of an International Trade Organization (ITO), but this proposal was not implemented. In view of the importance of international trade and keeping in mind the external effects of any nation's foreign-trade policy, there are good reasons to suggest a completely different approach recognizing that national sovereignty in this field is clearly nonoptimal. And, although the establishment of UNCTAD served a tactical purpose around the period of its birth, we wonder whether trade and development is a logical task description for a future World Trade Department. It seems more logical that the institution dealing with trade policies take into account all its consequences, not only its impact on development. If this is accepted, the implication is that an International Trade Organization may be considered again, this time preferably as a supranational agency, endowed with the competence to make binding decisions and the power to implement them.

The necessity to reform existing institutions is particularly clear for institutions whose optimal level of decision-making—the level with negligible external effects—is the world level. The three cases considered—World Bank, IMF, and ITO—belong to that category.

So does the institution in charge of environmental quality, the UN Environmental Programme (UNEP) in Nairobi, and here again decision-making and implementation should be made effective.

Similarly, the new Law of the Seas, once it is ratified, will introduce an "enterprise" with worldwide decision-making power with respect to the exploitation of ocean resources, especially manganese nodules, in such a way as to optimize world population's welfare.

The most important and also the most difficult subject belonging to the category under discussion is world security, and the agency in charge is the Security Council. This is going to be humanity's test case: Are we wise enough to survive, or don't we have leadership of that format? At the moment of this writing, the Soviet-American negotiations have not yet started. The technique adhered to is negotiations between at least two so-called sovereign powers. Although results are not excluded beforehand, the setting of this process is already suboptimal and will remain so as long as the mythical belief in sovereignty remains adhered to. Rightly, the Independent Commission on Disarmament and Security Issues (Palme Commission, 1982) emphasizes the action principle of common security.

Soviet philosophy is inspired by highly doctrinaire principles and therefore is extremely inelastic. The present American government is not much less inelastic, but American philosophy as a whole and traditionally (in its development over time) is certainly more flexible. What both superpowers and their alliances have to learn is to subordinate their thinking on social order and civilization to a necessary "security roof" accepted by all on the basis of common knowledge about the potentialities of a nuclear war. Since for doctrinaire minds real thinking is very difficult, an intensive exercise in creative discussion of the points indicated is the task we face.

5. The role of nongovernmental organizations (NGOs)

For a long time, the need for world institutions has been stated by farsighted individuals and by a number of nongovernmental organizations. An open letter by Albert Einstein (1932) is an example of the former and the existence of the World Federation of World Federalists an example of the latter. While for a long time only a few persons were involved, in recent years the acute changes in the superpowers' statements, arms build-up, and threats have led to mass movements of protest against the armament race. The policies propagated and the arguments used may not be optimal, but the importance of the phenomenon is that it shows the concern of large sections of society about the effects of the policies followed by today's governments.

Now that even in official circles some authorities (Under-Secretary of Defense Fred Ikle and Kenneth Adelman, Director of the Arms Control Agency, have been mentioned in the press) discuss whether or not a common security policy is the only way out, some pressure from the general public may be helpful to overcome conventional thinking and decision-making. Such pressure would be far more effective if there were a united front of the nongovernmental organizations involved. Unfortunately, a number of competing organizations exist—with the consequence that the efficiency of their effort is suboptimal. The integration of the existing organizations may enhance their impact. This may at the same time increase the number of supporters, which remained small as long as the aims seemed too utopian. The NGOs concerned need to be applauded for their persistence in the face of scepticism, if not worse. It looks likely that suddenly their activities have become less utopian and more realistic than many critics think.

References

Einstein, A. (1932), Open letter to S. Freud, *The Federalist* 26 (1984), p. 76.
Independent Commission on Disarmament and Security Issues (Chairman O. Palme), *Common Security*, New York, Simon and Schuster, 1982.
Jorgenson, D. W., and D. T. Slesnick, "Inequality in the Distribution of Individual Welfare," Disc. Paper no. 987, Harvard Institute of Economic Research, Harvard University, Cambridge, MA, USA, 1983.
Kravis, I. B., et al., *World Product and Income*, published for the World Bank, Johns Hopkins University Press, Baltimore and London, 1982.
Myrdal, G., *The Challenge of World Poverty*, New York, Pantheon Books, 1970.
Van Praag, B. M. S., "The Welfare Function of Income in Belgium: An Empirical Investigation," *European Economic Review*, 1971, and many more publications of the Leyden Income Evaluation Project.

Global Problems in an Interdependent World

by

József Bognár

It was still generally assumed in the 1960s that economic problems would be easier to handle as a result of the scientific and technical revolution. At that time, we already had some knowledge of the complex and contradictory "starting conditions" of the Third World, but the optimists confidently proclaimed that the enormous gaps between the different development levels could be reduced substantially within a few decades.

Contrary to these expectations, in recent decades mankind has been living through a dangerous development crisis that can be seen in its most serious form at present in the economy. The economic crisis has spread from the national economies to international trade and also to the international monetary system. It appears obvious that the protracted, severe crisis will radically transform the conditions for economic development and that survival and the further development of mankind depend on flexible adjustment to the new circumstances. At present, however, there is a sharp contradiction between the requirements of overcoming the economic crisis and establishing the new type of economic development on the one hand and the present evolution of the international political and security situation on the other.

Our intention here is to examine primarily the largest and most comprehensive group of phenomena: the global problems.

One of the characteristics of global problems is that they affect all inhabitants of the globe—even if not to the same extent—regardless of their social system, nationality, religious convictions,

József Bognár—Academician, Director of the Institute for World Economy of the Hungarian Academy of Sciences

or social situation. Another characteristic is that they can only be handled and solved on a global basis. In an international political system based on the independence of nation states and where the international bodies cannot adopt decisions binding on the nation states, a global basis can only mean broad international understanding and organized cooperation.

Among the global problems, we wish to place particular emphasis on the following:

- Evolution and distribution of world population in the coming decades, and the related food problems.
- The limitations of natural resources.
- The threat to ecological systems and our environment.
- The equivocal nature of technology and science.
- The present world political structure.
- Development of the Third World.
- The problems of economic interdependencies in a period of political "high tensions."

Population Growth

In this century, world population will increase four-fold and will be above 6 billion in the year 2000. The population of the developed countries—advanced capitalist countries and the European socialist countries—can be expected to stagnate or decline, and the great majority of the annual increase of 80-90 million will be in the Third World. Demographers and biologists agree that, even after 2000, the rapid population growth cannot be stopped abruptly, for "artificial" birth control comes up against strong religious and social prejudices. The position of the Roman Catholic Church in this respect is well known—it represents a very important factor, particularly in the case of Latin America—as is the very broad mass resistance that has been encountered in a number of Asian and African countries. It can be assumed that the growth in world population is not likely to be stopped before the level of 10-12 billion is reached.

It is obvious that the size of the world population influences all other economic areas: the quantity of the standard of living already attained or set as a goal.

The accelerated population growth in the Third World is the result of the contradiction between the scientific-technical and the social conditions for development. The mortality rate has been successfully reduced with the aid of methods developed in the advanced countries, but the historically determined reproduction habits of the population require a much longer time to adjust to the new situation.

The anticipated distribution of the population in the decades around the turn of the century also means a new situation, because in the year 2000, 81% of world population will live in the developing countries—including the People's Republic of China among the developing countries—and only 19% will live in the developed world. It is obvious that, under such circumstances, there will also be a change in the relative importance of the continents and regions: there will be a great increase in the economic and political aspects of the role of the Asian continent, where the outlines of an economic center (around Japan) are already beginning to emerge; the influence of the Latin American region is substantially increasing—despite all the difficulties, disorders, and inequalities—and new development energies are arising in the Middle East, too, which, for the time being, is struggling with very serious internal contradictions.

Pacific Ocean Nations

A shift is also occurring in the significance of the world oceans: development centered around the Atlantic Ocean is being shifted to the Pacific Ocean. Eleven capitalist countries can be found in the western Pacific basin: Japan, South Korea, Hong Kong, Taiwan, Singapore, Thailand, Malaysia, Indonesia, the Philippines, Australia, and New Zealand. The People's Republic of China also has a long Pacific coastal region.

Based on Japan as the technically and economically advanced Asian country, economic development in this region has greatly accelerated in recent years. This phenomenon merits attention because the basis of the upswing is not a region characterized by an abundance of energy resources and raw materials, but the acceleration of industrial development. Structurally, this industrial development differs from the traditional, because it did not begin with textile exports but with some advanced manufactured products.

The role of this Pacific Ocean region in world trade is increasing at a spectacular rate: in 1981, their share of world exports was 16.9% (of which Japan had 8%) and of world imports was 16% (of which Japan had 7.2%). Merely to give an idea of the relative magnitudes, it is worth noting that, in the same year, the share of the United States in world exports was 12.9% and of world imports 13.8%, while that of the CMEA countries in world exports was 8% and in world imports around 7%.[1]

Parallel to these processes, a marked shift is also taking place in the internal economic and population situation in the United States. Due to internal population migration and a change in the composition of the immigrant population (in favor of Asians and Hispanics), the population of the western and southwestern states is rising rapidly and, in economic terms, California has become the biggest state in the United States. The present world economic situation—the acceleration of the technological revolution and the sharp growth in the funds devoted to the armaments industry—favors the economy of the western states of the United States, while the steel crisis and the problems of the auto and other traditional industries are primarily affecting the eastern states.

The differences that can be observed in the distribution of population and new economic activities, as well as in economic dynamics, are also strongly influencing the internal and external policies of the United States. The result of the shift in internal politics has been that, in the last two elections, the president of the United States has not been selected from among the East Coast politicians, while, in the area of foreign policy, politicians from the West Coast tend to favor a Pacific, rather than an Atlantic, policy.

This shift is very significant and, over the long term, could affect the relationships established between Western Europe and the United States. It cannot influence the relationship with the Soviet Union since both countries are global powers. Naturally, this can (and does) give rise to problems in that politicians from the West Coast states are less familiar with Europe, including Eastern Europe. However, it can be assumed that this situation will change within one or two terms.

Food Supply

The rapid growth in world population and the change in its distribution raise new problems for the food supply, too. According to data of the FAO, 500 million people now face the threat of starvation, while the World Bank's estimate is 750 million. The number of undernourished and threatened is rapidly rising as a result of the rapid population increase. In addition, this growth is largely concentrated in the developing countries, where the agricultural productive forces are underdeveloped and where the social, economic, and organization mechanisms that encourage those on the land to commodity and surplus production have not yet taken shape. Nor is the most mobile factor in tropical agriculture, water, fully exploited, because either the repair of destroyed irrigation systems or the creation of new systems require vast and costly investments and certain international agreements. Nor is it an easy task to bring new areas under cultivation, for the destruction of forests on a large scale can result in serious—and not only regional— climatic dislocations.

The suitable handling of this global problem requires, in part, that:

• The advanced countries extend aid to the developing countries in the development of their agricultural production.

• The advanced countries ensure for decades in some form the quantity of food needed to cover the difference between the agricultural output of these countries and the effective consumption.

However, it must be clearly pointed out that, in the present world economic system, under the present commercial and financial conditions, this is not possible. Consequently, in order to avoid a catastrophe, an international institutional system must be established to promote the solution of these problems.

The limits of natural resources represent the second global problem. Earlier, in the spirit of "technological optimism," it was considered that natural resources are essentially unlimited; at the most, there is a deteriorating trend in the quality and extraction conditions of the minerals extracted. It follows logically from this concept that a steadily increasing volume of both nonrenewable and renewable raw materials is required for the growth of production and consumption.

This form of technological optimism can now be regarded as outdated, for evaluation of the limited or "unlimited" nature of natural resources cannot be independent of:

• How many people have to be supported.
• At what standard of living.
• And what influence the quantity and methods of extraction have on our natural environment.

Classical economics included the concept of free goods (air and water), which have no price. It is now obvious that there are no longer any free goods; air and water also have a price. Indeed, some forecasts even suggest that water requirements (for production and consumption) are rising so rapidly that they will become one of the most problematic factors in mankind's further progress.

It is well known that the per capita area of arable land is declining sharply in the developing countries. There is also increasing acceptance of the view that land suitable for agricultural production can no longer be gained at the expense of forests. However, it follows from this that the ruthless exploitation of timber resources carried out in certain tropical countries must also be stopped; in the future, logging and afforestation must be carried out simultaneously.

Similarly, restrictions must also be anticipated in the case of nonrenewable minerals.

Energy Resources

The market disruptions that occurred in the past decade in connection with energy resources (particularly with oil) are well known. The big fluctuations are now levelling out, although energy prices have stabilized at a very high level. Over the long term, however, this problem will obviously remain a serious one and will exert a great influence on possible economic-policy alternatives.

Further substantial changes can still be expected in the energy structure between 1980 and 2030, according to forecasts. The role of oil will decline (from 42% to 25%); the decline in the proportion of coal will continue (from 26% to 19%); nuclear energy will rise from 3% to 10%; and solar energy, hydro energy, and other renewable resources will rise to 19%.[2]

As a result of industrialization, the energy consumption of the developing countries will continue to rise sharply, and their energy-consumption structure will reach the 1980 structure of the advanced countries only by 2030.

It is obvious from all this that a rational evaluation of the limits of natural resources leads to an economic policy differing considerably from that followed hitherto. This does not mean that we face a catastrophe in the immediate future, but it is obvious that we must not threaten the future generations through ruthless resource exploitation. For this reason, we must make carefully considered use of natural resources; that is, they must be used efficiently. This implies:

• The rational protection of land areas suitable for agricultural production.

• Rational forestry management in the interest of protecting the climate and ensuring a supply of energy for populations in tropical regions.

• The development of resource-saving technologies.

• The establishment of interest and incentive structures that take these requirements into consideration in the national and international economies.

The following examples provide concrete illustrations of this. A resource-saving approach is naturally also essential in the extraction of natural resources (secondary oil production, recycling of pit-heaps, reduction of losses in long-distance high-tension lines, new "decentralized" energy forms—biomass, wind, solar energy—use of what were previously timber byproducts for the furniture industry, etc.). However, greater possibilities can be found in the rationalization of use (reduction of fuel consumption of internal-combustion engines, improved efficiency of boilers and other heating installations, proper insulation of homes, development of energy-sparing technologies and industries, etc.).

Since the oil crisis, all the major capitalist and socialist countries have achieved substantial savings in specific energy consumption. Nevertheless, there are still very substantial further possibilities in this area. The essential thing is that the energy and raw materials consumption index has now become one of the most important requirements for the modernity of different installations and technologies. All countries exporting and striving to achieve rapid technical progress must therefore take this into account.

The Biosphere

The biosphere is the field of organic life on the earth, approximately 15-16 km in thickness. This space is of enormous significance for man. However, the accumulated "side effects" of economic and industrial development in the past decades threaten the biosphere in a number of respects. The deterioration and destruction of the biosphere has numerous manifestations, appearing in increasingly serious forms: destruction of fertile soil; pollution of the biosphere, rivers, and oceans; the rising temperature factor related to the presence of carbon monoxide. Soil erosion also occurs in the most advanced countries. The destruction means a decline in the land area used for agricultural production.

Air pollution, especially in the big industrial agglomerations, is reaching enormous proportions. A recent phenomenon is acid rain, particularly in the Scandinavian countries; in the opinion of scientists and experts, this is caused in Europe predominantly by British and West German chemical industries.

In some cases, the deteriorating quality of waters is now threatening organic life in the water: the fish are dying out in many places, and especially species more sensitive to environmental conditions have disappeared from many rivers. These unfavorable trends are related to certain methods of industrial and agricultural production: bulk oil transport and the discharge of unpurified urban sewage into rivers.

The increased carbon-monoxide content of the biosphere referred to above can lead to a rise in temperature that will have an influence on the climate with catastrophic consequences even in the next decade.

These problems are global in nature, not only in their origin, but also in their effects, and reduction or elimination of the negative activities and influences can only be achieved through broad

international cooperation. The objectively necessary international cooperation should extend:
- To joint and coordinated investments carried out by the partners, together or in harmony, to prevent a further deterioration of the situation or to achieve an improvement.
- To scientific cooperation directed at identifying and observing certain currently or potentially threatened zones and at elaborating an action program to this effect.
- To the creation of bodies operating on the basis of international agreement, which could ban certain procedures in particularly serious cases.

Science and Technology

The equivocal nature of science and technology—which could be found, within certain limits, in the past, too, although no particular importance was attached to it in the general optimism of the time—has grown stronger over the past decades and will be even more marked in the future. Since the industrial revolution it has been considered that technology is a driving force of economic development that would solve all problems with time and whose effects could only be beneficial in social and political respects. It was assumed that certain conflicts may occur transitionally between forms of technical development and the established social relations, but society would gradually adjust to the changes, for they serve its interest.

At present, however, new developments must be anticipated because:
- There has been a great acceleration in scientific and technical progress; entirely different methods and means are now used to organize and encourage it from those applied in the first half of the twentieth century.
- The present state of human society is extremely sensitive: on the one hand, the higher level of development is accompanied by an increasingly extensive system of social relations and dependencies and, on the other, both the national economies and the international economic and political systems are passing through a structural crisis.
- These crises also extend to the international security systems whose operation and structure are inseparable from the scientific and technical background.
- In the course of technical progress, we are operating systems that exert an ever-growing influence on a deteriorating biosphere.

It is no longer a question of discoveries and inventions being beneficial but used by reactionary or inhumane political systems for bad purposes, since, in our present age, the majority of scientists and researchers in employment are working for the armaments industry; that is, the military invention is the primary goal and its application for peaceful purposes is a secondary by-product. If certain aggressive circles can dictate policy in one or more big countries, it is obvious that—in the interest of their security—other countries are also obliged to arm.

Science has been traditionally regarded as a problem-solving factor. However, the dialectic of our age shows that with the solution of old problems, we create new problems; that is, development is not leading towards a "problem-free" world. To date, concern has rather been caused by the fact that we have begun to threaten the equilibrium of our environment (the biosphere) as a result of the application of discoveries and inventions and their mass spread. This, too, represents "intervention" in the ecological systems, which, of course, should only be done with the greatest care. But the danger is increased by the fact that biology is becoming the leading science of the future, although, naturally, physics and chemistry are not declining in importance. But, through certain discoveries and capabilities of biology, fewer are now able to intervene directly in the operation of certain natural systems. Genetic engineering, gene banks, etc., are methods whose application has already begun or is only a step away. However, the appearance of biotechnology has created a new situation in the social, moral, and political sense. In this new situation, not only does the way in which we may intervene in functioning natural systems represent a problem, but also the relationship that exists between the possibility of intervention and the established social-moral attitudes and value systems. In this respect, it is not only political systems that we have in mind, but that, over the course of past centuries, it has been regarded as unacceptable to intervene artificially in the sex, abilities, and characteristics of an unborn individual, since the natural systems operated very well in one respect (the balanced proportion of the sexes), and intervention in other areas was regarded as dangerous. Whatever the solution brought for these questions in the future, it is obvious that the given state of society, the opinions established on the questions concerned, and the dangers that could arise with unsuitable application must all be taken into consideration.

It is thus obvious that there are obstacles to the application of biological discoveries in human society; public authorization and international agreements must therefore be required for their application.

Trade and Politics

We are living in a period when questions of the international economy and trade are in close interaction with international political questions. It was generally assumed earlier that cooperation among the national economies and the internationalization of certain processes lead to a decline and blurring of the differences between nations. However, at present, there are about 180 national economies in the world, and the national economic interest plays the decisive role in their activity.

This fact means that global questions or questions arising from interdependence could only be solved in well-organized cooperation sincerely supported by all participants. However, this cooperation—which is the decisive condition for the survival and development of mankind—cannot be achieved at present; indeed, it cannot be achieved at all under conditions of serious international tension, spreading conflicts, the arms race, and the cold-war atmosphere.

It must also be taken into account that—unlike the fifties—the rivalry between the two global powers extends to the whole world. In addition, many political crises, shifts of power, and conflicts are arising in the developing countries—as a characteristic combination of internal-political and foreign-policy factors—that are in the early stage of their national development. These changes undoubtedly affect, or could affect, the balance between the global powers; any steps taken by one side lead to counter-steps by the other.

The equilibrium system of "mutual deterrence" in the military field is extremely costly and, moreover, is very fragile.

There is an unquestionable need in the present world economic situation for new political decisions and new institutions, but their adoption, initiation, and operation require a certain degree of political trust and mutual goodwill. However, in the given international political system, under the conditions of arms race, it is hardly possible to talk of mutual trust or goodwill.

The limitations created by international political relations and the contradiction between the national economies and the requirements created by the international economy must be resolved through rational action, or else the world economy will collapse.

The economic and social situation of the developing countries is a global problem, not only because the developed and developing countries exist on the same planet, but also because the inequalities that have arisen and are as yet showing no decline are dangerous from the political viewpoint and irrational from an economic viewpoint. It is not the hunger uprisings or anarchistic clashes that make the problem politically dangerous in itself, but the fact that survival and development in such a dangerous world as ours are only possible if mankind realistically and correctly appreciates the dangers that threaten human lives. But the starving masses deprived of all hope, the millions who have grown indifferent in their sufferings and lack of prospects are incapable of appreciating the dangers for they have nothing to lose. It is the rich who fear nuclear annihilation; the poor must live in fear of starvation, as some spokesmen of the Third World point out.

The problems related to the economic development of the Third World or to acceleration of this development are complex. What is required for the acceleration of development is a system that places economic development in the center of social and political efforts, which is only possible if the productive forces—including the creative ability of individuals, groups, and small communities—can be genuinely released.

Experiences show that a politically organized power elite is needed to initiate and direct development—because of the low level of qualifications of the great majority of the population and their passivity, the weakness of the middle strata, and the lack of national cohesion. Naturally, the "power elite" cannot be uniform since it includes persons thinking in political categories and technocrats, revolutionaries and conservatives alike. The flagging of a particular development stage or the emergence of serious economic and social problems generally leads to a change of rulers. If the conflicts within the power elite become very acute, the army generally intervenes in order to avoid civil war or anarchy. There are indications that, in a large number of countries, the army represents the index of the scales. Naturally, the power elite cannot ensure development over the long term, but it is to be hoped that, with the advance of education and training and the establishment of economic interests on a broad scale, mass forces capable of ensuring democratic development will arise.

Nevertheless, however decisive may be the significance of development fed by "internal" resources, interest relations, and incentives, acceleration of the development of the Third World—which is essential because of the international political and economic interdependencies—can only take place with the carefully organized and coordinated aid of the developed world. The developing countries are demanding in the concept of the new world economic order that this aid must be made one of the decisive factors of the world economic system in the coming decades.

The essence of the concept of the new world economic order is thus that an integral harmony must be achieved between the problems of the developing countries and world economic processes. What is needed is not simply aid, credit, or transfers of technology, which are incidental and represent only a supplementary factor in world economic processes, but organs and institutional solutions whereby the transfer of means from one half of the world to the other is carried out as an integral and inseparable component of world economic processes.

Critics—mainly in the socialist countries—who support the notion of the new international economic order but also recognize its weaknesses, correctly pointed out that the transfer of resources can only bring the desired results if significant social and economic reforms are also introduced at the same time in the developing countries. For it is beyond question that the income distribution in the countries of the Third World is extremely uneven and hinders both accumulation on a social scale and the satisfaction of the basic needs of the broad masses. This means that the transfer of resources must be linked to the introduction of the necessary reforms.

The theory of the new international economic order has been embraced and further developed by certain progressive Western circles, most remarkably by the Brandt Commission, which has taken the question to mean that, in the case of economic stagnation of the Third World, the developed capitalist countries are unable to export, and, without exports, they are incapable of developing economically. At the end of the 1970s, the strengthening conservative circles adopted a firm position against the Brandt Plan and the transfer of resources and strove to redirect the dialogue and bargaining with the Third World back into the concepts and sphere of action of the free market and private investments. However, these methods represent, at the most, deferment or loss of time because the present economic crisis cannot be overcome without a suitable relocation of resources.

Interdependence

The economic problems of the Third World lead to the notion of interdependence. Economic contacts create relationships of mutual dependence among nations. The Communist Manifesto already referred to this fact. However, the relations of mutual dependence have been established in a world in which there are about 180 national economies, different socioeconomic systems, and extreme variations in the levels of economic development.

The relations of mutual dependence apply not only to commodity and money relations in this period, but also to economic policy.

At present, debts of 1,200 billion dollars have been accumulated in the world economy, and the debtor countries must pay 130 billion dollars a year in debt servicing. In practice, this means that the debtor countries must export much more than they import in the coming years. But how can the indebted countries export more when world trade is stagnating and the developed capitalist countries are not capable of importing more? Even if this could be achieved, it is obvious that the purchasing power of the indebted countries would be reduced by 130 billion dollars a year, which means that they could import that much less; but the advanced capitalist countries are not capable of recovering from their economic stagnation without increasing exports. Do the conditions now exist for globally considered and harmonized international economic policy?

There is now growing recognition that the restructuring of debts (transforming medium-term loans into long-term loans and short-term credit into medium-term credit) and the reduction of interest rates (which assumes the reduction of budget deficits) are unavoidable. The need for the introduction of a new monetary system has been raised in a number of quarters—not only in the developing countries, but also in France.

These ideas and aspirations cannot be put into practice overnight, but it is clear that the further deterioration of the economic situation and the deepening of the crisis will make the inevitability of these steps obvious for a growing number of experts and financial and business leaders.

However, it is also beyond doubt that economic changes of such major importance can only be introduced where there is a certain political agreement. And in the present situation, the outlook for this is not favorable.

State of Economic Emergency

If the international political situation does not improve, it is theoretically possible that there will be international recognition of a state of economic emergency and, consequently, tacit acceptance of the "depoliticization" of certain economic steps.

If acceptance of this state of emergency and attainment of the resulting economic "autonomy" also prove impossible, the individual countries will be obliged gradually to make their own external economic steps independent of the international political situation—depending on their concrete situation. This will naturally bring friction and clashes, but its neglect will lead to an economic catastrophe. Thus, in the majority of cases, taking these steps becomes a problem of survival.

Undoubtedly, the global problems—including, in particular, the system of interdependencies—are opening a new era in the system of international economic and political relations. Historically, these problems arise from the differing nature and speed of the various components in economic and social development and from the inadequacies and one-sidedness in our knowledge of the natural systems.

In this century—and especially since the Second World War—scientific and technical development has dictated the nature and speed of economic and social development. In keeping with the methods, degree of organization, and purposeful nature of scientific research, inventions have been made one after the other and rapidly applied and spread by the economy that is motivated under compulsion from international competition. And the industrial production and marketing systems that have been changed in this way have introduced the innovations into mass consumption through the new goods and services. The use of these goods and forms of consumption gave rise to new social habits and aspirations, but they also created new problems in society and in the way of thinking that subsequently came into conflict with different components of the existing values and institutional system.

The accelerated scientific and technical development created new interdependencies and a new set of relationships that could only be followed with a major transformation of the existing internal and external power and social structures. Moreover, certain effects of scientific and technical development are only felt in the case of accumulation, that is, when the goods and services concerned have already been introduced on a very broad scale. For example, the negative influences of automobile transport on the biosphere and on living conditions only became apparent by the time every second or third family in the developed world already owned a car and the majority of goods transportation was also handled by road transport.

The "ideology" of accelerated scientific and technological development did not devote sufficient attention to the questions of the natural systems. This was definitely a mistake, for man is not only a social being, but also a natural (biological) creature in many aspects of his basic nature and activity. Moreover, the natural systems only "serve" human aspirations adequately if their regularities are always taken into account. However, if the direct (e.g., mining, agriculture, the polluting effects of large-scale industry) and the indirect (biological) interventions in the natural systems greatly increase in quantity and intensity, certain forms of "intervention" cannot be applied because they threaten the equilibrium of the physical and chemical processes that form the basic conditions for human existence.

Solution of the global problems thus requires a new economic-development concept, harmonization of the different development factors, and the creation of new structures at both the national and international levels. It is naturally open to question whether these international structures suitable for cooperation can be created at all in the world today burdened with political tensions and the arms race. But if this is not achieved, the international economic and monetary system is threatened with collapse within the foreseeable future. And the collapse of the international economic and monetary system would be a catastrophe for most national economies and would create anarchy within the system of internal economic and financial relations.

Is there a way out of the present situation? Is it sufficient to feel a sense of danger and realize the situation for mankind (or the representatives of political and economic power) to adopt new forms of behavior and political norms in the questions concerned? Can the threat of economic collapse break through the political structure that is concentrated on other questions? Is it necessary for some local, regional, or partial catastrophe to occur first?

We naturally hope for the first because that in itself could initiate new actions. Unfortunately, we cannot exclude the other possibility: the occurrence of a local, partial catastrophe.

New Kind of Economic Action

We speak of a supplementary system because a new kind of economic action is needed, but the institutions and mechanisms that operate the present action system cannot be changed arbitrarily or very rapidly. However, there are two preconditions for the establishment of such a supplementary system of action: the elaboration on a scientific basis of the system of action concerned (in the present case, this means the global system of action) and the ability of national leaders to conduct talks on the world's present international political and economic system.

In the first case, a problem is raised from the scientific angle by the fact that, in the course of its few centuries of development, the science of economics has striven primarily to establish micro (enterprise) and macro (national economic) optimums. However, behind the micro and macro optimums and actions, there are real interest relations, plans, and institutions. There are no such interest relations, organizations, or institutions behind the global questions; there are no vehicles for rational global economic action.

Scientifically, therefore, the problems, influences, and consequences of global dimension must be elaborated; this must be done in the realization that there are no concrete interests in this respect. The elaboration of the global problems, influences, and consequences will naturally influence, in turn, the national and enterprise optimums, approximately in such a way that environmental factors will become the object of economic calculation in the future. From another angle, it is also obvious that the existing world economic situation is exerting a growing influence on the possibilities and limitations of action of the national economies. In a different approach, this means that the discipline of economics must develop methods of calculation and optimalization that reliably reflect these interactions.

Moreover, leaders of the different countries should discuss the questions of world political and world economic systems not only because the international political situation is tense and there is a serious world economic crisis, but also because the international political, security and economic systems set up after the Second World War have weakened in themselves and are no longer able to cope with the global problems. The United Nations unequivocally deals with the political problems that arise among nation states, and its point of departure cannot be global. Questions related to international security also come within the jurisdiction of the United Nations, but its ability to resolve conflicts has greatly declined.

There is no economic organization dealing with the full range of international economic processes, but GATT and UNCTAD analyze the different aspects of international trade and strive to set norms for the different countries. This system of norms is also weakening since, due to their indebtedness, individual countries are obliged to prefer bilateral barter agreements.

The international monetary system has also weakened, partly because of the change in the basic principles established at Bretton Woods and partly because financial processes have become separate from trade.

It is thus obvious that both survival and development call for a reexamination of international activities. The latter would also have the task of transferring part of the funds derived from the reduction of arms spending that has reached catastrophic proportions into a development fund that would be self-renewing, in such a way that the developing countries also undertake the introduction of reforms related to the transfer of resources.

A consultative body should be set up to handle this fund and deal with questions relating to its renewal; this body should have a broad scientific background and should begin its operation on an experimental basis so that its structure could be changed later in the light of experience.

References

1. IMF, *Direction of Trade Statistics,* Washington, various issues.
2. H.-H. Rogner, *IIASA '83 Scenario of Energy Development: Summary,* Laxenburg, International Institute for Applied Systems Analysis, p. 5. (no date)

The Problem of Unemployment

Global Unemployment: Challenge to Futurists

by

Bertram Gross and Kusum Singh

The specter of more and more jobless people haunts the modern world.

It is sired by uncontrolled transnational capital and mothered by revolutionary technologies that displace manual and mental labor. It is nurtured by business-cycle downturns brought on by the old contradiction of capitalist efforts to raise profit rates by raising prices and curbing real wages, thereby dampening the effective demand on which profitability is based. It is made worse by the export of jobs to, and the import of workers from, low-wage countries. It is hidden by doles for the jobless, statistical tricks, and other measures to render impotent, while enlarging, the so-called "reserve army of the unemployed."

In most countries of statist "socialism," the specter stalks silently in the corridors of bloated bureaucrats where people work unproductively. In China and Yugoslavia, the specter materializes through "market socialist" efforts to slim down bureaucracies.

Pre-industrial and industrializing countries face a tangle of contradictions. Population increases faster than the capacity to produce. Increased productive capacity usually grows faster than

---

Bertram M. Gross is Distinguished Professor Emeritus at Hunter College, City University of New York, and visiting professor at Saint Mary's College of California, Moraga, California (1982 to present), and University of California, Berkeley (1985-86). Kusum Singh is assistant professor, Institute of Communications, Muhlenberg/Cedar Crest College, Allentown, Pennsylvania.

the domestic capacity to consume. Production tends to be oriented toward the uncertainties of unequal exchange in world export markets. The number of unemployed and underemployed in Asia, West Asia, Africa, and Latin America already approaches half a billion people.[1]

With these tendencies throughout the world, global joblessness by the year 2000—with all the accompanying poverty, disease, and social breakdown—could easily victimize a billion people.

If Karl Marx were alive today, he would have to improve his analysis of the relative surplus population (or "reserve army of the unemployed") as an aid in capital accumulation.

In doing this, he would surely document the global growth of this huge, unarmed, and leaderless "army." He might even pay tribute to many capitalist "achievements" somewhat different from those celebrated in *The Communist Manifesto*. For example: (1) skillful avoidance of the army's size and significance, (2) the existence, side by side, of neoclassical, "Marxist," and tech- fix faiths, (3) policies that successfully expand the labor surplus, immobilize the jobless, and make rising unemployment more politically tolerable, (4) institutional and political supports for such policies, (5) "value-free" research that, in presenting part truths as whole truths, tends to protect existing power structures, and (6) crisis responses that succeed beautifully in distracting attention from the horrors of global unemployment and job insecurity. Fortunately, many people ponder different modes of creative action, seeking instead to

(1) uncover the painful realities of joblessness,
(2) design better models for fruitful discourse and action
(3) climb the "commanding policy heights" of moral vision,
(4) move from autocratic to democratic corporatism,
(5) uncover the kind of information that may help make power holders more accountable, or
(6) promote global dialogue on the hidden crisis of unemployment.

Let us now discuss some possible actions along these lines. We hope that our formulation may challenge others to do much better in trying to serve the needs of *all* people.

I. Confronting the Ostriches

"We have learned that we must live as men, and not as ostriches."—Franklin D. Roosevelt, fourth term inaugural address, January 20, 1945

The Chinese pictogram for "crisis," one often hears, has two characters: one for "danger," the other for "opportunity." But the ostrich is sometimes a better symbol for people who have not yet learned, in FDR's words, to "live as men" (or women).

We know of many people who, when confronted with genuine danger, promptly bury their heads in the ground. If power holders do not themselves know how to do this, many high-powered experts compete with each other in creating new opportunities for hiding from unpleasant realities.

Shunning Full Employment Commitments

"Every American able and willing to work has the right to a useful and remunerative job in the industries, or shops, or offices, or farms, or mines of the Nation."—from first draft of "The Full Employment Act of 1945," December 18, 1944[2]

"The full employment pledge in the United States Charter marks a historic phase in the evolution of the modern conception of the functions and responsibility of the democratic state ... It reflects the fundamental importance of the promotion of full employment ... first, as a condition of economic and social progress ... and secondly, as a necessary prerequisite for the maintenance and smooth working of an international economic system."
—U.N. Group of Experts, *National and International*
—*Measures for Full Employment*, (E/1584),
—December 1949.[3]

While World War II ended the Great Depression of 1929-1939, many people in Western Europe and America came to fear that victory in war would bring back the depression. In 1943, President Roosevelt's planning board proposed a New Bill of Rights that included the right to a job at fair wages. In January 1944, Roosevelt embodied most of these ideas in an Economic Bill of Rights message to Congress.[4] A little later, Sir William Beveridge proposed full employment as a postwar goal for the British government. For a while, full employment and the "right to a job at fair wages" became, in Herbert Stein's words, "a flag around which every one could rally."[5] By year's end, this flag was unfurled in a "Full Employment Bill" that tried to translate rhetorical pledges into statutory obligations. This measure was strongly opposed by those parts of the business community who saw, accurately, that truly full employment would strengthen labor and weaken corporate power. The bill was finally passed as the Employment Act of 1946. In essence, this law committed the federal government not to full employment but to preventing mass depression.[6]

In 1945, despite objections from U.S. conservatives, the U.N. Charter committed its members to promote full employment (Article 55). In 1948, the U.N.'s Universal Declaration of Human Rights strengthened this commitment: "Everyone has the right to work, to free choice of employment, to just and favorable conditions of work, and to protection against unemployment" (Article 23). The 1949 U.N. Group of Experts proposed policies to make these rights a reality.

For a while, the flag kept waving. But throughout the following decades, the idea of a right, or entitlement, was abandoned in most capitalist countries. In place of a commitment to full employment, more emphasis was placed on alleviation of the worst forms of unemployment. Policies in this direction tended to place simplistic overemphasis on job training without job creation, on limited job creation through localistic action to move employment from one region to another, and on ultra-expensive job creation through rising military budgets and subsidies to the rich. Meanwhile, the concept of "full employment" has widely been redefined (as discussed in the next section). "Frictional unemployment" has been widely replaced by "natural unemployment."

In turn, policies to "help" developing countries may provide greater help to transnational corporations. "Foreign aid" often taxes the poor in rich countries to enrich the rich in poor countries. The impressive rhetoric of "development," "growth," and "basic needs" is often used in a manner that distracts attention from the basic need for growth and development of useful employment. The reality of interdependence among nations is ignored, as discussions of "developing countries" proceed on the bland assumption that high goals can be obtained without structural changes within both "developed" and "developing" societies.

Regarding transnational formations, the Liberal International pays lip service to full-employment ideals under high-technology capitalism and closes its eyes to the rest of the world. The Socialist International has not yet directly grappled with the subject. The Third World's "Committee of 77" and the nonaligned movement avoid the subject. In his 1983 report to the nonaligned movement, Fidel Castro piously proclaims that "880 million jobs in the underdeveloped countries" are needed by the year 2000. But he confines himself to the old-style Third Worldism of trade and aid. He studiously avoided any discussion of economic rights or planning for full employment.[7]

As a combined result of these national and transnational orientations, full-employment commitments have been ignominiously deserted by the U.N. secretariat. Most U.N. agencies, even those originally set up to promote full employment, now hush-hush both the "full-employment" goal and the unemployment realities. Some actively support transnational corporate actions that sharpen the hushed-up crisis. Nor have many signatories of the U.N.'s more recent Covenant on Economic and Social Rights been very ardent in support of the full employment commitments formally restated in the covenant.

Hiding Un- and Underemployment

"The notion of measuring the labor supply, or the unused portion of labor supply as a residual, was abandoned [in the 1940 U.S. Census]... There was no demand for a measure of total supply as such, probably because labor supply seemed abundant for all possible demands."

—Gertrude Bancroft, *The American Labor Force,* —Wiley, 1968, pp. 185-188.

"The current definition of unemployment captures only the tip of the iceberg of potential workers; it is itself part of a grand cover-up of the shortage of jobs."

—Frank Furstenberg and Charles Thrall, "Counting —the Jobless," *The Annals,* March 1975.

Although statistics do not lie, liars can use statistics—and in the new information age, they use statisticians also. The most effective misinformation is provided by honest statisticians who apply concepts that serve the interests of the dominant forces in society. Indeed, the propensity of many social scientists—not only statisticians—is to prefer being professionally "sound," which often means being precisely wrong rather than vaguely right. Hence, major attention is paid to the tails of elephants and tips of icebergs.

During the Great Depression, battles raged around the world on how to measure the unemployment iceberg. In Europe and England, unions reported on their unemployed members and unemployment insurance offices on the people getting benefits. In the United States, with few unions and no social insurance, the field was wide open. One highly respected economist from the Brookings Institution estimated unemployment in a historic analysis of America's productive capacity.[8] For 1929, the peak year of pre-Depression prosperity, he estimated *unemployment at 19%.* Percent of what? Of the "gainfully occupied"—a concept very close to the total supply of available labor. In 1937, the federal government's National Resources Committee estimated that on the basis of "full time equivalents" unemployment during 1932-1934 averaged 45% of the total available labor supply.

But the political demand during the Great Depression period of extreme job shortage was *not* for a measure based on the "total available labor supply." Rather, it was for data that "would understate the degree of unemployment and thereby vindicate the effectiveness of government programs of job creation."[9] A group of brilliant technicians (including Gertrude Bancroft, quoted above) met this demand by inventing the "labor force." This artifact included as unemployed only the jobless of 16 years of age and over who were reported as actively seeking paid employment. This excluded millions of jobless "not in the labor force"—people who, although able and willing to work for pay, were not reported as actively seeking it. (If a similar method were used to estimate the number of unmarried people, no singles—not even Catholic priests—would be "unmarried" unless reported as actively seeking a spouse.) It also excluded many other groups: people working a few hours a month (who were classified as "employed"), people in institutions (often a haven for the jobless), those under 16, etc.

Ironically, the "labor force" concept was first used in the 1940 census, just as World War II was unfolding and the United States soon had to mobilize its unmeasured labor reserves. Eight million people "not in the labor-force" were quickly drawn into it. But with victory, the specter of massive joblessness returned. Postwar policies sent women back into the home, older people into retirement, young people to tertiary education—and many ethnic minorities into ghettoes. The labor-force concept came into its own—with many commissions and agencies involved in technical improvements. The U.N. statistical offices labored mightily to apply the concept in as many countries as possible. They succeeded beyond all expectation—except in socialist countries. Their greatest success was in developing countries whose best economists knew it was nonsense (since it could not cope with massive underemployment) but whose leaders relished statistics that would understate the horror of their vast surplus populations.

In the heat of World War II, President Franklin D. Roosevelt and the authors of the original Full Employment Bill of 1944 used a human-rights definition of full employment: *a situation in which there are job opportunities for everyone able and willing to work for pay*. This was close to Sir William Beveridge's original definition: a situation in which more employers seek workers than people seek employment. So for a while, *the essence of full-employment planning was to set goals for the number of people to be employed*: for example, FDR's famous 60 million postwar civilian jobs. Later, as more conventional minds prevailed, the idea of employment goals was buried. A new approach became dominant: measuring full employment by the amount of "frictional," and then "natural," unemployment. In the United States, these measures tended to rise over the decades:

1940s	2-3%
1950s	3-4%
1960s	3-5%
1970s	4-6%
1980	6-7%
1984	7-8%
1990 (est.)	9-10%
2000 (est.)	10-12%

As these conceptual changes became dominant, economists like Leon Keyserling, who spent decades calculating the loss of national output and government revenue resulting from officially measured unemployment, were labelled "unprofessional," exiled from the hallowed groves of academic economics, and ignored by the media. A brilliant heretic like John Kenneth Galbraith atoned for sins on other matters by piously accepting the infallibility of conventional concepts and abstaining from involvement in full-employment debates.

Generally, rising rates of unemployment were publicly justified by the entry of more women, younger people, and ethnic minorities into the labor force and the presumed need for more unemployment and recessions to control inflation by depressing labor costs. Less publicly stated was the demand for enhancing short-range rates of profit by weakening organized labor. Behind all these justifications, however, lay a more sober definition of full employment, as often lamented by Rep. Augustus Hawkins, chairman of the House Labor and Education Committee: *the highest level of unemployment that is politically tolerable.*

Dodging the Sources of Bank Crisis

The dominant elites in America and Europe look daily at a shaky banking system in which potential default by governments in Latin America and Eastern Europe could exceed the entire capital and assets of the world's largest banks. But they systematically ignore the vital links between the sickness of banks and the deeper diseases (spread by some bankers) of poverty, economic injustice, and self-centered greed.

Through a glass darkly, they may see the relevance of untamed business cycles, long-term tendencies toward stagnation, poverty-stricken markets, and oppressive social structures. But they close their eyes to the fact that higher interest rates make default more probable. They disregard the influence of austerity policies (forced on developing countries directly or through the International Monetary Fund) in converting potentially good loans into bad ones. While acknowledging that the enormous Reagan deficits boost nominal and real interest rates, they dodge other factors: an arms race financed by politicians who would rather borrow than ask for taxpayer support; the use of "tight money" to promote recession and "discipline" labor; private debt expansion; profligate speculation in mergers and takeovers; fears of more inflation in the future; and the bankers' own propensity (like many other corporate preachers of "free market" ideology) to work together in *setting* prices of their product—namely, credit.

Like their fellow deep thinkers in many transnational corporate board rooms, bankers concentrate on maximizing margins, profit rates, and short-term return on equity capital. They disregard the probability that widespread success in doing this undermines the effective purchasing power on which profitability is based. Sowing the wind, they pray that others—not they—will reap the whirlwind. This is an institutional *ostrich syndrome*. The justification for burying their heads in the sand is the expectation that whatever they do, national governments and their central banks will hear their prayers and bail them out. The expectation is well founded. Subservient public officials rush in to become lenders and subsidizers of first, not last, resort. Their bestowal of big welfare on an ultraprivileged minority is rooted in the efficiency of modern government in reducing the entitlements of, and raising taxes on, the lower-and middle-income majority.

II. The Need for Better Models

Throughout the world, the Left seems bereft, the Middle muddled, and the Right wrong.

Indeed, the old one-dimensional Left-to-Right spectrum—arising from the seating arrangements in the French national assembly almost two centuries ago—is itself obsolete. No single dimension could possibly describe the complex socio-political interests and posture of a person, group, party, nation, or transnational bloc. We need multi-dimensional models that build upon the best in different systems, practices, ideologies, and faiths.

Insolvency of the Old

The ideology of capitalism is an impressive historical asset. Although (like any ideology) it hides as well as guides, the ideology of entrepreneurial freedom and resistance to statism has much to commend it. Capitalist practice also has value—particularly its capacity for technological innovation, its combination of central planning with decentralized operations, and its well-planned use of state protection and intervention.

Socialist ideology is also a valuable asset. Its emphasis on human values, communal sharing, and the control of private greed is one of humankind's great heritages. Although these ideals have never yet been carried out, most countries of statist "socialism" have abolished the capitalist business cycle and provided better welfare-state minima than in most countries of "welfare-state" capitalism. In capitalist countries, socialist parties have pioneered in producing the welfare-state programs that, in softening the business cycle, have helped preserve capitalism.

Nonetheless, both capitalist and socialist countries are in acute crisis. Neither can meet their obligations. Although in different ways, each is incapable of guiding action to expand the supply of useful and productive jobs at adequate—let alone good—wages. The one bolsters markets with government, business, and consumer debt; the other with imports of food and technology from capitalist countries. The one nurtures a growing surplus population with little opportunity for earned income outside of the "underground economy" and the provision of illegal service. The other conceals unemployment within unproductive bureaucracies with many employees who make a living without really "earning" it. Both tilt toward "tech fix" solutions to problems that are basically political, social, and ethical. Neither has pioneered in using labor-saving technology to reduce substantially the hours of work per day, month, and year and to expand thereby the opportunities for creative and self-determined leisure. Both provide large amounts of employment in the armed forces and in enterprises provisioning them or producing weapons systems that threaten national and global security.

In Western Europe and Britain, socialist parties out of power are not yet offering full employment programs. In France, Spain and Greece, socialist or social-democratic parties *in* power seem to have learned little from the example of Scandinavian socialists. Rather, they have been vying with the British conservatives in demonstrating their incapacity. In the United States, the liberal wing of the Democratic Party and its organized-labor supporters (both essentially social democratic in nature) supported a presidential candidate who, despite depression conditions in many urban and rural areas and the imminence of another deep recession, totally abandoned his party's historic commitment to full employment.

By these standards of accountability, we suggest that in both practice and ideology in most countries, *capitalism and socialism are insolvent.*

We use "insolvency" in the sense given it by equity courts— namely, inability to meet debts as they mature. This is different from the bankruptcy concept of insolvency: assets worth less than liabilities. A currently insolvent system of thought and practice may include valuable assets that can yield larger benefits by reorganization within a better framework.

Essentials of the New

Unlike the Greek goddess of wisdom, improved models will never spring full-blown from the brow of Zeus-like thinkers. They will emerge rather from the real-life struggles of political leaders, citizen activists, and research workers to free themselves from the dead hand of obsolete modes of perceiving the world and trying to change it for the better. They will be borne of efforts—in the words of the World Future Society—to "think globally, act *locally*," and "plan for the long-range as a guide to acting *now*."

Thus the more creative futurists break away from dominating models that weigh like a nightmare on the minds of present generations. Those of us who have escaped the trap of technocracy seek models that, while using the best in the old, go much further in empowering human beings to meet needs for dignity, personal growth, and democratic freedoms.

Such a search leads one into the difficult question of what *new policies, power structures, research, or follow-up steps* may best respond to the global unemployment challenge.

III. Policy: The Commanding Heights of Moral Vision

For the Russian Bolsheviks in 1917, arsenals, police and railroad stations, and wireless offices were the "commanding heights" to be seized and kept. Later the term was used to refer to basic industry.

But it was the vision of "Peace, Bread, and Land" that commanded the hearts and souls of those who supported the Bolshevik "experiment." Indeed, the greatest strength of all socialist movements—evolutionary or revolutionary—has come from ethical values, not from the barrel of a gun or the charisma of a leader. One can say the same about the early capitalist revolutions that broke the bonds of agricultural feudalism and about present-day regimes and parties of constitutional capitalism. In this age of galloping secularism, paradoxically, some of the world's most decisive struggles focus on the commanding heights of the human psyche or, in Freud's language, soul.

These commanding heights cannot be reached merely through the desperately needed improvements in policies bearing on profits, government intervention, market controls, demand, supply, investment, consumption, wages, prices, trade, science, population, education, leisure, culture, etc. For this purpose, even "macroeconomic" policy is too "micro."

The transformation needed in the coming years cannot—to use a phrase from Marx that Marxists seem to have forgotten—"draw its poetry from the past, but only from the future." But the poetry of the future can rarely be found in the prose of economic and statistical analysis. The coming struggles for the "commanding heights" of public policy, we humbly suggest, will center around alternative ideals of peace, democracy, human rights, security, patriotism, and, above all, human freedom.

Some seek this "moral high ground" by playing the rhetorical game of competitive flatulence. Or else, in Orwellian terms, Big and Little Brothers use "peace" to justify war and "freedom," "democracy," "human rights," "security," and "patriotism" as covers for self-serving greed, mechanical formalism, the rights of corporate "persons," the insecurities of the arms race, and militaristic chauvinism.

A more constructive approach, we suggest, is to develop a moral vision that weaves the highest human values together with the strands of specific macro-and micro-policies. A fascinating example is provided by the American Catholic bishops' recent attack on "the morally unjustified" levels of current unemployment and poverty. Their draft pastoral letter on the American economy calls for "A New American Experiment."[10]

In it, the American bishops offer a "moral vision" that, while explicitly based on "Catholic social teaching," is also "catholic" in the sense of "universal." As a Jew and a Hindu, we find in their message the spirit of both the Hebrew prophets and the Holy Geeta. Like Lord Krishna, the bishops come done from the highest pinnacles of ideology to the lower plane of material philosophy and the point of view of worldly people. At both levels, these pillars of conservative religion have been attacked by free-market worshippers as radical "redistributionists," if not crypto-socialist enemies of the system they are trying to save. The give-and-take between the bishops and their opponents is already sparking a hot debate in the United States on some of the "meta-policies" we shall now touch on briefly.

Resurrection of Economic Rights

"Every adult American able and willing to earn a living through paid work has the right to a free choice among opportunities for useful, productive and fulfilling paid employment (part-or full-time) at decent wages, or self-employment.
"—Sec. 2(a), the Hayes "Income and Jobs Action Act,"
—H.R. 1398, 99th Congress

On March 5, 1985, Representative Charles Hayes (Democrat, Chicago), with the support of Representatives Augustus Hawkins, John Conyers, and many others, picked up the fallen flag of economic rights by introducing the "Income and Jobs Action Act." This measure re-states in vastly improved form the old "right to a job." It also sets forth a parallel right: "Every adult American unable to work for pay has the right to an adequate standard of living that rises with increases in the wealth and productivity of the society."

The growing support for this measure has probably been influenced by the leaders of almost all religious groups in America. Indeed, one may regard the entire bill as an effort to state in legislative terms the central theme in the draft pastoral letter of the Catholic bishops: "The nation must take up the task of framing a new national consensus that *all persons have rights in the economic sphere and that society has a moral obligation to take the necessary steps to ensure that no one among us is hungry, homeless, unemployed, or otherwise denied what is necessary to live with dignity.*" The bishops then went on to say that "there are forms of individual and group selfishness present in the nation that undermine social solidarity and efforts to protect the economic rights of all." The sins of indifference and greed have also "become embedded in certain of the economic institutions and cultural presuppositions of our society." To combat the "morally unjustified" levels of unemployment in the United States, they urged a "new national commitment" to reduce official unemployment to 3% or 4% and to "undertake a thorough reform of welfare and income support programs."

But the Hayes proposal is thus far strictly national in scope. Although the policies mandated in its overall planning section dealt with the problem of American corporations moving to other countries, they did not relate to the unemployment problems in such countries. The bishops, on the other hand, dealt at length with "The U.S. and the World Economy," while deploring poverty, hunger, and disease in "Third World" countries. Yet they followed the prevailing example in global discourse: they never mentioned unemployment in pre-industrial and industrializing countries. In neither case did the moral vision of the right to employment opportunities or any other economic rights include the world's largest pool of unemployed.

We find it hard to accept the idea that economic rights are the privileged heritage of industrialized countries only. Perhaps those with the courage to resurrect the idea of economic rights in the United States will proceed to call for U.S. ratification of the U.N. Convenant on Economic, Social, and Cultural Rights. Perhaps people in the many countries where ratification has already taken place will suggest that mere lip service to high ideals is not enough.

We wonder how much action is being taken or contemplated in Western European countries with mounting joblessness to strengthen demands for improved policies by rooting them in economic rights. And what about the industrializing countries of Asia and Latin America where "development" is used as the slogan to justify policies that uproot agricultural populations and lead to huge populations of displaced people with no future? The rights of government bureaucrats, native elites, and transnational corporations are both protected and expanded—in many countries, to the point of denying elemental civil and political rights. Can we not design—and win support for—future policies that would bolster economic and political rights for everyone, without sacrificing one in the name of the other?

Overall Planning for Freedoms

> "The word 'liberty'... may mean for some men to do what they please with other men."
>
> —Abraham Lincoln, 1864

Overall planning to protect the interests of a privileged minority is one of the basic facts or trends throughout the world. In countries of statist "socialism," it frees party bureaucrats from the threat of democratic accountability and competing power centers. In other countries—often hidden behind ideologies of so-called "free markets"—overall planning tends to guarantee greedy minorities the freedom to pollute the earth and air, break unions, move their operations to countries where free unionism is forbidden, swallow up small enterprises, buy elections, manipulate the media, and gratify personal additions to government-subsidized power and wealth.

This is one of the reasons why—in the words of the U.S. bishops—"the mere mention of the notion of economic planning is likely to produce a violent allergic reaction in the U.S." This allergy is not limited to any one country. It has also seriously afflicted economists throughout the world. On the other hand, many economists have themselves contributed to this negativism by discussing planning exclusively in terms of central decision-making by experts.

Fortunately, new attention is now being paid to the possibility of democratic planning in the interests of all the people. This is the heart of the Hayes-Conyers proposal—the way in which conditions might be created for the enjoyment of basic economic rights. It is also the heart of the proposed pastoral letter, which develops in some detail a recommendation by Pope John Paul II that "society make provision for overall planning." Both proposals emphasize the need for some kind of coordination among the many subgroups of society.

How can overall planning be initiated in neighborhoods, workplaces, cities, and regions? How can such locally-based planning be brought together in national plans and policies? How can localism and sectionalism be counterbalanced? How can the global context be kept in mind? This is one of the great challenges of the future.

Recent responses to this challenge are reviewed in "A Case for Democratic Planning" by Michael Harrington. "Planning is coming. Indeed, it is already here," he asserts, "and those who deny that fact, whether out of innocence or guile, are the true crackpots of the age. The real issue before us is not whether there will be planning, but who will plan, how, and for what purposes." [11] Many important ideas, he points out, are contained in the proposals by William Winpisinger and Richard Greenwood of the International Association of Machinists and Aerospace Workers.[12] He also refers extensively to a few of the ideas in legislative drafts prepared at the request of Rep. John Conyers: "The concept of a national needs inventory is already contained in draft legislation written by Bertram Gross and others for Representative John Conyers. It would involve planning agencies at every level of government in making an 'assessment of unmet needs'. . . . One of the most important features of the Gross-Conyers proposal is that mechanisms would be established to allow local and state governments to involve themselves effectively in the undertaking. . . . (It) suggests creating a Temporary Commission on Democratic Rights and Planning, which would use data from the inventory to formulate a proposed program of guaranteed opportunities for useful and productive employment."

In our "Democratic Planning: The Bottom-Sideways Approach" and in "Planning and Freedom," we suggest many other aspects of democratic—as contrasted with technocratic or oligarchic—planning.[13]

Jobs and Buying Power of the Poor

Compassion for the poor has always been part of humankind's moral vision. It has sparked the proliferation of both private charity and public-assistance programs. Yet both of these may have the effect—often unwittingly—of sidetracking efforts to strike at the roots of poverty and of making poverty (even exploitation) more politically tolerable. Each is consistent with widespread perceptions of the poor as lazy, stupid, and the victims of their own inherent incapacities. By themselves, both tend to preserve the low-cost labor that subsidizes the living standards of others.

One stands on higher moral ground, however, by not blaming the victims of circumstance and social structure. The greatest gene pool for the geniuses, artists, enterprisers, and productive workers of the future, it has been said, exists among the hundreds of millions of people who today see little or no escape from wretchedness.

But a few other things might be said with equal vigor:

1. The good jobs through which the poor could raise their incomes would also expand their purchasing power enormously.

2. The larger markets thereby created—particularly in Asia,

west Asia, Africa, and Latin America—would go a long way toward absorbing the goods and services that would be produced at fuller levels of employment in all countries.

3. The wasted labor power of the un- and underemployed can be seen as a vital source—along with others—of the new capital needed in industrializing countries.

In this paper, we shall bravely avoid the temptation to even list the enormous policy problems facing any who try to utilize the world's enormous pool of wasted labor.

Instead, we shall merely identify the "meta-policy" problem that most economists subconsciously recognize but, as well-behaved members of a "nonpolitical" profession, rarely mention: namely, *the intimate relation between purchasing power and political power.* If the poor have more money, they will have a larger voice in politics. While politics is not a zero-sum game, their gain would mean a loss for those who now have the most money and power. To paraphrase a remark by Jesse Jackson, people who now enjoy only three-fifths citizenship might rise to four- or even five-fifths. While those now enjoying seven- or eight-fifths citizenship would not necessarily be dispossessed, they might be reduced to the ignominious level of equality with "five-fifths people."

This is one of the reasons for inevitable resistance to any mix of policy proposals that would raise the income, self-respect and dignity of the poor.

IV. Power Democratization

> "America needs a new experiment in cooperation and collaboration to renew a sense of solidarity, enhance participation, and broaden the sharing of responsibility in economic society."
> —Ad hoc Committee on American Catholic Teaching and the U.S. Economy.

Throughout the industrialized, industrializing, and pre-industrial regions of the world—whether labelled capitalist, socialist, or "mixed"—power tends to be increasingly centralized. More and more people feel impotent in the face of huge forces beyond their control. This is particularly true of the un- and underemployed, the poor and all the so-called "wretched of the earth." Many more people feel their lives controlled by the impersonal power of giant bureaucracies, world-spanning corporations, mass media, and computerized monitoring. Intellectuals who want to do something about it by "speaking truth to power" can easily lose their precious illusions. "We are very rich," mused Walter Lippmann a little before his death. "But our life is empty of the kind of purpose and effort that gives to life its flavor and meaning."

Organization is the best way for the weak—whether in the

workplace, school, neighborhood, or region—to get power and participate in purposeful effort. Yet, as Robert Michels pointed out in his "iron law of oligarchy," there is an inevitable tendency for any organization—particularly a large one—to be run by a few.

Despite this risk, the organization of the otherwise weak is the only way to counter overcentralization and breathe more life into the valuable structures and procedures of constitutional democracy. No constructive policy can get anywhere without some kind of organizational infrastructure. Any such policies, in turn, imply—at least implicitly—some democratization of power.

Democratic Corporatism

The term "corporatism" has been given a bad reputation by the corporate-state theorists of "classic fascism." The power of old-time fascism under Mussolini, Hitler, and the Japanese imperialists was rooted in *exclusive partnerships* between the most powerful elements of big business and central government. Under these regimes, most people were rendered impotent through *mobilization* in support of imperial expansion. In many pre-industrial and industrializing countries, corporatism takes the form of "dependent fascism": exclusive partnerships between military dictators and transnational corporations. A special kind of elitist and technocratic corporatism is found in countries of state "socialism."

Incipient exclusive corporatism is to be found in many countries of constitutional and democratic capitalism. This tendency is brilliantly set forth in many writings by Manfred Schmidt of the Free University of Berlin. Schmidt refers to the "corporatism without labor" in Japan and the "quasi corporatism" of Switzerland.

On a more hopeful note, Schmidt discusses "corporatist and welfare statism" in Austria, Norway, and Sweden, countries that —like Japan—enjoy what he describes generously as "real full employment." Part of his sophisticated and highly original explanation is that in Austria, Norway, and Sweden, "trade unions are highly organized, politically united, and ideologically moderate. Moreover, they participate in tripartite-corporatist arrangements...Cooperation between trade unions, employers, and the state is based on the principles of compromise and equal exchange. In these countries, full employment is part of political orthodoxy."

We are almost prepared to call this democratic corporatism. Our hesitation is this: *the magic number three is too exclusive.* Inclusive corporatism must also make provision for (a) *many* sectors of business, (b) *many* private, non-business, and non-government sectors such as labor, religious groups, cooperatives, neighborhood associations, and foundations, and (c) local and state government.

Stronger Transnational Labor Movements

A clear implication of Schmidt's analysis is that a strong labor movement is the first institutional and political requirement for any policy of fuller employment and any structure of democratic corporatism. We accept this idea. But we add two others.

First, any serious attack on unemployment requires much more transnationalism in labor movements. In the modern world, big capital has become transnational. It is supported by impressive complexes of government agencies, consulting firms, media specialists, think-and-talk groups, and U.N. agencies. But no matter how strong it may seem at home, *a national labor movement cannot bargain very effectively with transnational capital.* It needs the help of other national labor movements which, in turn, get its help. How can the first feeble moves toward labor transnationalism—already discernible in Western Europe but almost nonexistent in industrializing countries—be strengthened?

Second, no labor movement can be strong enough to cooperate with labor in other countries if it remains weak—or allows itself to become weaker—at home. The now traditional combination of bread-and-butter unionism with national policy involvement is no longer enough. Among the great new frontiers for organized labor are: (1) reaching out to all types of workers (manual and mental, "underground" and "guests"); (2) maintaining as members those who have been laid off and can no longer pay regular dues; (3) providing many services to all members, including training, re-training, and education in public policy, planning, management, and budgeting; (4) *organizing the un- and underemployed;* (5) adopting "solidarity wage policies" that reduce the differentials between the highest- and lowest-paid members (even between full professors and instructors); and (6) avoiding the stagnation of "headquarters unionism" by encouraging activism and participation in decision-making by all their members—even at the risk of much more turnover among union officers.

Labor movements moving in this direction can best develop coalitions for empowerment of the weak (including small enterprises), infrastructures for "botton-sideways" planning, partnerships—as equals—with government monopolies and private corporations, and improved policies by political parties.

Political Leaders for Economic Rights

Economic policy making, we often hear, should be above politics and pressure groups. This is a favorite political ploy of powerful pressure groups that seek some form of oligarchic corporatism divorced from the electoral and legislative processes of constitutional democracy.

A similar ploy is subconsciously incorporated in economic planning theories that assume the existence of an all-powerful central planning board and then raise the question of what decisions this board should make. Where and how the board gets its power—and even the effect of alternative policies on the structure of power—is conveniently overlooked.

"Stay out of party politics" is a major premise of almost all technocratic planners, not merely economists. It is reinforced by the relentless march of specialization. Many liberal and even radical planners see themselves as health planners, housing planners, land-use planners, economic-development planners, etc. If they associate themselves with popular action (directly or indirectly), they usually do so in the context of single-issue movements.

The single-issue movement, however, is the activist counterpart of technical specialization. Just as researchers must specialize to get results, activists must specialize to arouse people out of apathy and toward self-empowerment. By so doing, they develop specialized political understanding on, say, a nuclear freeze, plant closings, utility costs, etc.

But despite all its advantages, single-issue activism has the same disadvantage as technical specialization. Unless counterbalanced in some way, it creates social fragmentation. The remedy is not to destroy either technical or activist specialization. It is to bring both kinds of specialties together into a broad coalition. The broadest coalition is a political party (in some countries, a coalition of parties) with the capacity to take control of the top positions of government. This kind of control is essential for planning in the service of public interests.

All single-issue drops (or cups) in the progressive bucket are important—*but only if there is a bucket to hold them together*. Otherwise, vast local and national efforts may evaporate into thin air. The political party or movement is the best bucket. Whether in power or in opposition, it can hold together the precious drops or cups of otherwise isolated actions and theories. As Paul David has pointed out, "party platforms have become important as alternative and partially overlapping national plans on which a substantial degree of execution can reasonably be expected."[14] Party building, therefore, becomes an inescapable part of national planning for fuller employment.

And the building of transnational party groupings for fuller employment requires, in turn, national party leaders capable of seizing the commanding heights of a moral vision that includes economic rights for all and overall public-interest planning.

V. Research: Information and Accountability

Information has always been a strategic source of power. It can be used to hold power holders accountable or—when part truths are presented as whole truths—to protect them from accountability.

A part of democratic planning, therefore, should be an effort to develop a "social calculus," or what is now often referred to as "social indicators," but might better be referred to as "social system" (or societal) accounting.[15] For this reason, overall democratic planning for fuller employment requires a research program based on continuous improvements in concepts, definitions, collection, analysis, and distribution of quantitative and qualitative data, including the data used in local and national budgets. Here, however, we shall touch on only a few items.

More Truth on the Jobless

> "The relative surplus population exists in every possible form... now an acute form during the crisis, then again a chronic form during dull times—it has always three forms, the floating, the latent and the stagnant.
>
> "—Karl Marx, *Capital*, Vol. I, Chapter 25.

While the distinctions made by Marx in 1867 were ahead of his time, the data now available is far behind what is needed in our time.

To get a broader view of unemployment and its implications, a new burst of socioeconomic research is needed. But not the mere collecting of more data to stuff into old boxes. By itself, that promotes a hardening of the categories. What is needed is a more effective use of presently collected data and, above all, a broader array of concepts and definitions. This requires, of course, more effective demand for the output of data producers willing and able to swim against the stream.

As a bare minimum, constructive research in this area would require fuller use of official data collected but not well publicized. Thus, for the third quarter of 1984 in the United States, the official figures showed 8.5 million people unemployed, or 7.4% of the labor force (including the resident and armed forces). But the official figures also showed that, of the people "not in the labor force," 5.5 million "want a job now." This raises the official total from 8.5 to 14 million. Also, for each unemployed jobseeker in a monthly average, there are two and a half such people during an entire year. This means that an 8.5 million average for a month implies an estimated 21.3 million people (or 18.5% of the labor force) unemployed at some time during the year.

The data become more startling when attention is paid to specific groups of people. In depressed localities and industries, the general indicators are much higher than the above. And in general, without reference to specific areas and sectors, the official rates show the following: 10.4% for all people of Hispanic origin, 16.1% for all blacks, 19.3% for all teenagers, and over 36% for black teenagers. For all these groups, moreover, and also for all older men, the official data show declining labor-force participation: in other words, large numbers of labor-force "drop-outs," "kept-outs," or "pushed-outs."

In addition to these official data, let us present some estimates based on concepts that might serve as a starting point for new research in many other countries:

Table 1

Victims of Joblessness United States

Official data:	U.S., 1984 (in millions)
Jobless jobseekers (the official unemployed)	8.5
Part-time employees seeking full-time work	5.1
Jobless job wanters	5.5
General jobless	19.1
Hypothetical estimates (as guide for new-style sample surveys):	
Dependents of the jobless (at least 1-to-1)	19.1
The insecure employed, those fearing termination (1-to-1 for jobless and dependents)	38.2
Total victims: (= 32% of U.S. population)	76.4

The above indicators could be serious understatements. They do not include the local government, landlords and storekeepers adversely affected by declining tax bases, rent payments, and consumer purchases. Moreover, the first three indicators are official estimates. Not relying on the official reports, the Center for Urban Studies of Youngstown University, Ohio, did its own door-to-door survey using the official definitions. While the government reported unemployment of 15.2% in this depressed area, the university's figure was 29.3%.[16]

Other research that has been occasionally attempted (but still only skims the surface) relates to the impact of joblessness and job insecurity on workers' morale, productivity, physical and mental health, alcoholism, drug addiction, violence in the family, suicide, low-income crime, racism, anti-Semitism, sexism, and other forms of institutionalized or spontaneous discrimination.

Still less attention has thus far been given to the other side of this huge coin: *those people and groups who see concrete benefits in both large pools of joblessness and business-cycle downturns.* "There's no insurance against inflation, strong labor movements, and higher wages like a pool of genuine unemployment—and no better way to raise productivity in competition with low-cost labor. There is no better way to squeeze the water out of the economy and pick up depression bargains than a downturn in the business cycle." Strong statements of this type with respect to the benefits of unemployment are to be found throughout business journals and in the more candid statements of many "free market" theorists. Are these benefits real? Are they short-run only? What is their relation to the structure of power?

From a more positive point of view, creative research is needed to articulate:

1. Full-employment goals in terms of desirable reductions in the hours of paid working time per day, week, and year, and expansions in opportunities for self-determined leisure as well as part-time and irregular employment.

2. Full-employment goals for various groups of people, by sex, age, and race in different geographical areas, occupations, and sectors of output.

3. The role of high employment levels in expanding purchasing power and market demand (particularly in pre-industrial societies), reducing the birth rate, promoting technological innovation, and combining stabler returns on invested capital with reduced rates of unit profits.

Clashing Corporatisms

In a recent report on social indicator research in the United States, Murray Aborn of the National Science Foundation pays "tribute to the 25 or so principal investigators who attempted implementation of the incredibly complex and extraordinarily ambitious research prospectus set forth [in *The State of the Nation: Social Systems Accounting*] by Bertram Gross in the mid-1960s."[17]

Unfortunately, before getting federal research funds, the investigators donned a powerful Cap of Darkness. They could thus make believe that without looking at power structures they could account for changes in social systems. They could also avoid looking at any monsters in the flesh or in the making.

In our times, we suggest, there are many more monsters— and more terrible ones—than Marx ever dreamed of in 1867.

In *Friendly Fascism,* one of us—with considerable help from the other—tried to produce a personal report on the changing state of American society. In it, he contrasted two trends:

1. A powerful drift toward greater concentration of power and wealth in a repressive Big Business-Big Government partnership.

2. A slower and less powerful tendency for individuals and groups to seek greater participation in decisions affecting themselves, their nation, and their world.

Today, with the benefit of more research and dialogue, we feel that this earlier distinction is not clear enough. Both trends, we suggest, deal with patterns of social organization. But the first is toward exclusive—and fundamentally authoritarian, if not repressive—corporatism. The other is toward inclusive—and democratic—corporatism.

More sophisticated attention to these clashing alternatives — and the variety within each—would undoubtedly produce more useful frameworks for deciding what concepts and styles of data collection are needed for the information in the service of accountability.

VI. Poetry of the Future: Global Dialogue

Who can hear the whimper of a hungry child?

Can such a small sound be heard in the halls where secure, well-fed leaders and experts convene to talk at and with each other?

Perhaps. But not with a mere continuation of endless meetings dealing with "basic needs" that exclude the need for productive employment and with "development" that excludes the development of human dignity through useful and fulfilling work.

People-to-People Communication

The importance of East-West and North-South summitry should not distract attention from the need for less top-top communication and more lateral communication by people at the middle and lower levels of social pyramids.

Thus, in any country considering progress toward dealing with the global unemployment crisis, consideration should be given to "People-to-People Planning Forums" legislation. A measure of this type, with appropriate wording to suit the country involved, might include such ideas as this:

1. The government hereby finds that: (a) managers, professionals, and scientists associated with transnational corporations and

national governments benefit from continuing communication through travel, meetings, electronic information exchange, membership in associations, and formal and informal networks; (b) the great majority of the people in most countries, particularly those at the lower and middle levels of income and wealth, have little or no opportunity to benefit from such forms of continuing communication; and (c) that the opportunities for such continuing communication on a people-to-people basis would facilitate democratic planning to reduce involuntary unemployment, attain sustainable recovery from recession or depression, and move toward full employment.

2. Upon the enactment of this law, the appropriate agency of government shall promote the convening in this country or elsewhere of global or regional conferences on coping with unemployment, attaining sustainable recovery from recession or depression, and moving toward full employment.

3. Toward this end, the appropriate agency of government shall provide financial and technical assistance to organized labor and profit-seeking, non-profit, cooperative, and voluntary organizations, with priority for widespread communication on how best to (a) control facility closing and capital flight by large business and otherwise, and (b) facilitate transnational labor organization and collective bargaining.

In other words, to modify the terms of international discourse, the action needed to cope with unemployment should be debated in neighborhood forums, union halls, political meetings, classrooms, regional conferences and workshops, and international sessions in many parts of the world. To facilitate such communication, published proceedings, books, and articles in many languages would be immensely helpful.

During the next four years, however, no action along these lines may be expected from the U.S. government. It remains, therefore, for nongovernmental groups or *other governments* to act on—and improve—ideas of this type.

A U.N. Full Employment-Technology Conference

Another possible measure might contain such provisions as these:

1. The government hereby finds that: (a) despite many valuable international conferences on trade, aid, currencies, labor-management relations, and working conditions, there have been no international conferences concentrating on the growing challenge of large-scale and persistent unemployment in many parts of the world; and (b) a series of global and regional conferences on coping

with unemployment and moving toward full employment could (i) help expand the markets for both domestic and foreign goods and services, and (ii) provide a more logical framework for international conferences on trade, aid, monetary matters, labor-management relations, and working conditions.

2. Upon the enactment of this law, the government shall propose to the United States the prompt beginning of a series of international and regional conferences on alternative methods of planning for the reduction of involuntary unemployment.

This action, also, cannot be expected to originate in Washington, D.C. But if other governments propose a U.N. conference on fuller employment, it is likely that the United States would go along.

If not dominated by the orthodox "Right" and "Left," technical groups or task forces under the auspices of college, labor, business, and political parties—or even the I.L.O.— could be enormously helpful in preparing the way.

It might even be feasible to plan for one or two modest regional U.N. meetings on unemployment and full employment during the next few years. This could lay the groundwork for a multi-regional U.N. conference before the end of the 1980s.

Notes

1. We reject the vulgar use of "Third World," despite its widespread usage, to identify these areas. In addition to being *first* in terms of population, these were the *first* areas where human beings came into existence and the homes of humankind's *first* civilizations. First, Second, and Third "worlds" is not like grades in primary school. They express, rather, half-conscious, patronizing assumptions of all-around Euro-U.S. superiority.

2. Drafted by Bertram Gross for Senate Military Affairs Subcommittee composed of Senator (then Vice President-elect) Harry Truman and Senator James Murray, Year End Report, War Contracts Subcommittee, December 18, 1944.

3. Its members: John Maurice Clark, Nicholas Kaldor, Arthur Smithies, Pierre Uri, and E. Ronald Walker.

4. State of the Union message, January 20, 1944.

5. Herbert Stein, *The Fiscal Revolution in America,* 1969.

6. This interpretation is explained in " 'Full' Employment Growthmanship and the Growth of the Labor Supply," *The Annals,* March 1975.

7. Fidel Castro, *The World Economic and Social Crisis,* Report to the Seventh Summit Conference of Non-Aligned Countries, Havana, 1983.

8. Edwin G. Nourse, *America's Capacity to Produce.*

9. Stanley Moses, "Labor Supply Concepts: The Political Economy of Conceptual Change," *The Annals,* March 1975.

10. Ad Hoc Committee on Catholic Social Teaching and the Economy, *Pastoral Letter on Catholic Social Teaching and the U.S. Economy.*

11. Michael Harrington, "A Case for Democratic Planning," in Irving Howe, ed., *Alternatives,* Pantheon, 1984.

12. *Let's Rebuild America,* Machinists Building, 1300 Connecticut Avenue, N.W., Washington, D.C.

13. Bertram Gross and Kusum Singh, "Democratic Planning: The Bottom-Sideways Approach," in Gartner et al, eds., *Beyond Reagan,* Harper and Row paperback, 1984, and "Planning and Freedom" in Barry Checkoway, ed., *Strategic Approaches to Planning Practice* (in press).

14. Paul David, "Party Platforms as National Plans," *Public Administration Review,* May/June 1971. This article draws heavily not only on Professor David's own research but also on the work of Gerald Pomper in *Elections in America,* Dodd Mead, 1968.

15. Bertram Gross, *The State of the Nation: Social Systems Accounting,* Tavistock, 1966; also in Raymond Bauer, ed. *Social Indicators,* MIT Press, 1966.

16. *Daily Labor Report,* Bureau of National Affairs, Washington, D.C., Nov. 5, 1984.

17. Murray Aborn, "The Short and Happy Life of Social Indicators at the National Science Foundation," *Items,* publication of the Social Science Research Council, Vol. 38, November 2/3, 1984.

Social Values, Political Goals, and Economic Systems: The Issue of Employment in European Societies

by

Jacques F. Lesourne

Around 2020, when economic historians consider the rise of unemployment in the European societies of the 1980s, there is little doubt that they will be as amazed about the inadequacy of our analysis, the inconsistency of our projections, or the inefficiency of our policies as we are when we study the reactions of our grandparents to the economic situation of the 1930s. They will have, of course, the advantage of better access to the facts of the period, the superiority of their knowledge of the following decades, and the benefit of an absence of involvement in our ideological or political debates. As observers of the present, in spite of our handicaps in comparison with future historians, we may try, however, to examine without complacency the employment issue in our contemporary European societies in order to understand how this situation has developed since the end of the 1960s, which scenarios are conceivable for the future, and why our policies have been ineffective. Since we shall avoid subtleties to keep the picture as clear as possible, the result will, of course, be somewhat provocative and debatable, but it should contribute to a better formulation of the problem. This paper will essentially refer to France, but most of the analysis seems to remain valid when transposed to other Western European economies.

Jacques F. Lesourne is professor of Economics at Conservatoire National des Arts et Metiers, Paris, France.
His paper was originally presented at a workshop organized by SNS - Business and Social Research Institute and Swedish Secretariat for Future Studies. Stockholm, 1985.

Unemployment Genesis

To adequately discuss unemployment genesis, a few preliminary distinctions have to be introduced: (1) one may refer to a static or to a dynamic description of the economy, (2) one may consider a closed or an open economy, and (3) one may select a macroeconomic framework with only one category of labor or a microeconomic context with a whole variety of labor categories.

Let us start with the simplest situation: a static and macroeconomic analysis of a closed economy. In that case, modern economic theory shows (Malinvaud, 1980, 1983) that two kinds of unemployment may exist:

- Keynesian unemployment—firms do not hire workers because of insufficient demand.

- classical unemployment—firms do not hire because they consider the expected additional cost generated by hiring workers as higher than the savings or the supplementary income it would produce. In their evaluation, firms take into account not only the present and future wages, but also the social levies and the monetary cost of regulations related to employment.

While a higher growth rate would eliminate Keynesian unemployment, marginal labor cost flexibility is necessary for the restoration of classical unemployment and the restoration of equilibrium on the labor market.

The openness of the economy adds to this description two well-known considerations:

- At a given exchange rate, the higher the exported percentage of the national production, the more sensitive is the production level to the volume of activity of the main foreign partners. As a consequence, Keynesian unemployment may be generated from outside.

- As for the real exchange rate, it influences the volume that can be profitably exported by the firm and, hence, the demand for labor at various labor costs. In other words, it may have an impact on the level of classical unemployment, though the true cause of this unemployment lies in domestic rigidities.

The analysis becomes, of course, much more complex when the dynamics of economic evolution are introduced. Depending on the assumptions made, unemployment may then occur as a permanent or a transitory phenomenon. For instance, the Keynesian unemployment volume will be altered by changes in economic agents' expectations; classical unemployment will decline if the excess of labor generates a decrease in the real cost of labor, which progressively induces a substitution of labor to other inputs and an increase in the production level considered profitable. [1]

Of course, the speed at which a transitory phenomenon would spontaneously disappear is a crucial element for the choice of an economic policy.

But an economy cannot be reduced to a unique production sector and to a unique category of labor. When microeconomic considerations are taken into account, structural change becomes possible, which means that labor demand increases in some sectors and for some categories while it decreases for other sectors and categories. Hence the existence, even if labor costs were not rigid, of a third type of unemployment, sometimes called frictional and due to the reallocation of the various categories of labor throughout the production sectors.

Let us keep in mind these theoretical elements and consider what has happened in the European economies since the end of the 1960s:

1) Almost everybody would agree on the first part of the analysis: the sustained postwar economic expansion has only been made possible by an exceptional conjunction of historical factors: European reconstruction; Japanese take-off; flexibility in domestic reallocation of resources, facilitating a balanced growth in supply and demand without important tensions in prices; high growth of foreign trade within the frame of a stable monetary system; low levels of indebtedness of economic agents at the start of the period; etc. The progressive disappearance of these conditions since the second half of the 1960s has contributed to the seriousness of the recession generated by the first oil shock, the OECD growth rates being reduced from 5.0% on the average during the decade 1963-1973 to 2.7% between 1974 and 1978 (corresponding figures for France are 5.5% and 3.2%). The second oil shock has not been a pure repetition of the first because the magnitude of the balance of payments disequilibria and the strength of inflationary pressures have led to restrictive policies aggravating the recession: in the period 1979-1983, the OECD growth rate went down to 1.1% (the French rate being around 0.9%). Therefore, there is no doubt that unemployment in Western Europe is, to a significant extent, due to the reduction in the rate of economic growth. There exists in 1984 a sizable amount of Keynesian unemployment.

2) But this is only the beginning of the story: in a country like France, unemployment rates started to increase as early as 1967, and they almost doubled between 1967 and 1974 during a period of exceptionally high growth. A study from Professor Allais (Allais, 1980), covering the period 1952-1978 and based on an econometric model, concludes that classical unemployment, which had probably been negative during most of the 1960s, had

become positive around 1967 and has regularly increased during the 1970s. For 1978, Professor Allais evaluates the volume of this type of unemployment to be on the same order of magnitude as Keynesian unemployment. This conclusion is supported by many other microeconomic studies—for instance, by the analysis of firms' employment policies.

Two elements have contributed to the relatively high level of real labor marginal costs in European societies:

• The need to extract more and more resources to finance the welfare-state—in France, for instance, the welfare-state expenditures are essentially covered by contributions related to wages. As a consequence of the growth of these expenditures, the cost of labor for the firms has increased during the 1970s even when real wages were constant. Not only has the cost of the labor induced firms to adopt more restrictive recruitment policies, but it has also favored the development of the informal economy, with households buying labor at a reduced price on the black market or substituting their own time for external labor.

• The development of what I have called the social oligopoly—in other words, the fact that, in order to negotiate between themselves and with the government, the social groups (from peasants to physicians) have created bureaucratic superstructures whose objectives have constantly been to obtain an indexation of compensations, an increase in minimum wages, a decrease (at constant incomes) of the number of hours worked per year, and/or a reinforcement of labor regulations. Quite understandable throughout the 1960s, this attitude has persisted during the 1970s, the employed people preferring the preservation of their advantages to a hypothetical decrease in classical unemployment and the unions not being ready to give priority to the fight against unemployment (in spite of some desperate struggles to try to prevent the unavoidable closure of unprofitable firms). Hence, our societies have rigidified the formal labor market to a point at which any reasonable employer should try to avoid any permanent recruitment by any means. To stop growth or to substitute capital for recruitment through productivity investment will often appear more profitable and less risky. Firing has also become so difficult that it is delayed as much as possible and concentrated in big operations that give rise to major social conflicts.

But what is remarkable is the blindness of the European societies (at least the French one) with respect to classical unemployment. They positively refuse to see it. For reasons that are, of course, easily understandable: the improvement in labor conditions has been an aspiration for decades, and to relate it to unemployment is a crime of lèse-majesté; the corporatist democracy (i.e., the system of relations between the government and the members of the social oligopoly) is considered as legitimate, and not many are ready to challenge the strategies of its agents.

3) The genesis of classical unemployment interferes, of course, with structural change. The forces that are modifying the productive structures of the European societies are well-known: competitive pressure from the NICs and from other industrial countries, technical progress, and evolution in the composition of demand. As a consequence:

• There is a decrease in the relative scarcity of those categories of labor that are abundant throughout the world or which can be easily replaced by automation, while, on the contrary, other Europeans see their professional abilities becoming more and more valuable; in other words, the dispersion among the various categories of the equilibrium labor costs is probably becoming greater, which makes some categories very sensitive to classical unemployment.

• While production increases in some sectors, it shrinks in others, but, because of the cost of labor, the expansion in the new activities is more capital intensive than it could normally be. Hence, structural change reveals a certain amount of classical unemployment that would remain hidden in a non-changing economy (as long, at least, as the firms are not compelled to fire to avoid bankruptcy).

• Economic interdependence aggravates the negative consequences of rigidities: in the declining industries, the more difficult it is for a country to adapt its costs and its production levels, the harder it becomes to find a stable and profitable level for these activities and the heavier it turns out to be to support the corresponding financial losses that represent amounts subtracted from investment in promising activities; simultaneously, the slower development of the new activities decreases the advantages of learning and makes, therefore, capturing a significant part of the international markets more difficult. As a result, the equilibrium real cost of labor tends to decline (or to increase more slowly) in the country, which, in presence of rigidities, tends to stimulate classical unemployment.

4) These mechanisms are so unpleasant that many observers prefer to look for other explanations. Two of them are frequently proposed, jointly or separately.

According to the first explanation, we face global demand saturation, and it is the lack of needs that limits employment. But, if this were so, the majority of people would be ready to accept a stagnation (or a decrease) of their income in exchange for a reduction of their working time, which would decrease the level of employment demand and diminish unemployment. However, though some groups support such an arbitrage, they still constitute a minority (in a country like France), as has been clearly shown by the refusal of the workers to accept a decrease in their income when the length of the working week was reduced in 1981/2. Hence, in spite of the fact that final demand is near saturation for some commodities in the European societies, the thesis of a global demand saturation is, at least at present, in contradiction with the facts.

As for the second explanation, it designates technical progress as one of the main causes of unemployment in our societies, stressing rightly that, with microelectronics, we are in the middle of a technological revolution of unprecedented scale with far-reaching consequences: the emergence of an information society, the replacement by robots and computers of many individuals' physical and mental activities, and the development of new capital goods and consumer durables. It is difficult to deny that technical progress is destroying many production jobs in the secondary sector. As such, in a flexible society, it would contribute, in any case, to a rise in frictional unemployment, since the new jobs would demand different abilities and would not necessarily be created at a sufficient speed. But that does not mean that technical progress would generate permanent unemployment, since there would be either no new demand and, as we have seen above, employment demand would decline, or technical progress would give rise to an economic surplus that would be devoted to an increase in the demand of traditional goods (the cost of which having become lower) or to the appearance of a demand for new commodities. In the course of the process, one would observe, however, significant changes in the equilibrium real costs of the various categories of labor. As Herbert Simon wrote years ago, a full-employment situation is perfectly conceivable in a world in which computers have an absolute advantage over individuals in all their abilities. In such a world, people would be employed in the activities in which they keep relative advantage over computers. But the present situation is not as desperate for individuals since they retain, in many fields, absolute advantages over microelectronic devices.

As stressed by Alfred Sauvy, technical progress has never given rise to permanent unemployment since the dawn of the industrial revolution. If the evolution seems to take a different course in Western Europe in the 1980s, it is due to the constraints preventing real labor costs to adapt, inasmuch as technical progress changes the equilibrium prices for the various categories of labor and, in the presence of rigidities, aggravates classical unemployment.

The forecasting errors made a few years ago in some sectors like steel—partly due to an underevaluation of the new technical possibilities and the fact that many firms have delayed firing as much as possible—have, of course, amplified the recent increase in classical unemployment.

This analysis puts into evidence two related phenomena:

(i) Rigidities play a central role in the present unemployment situation within European societies. This situation is the consequence of the emergence of a strong social oligopoly during the postwar growth period. This oligopoly tends to reinforce the demands for security and protection that exist in society. Though it constantly proclaims its commitment to full employment, it is not ready to accept any change in the rules of the game, since the unemployed are not a very strong pressure group and since the employed still prefer to keep all the advantages they enjoy while being employed.

(ii) Simultaneously, the intellectual pressure of the social oligopoly is so strong that many observers and almost all political leaders remain blind, consciously or not, to the importance of social rigidities. Rather than trying to see the unseeable, they prefer to accept comfortable, inconsistent explanations, preventing themselves from looking for policies that would keep the goals of the welfare society but would change the instruments through which these goals are pursued.

But, before discussing policies, it will be useful to present a few scenarios about the possible evolutions.

A Few Scenarios for the Future

From the preceding analysis, we may deduce that four main dimensions have to be taken into account in the construction of any set of employment scenarios over a period of ten to fifteen years: the rate of growth of the international economy, the evolution of attitudes with respect to work and income within the country, the amount of rigidity of the labor markets, and the rate of growth and the financing of welfare expenditures. Other dimensions also have to be introduced (such as the quality of education and training, the rate of technological progress, the regulations about the working time), but it will be easier to consider them in the course of the discussion.

(i) The future level of world economic growth seems essentially conditioned by the ability of nations to implement efficient economic regulation systems: exchange-rate regulation to avoid the uncertainty generated by the fluctuations in the big currencies' relative values; international financing regulation to avoid the insolvency of debtor countries; internal regulations to permit a smooth simultaneous development of consumption and investment; and internal flexibility in inputs allocation and in prices and incomes evolution.

Since the introduction of these regulations will take time, the probability is high that the world economy will experience reduced and irregular growth at least for the next decade. Hence, we cannot expect, from a revival of growth, an almost complete elimination of unemployment. At most, it may reduce Keynesian unemployment (as observed at present in the United States), but it should not be sustained enough to contribute as such to a major decrease in classical unemployment.[2]

All the scenarios proposed hereunder will postulate the same assumption of modest world economic growth.

(ii) The evolution of individual attitudes with respect to work and income is, of course, central to the construction of unemployment scenarios. To simplify a rather complex matter, we are interested in the two following trade-offs:

- the trade-off between income (direct or indirect) and free time.
- the trade-off between direct (or monetary) income and indirect income (i.e., free access to collective services).

At the individual level, several extreme attitudes are conceivable: a) the individual prefers direct income and is not ready to accept a decrease (or a smaller increase) of this income in exchange for more free time or better collective services; b) the individual chooses "quality of life" and is ready to consider a limitation of his income if he may improve this quality through an increase in the free time available; or c) the individual agrees to sacrifice a part of his direct income or a part of his free time to enjoy better collective services.

Such attitudes give rise to a whole set of assumptions at the level of society. Let us consider, in the following discussion, those that are the most characteristic.

In the first possibility, the vast majority of individuals stick to attitude (a), preferring direct income.

In the second one, on the contrary, a general move takes place towards attitude (b), free time being preferred.

In the third one, almost all society members accept priority being given to an increase in indirect income.

Finally, the last assumption corresponds to a fragmented society, in which different attitudes are adopted by various groups within the society.

(iii) As far as rigidities are concerned, two paths have to be explored: either the social oligopoly is so strong that it succeeds in maintaining the real cost of labor and the absence of flexibility of labor markets, whatever the employment situation, or, under the pressure of the external economic environment, European societies accept quicker adjustments in their prices and resource allocations.

(iv) The evolution of the welfare state may be characterized by two parameters: the rate of growth of welfare expenditures with respect to the rate of growth of GNP, and the discrepancy between the cost of labor to the firm and the net income drawn from labor by the individual. These two parameters do not necessarily follow parallel paths, though an increase of the first tends generally to increase the second.

Many scenarios can be built out of combinations of the preceding assumptions, but we shall only analyze briefly those indicated by a circled number in table 1.

Table 1

A Few Employment Scenarios for European Societies

Labor Markets

Prevailing attitudes	Flexible		Rigid	
	Welfare state expenditures		Welfare state expenditures	
	slow growth	rapid growth	slow growth	rapid growth
A	scenario 2			scenario 1
B			scenario 3	
C		scenario 4		
Mixed	scenario 5			scenario 6

Scenario 1: In this scenario, people essentially look for direct income. They resist a reduction of working time and fight for high real salaries. The simultaneous rapid growth of private consumption and welfare expenditures reduces the firms' profitability and hence limits investment. The discrepancy between the marginal cost of labor and salaries tends to increase, and firms limit recruitment and concentrate their investment on labor-saving projects. As for the unemployed, they look actively for an income in the informal economy—not without success, since it is highly profitable to avoid social levies. Hence, this scenario cor-

responds to a high level of classical unemployment and to an active black market.

Of course, the harder the international competition, the less efficient, the training processes, the quicker the technological evolution, and the unemployment level will tend to be higher.

Scenario 2: Individual attitudes are the same as in scenario 1, but the labor markets are flexible and the welfare-state expenditures do not grow as fast as GDP. It may be supposed, in addition, that the discrepancy between labor costs and wages is progressively reduced. In such a scenario, frictional unemployment remains, but classical unemployment significantly decreases and informal-labor markets do not develop. However, because of the great differences between the relative scarcities of the various abilities, wage dispersion tends to increase within society. Hence, a question that we shall consider later: To what kind of redistribution policy is it possible to associate such a scenario?

Necessarily, such a scenario has less adverse distributional effects when the training processes are able to quickly produce individuals with scarce abilities out of those whose abilities are becoming relatively more and more abundant.

Scenario 3: People are now supposed to accept a simultaneous reduction of their working time and of their income. In addition, the welfare-state expenditures are controlled and do not increase the labor costs to the firm. In this scenario, one observes, at the same time, a decrease in the final demand for commodities and a decrease in the demand for employment (expressed in working hours). The firms accept a reduction of the working time, or part-time work, in exchange for a better use of the equipment and without any increase in their total labor costs. Of course, the length of the working time has to be maintained for the scarce labor categories (as long as people are not trained in sufficient numbers), but, for the other categories, the amount of labor available is divided among more people. Unemployment decreases. Expressed in GDP terms, growth is, of course, lower than in scenario 2. As for the black market, it is not very active. What develops, on the contrary, is the amount of unpaid informal activities (transformation of goods into services by the individuals themselves, creation of associations, production of some of the services of the welfare-state by small groups of individuals).

Scenario 4: In this scenario, flexibility of the labor market facilitates a resorption, at least partially, of unemployment. Simultaneously, the rapid growth of welfare-states expenditures probably increases the difference between labor costs and wages, which implies a very unfavorable evolution of direct income (and, hence, of private consumption), but such an evolution is accepted by the individuals who privilege collective services. Working time is not reduced, and unpaid informal activities do not develop much. It is more difficult to conclude for monetary informal activities since the incentives are high, but the population concerned is not as big as in other scenarios.

Scenario 5: This is the first of two scenarios with heterogeneous attitudes among the individuals. Since the labor markets are flexible and the welfare-state expenditures do not grow too much, the scenario is favorable to the appearance of a great variety of solutions with respect to the nature of labor contracts. Part-time work develops, and many forms of it coexist with full-time work without any reduction in working time. On the whole, firms are favorable to such experiences, since the cost of labor can be adapted in each case. As a consequence, paid informal employment does not expand, but non-monetary informal activities, though not increasing as much as in scenario 3, present significant development.

Scenario 6: This scenario differs from the preceding in two respects: first, labor markets are rigid, and second, welfare expenditures grow rapidly. Because of these two features, the adaptation of labor supplies and demands in volume and nature becomes much more difficult than in the preceding scenario. Firms are generally reluctant to explore new forms of employment, their main effort being to limit labor costs. Hence, in this scenario, classical unemployment coexists with an active black market and with some development of unpaid informal activities.

What are the probabilities of these various scenarios?

- The French CFDT union is actively promoting the third, but the reaction of the workers to a decline in working time two years ago does not support the assumption that, in the medium term, attitude (b) will become dominant among individuals.
- The probability of scenario 4 does not look high: a growing resistance to welfare-state expenditures seems to be observed, and the future flexibility of labor markets is also at question.
- On the contrary, scenario 1 (or a combination of scenarios 1 and 6) seems the most probable development, at least in the coming decade. The social oligopoly fights to maintain the rigidity of markets. Governments have the greatest difficulties in restructuring the welfare-state, and the majority of individuals still demand income. If this analysis is true, we have to admit that the unemployment prospects remain gloomy in Western Europe.

These prospects would be, of course, much more favorable in scenarios 2 and 5, though perverse effects could appear in income distribution. In these scenarios, the European growth rates would be higher, and unemployment would progressively decrease.

These scenarios have, however, a rather low probability of occurrence since, as we have explained in the first part, European leaders are totally blind to some of the mechanisms generating unemployment.

We have now all the necessary elements for a useful discussion of employment policies.

Employment Policies

Two questions may be raised about employment policies: (1) Which opinion to express about the policies that have been followed since the first oil shock? (2) In which directions to search for more adequate policies in the future?

(1) To consider the first question, it is, of course, necessary to realize that the goals of government cannot be limited to the pure restoration of full employment. They also have to avoid social explosions, take into account distributional aspects, fight inflation, and maintain the balance-of-payments equilibrium. We must keep this in mind in the following discussion.

In France, three periods have to be distinguished: 1974-81, 1981-83, 1983-84.

During the first period, the policy has been characterized by:

• A great improvement of unemployment compensation for individuals who have lost their jobs as a consequence of the economic situation.

• A sustained increase in real wages from 1974 to 1976, followed from 1976 to 1980 by an increase in the social levies included in the labor costs, the consequence being a regular increase in real labor relative marginal costs; simultaneously, from 1974 to 1976, labor regulations were strengthened.

• A moderate acceptance of the decline in productive capacity and employment in the noncompetitive industries, their restructuration being largely financed through government funds.

• A moderately restrictive macroeconomic policy.

• Efforts to ameliorate training procedures.

In other words, most of the measures taken (consciously or not) could only aggravate classical unemployment, while the government preferred not to stimulate demand in labor-intensive sectors with low import-content (for instance, housing).

The second period corresponds to the first policy of the socialist government. During 20 months, the main policies that had an impact on employment were:

• A stimulation of global demand through budget deficits in order to limit Keynesian unemployment (but, partly because of the recession in the United States, it has generated a massive balance-of-payments disequilibrium).

- A wave of recruitment in the civil service.
- A reduction from 40 to 39 hours of the weekly legal working time, generally not compensated by a decrease in total wages.
- A general increase of real labor costs through various measures (increase in the length of paid holidays, augmentation of minimum wages, constraints on temporary work or on fixed-term labor contracts, additional labor regulation).
- A reduction in the job seeking among people above 55, various incentives having been given to these people to retire earlier (what the government has called the social treatment of unemployment).

From this enumeration, it is quite clear that the government has stimulated classical employment and has had only a transitory influence on Keynesian unemployment. The only efficient action has been to relabel some unemployed persons by calling them retired (which may be positive from a social point of view).

The third period started at the beginning of 1983 when the government was compelled to reverse completely its macroeconomic policy because of the balance-of-payments situation. As a consequence, the rate of growth has been strongly reduced. Keynesian unemployment has begun to increase again, and the financial situation of the firms has compelled them to readjust their staff volume. Hence, a certain amount of classical unemployment that had remained hidden for one year has become reality. At the same time, the possibilities of a social treatment of unemployment have been exhausted. Therefore, a rapid increase of the unemployment volume is considered probable over the next five years (approximately 200,000 more unemployed per year).

From this summary of French employment policies, a conclusion may be drawn: under the pressure of the social oligopoly and the prevailing weltanschauung, the French governments, whether from the right or from the left, have not made a correct diagnosis of the nature of employment. Consequently, their employment policies have combined some measures likely to have a positive impact on employment with many others that could only have negative effects.

(2) At this stage, we may ask ourselves: Which avenues could governments explore in order to improve the employment situation?

To begin with, it should be clear that the present level of economic interdependence excludes any stimulation of global demand limited to a given national economy. Hence, in that direction, the only possibility is a concerted action of the main OECD governments.

This being said, the governments should try to favor the

emergence of a scenario of type 2 or 5, the outcome depending, of course, on a change of individual attitudes, which cannot be controlled. Therefore:

- They should progressively (it will take years) change the financing of welfare expenditures in order to reduce significantly the discrepancy between the labor cost to the firm and the labor income for the individual.
- They should consider a reform of the welfare-state, not to destroy what has been a marvelous achievement of postwar European societies, but to adapt this institution to a totally new environment. For instance, it is conceivable for France to separate health expenditures into two categories, the hospital expenditures being taken in charge by the welfare system and the other expenditures being covered by personal insurance (the premium being reimbursed to the low-income households). Simultaneously, a better control of welfare expenditures could seriously reduce their growth rates.
- They should promote a greater flexibility of labor markets and avoid at least any reinforcement of existing constraints. For the same reason, they should be careful about any increase in minimum wages. (In the long run, it is less destructive for a society to have people with a lower income than people practically excluded from the economic system.) They should also eliminate distortions against temporary work or part-time work.
- Since the result of such policies could be a greater dispersion of income, the possibility could be considered of a progressive and partial replacement of minimum wages by a minimum family income (with a negative income tax at low-income levels).
- Finally, great efforts should be made to implement training policies as efficiently as possible in order to transfer individuals as quickly as possible from relatively abundant labor categories to relatively scarce labor categories.

That these guidelines are insufficient to define, in practice, a detailed employment policy is obvious. They indicate, however, errors to avoid and avenues to explore. Nevertheless, we must not underestimate the great difficulty for a government to implement adequate employment policies, on two grounds:

- Such policies imply reforms that have to be introduced progressively and pursued over many years.
- Such policies may not be supported by public opinion and will be resisted by many members of the social oligopoly (this suggests that a condition of their success would be a direct appeal by the government to these numerous citizens who are dissatisfied with the present employment prospects).

At any rate, success is far from assured.

The issue of employment in European societies is, of course, crucial for the future of these societies, but, for the observer, it also has another interest: it illustrates how the weltanschauung and the institutional setup that have developed during the high-growth postwar period make us blind to some key features of the functioning of the economic system. The fact that simultaneously we probably enter a period of fragmentation in social values and individual attitudes adds to the confusion. The governments, therefore, tend to respond to the short-term demands of their electorate and of the social oligopoly, without basing their action on a consistent interpretation of the evolution and without asking themselves what would be the appropriate instruments that, in the new context, would enable them to approach, at least partially, their goals.

But we should not forget that this inability of European societies to cope with the issue of unemployment means, for the future, a lower monetary income growth, a relative decline in the world economy, more suffering for the underprivileged groups, and greater risks of social explosion. If nothing changes, the European societies will have to pay the price of their incapacity to adapt.

Notes

1. While the impact of real labor costs on classical unemployment is clear, the influence of real interest rates is more ambiguous; since an investment may increase the productive capacity and/or improve productivity, a rise in the real interest rate will simultaneously reduce capacity investments (and, hence, will unfavorably affect labor demand) and delay productivity investments (and, hence, will maintain jobs). But, because capacity investments are more sensitive to the interest rate than productivity investments, the first impact is probably bigger than the second, and the resulting influence is negative. High real interest rates also generate Keynesian unemployment through the usual mechanism of reduction of global demand.

2. Classical unemployment is easier to limit in a growing economy, since the equilibrium real cost of labor is increasing, which may diminish the discrepancy with the effective real cost of labor, if this latter remains constant or increases only very slowly.

References

Allais, M., *Rapport d'activité scientifique du Centre d'Analyse Economique*, Juil. 1978/Juin 1980. (Document non publié).

Dubois, P., *Expansion et repartition: quels choix stratégiques pour la France* (à paraitre dans un ouvrage collectif), Nov. 1983.

Lesourne, J., Les mille sentiers de l'avenir, Seghers, Paris, 1981.

Lesourne, J., "L'avenir des économies européennes: évolutions autononomes et pressions extérieures," *Communication a l'Académie des Sciences Morales et Politiques*, Sept. 1982.

Lesourne, J., Le chômage et la théorie économique, Projet, no. 156, Juin 1981.

Malinvaud, E., *Réexamen de la théorie du chômage*, Calmann-Lévy, Paris, 1980.

Malinvaud, E., *Essais sur la théorie du chômage*, Calmann-Levy, Paris, 1983.

Olson, M., *The Rise and Decline of Nations: Economic Growth, Stagflation and Social Rigidities*, Yale University Press, 1982.

Sauvy, A., *La machine et le chômage: Le progrès technique et l'emploi*, Dunod, Paris, 1982.

The Prospect of Work in the Western Context

by

David Macarov

Discussions of the future of work tend to be inconclusive, not only because they deal with the unprovable yet-to-be, but also because the very concept of work is unclear and complex—definitions abound, ideology intrudes, circumstances alter cases, and the surfeit of research findings makes it possible, through judicious picking and choosing, to prove almost any thesis. It should be no surprise, therefore, that there is little general consensus concerning many of the elements which make up the future of work.

Yet certain factors regarding the future of work are becoming more clear and less controvertible, although no less controversial. New technology will bring about an even more rapid increase of per-person productivity than has been known in the past, resulting in more goods and services, as well as shorter hours and more unemployment. Needing more jobs but less work, society will attempt to maintain the present emphasis on human labor as its central value and structural base by dividing jobs into smaller and smaller components; by condoning, if not encouraging, the maintenance of useless jobs and the growth of unproductive work time; and by engaging in various job-creation and job-sharing schemes.

Ultimately, after a transition period which will probably be chaotic, if not anarchic, the recognition that human labor need play only a minor role in a healthy economy will result in the emergence of values other than work as the touchstone of the

---

David Macarov is associate professor, Paul Baerwald School of Social Work, The Hebrew University, Jerusalem, Israel.

desirable citizen, as well as a structure for distributing the resources of society other than on the basis of the kind or amount of work performed.

Arriving at the almost-workless society with as little individual and social upheaval as possible will require not only planning and determination, but the ability and courage to strip work of the moral values with which it has been endowed over the ages and to view it as a purely instrumental activity which has outlived its usefulness.

The latter will not be easy, for even scientifically-trained researchers, academics, professionals, and planners have been known to literally bristle at the very idea that work is not in and of itself a moral act. Despite their training to be objective and value free, they are unable to examine the evidence—let alone draw conclusions from it—because they have been conditioned to see work in moral terms. Thus, they confuse desires with expectations—and from such a matrix, historical tragedies emerge.

Definitions

Work: About the fifth century B.C., the Bhagavad Gita posed the questions:
"What is work? And What is not work? These are questions that perplex the wisest of men."

Since that time, the answers continue to elude us. The Oxford English Dictionary devotes nine pages to the definition of work, and Webster's Unabridged, 12. The difficulties inherent in trying to define work have been discussed extensively—by Parker, O'Toole, and others. Consequently, throughout the literature, definitions range from the simplistic through the esoteric to the very complex. For example, a definition such as "Any useful activity" (Plamore) not only contains a value judgment, but is so wide as to be inapplicable. Similarly, O'Toole's "An activity that produces something of value for other people" not only contains the same value judgment regarding usefulness, but admittedly includes activities of unpaid people, such as housewives and volunteers, and consequently cannot be used in discussions of employment and unemployment, for example. As definitions become more specific, they become more restrictive; e.g., "An obligatory economic action involving physical energy with the intention of perfecting or bettering something, which is useful and respectable" (Schrecker). This would rule out those engaged in demolishing houses or wrecking cars, since they are not perfecting or bettering something, as well as the writers and publishers of literature containing erotic—and hence not respectable—passages. It would also omit those engaged in intellectual, rather than physical, endeavors.

On a more conceptual level, Arendt's oft-quoted distinction between work and labor is elegant but hardly functional. In her formulation, work produces articles that are lasting and a source of satisfaction, while labor produces articles that are immediately consumed and must be renewed. Thus, it should be possible to distinguish between a work of art and a labor of love. However, in trying to apply this definition, the physical activity involved in planting a pine tree becomes work, since pines are for beauty; but the same activity applied to a tomato plant is labor, since tomatoes are for eating. But what becomes of this distinction if it is later decided to cut down the pine tree to use its lumber, or to leave the tomato plant unpicked, as a decoration? Definitions which depend on intentions and can be changed by subsequent actions are of doubtful validity.

Neulinger goes even further with this type of distinction, distinguishing between work, the job and leisure. Depending upon the source of satisfaction and the amount of coercion, one may be at leisure on or off the job, or working during one's free time. Again, an interesting formulation but of doubtful applicability to most discussions of work in the real world.

As a final example of the difficulties inherent in defining work, take Mouly's comment that work is characterized by being perceived as unpleasant, being a duty, and giving no direct satisfaction—an exact description of putting a diaper on one's grandchild.

Other definitions emphasize elements such as payment, coercion, time frames, supervision, lack of autonomy, societal expectations, and so forth. Due to this welter of definitions and the difficulties inherent in each of them, there is a tendency for definitions of work to be idiosyncratic to the article or purpose for which they will be used. Consequently, for the purposes of this article, work will be operationally defined as *those activities in which people engage in order to acquire the goods and services that they want*. Admittedly this definition does not distinguish between physical and intellectual activities, or between those that are legal and illegal, socially useful or socially destructive; nor does it distinguish between self-employment and working for others. It also eschews activities undertaken for emotional, psychological or social ends alone, such as volunteering, rehabilitation workshops, and leisure-time activities. It has been found functional, however, for discussions of employment, unemployment, full employment, and various aspects of work patterns (Macarov, 1982).

The Future

It can be argued that for all practical purposes there is no present (Cornish). The present is an abstraction postulated to exist between the past and the future, but it is of such fleeting existence that—like the distance between Achilles and the tortoise—it is only theoretically present. It is of such minute quantity that it can neither be measured nor have an effect. Thus, as we pronounce the very word "present," one syllable is already in the past while the other is still in the future. Even when we arbitrarily designate a time period as the present, it is a combination of the past and the future.

And since we cannot influence the past (although we may change our knowledge about the past or our interpretation of it), we can only be part of, and try to influence, the future. Indeed, we live our lives on the basis of assumptions as to what will take place next year, next week, tomorrow, in five minutes, or in the split-second from what we think of as "now." As Lamm points out, "One of the dilemmas of the human condition is that our experience and knowledge is about the past, while our decisions are in the future." Consequently, there is no question as to whether we *do* try to predict the future, but rather within what time frame, on the basis of what information or assumptions, and how successful we are.

Insofar as time frames are concerned, the year 2000, or the beginning of the 21st century, is beguiling, and it has been used for a number of studies and articles. It is, however, only 15 years in the future, and—as a glance back at 1970 will reveal—although some things will change radically, most things will remain pretty much as they were. This is perhaps why Jaffe and Froomkin's study found that 10-year projections tend to be pretty accurate.

On the other hand, students graduating from universities today, at about 25 years of age, may work in their professions or occupations until they are 65, if not longer, which means another 40 years, or until 2025. Or, if we take children being born now, who will probably have a life expectancy of 90 years, we are projecting until 2075. Consequently, if we take as our time frame the lifetimes of people alive today, or the working life of those entering the labor force now, we are speaking of a period from 2025 to 2075. Such projections are not unimaginable—in 1974, the United Nations predicted minimum and maximum world population figures for the year 2075. On a shorter range, Goodman found that of the 137 devices concerning information technology alone imagined by George Orwell over 30 years ago, about 100 are now practicable. In any case, it has been observed that the unanticipated usually happens in addition to the expected rather than in place of it, so there is utility in planning for the expected (Ferkiss).

As for the instruments used for predicting the future, these have been listed as:
  trend extrapolation
  scenarios
  expert consensus
  relevance tree
  cross impact matrix
  models, games, simulations
  systems analysis
  technology assessment (Cornish).

Each of these must be used with caution, logic, an understanding of the variables involved, and common sense. Each is merely an instrument, and none of them—or any combination of them—is infallible. Hence, it is salutary to try to weigh the possibilities of an event occurring against its consequences. Thus, if something seems almost certain to occur, but the results will be trivial, planning is hardly indicated. On the other hand, even if there is only a small probability of something happening, but the results if it does occur will be either catastrophic or utopian, it would be wise to at least take it into account. This, incidentally, is what military planning units try to do—to assess probabilities in the light of outcomes. In other words, although prediction is fallible, it is better to plan even for the improbable than to have to meet it without prior thought.

The West

For purposes of this paper, work will be discussed within the general context of the Western industrialized nations, with specific attribution to individual countries where necessary. Generally speaking, both Japan and Israel are exceptional cases, for different reasons and are not included in this discussion unless specified. Similarly, although trends in the Eastern or Communist-bloc countries have a great deal in common with those in the West, the implications and manifestations differ due to structural, attitudinal, and ideological reasons, and consequently will not be included here.

The Growth of Productivity

Despite short-term fluctuations and differences in various countries, per-person productivity has been rising over the long term throughout the West at least since the Industrial Revolution. This has been estimated by the International Labor Office to be currently about 2.7 per annum, which aggregates to about 35%

in 10 years. Levitan and Johnson hold that during this century alone, productivity has at least quintupled. Looked at differently, between 1972 and 1982, the real product per employed worker rose in industrial countries, from a minimum of 14% in England to a maximum of 37% in Japan (*Jerusalem Post,* November 15, 1983).

The steady increase in productivity is even more striking when it is realized that it has occurred despite a number of factors which should have—and perhaps did—reduce per-person productivity. The entrance of a growing number of women and members of minority groups into the labor force, without prior experience and generally without much training, should have had such an effect. The growth of part-time work, as well as the growth of the labor force itself, should have added to this brake on productivity. But if these have reduced the trend, they have not, and probably will not, bring it to a halt.

It should not be assumed, of course, that individuals continually work harder, or work harder or better now than they did in the past. Rosow estimates that only 10% to 25% of changes in productivity are accounted for by changes in human labor. Increases in productivity arise from changes in methods, machines, and materials—not manpower. Ultimately technology—whether through capital, investment, efficiency, or better use of energy—is the single largest factor in productivity growth. Again, it would be a mistake to see technology as simply providing a machine in place of a human being. Technology makes possible entirely new systems and methods of doing things, which need less human labor. The milkman who places a bottle on the porch, whom Gabor saw as irreplaceable, has not been replaced by a machine which does the same, but by an entirely different way of acquiring food and keeping it in the house—supermarkets, freezers, powdered milk, pasteurization, sterilization, the proliferation of public and private transport—all have played a part in transforming the system. There is very little doubt that the postman will go the same way, as information technology continues to develop, and so will many other jobs for which human beings seem indispensable today.

Increases in productivity make themselves felt in many ways. Among them is the abundance of material goods available throughout the West. There is practically no material good which is in short supply due to technical inability to provide it. The factor which controls the amount of production is customer demand, coupled with purchasing power. Indeed, productive capacity so outstrips customer demand that immense industries are devoted to creating more demand through advertising, public relations, and the like.

The same is true of services. Although productivity is harder to define and measure in the services, those studies that have been done indicate an almost parallel growth in productivity (Carey; Carnes: Carnes and Band; Mark). There is little question concerning the impact of technology on certain areas of the service sector. It has been estimated that automation in offices could easily result in 15% more productivity within five years (*World of Work Report,* November 1980). Over 30% of current middle management positions in banks could be eliminated without any appreciable effect on service (*World of Work Report,* June 1982). The word processor and the computer memory make the typist and file clerk infinitely more efficient.

Within the human services, too, the inroads of technology are evident. In medicine, changes ranging from electronic blood pressure measurements through use of finger caps, to CAT scanners, to microsurgery with laser beams, are cases in point. Even in counseling, Schoech and Arangio find technology equal to, if not better than, human therapists in some cases: "Individuals with thoughts of suicide were interviewed by a computer, which was able to predict suicide attempts more accurately than experienced clinicians."

Insofar as information and communication jobs are concerned, the OECD says that information-processing machinery has been increasing its capabilities about 10 times every five years. Hillard points out that if the creation and acquisition of new knowledge continues at its present rate, a child born today will find that the amount of knowledge in the world will be four times as great when he or she graduates from college; 32 times as great when he or she is 50 years old; and 97% of everything known in the world at that time will have been discovered or learned during his or her lifetime.

This is not to say that technological change is without its economic, social, and human costs. Indeed, there are those who wonder whether the gains are worth the costs (Tévoédjrè). Nevertheless, from the point of view of increased productivity, nothing else has anywhere near as great an impact. Technology accounted for 54.5% of the growth in national income per employed person in the United States from 1948 through 1969. As a factor in the postwar growth of the American economy, technology was four times greater than business capital investment, 2.8 times greater than investment in education, and 3.8 times greater than improvements from more efficient use of resources. Without technology the growth rate of the postwar economy would have been cut in half (J.O. Wilson).

Insofar as continuation of technological change is concerned, there is an opinion that we are nearing the point of having exploited the bulk of opportunities opened by the impact of science since the end of the last century (Tévoédjrè). There is a contrary opinion, however, based upon a study of "waves" of seminal inventions, that the next cluster of basic innovations may be expected around 1989, plus or minus five years (Mensch). It is certainly true that the pace of change is unequal. As Freedman has pointed out, if airplanes had developed at the same pace as computers, the time from the Wright brothers to the Concorde would be about six months. Or, if automobiles had developed like computers you could buy a Rolls Royce for $2.75, get more than 3 million kilometers a litre, and have enough power to drive the *Queen Elizabeth II* (Evans).

However, on balance, there seems little chance that technological change will cease, or even slow appreciably. Many inventions are synergistic, not only applicable to a broad number of situations, but making possible and calling forth even further changes. And the speed of change seems to be increasing. There were more profound changes in the last four decades than there were in the previous six centuries (Shane and Sojka). Mensch holds that 80% of the industrial products and processes now sold in the markets will be phased out by 1990 and replaced by some alternatives; further, that about 60% of present industrial produce will be replaced during this century by something still to be developed or to be specified. Indeed, to believe that technological change has come to an end is to be in the position of the British lord in the eighteenth century who proposed that the Patent Office be closed, since everything conceivable had already been invented.

If the continuation of technological change were only to result in the production of more goods and services—and new goods and services—one could simply argue as to whether these were necessary and/or desirable. Technology, however, and its concomitant, productivity, have efffects other than these.

Reduction in Working Time

That increased productivity has not been completely absorbed by the provision of more and novel goods and services is obvious by its effect on working time, on the one hand, and unemployment, on the other.

A few figures will suffice, for it seems obvious that most people do not work as many hours today as did their grandparents. In 1900, the average workweek in the United States was 53 hours;

in 1980, 35.5 hours. From 1948 to 1981, work hours in the United States dropped from 42 to 35; work hours in France were 47 in 1957, and 40 in 1981; during the same time period, work hours shrank in Germany from 46 to 41; and in Britain from 48 to 43; in Japan from 46 to 40; and in Israel from 44 to 36. The phenomenon is almost universal in industrialized countries *(Yearbook of Labor Statistics)*.

Vacations are longer, there are more workless holidays, entry into the workforce is later, and retirement is earlier. These figures, taken from ILO publications, include part-time workers and take into account overtime work. Even insofar as workers holding second jobs are concerned, this has remained constant at about 5% for many years (Michelotti; Rees: Taylor and Sekscenski).

There is little reason to believe that work times will increase in the future. The recent steel strike in Germany, which had as its sole aim a reduction in working hours, is a case in point. Bell predicts a 30-hour week and 13 weeks of vacation a year in the year 2000. Emery foresees a week of four 8-hour days, with summer and winter vacations, while Albus predicts a 10-hour week. Others use different figures and different time frames, but no one predicts stabilization of hours at present levels, much less a return to longer work hours.

In short, technology, which leads to productivity, has made it possible—if not necessary—to reduce the amount of human labor expended, and this trend promises to continue into the indefinite future. However, there are limits to this trend: Durkheim predicted long ago that dividing jobs into smaller and smaller segments would lead to worker alienation and anomie, with subsequent individual and societal problems. Homans points out that a situation is eventually reached where it is simply no longer economical to segment jobs, due to the costs of planning, record keeping, coordination, and supervision. When these limits are reached, there will be no alternative to the elimination of jobs entirely.

Unemployment

Despite efforts to spread the work available by reducing each worker's hours, the phenomenon of unemployment is not only ever present, but growing. Of the 18 countries reporting unemployment figures to the ILO in 1955, only one—Austria—had a lower figure in 1982; and the latter figure was higher than any intervening report. In all 17 of the other countries, 1982 rates were much higher than the 1955 rates. In some countries— Australia, France, Netherlands, Spain, Great Britain, and Yugoslavia—the 1982 unemployment figure was 10 times greater than that of 1955. Similarly, whereas a 4% unemployment rate was seen as "acceptable" (read: inevitable) in the United States during the 50s, the actual rate was at least 5% (McGaughey). In 1979, many economists were arguing that the economy was at full employment despite a 6% rate (Thurow). When 4% is the figure used in Congress, liberal economists argue for a 5.5% rate, and conservative economists speak of 6.5% unemployment as full employment (*World of Work Report,* April 1979). In 1982, *The New York Times* spoke of 6% to 7% unemployment as "built into the economy." The Council of Economic Advisors now speaks of a "natural" rate of 6-7%—12 years ago, they spoke of 3.5% in the same terms.

Within these figures, there are pockets of much higher unemployment—minorities, people living in depressed areas and, increasingly, youth. Unemployment in these groups can rise as high as 60% in some places. The matter of youth unemployment has become one of special concern in a number of countries, for these are people who have not built up vestedness in compensation programs through previous work; nor acquired savings and/or pensions; or even attained job skills or work-related behavior patterns. There is fear that many of these young people will *never* find work, or, at most, only transient and temporary employment.

It should be noted, incidentally, that all of the figures given above are from official sources and are by many criteria understated. Unemployment is beset with many definitional and enumerative artifacts. These include listing only those who receive compensation, or who report daily to employment offices, or who fill out forms, or who prove that they are actively looking for work. Exclusions contain those on waiting time, those who have exhausted their benefits, those declared "unsuitable for employment" (Field), those holding part-time jobs but seeking full-time work, and those who are discouraged to the point of no longer seeking work. There is also the widely used artifice of enrolling the unemployed in training courses, thus listing them as students receiving stipends rather than as the unemployed being paid compensation. As a result of these many methods to hide the extent of real unemployment, it has been estimated by a number of researchers that the real unemployment figure is invariably from 50% to 300% higher than the official ones (Kogut and Aron; Field; Livitan and Taggart; Macarov, 1980).

Nor has unemployment risen due to lack of efforts to contain it. Attempts to reach full employment—or, at least, to reduce unemployment—have occupied governments from time immemorial (Garraty; Kumar; Macarov, 1985). Mendelssohn holds that the later pyramids in Egypt were basically public works projects to contain unemployment. The same can be said of a road—still visible—that Herod started to occupy the builders of the recently completed Second Temple. Taggart lists efforts to increase employment as tax cuts, wage subsidies, reduced work time, public works projects, and public service—none of which have been very successful—to which can be added training and retraining schemes, job sharing (Best), and inducements for geographical mobility. Rubenstein takes what is perhaps the most extreme position, saying that when mass unemployment and destitution no longer serve the national interest, strategies for the physical elimination of the unemployed will then begin to form.

Covert Unemployment

In addition to those unemployed in the traditional sense, there is evidence of the lack of need for human labor among those holding jobs. The two basic phenomena of this type are known as featherbedding and goldbricking. Featherbedding consists of maintaining useless jobs or inefficient methods in order to spread employment. For example, Vespasian forbade the use of rivers for conveying building materials since it deprived people of work (Garaty). Later examples include firemen (coalshovelers) on diesel trains; printers setting up type only to break it up again; and the third and sometimes fourth person in an airline pilot's compartment built for two (Jacobs).

More recent examples are the 630 printers given lifetime contracts by *The New York Times* to do work for which 350 were required (Zimbalist), or contracts such as those given New York longshoremen, which guaranteed them pay for 38 hours of work a week whether they perform it or not. Indeed, the introduction of new machinery or new methods in many places must be accompanied by a pledge not to dismiss any workers, which means in effect that while the machines do the work, the workers continue to draw salaries.

Perhaps even more revealing are the instances when the government subsidizes a failing company not because its products are irreplaceable but in order to save jobs. Thus, when a shipyard is threatened with closure, no one argues that there will be insufficient ships, but that there will be fewer jobs. This even becomes a dangerous situation when it is recognized that much of the current make-work necessitated by unemployment is not the harmless leaf raking of bygone days, but rather the production of armaments—even doubtful armaments—because of the jobs that it gives (Silk).

Finally, featherbedding has given rise to neo-Luddism, in that machinery which would do the work easier, faster, safer, cheaper, and cleaner is resisted, in favor of much less efficient and more expensive human labor.

Goldbricking, the second element in covert unemployment, consists of work time not used for work. Sometimes termed "unproductive work time," or "time theft," this is more familiarly known as loafing. Measuring the extent of this phenomenon is not easy, but Walbank's study indicates that most people use about 44% of their potential at work. Seventy-eight percent of Yankelovich's respondents said that they could work harder than they do. Cherrington had building workers watched for two years and found that 49% of their time was used for something other than the job. Nor are executives immune; Olson found that the average white-collar management staff wastes four hours out of eight. This does not necessarily mean that workers are deliberately holding back: in this author's research in an Israeli kibbutz, almost every member reported that they could work harder than they did. When asked why they did not work harder, they replied that the job didn't require it. Others have found the same—Berg concludes that "keeping a job usually requires performance far short of the potential of the worker." One of Terkel's respondents put it more succinctly: "Jobs are not big enough for people."

The combined effect of featherbedding and goldbricking is not confined to measurements of work actually needed. They have profound effects on the workers themselves. Not only do great masses of people get little satisfaction from their work—they also know that they are not working hard. However, they must keep up the pretence of working, or at least put in their hours, regardless of what they do. The result is widespread socially sanctioned corruption in which one appears to keep busy although not really working hard; overlooks others engaged in the same make-believe; and conspires with superordinates or subordinates to conceal the true situation.

Perhaps even worse, in terms of workers' self-images and mental health, is the knowledge on the part of many of them that their jobs could be done better, faster, and cheaper, for 24 hours a day and 365 days a year, by a machine—a machine that takes no vacations, wastes no time, participates in no strikes, needs no fringe benefits, and never asks for a raise. And yet such people are expected to feel that their work is important, useful, and self-fulfilling—or to at least pretend that they do.

Incidentally, the goldbricking system is not confined to the West. Shop hours in the Soviet Union are being changed to keep workers from slipping away from their jobs to shop and run errands; and raiding parties visit bars, restaurants, barber shops, and stores looking for workers who have ducked out of the office (*The New York Times,* February 6, 1983). In any case, there is evidence that unproductive work time is not only expensive, costing the United States about $125 billion in 1981 *(Working Woman),* but seems to be on the increase (Kendrick).

Adding the unemployment figures (corrected from the official to the real) to the covert unemployment figures and taking into consideration the reduction in working hours, it is clear that less human labor is required today than it was in the past, and that this demand gets steadily smaller. To the extent that this demand is based upon technological changes, and to the extent that technological change will continue, there seems to be real reason to question the role of human labor in the world of work in the future. However, two counterarguments can be, and often are, adduced.

New Goods and New Services

One of the possibilities that argue against any severe reduction in the amount of work needed is that the creation of new goods and new services, including technology itself, will absorb redundant workers from previous areas. It is certainly true that technology is creating new goods and new services. However, these are themselves subject to technological unemployment in relatively short order. Atari, producing a relatively new product, now turns out a computer every 27 seconds, and its labor cost is about 1% of the total. The reason for this efficiency is the massive use of computers in the manufacturing process. Indeed, most electronic devices have many fewer moving parts than do their predecessors, and thus are easier to manufacture and to repair. An electronic telex machine has one microprocessor in place of 936 moving parts; an electronic cash register requires only 25% as much labor to produce as its previous version (Norman). Jobs for computer programmers, once heralded as the employment boom of the future, are dwindling as standardized programs proliferate, and as computers program themselves.

Further, many of the new devices replace, rather than augment, existing items. Video games practically wiped out pinball machines; ballpoint pens did the same to fountain pens; word processors are replacing electronic typewriters, which replaced electric typewriters, which replaced manual typewriters. And sound transcribers will eliminate word processors. The Swiss watch industry lost 46,000 jobs, and seventeen manufacturers went bankrupt with the introduction of digital watches. An Israel report says: "Of the 60,000 persons employed in textiles today, some 55,000 can never be retrained for electronics or high technology" (Dean). It is because of such reasons that Reich concludes: "High technology standing alone promises to generate relatively few jobs," and an AFL/CIO report says flatly: "There won't be enough high-tech jobs to replace the jobs lost in declining industries" *(The Future of Work.)*

The second possibility advanced against the postulation that less work will be needed has to do with the services, and particularly the human services. Here the thinking is that as people are redundant in industry, they can be trained to provide services not now offered or not offered in sufficient quantity. This viewpoint postulates more services for the aged, the handicapped, the ill, the troubled, the deviant, and so forth.

It is certainly true that one of the most profound shifts in Western economies has been going on for about fifty years now, with more and more employment being offered and found in service occupations. Despite severe problems in defining and categorizing service occupations (Shelp), it has been estimated that the service sector now constitutes over 80% of the jobs in the United States, for example (Thurow) and there are estimates that this will grow to 95% (Stellman) or 97% (Best) by the end of the century.

However, despite the extent to which the services have absorbed the fallout from industry, the facts remain that unemployment is high, hours are short, and featherbedding and goldbricking remain. Thus, the shift to services must be seen as only a partial solution of the problems created by technology-induced productivity. And, as pointed out previously, the services themselves are subject to the same inroads by technology.

The question that remains is whether there are areas of need—and therefore employment—that have not as yet been covered or saturated, and that can develop in a manner that uses surplus manpower. An examination of the purported need indicates, however, that there is no shortage of the professionals operating in the human service areas. Or, to put it more precisely, if there are unmet needs in the human service areas, it is not because there has been a manpower shortage and people have not been available to train for or fill such jobs. The manpower is available—sometimes in surplus numbers—but the jobs, or the jobs offering proper conditions, are not.

For example, of the registered nurses in the United States, one-third are not working, and one-third work only part time (Flick). In Israel, too, one-third of the nurses work part-time

(Handless et al.). Although nurses, teachers, and social workers may be in short supply in certain geographic regions, such as outlying districts or slum areas—or in certain professional specialties, such as renal social workers—there is no aggregate manpower shortage which needs to be relieved by infusions of more people.

Indeed, the popular conception of manpower shortage in the services focuses on the unskilled and the untrained—those who push the wheelchairs, empty the bedpans, change the linens, do the laundry, serve the food, clean the floors—in short, those who do what Gans has called the dirty, dead-end jobs of society. Again, in view of current unemployment figures, there is no shortage of people for such jobs, but there are the jobs that nobody wants. And experience in industry indicates that it is precisely into the dirty, dangerous, disagreeable jobs that automation creeps.

Consequently, electronic wheelchairs, operated by push buttons or joysticks, are replacing manually-operated chairs; there are robots that prepare food and perform other household chores for quadriplegics (*Jerusalem Post,* June 1, 1983) and beds in which patients can blow into one of a series of tubes and have the bed tilted or get a glass of water, among other things (Stokes). Thus, for a number of reasons, it would not do, as McKinlay warns, to overestimate the extent to which the service sector can absorb otherwise unemployed workers.

There seems little reason to believe, therefore, that either new goods and services, or expansion of existing ones, will absorb the additional productivity that technology will make possible. Leontief, the Nobel economist, has developed a "fully integrated, dynamic input-output" model, taking into consideration not only technological change, among other things, but also the new industries that such change might create. He concludes: "The intensive use of automation over the next twenty years will make it possible to conserve about 10% of the labor that would have been required to produce the same bills of goods in the absence of increased automation." Thus, if current trends continue, in 40 years we can expect a 20% further decrease in work times and a 20% increase in useless jobs, time wasted on the job, and official unemployment. That would make unemployment between 27% and 35% in many countries, with real unemployment reaching 40% to 52%.

Crying Wolf

A much-used counterargument to the postulation of enormously reduced human labor due to technology is that such predictions are crying "Wolf!" In other words, such predictions have been made in the past, but they have not come to fruition, so current efforts should be viewed as additional false alarms. However, if one views overt unemployment, covert unemployment, reduction in work time, featherbedding, and goldbricking together, it is clear that, in some measure the previous predictions have borne fruit. Further, to argue that because something has not happened in the past it will not happen in the future is akin to arguing that since some natural resource has never become depleted it never can be (Rada). Thus one dodo and one dinosaur must have reassured another. Finally, it is salutary to remember the end of the story of the boy who cried "Wolf!" The wolf came, and the society was not prepared.

An OECD report asks, "Is there something really new about information technology which may make it qualitatively different from past technology changes?" And answers itself: "There are two such unique features. One of them is the unprecedentedly rapid *rate* of improvement in information processing capacity... The other is that information technology may have its greatest impact on the services sector." *(Science and Technology Policy for the 1980s)*. Hence, it will not do to dismiss predictions of future reductions in the need for human labor on the basis of past performance, nor in the hope that the services will demand more, rather than less, work.

Attitudes Toward Work

Past changes in the world of work have both impacted upon and been caused by peoples' attitudes toward work. In fact, an enormous literature has been built up, based upon tens of thousands of studies, descriptions, experiments, and experiences. In 1976—almost ten years ago—Locke found over three thousand published studies, while others feel that there is at least an equal number of unpublished reports or undocumented experiments (Katzell, et al.; Cummings and Molloy). In the interim, there have probably been just as many published and unpublished studies.

Generally speaking, the thrust of the bulk of those studies (which are relatively superficial surveys, simply asking workers whether, or to what extent, they are happy) indicates a high level of satisfaction. So high, in fact, that many researchers caution that satisfactions cannot be measured on an absolute basis, but only relatively. Others point out that high levels of work satisfaction say very little because there is a very strong tendency in survey research to report satisfaction with every aspect of life, even when it is obvious that problems are present (Haavio-Manila; Gutek).

Other researchers have found, however, that when one goes

deeper than superficial questions, either with in-depth interviews or using facet-questions, a different picture emerges (Garson; Kanter and Stein; Lasson: Terkel; Rubin: Schrank: Yankelovich). Few people get active pleasure from their jobs or their work. Their attitudes have been described as "resigned acceptance" (Macarov, 1982) and "fatalistic contentment" (Lasson). And since satisfaction can be described as fulfillment of expectations, Robinson points out that as workers come to recognize the reality of their jobs, a "surrender process" sets in as original expectations from work are lowered. Price found that older workers tend to report themselves as more satisfied, but this is due to the "lowered rising expectations" reported by the Opinion Research Corporation. Few people in all of the reported studies speak of their work as challenging, exciting, or fulfilling, and those that do tend to be in ego-satisfying, power-wielding, policy-determining positions—and constitute a small minority of all workers.

Even more revealing than what people say about their work is what they do. The previously discussed reduction in work time did not come about over the objections of the workers. Despite the societal norm that people want to work, need to work, and are happy at work, the behavior indicates that almost nobody is willing to work more hours than he or she is paid for. The few workaholics (Machlowitz) are far, far outnumbered by those at the other end of the continuum, who constantly seek methods of reducing the amount of work they do.

Take, for example, the matter of retirement. In Sweden, in 1982, 40% of all workers in the 60-64 age group retired early (*European Industrial Relations Review.*) In the United States, given the choice of a full pension at age 65, or the loss of three-years' salary and 30% of their pensions for life, the number of Social Security recipients opting for the latter has increased since this option was offered, and now accounts for over half the retirees (*Statistical Abstracts of the United States,* 1981.) Men are leaving the work force with greater frequency than ever before. In the 1950s, nearly nine out of 10 men aged 55 to 64 worked. Thirty years later, less than three in four did (Levitan and Johnson). Nor is this decrease due to mandatory retirement or to health reasons. Parnes found that 60% of retirees are healthy and volunteer voluntarily, and 68% of them are not interested in working. His evidence is fairly conclusive that the vast majority of covered workers retire early or at the mandatory age with no desire to work longer (Parnes). Indeed, despite mythology to the contrary, 25% of blue-collar retirees in Eisdorfer and Cohen's sample reported improved health after retirement, and only 10% reported a decline. Further, a very large majority of retirees report that their experience in retirement has equalled or surpassed their expectations. In short, more and more people are acting on their real feelings about their work and retiring as soon as possible. Those with enough money are happy in their retirement, glad they retired, and wish they had retired sooner (Barfield and Morgan; Heidbreder; Atonley).

In summarizing the way great masses of people feel about their work, one cannot do better than to quote Jenkins and Sherman: "If religion was the opium of the masses, work is the castor-oil of the population."

The paradox of a society that postulates work as both necessary and desirable, and of individuals who share that belief, while at the same time people get little satisfaction from their work and try to reduce or avoid it as much as possible, is handled by individuals in a number of ways: ambivalence, goal displacement, cognitive dissonance, cultural lag, projection, and separation of norms from behavior (Macarov, 1970). Ultimately, however, the fact that people do not like to work, do not like their jobs, their workplaces, or their work, might have an effect on their readiness to accept a different set of values, activities, and sources of income.

Changes in Work

The amount of human labor which will be required in the future cannot be pinpointed, either as to amount or as to time. However, whether future society will be almost workless, or whether the number of people without jobs will simply be much larger than it is today, there will probably always remain some work requiring human hands or brains. What kind of work it will be, and its implications, lead to divided opinions.

One opinion holds that technology will wipe out the dull, dirty, difficult, disagreeable, dangerous jobs (Glenn and Fielding; Zimbalist; Kraft)—or, in Foulkes' terms, hot, heavy, and hazardous work. This is the way much technology starts. A second view is that although the new jobs will probably be white-collar rather than blue-collar, they will require fewer skills, and many people will be over educated for such jobs (Foulkes). Still another opinion holds that technology will remove the interesting aspects of work, thereby increasing lack of satisfaction and alienation (Richardson). A study by Gabel and Meers found that mechanization of a bank led half the workers to want more enriching work, but England and associates studied fifteen countries and found that, among industrial workers, the level of technology did not account for differences in amounts of satisfaction.

The bulk of opinion, however, seems to agree with the AFL/CIO report that foresees an increasingly polarized, two-tiered work force, dominated with low-paid workers at the bottom performing routine, high-turnover jobs, with a few professionals and executives at the top performing highly paid creative jobs *(The Future of Work.)*

The workers at the bottom may find their situations even less satisfying than similar workers today. Telecommunications equipment makes it much easier to monitor work—the words per minute typed, the number of errors, amounts of non-work time, units produced, and so forth. Richardson says that automation leads to less time for what Schrank calls *schmoosing* on the job: "We can expect to find an increase in worker alienation and a decline in job satisfaction as workers spend less time informally socializing both inside and outside of the work setting." They may also find new health hazards in their jobs—there is some fear of the radiation from visual display terminals, and some tentative findings of its effect on pregnancies (Hiller). Ergonomics, the study of the physical relationship of people to machines, has entered this field mostly at the request of manufacturers, who seek "user friendly" machines. On balance, however, automated equipment has been found to be much less hazardous, in terms of work accidents, than its predecessors.

There will undoubtedly be other important changes in the content of work and the way work is done, only a few of which can be mentioned briefly here. The spread of flexitime, for example, may bring into the labor force many people who would not otherwise be available for work due to their normal time commitments: parents who can work only while their children are in school; people who must be home for a number of reasons during the day, but who can work at night; those who can free themselves for blocks of time, but not as a schedule; and others. Such people will, by increasing the labor force, also increase the pressure for jobs, and unemployment. Technology makes possible such flexitime arrangements, as demonstrated by the number of university personnel who use computers in the wee hours of the morning, when they are not confined by class schedules and domestic arrangements.

Swart, incidentally, found that the great majority of the firms that he studied viewed flexitime as a positive development. Workers in 62.5% of the utilities in his sample reported higher satisfaction when given flexitime opportunities, and 37.5% reported much higher satisfaction. No one indicated less satisfaction. The firms involved also reported higher efficiency under this arrangement.

Flexiplace, too, will have enormous implications. The ability to work at home, or reasonably near home, can change child-care arrangements, such as nursery schools, enormously. The same may be true of institutions for the care of the aged; and the chronically ill. The opportunity to stay home, or near home, may make it possible to deal with many situations differently than at present. Some of the implications of flexiplace are already evident: firms that no longer find it necessary to be in mid-city, but which can locate in suburbs, or even in open country, due to enormously improved communications methods; neighborhood work centers, which are a compromise between working in the city and working at home (Salomon and Salomon; Simmie); and changes in traffic planning and city planning. There are also implications concerning traffic, pollution, housing design, and others, inherent in flexiplace.

A negative implication of flexiplace, or the cottage workshop, is the danger in which these can become a return to the old sweatshop, piecework system. If production in the home is recompensed in terms of units turned out, and if the work involved is made simple enough through technology, there is a danger that the entire family, including children, will put in all available time, to the neglect of other things, in order to acquire more income. And as output increases, per-unit payment usually decreases, so the family has to work harder and harder to maintain their income.

This situation reflects the danger to labor unions inherent in home production and, conversely, the danger of weakened unions to workers, especially under such conditions.

The entrance of growing numbers of women into the labor force, alluded to several times previously, also has many implications. The reduction in industrial jobs means a loss of the traditional "men's jobs," and the remaining jobs tend to be seen in less sex-discriminating contexts. That women can perform high technology jobs, when this involves button punching and gauge guarding, is obvious even to diehard male chauvinists. The jobs that will remain in the high-tech era will be much more available to women, which, in turn, will influence family patterns, child-care methods, individual roles, and self-images, among other things.

Finally, in this necessarily abbreviated foray into the meaning of changes in the world of work, there may be that which Naisbitt has termed the "high-tech/high-touch" syndrome. In this scenario, the growing relationship of people to machines will necessitate and bring forth new methods, or renew old methods, of person-to-person contacts. Naisbitt believes that the impersonality of work in the future will cause that which Mitchell terms "the belonging society," in which human contacts outside work will be sought out and treasured as compensation for their lack at work. This lack seems to be borne out by Foulkes' finding that workers tend to give robots names in order to humanize them (and that at least one factory forbids such practice in order, presumably, to discourage such efficiency-disturbing relationships).

A number of questions must remain unanswered, and even undiscussed, at this point: Will work in the future require more or less education? A different kind of education? Will a high-tech economy require less concern for other people? Are different personal characteristics required? Will work offer more or less prestige than it does today? Will it pay more or less? Will people get satisfaction from the work they do? If only a minority of people work, how will they be chosen? If the majority do no work, what will they do with their time? These are serious questions (Macarov, 1983), and each deserves serious study in its own right.

Underlying each of these questions, however, are two areas that any discussion of a future reduction in the amount of work must address: What societal value will take the place that work now holds; and what structure for distributing society's resources will replace that of job holding?

Value Changes

Values and structures are inextricably linked. Values bring forth and support societal institutions, and those institutions support and solidify values. They can be discussed separately only for heuristic purposes.

The major and central value in Western society is that of work. "The concept of work is one of the most widely spread and deeply embedded elements in individual psyches, the structure of societal institutions, and the value system of industrial civilizations. It is the measuring rod of individuals, the goal of organizations, and the basis of society. It is almost as encrusted with value-orientations and transcendental meanings as is religion. . . . Work is seen. . . . as both necessary and desirable for the individual and for society" (Macarov, 1981).

The reasons for this worship of work extend far back in history (Macarov, 1980). Suffice it here that work, once seen as purely instrumental, took on affective values with Luther's equating work with serving God; with Adam Smith's insistence that everyone compete with everyone else for the good of all; from the concept of mercantilism, which put the wealth of the nation ahead of the individual; and from Freud's dictum that happiness consists of the ability to love and to work. In this manner, work took on elements of religiosity, good neighborliness, good citizenship, and mental health. As a consequence, all the instruments of socialization—the church, the state, the marketplace, the educational system, the family, even the criminal justice system—are brought to bear on the individual to motivate him or her to enter the world of work and to equip the individual to do so.

Yet there are those who question the centrality of work in life, even under present circumstances. A.D. Smith holds that people should be entitled to provisions making for a decent life without regard to what they do, have done, believe, or belong to—that people have a "right to life," simply by virtue of being alive. Indeed, one of the philosophic or ideological underpinnings of the welfare state is the belief that the collectivity, the body politic, the polity, should undertake the risks of the exigencies of life, rather than the individual or designated members of his or her family. This finds clear expression in an American court ruling that selecting certain relatives as financially responsible for others deprives them of equal protection under the law because family membership is an unreasonable classification for separating the liable from the nonliable (Eagle). Similarly, according to Smith and others, welfare policies based upon whether one has worked, does work, or can work, and limited to or by the amount that one has worked, are essentially immoral (Macarov, 1981).

Others have begun to question the role of work as a value, due to the inherent dissatisfaction that great masses of workers experience (Macarov, 1982; Schrank; Rubin; Garson; McGaughey). Even the shibboleth that workers find self-fulfillment, in Maslow's terms, in their work—or that self-actualizing activities lead people to work harder or better—has been questioned both through empirical studies (Macarov, 1976) and through experience, as voiced by Fein: "It is only because *workers choose not to find fulfillment in their work* that they are able to function as health beings . . . By rejecting involvement in work which cannot be fulfilling, workers save their sanity."

Still others feel that value changes regarding work will come about whether they are desired or not, due to the structural changes to be expected. Kaplan, for example, says that as leisure time expands, people come to be defined in terms of their leisure pursuits rather than their work. Similarly, Jamal et al., hold that the demands of work will have to be subordinated to the demands of nonwork activities as the latter become more prominent and important. R.M. Wilson acknowledges that seeking this kind of value change will not be easy: "The avowed, conscious pursuit of leisure is . . . a genuine test of personal courage."

There are in history, and throughout the modern world, many examples of civilizations which had values other than work as their core value. The ancient Athenians, for whom work was done by slaves, disparaged work. In Jewish life, Torah study was—and in some places, still is—the most important activity in which a person can engage. In Brazil, life is said to revolve around football, Carnival, and the Church (Cardoso). There are places in Africa in which cooperation with others is the highest value (Social Reconstruction ...). Japanese society is said to rest on a sense of duty, to the Emperor, to the employer, to the family—rather than on a sense of rights (De Vos). There have been societies based upon military prowess, athletics and, of course, religion. Thus, as Meenaghan and Washington put it: "The prevailing conception of work is not ancient nor is the way work [is] organised necessarily natural."

It is within this general framework that Werneke and Broadfield argue for a needs-oriented approach to manpower: needs being defined as income, value to society, and satisfaction to individuals. These are the values to which societal structures should be directed. Freedman also argues that even if a return to full employment were possible, broader approaches to employment and work life would be warranted.

Most writers stress the difficulty of changing morals or values, but there are also those who feel that such change can and will come about relatively easily. Penicillin and the pill, in recent years, and the automobile before them, led to major changes in sexual mores within one generation, causing St. George to comment, "How shallow are our values." Others put it succinctly: "Values change to fit the world which technology presents" (Gordon).

Structural Changes

The major structural change that enormous increases in permanent unemployment will require will be in the income-distribution method. In short, there will have to be a method of dividing the resources to be made available by technology, other than through the medium of holding a job.

There are a number of alternatives. One is to re-define work and pay people for doing many things which currently are unpaid. This has been termed the "provision of meaningful alternatives to [current] paid work" (Freedman). Just as professional ballplayers, musicians, entertainers, writers, etc., are currently paid, so it might be desirable to pay everyone who engages in sports, music, the arts, or entertainment, among other things. Indeed, the list is endless—people could be paid for doing anything they wanted to do, provided it was not socially or personally destructive. The Canadian government currently makes grants available to aspiring writers, rather than to successful ones. Students are given stipends on the basis of grades and need in many countries; they could be paid to study regardless of these conditions. This is what Mouly and Broadfield call for: acceptable remunerated substitutes for work. Or, as Duboin puts it, "Life is not only a matter of creating wealth . . . There are other things: study, the arts, science, sport, in short, everything that makes life worth living." These are the things that can be encouraged and supported as alternatives to work as currently conceived.

A second possibility is to divide the resources of society more or less equally, with everyone getting a share. Income in this case would not be based in any way on what people do but would be theirs as of right. Again, this is not fanciful: cooperatives almost always operate this way, and there are countries in which cooperatives are very large, income producing, and of long standing. A further step in this direction is the collective, in which members are provided with all their needs, i.e., equity rather than equality.

Other methods present themselves. Schrank suggests that workers—individually or as a group—buy machinery to replace themselves, living on the difference between their wages and the cost to them of the machine. Casner-Lotto points out that a robot costing $45,000, amortized over eight years, will cost $5 an hour as compared to $15 an hour now paid a human worker, and by the turn of the century, the cost of robot labor may be down to about 70 cents an hour (Bylinsky). In Japan, a robot leased for $90 can turn out work that would cost $1,200 if done by humans. As Albus points out, "If all humans could own the equivalent of one or two robots, they would be financially independent regardless of whether they were employed or not."

Ingenious minds can probably devise other means for distributing income outside the mechanism of work and jobs, but in a society based upon very little human labor, and therefore, few jobs, some such system will of necessity be put into operation. When a majority of the labor force is unemployed, seeing such persons as responsible for their own situation—"blaming the victim," in Ryan's terms—will no longer be possible. Or, as Cunninrham points out, when 10% of the people do all the work necessary, "Shall we continue to regard the other 90% in the same light that we viewed yesterday's 4% or 5% unemployed? The question answers itself." It is in this sense, that quantity does change quality, that both Theobald and Griffiths call for "full unemployment" as a catalyst that will lead to new definitions and new structures.

The Transition Period

As difficult as it will undoubtedly be to adjust to the envisioned state of affairs when it comes about, it will be infinitely more difficult to move from the present situation to the expected one. Adams points out how the struggle for jobs will intensify as they become scarcer, and Jackson outlines the methodology of "guerrilla tactics in the job market." The transition period might be marked by cataclysmic processes—riot, rebellion, revolution, and anarchy (Koch; Ferkiss). Consequently, as Senator Gary Hart says, "We must find a way to shift from the economy of the past to the economy of the future with as little pain and as much excitement as possible."

A second possibility is a relatively peaceful move. This might come about by building on existing situations and enlarging them. Thus, shorter hours, longer vacations, more holidays, later entry into the work force, and earlier retirement might be continually but gradually emphasized, while value changes and structural changes begin to take place more as a resultant than as a goal.

Or, along these lines, existing children's and family allowances—which exist in almost every Western country except the United States—can be gradually increased until they become, in effect, a guaranteed minimum income. In those countries where the program is confined to families with children, this can be shifted to family allowances, regardless of whether they have children. This can then be further shifted to individual allowances, regardless of family status. Further, students' stipends could be made universal, to all students, as could grants to aspiring and practicing artists, entertainers, athletes, etc., regardless of financial need or personal ability. Guaranteeing lifetime salaries to all workers, whether work is available or not, is a more limited proposal, but it is based upon existing practice in some places, for some groups, under certain circumstances. Finally, it would be possible to enormously increase unemployment insurance, without restrictions as to waiting time, vestedness, time limitations, or job seeking.

A third scenario has been termed the "passion scenario" (Macarov, 1980), in which there is an active, passionate attempt to achieve a workless world as soon as possible. Here, every effort would be made to invent and use labor-saving devices. Inventors, scientists, and workers would be offered large bonuses, in addition to salary continuation, for labor-saving devices and methods. Rather than fear job losses, workers could look forward to carefree futures by inventing themselves out of jobs.

The goal of a workless society would be supported in every way that work is glorified today. The release of human creativity and the increase of human happiness which would result would become societal goals of the highest importance. Mechanization and the desire for efficiency would not be stifled by fear of job losses. As Freedman holds, technology freed from all restraints arising from fear of job loss and unemployment would reduce to a small fraction the paid work performed today.

There is one more important factor to consider. Even if people were paid to engage in activities not presently considered work—and certainly if they were simply provided income without requiring an activity—there would probably be much more free or leisure or non-work time than there is today. Many people see this as a problem. In some cases, it is posed as a societal problem, almost in the moral terms that the devil finds work for idle hands to do. In other cases, this is seen as a problem for individuals, who would be bored. It is interesting, although not important, that most people who pose this problem put it in terms of "What will they do with their time?" Rarely is it termed, "What will I do with my time?"

The use of vastly expanded leisure time can indeed require societal intervention, perhaps in terms of providing a cafeteria array of interesting things that are not presently within the reach of many people. It can institute courses of study, exhibits, etc., to interest people in areas that have previously been unknown or foreign to them. It can adopt some of Best's ideas about lifelong learning experiences. It can also change its own ideas as to the need for leisure time activities to be "productive" or "constructive."

However, as Kaplan has pointed out, most people have tried out different types of leisure-time activities throughout their lives—on weekends, on holidays, on vacations, and during daily non-work time. They know what they like and what they don't like to do. Freed of both financial need and guilt feelings about not working, most people would probably find enjoyment in life. Those that didn't, of course, would be able to seek the same kind of counseling, psychotherapy, or religious help that unhappy people in today's work world have available to them.

It is interesting that despite personal pleasant anticipations of more leisure time, many people still fear what "they"—the amorphous, faceless mass of people different from themselves—will do, or find to do. This "ideology of mistrust" (Macarov, 1978), which is somewhat similar to an earlier societal postulation of a separate "culture of poverty" (Macarov, 1970), is based upon an essentially pessimistic view of people's potentials and intentions.

Yet the ancient Greeks, freed of the necessity to work, enjoyed a period of creativity on which most of modern civilization is based—government, science, the arts, philosophy, and other aspects too numerous to mention. The Jewish community of past periods, devoting itself almost exclusively to Torah study, was singularly free of crime. Both of these factors exist in today's kibbutz where, all the basic needs of life and many of its luxuries provided, there is a revival of many art forms and almost complete absence of crime. Even the WPA during the Depression in the United States, with all of its deficiencies, unleashed a creative outpouring that remains until today in the form of murals, plays, literature, and much else.

There is no reason to believe that modern men and women are any less capable of using leisure constructively than are their forebears. As Passmore says:

> It is very hard to shake off the feeling that man is capable of becoming something much superior to what he is now. There is certainly no *guarantee* that men will ever be better than they now are; their future is not ... underwritten by Nature. Nor is there any device.... which is certain to ensure the improvement in man's condition.... But we know from our own experience, as teachers or parents, that individual human beings can come to be better than they once were.... We know, too, that in the past men have made advances, in science, in art, in affection. Men, almost certainly, are capable of more than they have ever achieved.

The coming technology era has the possibility of releasing men and women from the tyranny of work—and releasing them gradually, peacefully, beautifully—if there is both the courage and the intention to grasp the opportunity.

References

Adams, W., "Economic Theory and Economic Policy," *Review of Social Economy,* 40(April, 1982):1-12.
Albus, J.S., "Robots in the Workplace: Key to a Prosperous Future," *The Futurist,* 17(February, 1983):22-27.
Arendt, H., *The Human Condition.* Chicago: University of Chicago Press, 1958.
Atchley, R.C., *The Sociology of Retirement.* New York: Wiley, 1976.
Barfield, R.E., and J.N. Morgan, *Early Retirement: The Decision and the Experience and a Second Look.* Ann Arbor: University of Michigan, 1975.
Bell, D., *Toward the Year 2000: Work in Progress.* Boston: Beacon, 1967.
Bell, D., "The Future That Never Was," *Public Interest,* 5 (1978):35-73.
Berg, I., M. Freedman and M. Freeman, *Managers and Work Reform: A Limited Engagement.* New York: Free Press, 1978.
Best, F., *Work Sharing: Issues, Policy Options and Prospects.* Kalamazoo: Upjohn, 1981.

Best, F., *The Future of Work*. Englewood Cliffs: Prentice-Hall, 1973.
Best, F., *Preparing California's Workforce for Jobs of the Future*. Unpublished paper prepared for meeting of California Commission on Industrial Innovation, 1982.
Bylinsky, G., "The New Robots: Nimble—and Far Brainier," *Fortune*. (December 17, 1979).
Casner-Lotto, J., "Robots Expected to Boost Productivity," *World of Work Report*, 5(March, 1981):17.
Cardoso, F.H., "Social Development: A Latin-American View," in C.A.O. van Nieuwenhuijze (ed.), *The Quest of Another Development: A Social Approach?* The Hague: Institute of Social Studies, 1981.
Carey, J.L., and P.F. Otto, "Output per Unit of Labor Input in the Retail Food Store Industry," *Monthly Labor Review*, 100(January, 1977): 42-47.
Carnes, R.B., "Laundry and Cleaning Services Pressed to Post Productivity Gains," *Monthly Labor Review*, 101 (1978):38-42.
Carnes, R.B., and H. Band, "Productivity and New Technology in Eating and Drinking Places," *Monthly Labor Review*, 100(September, 1977):9-15.
Cherrington, D.J., *The Work Ethic: Working Values and Values That Work*. New York: Amacom, 1980.
Cornish, E., *The Study of the Future*. Bethesda: World Future Society, 1977
Cummings, T.C., and E.S. Molloy, *Improving Productivty and the Quality of Work Life*. New York: Praeger, 1977.
Cunningham, R.L., *The Philosophy of Work*. New York: National Association of Manufacturers, 1964.
Dean, M., "Textiles Are Also High-Technology," *Jerusalem Post*, July 30, 1984, p.6.
De Vos, G.A., *Socialization for Achievement: Essays on the Cultural Psychology of the Japanese*. Berkeley: University of California Press, 1973.
Duboin, J., *la grande releve des hommes par la machine*, Paris, 1932; quoted by Garraty, J.A., *Unemployment in History*, New York: Harper and Row, 1978.
Durkheim, E., *The Division of Labor in Society*. New York: Free Press, 1933.
Eagle, E., "Charges for Care and Maintenance in State Institutions for the Mentally Retarded," *American Journal of Mental Deficiency*, 65 (September, 1960):199.
Eisdorfer, C., and D. Cohen, "Health and Retirement: Retirement and Health: Background and Future Directions," in H.S. Parnes (ed.), *Policy Issues in Work and Retirement*. Kalamazoo: Upjohn, 1983.
England, G.W., I. Harpaz amd I. Norvath, "Worker Satisfaction: Its Nature and Causes Among Production Workers in Fifteen Countries," in Jacob, P., et al., (eds.) *Automation and Industrial Workers: A Cross National Comparative Perspective*. Oxford: Pergamon, in press.
Emery, F., *Futures We Are In*. Leiden: Martinus Niijhoff, 1977.
European Industrial Relations Review, 122(March, 1984):5.
Evans, E., *The Micro Millennium*. New York: Washington Square Press, 1979.
Fein, M., "Motivation to Work," in R. Dubin (ed.),*Handbook of Work, Organization, and Society*. Chicago: Rand McNally, 1976.
Ferkiss, V.C., "Technological Man," in Inciardi, J.A., and H.A. Siegel (eds.), *Emerging Social Issues: A Sociological Perspective*. New York: Praeger, 1975.

Field, F., "The New Feminism and the World of Work," *The Public Interest,* 71(1983): 33-44.

Foulke, F.K., Quoted in "Robots and Technology: How to Manage Technostress," *Personnel* 61 (July/August, 1984): 51-52.

Freedman, D.H., "Grounds for Pessimism," in Freedman, D.H. (ed.), *Employment Outlook and Insights.* Geneva: ILO, 1979.

Freedman, D.H., "Seeking a Broader Approach to Employment and Worklife in Industrialised Market-Economy Countries."*Labour and Society,* 8(April/June, 1983): 107-122.

The Future of Work. AFL-CIO. Reported in *World of Work Report,* 9(January, 1984):5.

Gable, R. and A. Meers, "Impact of Two Successive Mechanization Projects on Motivation and Work Organization in a Bank," in G.O. Mensch and R.J. Niehaus (eds.), *Work, Organization, and Technical Change.* New York: Plenum, 1982.

Garraty, J.A., *Unemployment in History: Economic Thought and Public Policy.* New York: Harper and Row, 1978.

Garson, B., *All the Livelong Day: The Meaning and Demeaning of Routine Work.* Harmondsworth: Penquin, 1975.

Gorz, A., *Farewell to the Working Class: An Essay in Post- Industrial Socialism.* Boston: South End Press, 1982.

Glenn, B.N., and F.L. Feldberg, "Proleterianizing Clerical Work: Technology and Organizational Control in the Office," in A. Zimbalist (ed.), *Case Studies on the Labor Process.* New York: Monthly Review Press, 1979.

Goodman, D., "Countdown to 1984: Big Brother May be Right on Schedule," *The Futurist,* (December, 1978): 345-355.

Gordon, T.J., "The Feedback Between Technology and Values," in Baier, K., and N. Rescher, *Values and the Future: The Impact of Technological Change on American Values.* New York: Free Press, 1969.

Griffiths, D., *Whither Work.* Bundoora: Preston Institute of Technology Press, 1977.

Gutek, B.A., "The Relative Importance of Intrapsychic Determinants of Job Satisfaction," in K.D. Duncan, M.M. Gruneberg, and D. Wallis (eds.), *Changes in Working Life.* Chichester: Wiley, 1980.

Haavio-Mannila, E., "Satisfaction with Family, Work Leisure and Life Among Men and Women," *Human Relations,* 24(1971): 585-601.

Handless, Y., L. Appel and M. Sagin, *Satisfactions of Nurses at Work.* Tel Aviv: General Federation of Labour, 1982.

Hart, G.,, "Investing in People for the Information Age." *The Futurist,* 17 (February, 1983):10-14.

Heidbreder, E. M., "Factors in Retirement Adjustment: White- Collar/Blue-Collar Experience," *Industrial Gerontology,* 12 (1972):69-79.

Hillard, R., quoted in W. Abbott, "Work in the Year 2001," in E. Cornish (ed.), *1999: The World of Tomorrow.* Bethesda: World Future Society, 1978.

Hiller, J., *The Video Display Terminal in the Office.* Baltimore: Johns Hopkins University, 1981.

Homans, G. C., *The Human Group.* London: Routledge and Kegan Paul, 1951.

Jackson, T., *Guerrilla Tactics in the Job Market.* New York: Bantam, 1978.

Jacobs, P., *Dead Horse and the Featherbird.* Santa Barbara: Center for the Study of Democratic Institutions, 1962.

Jaffe, A. J., and J. Froomkin, *Technology and Jobs: Automation in Perspective*. New York: Praeger, 1968.
Jamal, M., V. V. Baba and V. F. Mitchell, "The Nature and Structure of Nonwork," *Relations Industrielles*, 37(1982):618- 633.
Jenkins, C., and B. Sherman, *The Collapse of Work*. London: Eyre Methuen, 1981.
Jerusalem Post, June 1, 1983, p. 4; November 15, 1983, p. 6.
Kanter, R. M., and B. A. Stein (eds.), *Life in Organizations: Workplaces as People Experience Them*. New York: Basic, 1979.
Kaplan, M., *Leisure in America: A Social Inquiry*. New York: Wiley, 1960.
Kaplan, M., *Leisure: Theory and Policy*. New York: Wiley, 1975
Katzell, R. A., P. Bienstock and P. H. Faerstein, *A Guide to Worker Productivity Experiments in the United States 1971-1975*. New York: New York University Press, 1977.
Kendrick, J. W., "Productivity Trends and the Recent Slowdown," in W. E. Fellner (ed.), *Contemporary Economic Problems*. Washington: American Enterprise Institute, 1979.
Koch, E., *The Leisure Riots*. Montreal: Tundra, 1973.
Kogut, A., and S. Aron, "Toward a Full Employment Policy: An Overview," *Journal of Sociology and Social Welfare*, 7(1980): 85-99.
Kraft, P., "The Industrialization of Computer Programming: From Programming to 'Software Revolution'," in A. Zimbalist (ed.), *Case Studies on the Labor Process*. New York: Monthly Review Press, 1979.
Kumar, K., "Unemployment as a Problem in the Development of Industrial Societies: The English Experience," *The Sociological Review*, 32(1984): 185-233.
Lamm, R. D., "Why the U.S. Closed Its Border," *The Futurist*, 16(1982): 4-8.
Lasson, K., *The Workers*. New York: Grossman, 1971.
Leontief, W. and F. Duchin, *The Impacts of Automation on Employment, 1963-2000*. New York: Institute for Economic Analysis, New York University, 1984.
Levitan, S. A., and C. M. Johnson, "The Survival of Work," in J. Barbash, et al, (eds.), *The Work Ethic: A Critical Analysis*. Madison: IRRA, 1983.
Levitan, S. A., and R. Taggart, quoted in Levison, A., *The Full Employment Alternative*. New York: Coward, McCann and Geoghegan, 1980.
Locke, E. A., "The Nature and Causes of Job Satisfaction," in M. D. Dunnette (ed.), *Handbook of Industrial and Organizational Psychology*. Chicago: Rand McNally, 1976.
Macarov, D., *Incentives to Work*. San Francisco: Jossey-Bass, 1970.
—"Reciprocity between Self-Actualization and Hard Work," *International Journal of Social Economics*, 3(1976): 39-44.
—*The Design of Social Welfare*. New York: Holt, Rinehart and Winston, 1978.
—*Work and Welfare: The Unholy Alliance*. Beverly Hills: Sage, 1980.
—"Welfare as Work's Handmaiden," *International Journal of Social Economics*, 8 (1981): 21-30.
—"Work and the Prospect of Development in the West and Elsewhere," in C.A.O. van Nieuwenhuijze (ed.), *The Quest of 'Another Development': A Social Approach?* The Hague: Institute of Social Studies, 1981 a.
—*Worker Productivity: Myths and Reality*. Beverly Hills: Sage, 1982 b.
—"Changes in the World of Work: Some Implications for the Future," in H. Didsbury, Jr. (ed.), *The World of Work: Careers and the Future*. Bethesda:

World Future Society, 1983.
— "Overcoming Unemployment: Some Radical Proposals," in H. Didsbury, Jr. (ed.), *Creating a Global Agenda: Assessments, Solutions, and Action Plans.* Bethesda: World Future Society, 1985.
— "The Concept of Employment in Social Welfare Programs: The Need for Change in Concept and Practice," *Journal of Sociology and Social Welfare* (in press).
McGaughey, W., Jr., *A Shorter Workweek in the 1980s.* White Bear Lake, MN: Thistlerose Press, 1981.
Machlowitz, M. M., *Workaholics: Living With Them, Working With Them.* New York: Mentor, 1981.
McKinlay, J. B., "The Limits of Human Service," *Social Policy,* 8(1978): 29-34.
Mark, J. A., "Measuring Productivity in Service Industries," *Monthly Labor Review,* 105(June, 1982): 3-8.
Meenaghan, T. M., and R. O. Washington, *Social Policy and Social Welfare: Structure and Applications.* New York: Free Press, 1980.
Mendelssohn, K., *The Riddle of the Pyramids.* London: Sphere, 1977.
Mensch, G. O., "The Co-Evolution of Technology and Work Organization," in G. O. Mensch and R. J. Niehaus (eds.), *Work, Organizations, and Technological Change.* New York: Plenum, 1982.
Michelotti, K., "Multiple Jobholding Rate Remained Unchanged in 1976," *Monthly Labor Review,* 100(June, 1977): 44-48.
Mitchell, A., "Human Needs and the Changing Goals of Life and Work," in F. Best (ed.), *The Future of Work.* Englewood Cliffs: Prentice-Hall, 1973.
Mouly, J., "Employment: A Concept in Need of Renovation," in D. H. Freedman (ed.), *Employment Outlook and Insights.* Geneva: ILO, 1979.
Mouly, J., and R. Broadfield, "Objectives and Policies: A Reassessment in the Wake of the Recession," in D. Freedman (ed.), *Employment Outlook and Insights.* Geneva: ILC, 1979.
Naisbitt, J., *Megatrends: Ten New Directions Transforming Our Lives.* New York: Warner, 1982.
Neulinger, J., *The Psychology of Leisure.* Springfield: Thomas, 1974.
New York Times, March 21, 1982, p. 26F; February 6, 1983, p. 41E.
Norman, C., *Microelectronics at Work: Productivity and Jobs in the World Economy.* Washington: Worldwatch Institute, 1980.
Olson, V., *White Collar Waste: Gain the Productivity Edge.* Englewood Cliffs: Prentice-Hall, 1983.
Opinion Research Corporation. *National Executive Briefing on Changing Work Values in America,* 1977.
O'Toole, J., *Work, Learning, and the American Future.* San Francisco: Jossey-Bass, 1977.
Parker, S., *The Future of Work and Leisure.* New York: Praeger, 1971.
Parnes, H. S. (ed.), *Policy Issues in Work and Retirement.* Kalamazoo: Upjohn, 1983.
Passmore, J., *The Perfectability of Man.* London: Buckworth, 1970.
Plamore, E. B., "Physical, Mental and Social Factors in Predicting Longevity," *The Gerontologist,* 9(1969): 103-108.
Price, C. F., *New Directions in the World of Work: A Conference Report.* Kalamazoo: Upjohn, 1971.
Rada, J., *The Impact of Micro-Electronics.* Geneva: ILO, 1980.

Rees, A., *The Economics of Work and Pay.* New York: Harper and Row, 1979.
Reich, R. B., "An Industrial Policy of the Right," *The Public Interest,* 7(1983): 3-17.
Richardson, V., "Social Change in Perceptions of Work Relations," *Social Service Review,* 56(1982): 138-148.
Robertson, J. P., "Occupational Norms and Differences in Job Satisfaction: A Summary of Survey Research Evidence," in J. P. Robinson, R. Athanasiou and K. B. Mead, *Measures of Occupational Attitudes and Occupational Characteristics.* Ann Arbor: University of Michigan, 1969.
Rosow, J. M., "Productivity and People," in J. M. Rosow (ed.), *Productivity: Prospects for Growth.* New York: Van Nostrand Reinhold, 1981.
Rubin, L. B., *Worlds of Pain: Life in the Working Class Family.* New York: Basic Books, 1976.
Rubenstein, R. L., *The Age of Triage.* Boston: Beacon, 1983.
Ryan, W., "Blaming the Victim: Ideology Serves the Establishment," in P. Roby (ed.), *The Poverty Establishment.* Englewood Cliffs: Prentice-Hall, 1974.
Saint George (Szent Gyorgyi), A., *The Crazy Ape.* New York: Philosophical Library, 1970.
Salomon, I., and M. Salomon, *Telecommuning—The Employee's Perspective.* Jerusalem: Hebrew University, 1982.
Schoech, D., and T. Arangio, "Computers in the Human Services," *Social Work,* 24(1979): 96-102.
Schrank, R., *Ten Thousand Working Days.* Cambridge, MA: MIT Press, 1979.
Schrecker, P., *Work and History: An Essay on the Structure of Civilization.* Gloucester, MA: Peter Smith, 1967.
Science and Technology Policy for the 1980s. Paris: OECD, 1981.
Shane, M. G., and G. A. Sojka, "John Elfreth Watkins, Jr.: Forgotten Genius of Forecasting," *The Futurist,* 16(1982): 9-12.
Shelp, R. K., *Beyond Industrialization: Ascendancy of the Global Service Economy.* New York: Praeger, 1981.
Silk, L., "Cost-Effective Job Creation," *New York Times,* September 22, 1982, p. D2.
Simmie, J. M., "Beyond the Industrial City?" *Journal of the American Planning Association.* 49(1983): 59-76.
Smith, A. D., *The Right to Life.* Chapel Hill: University of North Carolina Press, 1960.
Social Reconstruction in the Newly Independent Countries of East Africa. New York: United Nations, 1965.
Statistical Abstract of the United States, 1981. Washington: United States Department of Commerce, 1981.
Stellman, J., *Human and Public Health Aspects of Telecommunications.* Paper delivered at Fourth General Assembly, World Future Society, Washington, D.C., 1982.
Stokes, H. S., "Japan's Love Affair with Robots," *New York Times Magazine,* January 10, 1982, p. 24.
Swart, J. C., "Flexitime in the Utilities Industry," *Personnel,* 61(March/April, 1984): 43-44.
Taggart, R., *Job Creation: What Works?* Salt Lake City: Olympus, 1977.
Taylor, D. E. and E. S. Sekscenski, "Workers on Long Schedules, Single and Multiple Jobholders," *Monthly Labor Review,* 105(May, 1982): 47-53.

Terkel, S., *Working*. New York: Random House, 1972.
Tévoédjrè, A., *Poverty: Wealth of Mankind*. New York: Pergamon, 1979.
Theobald, R., "Guaranteed Income Tomorrow: Toward Post-Economic Motivation," in F. Best, *The Future of Work*, Englewood Cliffs: Prentice-Hall, 1977.
Thurow, L. C., *The Zero-Sum Society: Distribution and the Possibilities for Economic Change*. Harmondsworth: Penguin, 1981.
United Nations, *Concise Report on the World Population in 1970-75 and Its Long-Range Implications*. New York: United Nations, Department of Economic and Social Affairs, 1974.
Walbank, M., "Effort in Motivated Work Behavior," in K.D. Duncan, M. M. Gruneberg and D. Wallis (eds.), *Changes in Working Life*. Chichester: Wiley, 1980.
Werneke, D., and R. Broadfield, "A Needs-Oriented Approach to Manpower," in D. H. Freedman, *Employment Outlook and Insights*. Geneva: ILO, 1979.
Wilson, J. O., *After Affluence: Economics to Meet Human Needs*. New York: Harper and Row, 1980.
Wilson, R. N., "The Courage to be Leisured," *Social Forces*, 60(December, 1981): 282-303.
Working Woman, September, 1983, p. 48.
World of Work Report, 4(April, 1979): 29; 5 (November, 1980): 77; 7(July, 1982): 49.
Yankelovich, D., H. Zettenberg, B. Strumpel, and M. Shanks, *Work and Human Values: An International Report on Jobs in the 1980s and 1990s*. New York: Aspen Institute, 1983.
Yearbook of Labor Statistics: Sixteenth Edition: Twenty-Sixth Edition; Thirty-Sixth Edition. Geneva, ILO, 1956; 1966; 1976; 1978.
Zimbalist, A., "Technology and the Labor Process in the Printing Industry," in A. Zimbalist (ed.), *Case Studies on the Labor Process*. New York: Monthly Review Press, 1979.

The Search for Appropriate Development Models

Japanese Development Model [1]

by

E. Wayne Nafziger

Japan, whose 1868 level of economic development was only slightly more than other Afro-Asian countries, has had the world's fastest growth in real GNP per capita since then,[2] or second fastest to Sweden if computed through the early 1950s. Noncommunist developing Asia is "looking East" to learn development lessons from the major non-Western industrialized country, Japan. With recent U.S. slow growth, "modernizing" theorists have emphasized capitalist Japan as an alternative model to the Soviet Union.

Though the Tokugawa shoguns isolated Japan from foreign influence from 1638 to the 1860s, they provided a more favorable legacy for modernization than many present LDCs. Mid-nineteenth-century feudal Japan had a literacy rate about as high as England, a well-integrated transport system, a well-developed tax system, a highly commercialized agriculture whose productivity per acre exceeded southeast Asia today, and guild and clan-monopoly workshops producing silk textiles, *sake*, rapeseed oil, cotton cloth, candles, and other processed products for a national market, especially the large urban populations of Edo (Tokyo), Osaka, and Kyoto.

I. The Focus of the Study

The Japanese development model (JDM) from 1868, following the restoration of the Meiji emperor, through the late 1930s is different from the JDM after the 1945-1947 U.S. occupational land, educational, labor union, antitrust, and political reforms. Doubtless, South Korea, Taiwan, and Hong Kong, newly indus-

---

E. Wayne Nafziger is professor and Mid-America State Universities Honor Lecturer, Kansas State University, Manhattan, Kansas.

trialized countries that account for more than one-third of total LDC manufactured exports, have learned from post-World War II Japanese development. But I limit the JDM's application to low-income and lower-middle-income countries from noncommunist sub-Saharan Africa and south and southeast Asia.[3] These countries are in earlier stages of industrialization, account for over 76% of the noncommunist less-developed countries' (LDCs') 1982 population, and have an average real income perhaps comparable to 1868 Japan. Thus, the appropriate period for testing the JDM's application to these countries is from 1868 through the late 1930s, rather than the period after 1945.[4]

This paper concentrates on major ways in which the pre-1940 JDM differs from other non-Western development approaches and how this JDM applies to today's LDCs. The major focus—sections III-VIII—is capital formation and technology policies that contributed to Japan's rapid industrial capitalist growth: technological borrowing, education, business assistance, financial institutions, transfer of agricultural savings to industry, and wages. These policies even benefited the traditional sector of the dual economy (section IX); most contemporary LDCs are also dualistic. Growth in productivity per person was increased substantially by Japan's policy of participating in the growing international specialization in the decades following the 1868 Meiji Restoration (section X). But a key to the ability of Japan to pursue these favorable policies was that, unlike most non-Western countries of the time, she was not dominated by Western imperialism (see section II).

II. Self-Directed Development

Despite unequal treaties with the West, from 1858 to 1899, Japan had substantial autonomy in economic affairs compared to other Afro-Asian countries, either colonized or subject to informal imperial economic controls. Although the West limited Japanese import tariffs to 5%, Japan partially circumvented these protective limits through tax rebates, subsidies, government purchase contracts, and state industrial enterprises. Furthermore, the 1868-1912 Meiji government was committed to economic and military development. It promulgated laws encouraging joint-stock organization and freedom of enterprise. The Act of 1872 established a national system of education stressing scientific and technological education, rather than skills for the junior civil service like schools in the European colonies. Unlike colonial India, Japan discouraged foreign investment between 1868 and 1899 (with minor exceptions like coal mining and shipbuilding in 1870-1872), hiring thousands of foreigners to adapt and improve technology under ministry (or local business) direction. The Meiji government invested large amounts in infrastructure—telegraphs, postal service, water supply, coastal shipping, ports, harbors, bridges, lighthouses, river improvements, railways, electricity, gas, and technical research. In the last quarter of the nineteenth century, Japan organized a banking system (with the Bank of Japan, semiofficial development banks, and locally-run private banks), expanded bank credit for government infrastructure and private investment, regulated banks, and stabilized the currency. In contrast, even after 1935, the Indian colonial government interfered little in private foreign-dominated banks, whose power was only gradually eroded even after independence in 1947. Nor did a colonial government and foreign trading houses thwart industrial exports and import substitution, as in early twentieth-century Nigeria. The post-1868 Japanese government, in contrast, helped domestic business find export opportunities, exhibit products and borrow abroad, establish trading companies, and set marketing standards.

The JDM indicates the clear advantages of domestic political and economic control. But the policy implications for today's LDCs, most of which are politically independent but economically tied to developed capitalist countries (DCs), are not clear. Cutting economic ties with DCs, while feasible for large countries with wide resource bases, has been costly for small countries like Ghana (1961-1966) and Cuba, whose economic growth stagnated. But the JDM does have lessons indicated below for how technological borrowing can be more self-directed.

III. Borrowing and Modifying Foreign Technology

To maintain independence, the Meiji rulers tried to "enrich the nation and strengthen the army," goals requiring adopting Western technology. But since Japan could not rely on foreign aid then, the central government and private firms had to pay the full cost of foreign technical expertise. This cost, together with introducing universal primary education and compulsory adult male military service, caused a serious financial strain. Between 1868 and 1892, the central government spent 1.5% of its total expenditures for foreign employees and an additional 0.4% for expenses to send more than 4,000 students and government officials for training and education abroad. The Ministry of Industry, which invested in heavy and chemical industries, mining, and infrastructure, employed almost 1,000 foreign advisors and teachers from 1870 to 1885. The Ministry of Home Affairs hired almost 250 foreigners from 1873 through 1895 to establish agricultural experiment stations to introduce Western farming methods and products and to establish model factories to transfer technology to light industry. During the same period, the Ministry of Finance drew on about 125 foreign experts to help set up a modern monetary system and introduce corporate business organization. Other ministries and public enterprises hired almost 5,000, and the private sector about 12,500, foreigners during 1870-99.

Japan learned a lesson in the 1870s that many contemporary LDCs learned only recently or not at all: that importing replicas of Western institutions and capital-intensive technology may fail if the LDC lacks the capital and skills needed. Foreign techniques were modified—substituting hand-powered machines in silk reeling factories and wood for iron in Jacquard weaving machines—to save capital. Japan's Ten-Year Plan of 1884, the Kogyo Iken, advocated projects conforming to local conditions and capital, urging improvement engineering, i.e., upgrading indigenous (including artisan) production, rather than importing Western replicas.

In agriculture, two German experts at the Komaba School of Agriculture in the early 1880s advised that Japanese farms, with a small average size, should rely on biological and chemical, not Western mechanical, innovations. Beginning in 1885, the Ministry of Agriculture and Commerce used foreign farm scientists to develop technology to suit small farms and local soil, and it sent veteran farmers and new Japanese agricultural school graduates to diffuse the best seed varieties then used on Japanese farms. For most LDCs, with high worker-land ratios, the Japanese biochemical emphasis is more sensible than the capital-intensive approaches of the United States and Canada.

Many Japanese agricultural innovations, like better seed varieties (a green revolution in rice began around 1911), improved irrigation, improved seedling beds, and deeper plowing increased labor used per acre. Filipino innovations of high-yielding rice varieties and chemical fertilizers, following the JDM, almost doubled labor requirements per acre between 1966 and 1975.

In industry, both in government training schools and private firms, foreign experts were often unsuitable, importing techniques they were acquainted with, regardless of their relevance. In the raw silk industry, imported machines and equipment were too costly and mechanically sophisticated, and their capacity was inconsistent with the inadequate storage facilities for the perishable cocoon. In flood control, Dutch experts introduced a system identical to that in Holland, where flood water rises from sea level, overlooking the fact that Japan had to handle flood water coming down the mountains. Repeated failures of

Dutch technology to control floods finally convinced the Japanese government to change control measures completely. By the last two decades of the nineteenth century, the Japanese realized the necessity of questioning foreign industrial and flood-control experts in light of differing local conditions.

The Meiji government hired foreign experts directly and restricted foreign direct investment. While the immediate financial cost of limiting investment was substantial, Japan avoided the foreign restrictions placed on the transfer of technical knowledge and also avoided the continuing technological dependence on foreign sources and associated foreign technical concentration that many contemporary LDCs face. Regarding foreign experts, the Japanese learned by the 1880s the necessity of ensuring that technology introduced by foreigners be modified to fit local conditions and factor proportions.

During the Meiji period, labor was relatively more abundant in Japan than in the most advanced economies of Western Europe and the United States. Accordingly, Japan frequently substituted more appropriate labor-intensive technology for the "best-practice" techniques available from capital-abundant Western countries.

Following are some major patterns of Japan's appropriate technology, 1868-1939:

1. Emphasizing the production and export of more labor-intensive goods like raw silk, and silk and cotton textiles.

2. Labor-intensive adaptation where the production process is simplified. Silk-reeling equipment appearing in 1875 consisted of a blacksmith-made steam boiler, ceramic cocoon-boiling and silk-reeling kettles, and a frame built by a village carpenter. Additionally, many Japanese manufacturing firms purchased secondhand machinery in good condition from Western countries. The cotton textile industry used two shifts and substituted labor in ancillary and peripheral processes. Furthermore, much of the ancillary activities, like transport and machine repair, for large manufacturing units, were done cheaply by small firms using simple equipment and labor-intensive processes.

3. Using manual labor instead of Western-type ancillary equipment in coal and mineral mines.

4. Adoption of technology used in an earlier stage in the West.

5. Adaptation of foreign technology to industries catering to tastes unique to the indigenous market, including traditional soybean sauce, and indigenous dyeing houses. As these enterprises learned through experience, many made the transition to technology needed for export markets.

6. Substituting labor-intensive techniques to produce goods of

lower quality and performance than imported goods, like bicycles (beginning in 1890), machine tools, three-wheel trucks, and small-sized cars (Datsuns in the 1930s).

If anything, contemporary LDCs have to be even more cautious than Meiji Japan in importing foreign capital and technology. Since present LDCs are even more technologically backward relative to the most technologically advanced economies than Japan was relative to the West in the late nineteenth century, it is probably more difficult to adapt technology to local conditions and indigenous production. For example, most internationally available yield-increasing farm inputs for early developing Japan were labor-using, while most yield-increasing inputs for today's latecoming LDCs are labor-saving.

Today's developing countries are also less likely to directly control experts transferring technology than the Japanese were. Finally, contemporary LDCs are more likely to face unalterable capital-labor ratios in production processes and to pursue policies creating factor-price distortions (subsidized capital and foreign exchange prices, and above-market wage costs) than the Japanese a century ago.

IV. Education

The 1980 literacy rate for lower and lower-middle income countries is 54%, a level reached in Japan about the first decade of the twentieth century. Japan's primary enrollment rate, 28.1% in 1873, reached virtually 100% by 1911. Furthermore, the state made serious efforts to expand primary and vocational education and to stress Western scientific and technical education in the last three decades of the nineteenth century, when Asian countries like Siam were only educating elites for government service. Starting with a common language, the Meiji government developed a relatively uniform primary education that fostered national unity as well as speeding up acquiring Western ideas and technologies.

The emphasis on "Japanese spirit and Western technology" meant that Meiji education stressed subserviency to superiors and the state, superiority to other Asian countries, and the acquisition of Western technological expertise, but not human dignity or the method for developing science in Japan. While the Meiji Japanese experience reinforces studies indicating a high rate of return to LDC investment in primary, science, and vocational education, it provides no model for countries using the educational system to promote democracy, human rights, and female equality.

V. An Indigenous Capitalist Class

Political revolutions in Western Europe (England, France, and Holland) in the seventeenth and eighteenth centuries reduced the power of the church and landed aristocracy, and eventually the industrial and commercial capitalist classes took over much of this power. Since most LDCs, like nineteenth-century Japan, do not have the strong middle- and capitalist-class leadership for capital accumulation and technical progress, can they look to Japan's "guided capitalism" as an alternative model to Soviet state capitalism?

Following the fall of the Tokugawa shogun from 1860 to 1868, the Meiji government was controlled primarily by lower-ranking samurai, not merchants and industrial capitalists. From 1870 to 1885, this government owned and operated factories and mines, many expropriated from the shogunate and feudal lords. Throughout the late nineteenth century, the Meiji regime accounted for about half the investment outside agriculture, including not only infrastructure, but also shipbuilding, iron and steel, other heavy industries, and arms factories to strengthen the military, as well as mines and construction, engineering, cement, soap, and chemical industries. After private-sector skills improved, government profits proved meager. The state needed funds for armament and it sold most industrial properties, often at bargain prices, to private businessmen, many of whom were samurai. Additionally, in 1876, the state strained its public credit to commute the pensions of 400,000 feudal lords and samurai to cash and bonds, and to pay off debts owed to relatively privileged merchants and moneylenders (like the House of Mitsui) who had financed the 1867-1868 coup restoring the emperor. The more enterprising recipients used these funds to invest in new industrial enterprise. Moreover, the state aided private industry through a laissez-faire labor policy (low wages and child labor), low taxes on business enterprise and high incomes, a favorable legal climate, destruction of economic barriers between fiefs, lucrative purchase contracts, tax rebates, loans, and subsidies. (For example, the government imported spindle spinning machines during 1878 and 1879, to sell on lenient credit terms to private enterprise in the textile industry, Japan's leading export sector.)[5] From these state-assisted entrepreneurs came the financial cliques or combines (*zaibatsu*) that dominated industry and banking through World War II. The zaibatsu's concentration of wealth helped perpetuate high income inequalities at least 75 years after the Meiji restoration. To be sure, the zaibatsu reaped large-scale economies, managed ably, were generally frugal, invested productively, provided assistance to small industry (see below), and were partners in building national power.

Perhaps as many as one-fourth to one-fifth the farmers in the late Tokugawa and early Meiji periods managed second businesses such as small bars, rapeseed-oil selling, lumber vending, eating house management, bean-curd making, confection making, tobacco selling, sundry shopkeeping, carpentry, and plastering. Landlords were fertilizer merchants, pawnbrokers, moneylenders, doctors, dry-goods merchants, and brewers of *sake,* soy sauce, and bean paste. Furthermore, many merchants became landlords.

Yet empirical studies on entrepreneurship indicate that landowners and wealthy farmers in today's LDCs rarely invest in industry. LDC landlords tend to highly value consumption and real estate expenditure and to lack experience in managing and coordinating a production process with specialized work tasks and machinery and in overseeing secondary labor relations.

Many economists, noting the disproportional samurai representation among early Meiji industrialists and bankers, stress the spirit of the community-centered samurai entrepreneur who sacrificed for national economic progress. But Yamamura's evidence (1968) indicates that samurai status in the early Meiji period was blurred, as many from peasant and merchant families purchased this status during the late Tokugawa period. The major force to establish banks and factories came from merchants and landlords motivated by profit, not longstanding samurai motivated by nationalism.

Meiji Japan's policies illustrate an alternative to the Soviet approach for accumulating capital where there is no strong bourgeois class. And selling government-owned industrial properties to private firms reduces public financial loss since their bankruptcies eliminate inefficient enterprises. Yet this selling may, as in Japan, contribute to high industrial concentration, high income inequalities, and slow growth of a politically independent middle class. Moreover, today populist pressures prevent most LDC political elites from pursuing the low-wage policies, unrestricted labor rules, low welfare spending, and large subsidies that nineteenth-century Japan used to foster indigenous capitalist development. Furthermore, few LDC societies have the Japanese nexus of community reciprocal obligation that reduces the destructive power of capitalist rivalries.

Yet Meiji Japan's bourgeoisie, though weaker than that in Western Europe and the United States, were more experienced in large commercial ventures and were not as far behind the most technologically advanced economies in LDCs today. The Japanese capitalist class was capable of responding to government policies to encourage private industrial ventures. Furthermore, Meiji government bureaucracy had the vision and skills to plan programs to abet private entrepreneurs. The irony is that while the weakness of today's LDC bourgeoisie indicates the need for stronger government intervention and more skilled government planning to spur entrepreneurial activity, technical progress, and capital accumulation in industry, few LDC government bureaucracies have the capabilities to facilitate these in the private sector or manage these in the public sector.

VI. Financial Institutions

Goldsmith thinks a knowledgeable 1870 economist would have indicated India as more likely to be economically developed by 1970 than Japan. India, a British colony, possessed unified currency, rudiments of a Western-type banking system, access to the British capital market, and British financial technology, while Japan, just emerging from feudalism, had a negligible modern sector, a chaotic currency, and no modern financial institutions.

But Britain constructed India's modern financial system, while the Meiji government created Japan's system through conscious selective adaptation of features of the American, British, French, and German systems. British civil servants, entrepreneurs, and investors operated, owned, and organized India's modern financial institutions, while foreign ownership or management of Japan's institutions was practically nonexistent. Furthermore, the British colonial government in India intervened little in regulating bank and financial institutions, had little contact with the small number of indigenous bankers, and in the half century before World War II created few new financial institutions. In contrast, the Meiji government organized most of the modern financial institutions during the first two to three decades after the 1868 restoration and cooperated with and supported local private bankers and financiers.

In contrast to India, Meiji Japan's development of currency and credit institutions through the mid-1890s was "supply-leading," created in advance of demands for industrial loans and financial services, and private-saver deposits. In 1872, the government set up national banks, and in 1876, it permitted private commercial banks. Other major financial reforms were the conversion of the rights of feudal lords to negotiable government bonds, and the land tax, which provided the revenue for the government's Reserve Fund (RF), 1873-81, and the Industrial Promotion Fund (IPF), beginning 1878, for loans to industry.

Other special banks established included the Yokohama Specie Bank (1880) for foreign exchange for importers, the Hypothec Banks (1896) at the prefectural level to make long-term loans to industry and agriculture, and the Industrial Bank (1900) to make medium-to long-term loans to industry.

The national and private banks' high ratio of currency issues to specie, as well as the RF and IPF liberal lending policies, contributed to rapid inflation from 1876 to 1881, reducing peasant and former military real income and increasing capitalist speculative profits, thus forming substantial initial capital accumulation for industrialists.

Finance Minister Matsukata Masoyoshi created a central Bank of Japan in 1882 (54 years before the Reserve Bank of India) to limit paper currency, levied new consumption taxes, restrained RF lending except to export industries accumulating specie, and balanced the government budget, bringing about more stable expectations among capitalist investors.

All in all, the new financial institutions standardized the currency, integrated the national market, and channeled savings into industry. By 1897, Japan's credit standing had improved to the point that she could borrow in foreign capital markets. With few exceptions, the money supply grew rapidly from 1880 to 1940, enabling rapid though fluctuating growth *rates*, but virtually avoiding recessions with negative growth.

The symbiotic relationship between government and private finance strengthened zaibatsu bank concentration, contributing to the 1920s' sharp decline in small banks. While banks collected private savings for affiliated zaibatsu enterprises and helped determine which firms survived, these large financial concentrations still supported traditional small-scale industry and trade. Bank concentration was not reduced until the post-World War II occupational antitrust reforms.

The rapid growth of Japan's banking and credit institutions in advance of industrial and saver demands indicates the advantage of more than a century of self-directed financial development. However, the Japanese government, in its drive for national economic and military power, tolerated growing financial concentration, a pathology of growth that LDCs may want to avoid.

VII. Transfer of Agricultural Surplus

Economic historians differ on the relationships between agriculture and industry in the development process and on the timing of initial sustained growth in both sectors. As in England, where an agricultural revolution preceded the industrial revolution, in Japan late Tokugawa agricultural growth preceded the beginning of the early industrialization spurt of the 1880s. Agricultural growth accelerated through the Meiji period before slowing down beginning in the 1910s. During the Meiji period, agriculture contributed to and benefited from rapid industrialization (Minami, 1985). Sections VII and VIII look at how capital, labor, and food from agriculture helped industry.

A major concern for newly industrializing countries is the source of early investment capital for industry. Many economists advocate relying heavily on agricultural surplus for industrial capital, since agriculture is usually an LDC's largest sector; for example, before 1915, it contributed more to Japan's NDP than any other sector. Agricultural surplus refers to an excess of savings over investment in agriculture, an amount transferred to nonagriculture (or industry). This transfer includes both taxes and private savings.

Meiji centralized government replaced the feudal landed gentry *(daimyo)* who politically controlled large fiefs with smaller, capitalist village landlords who had purchased their land. These gentry remained wealthy, but they lost their land and political power. The village landlords, who were often themselves farmers during the early Meiji period, frequently improved productive methods.

The Meiji bureaucrats controlling policy had no personal interest in protecting agricultural incomes at the cost of slowing industrial growth. They imposed a land tax in 1873 to squeeze investment capital from agriculture, partly through a moderate inflationary policy redistributing resources to finance state and private industrial ventures. In that year, the land tax accounted for 94% of central government revenue, appropriating one-third of the total crop, nearly as much as the share appropriated by the feudal lord under the pre-1868 Tokugawa shogun. The land tax continued to provide more than 80% of total government revenue through 1882 and contributed to continuing, though reduced, net resource outflows from agriculture to government through 1922. Government investment in agriculture was only a small fraction of agricultural tax revenue used for nonagricultural investment.

From 1888 to 1937, the significant surplus flows of private savings from agriculture to industry are concentrated during the period from 1903 to 1922, when cultivator-landlords were being replaced by "parasitic" landlords using tenant rents to accumulate capital for industries like brewing, pawnbroking, retail shops, and village moneylending. But the amount of net capital private flows from agriculture to industry is not certain, since price indices to estimate the effect of changing terms of trade on net resource flows from agriculture and figures on private inflows to agriculture are not reliable.

Part of this intersectoral resource transfer was from colonies Korea and Taiwan, 1911-40. During this period, Taiwan's net resource outflow from agriculture equaled its balance of trade surplus (with exports predominantly agricultural) with metropolitan Japan. Japanese investors in the colonies acquired prime agricultural land for producing food exports to Japan. These cheap rice imports from Taiwan and Korea kept Japanese food prices low, keeping industrial wages low and increasing industrial profits.

Meiji Japan, like the Soviet Union subsequently in the 1930s, accumulated industrial capital by squeezing it from agriculture. With the possible exception of the Soviet Union, where the collectivization of 1929-1933 involved forcible collection of grain, confiscation of farm property, destruction of tools and livestock, class warfare between peasants and properous kulaks, administrative disorder, disruption of sowing and harvest, and an accompanying famine that led to the deaths of about five million people, Japan has probably relied more on a strategy of using agricultural savings for initial industrial capital formation than any other presently industrialized country.

The land tax had little or no effect on farm output. The owner, unable to shift the tax forward to farm-good middlemen or consumers, could only shift the tax incidence to tenants, who rarely had alternative employment. The high and regressive land taxes, required in cash, the growing burden of other taxes (1890- 1910), and high rents reduced farm disposable income and consumption, especially among tenants and peasants, the last of whom faced heavy debts, frequent bankruptcies, and abject poverty.

Dore (1959) argues that the agrarian poverty and distress from taxes and tenancy contributed to the rise of Japanese totalitarian and military expansion abroad in the following ways: (1) tenant distress and farm population pressures provided a powerful motive for securing emigration opportunities through expansion; (2) rural poverty and the interrelated low industrial wages (see below) limited domestic market size, spurring Japan to use force to acquire external markets for its industry; (3) ruling elites used overseas expansion to divert attention from agrarian distress and foster national unity; and (4) landlord paternalism and agrarian pressures for social conformity facilitated susceptibility to authoritarianism.

Other countries may find it difficult politically to extract agricultural surplus through land taxes. In England, unlike Japan, the landed aristocracy maintained political influence until a relatively advanced stage of industrial development. Likewise, landlords in many contemporary Latin American countries are too powerful for the state to capture an agricultural surplus. Few low-income Afro-Asian countries have enough rural political tolerance to allow the squeezing of agriculture in excess of the substantial agriculture-industry transfers already being made.

Additionally, Japan's agricultural technological progress was fast, contributing to the rapid annual growth rates of 1.8% in agricultural gross value-added and 2.0% in farm productivity per worker, 1880-1920, that facilitated substantial surplus transfer to industry. The agricultural surplus in many low-income Afro-Asian countries is too small and growing too slowly for industry to exploit without severe political costs.

LDCs need a thriving agriculture to produce adequate food and raw materials for other sectors. Should we not discourage the following policies African and Asian LDCs frequently use today to transfer a large share of the agricultural surplus to industry: (1) food price ceilings and industrial price floors to raise industrial prices relative to the prices of farm goods; (2) concentration of government investment in industry; (3) tax incentives and subsidies to pioneering firms in industry, but not in agriculture; (4) setting below-market prices for foreign currency, reducing domestic currency receipts from agricultural exports, but lowering the price of capital goods and other foreign inputs to large industrial establishments; (5) tariff and quota protection for industry, raising its prices to farmers; and (6) spending more for education, training, housing, plumbing, nutrition, medical care, and transport in urban areas than in rural areas. These policies of urban bias have contributed to farm production disincentives and high rates of rural poverty and undernourishment in low-income countries.

These disincentives in many of today's LDCs are perhaps as great as those that threatened widespread rural rebellion in Meiji Japan. Rural poverty and undernourishment rates are probably no less than those in Meiji Japan. Additionally, rural populist pressures in many contemporary LDCs are greater and more politically destabilizing than peasant pressures in 1870s Meiji Japan.

In Pakistan, a below-market foreign exchange price coupled with industrial price guarantees resulted in the transfer of about 70% of savings in agriculture and over 24% of its gross product to the nonagricultural sector in 1964 and 1965—a transfer largely from poor to rich and from East Pakistan to West Pakistan. This transfer exacerbated the East Bengali peasant discontent that contributed to Bangladesh secession. Few low-income Asian countries have the rural political stability sufficient to squeeze agriculture in excess of surplus transfers already being made.

In fact, some—like democratic India—faced with fast population growth, low agricultural incomes and savings, and potential farmer discontent, have no income tax on agriculture and a net resource inflow to agriculture since independence in 1947.

VIII. Low Industrial Wages

From 1868 to 1915, agricultural unskilled *real* wages remained at a subsistence level. Unlike the Lewis-Fei-Ranis models (LFR), the marginal productivity of labor (MPL) was positive, though less than the wage, since the village supplied subsistence to those with a MPL below it. As in LFR, employers in the formal (or organized) industrial sector paid a premium (say 30% more than the agricultural wage) to compensate for migration costs, psychological costs of city life, etc. This premium remained low partly because much of industry's wage labor—female, second and third sons, or off-farm part-time—merely supplemented household income. But subsistence levels rose over time as the minimum maintenance level expected by society increased. The relatively stable agricultural (and thus industrial) real wages can be attributed partly to technical progress and increased productivity in agriculture (and cheap food from colonies after 1911) that enabled the industrial sector to buy food without declining terms of trade. These low real industrial wages increased industrial profits, business savings, and labor-intensive manufactured-export competitiveness.

Over a normal range, where product and labor demand increase gradually, labor supply elasticities were high (though not infinite as in LFR), benefitting from vast reserves in the rural and informal industrial sectors. But the 1915-1919 increase in demand for industrial products and labor resulting from World War I was too substantial to be satisfied by labor from the elastic portion of the supply curve. Wage equilibrium could only be attained at the inelastic portion of the labor supply curve, thus increasing industrial wages and subsequently, through greater food demand by new workers, increasing agricultural product (especially rice) and labor prices. In the 1920s and 1930s, industrial wages, sticky downward with emerging unions, remained high, while agricultural (and informal industrial sector) wages declined from their war peak. Following war and recovery years, (1935-1955), the labor surplus ended, and the industrial formal sector labor supply turned inelastic permanently, as innovation-led demand for industrial products and labor increased rapidly, while labor supply growth from agriculture and population growth was drying up.

The labor supply in developing Japan grew slower than in today's LDCs. Late nineteenth-century Japan's birth rate, 22 per 1,000, kept down by farmland shortages, extended-family dissolution, and high literacy levels, was lower than the LDCs' 32 per 1,000 (1982), while Japanese death rates, 18 per 1,000, were higher than LDC rates of 11 per 1,000, lowered by access to the nutritional, medical, health, and production techniques of the past century. Japan's labor growth, which never exceeded 1% per annum during the nineteenth century, rose to a peak of 1.3% per annum in 1930, slowing to less than 1% by 1955. In contrast, LDC labor force growth was 1.8% per annum in the 1960s, 2.1% annually in the 1970s, and 2.0% the early 1980s (each figure slightly less than population growth). Yet Meiji Japan's density of farm population per cultivated acre of land (higher than India, Taiwan, and most other Asian LDCs today) put pressure on the nonagricultural sector. But Japan's annual industrial-employment growth rate from 1878 to 1914, was 3.9% of the total labor force, compared to the LDC figure in 1980 of about 0.4% to 0.7%. While LDC industry in 1980 absorbed only 20% to 35% of the increased labor force, Japanese industry at the turn of the twentieth century absorbed 4.5-5.0 times the labor increase. Crucial in Japan's successful absorption was slower population growth, together with highly labor-intensive industrialization, spurred by government's low-wage and appropriate technology policies, but *not* a faster annual industrial growth rate than LDCs from 1960 to 1981.

While Africa and south Asia face labor surpluses today from rapid population growth and slow industrial-employment demand, these surpluses are more likely to be reflected in urban unemployment instead of low wages, due to political pressures for minimum wages, labor union strength, factor-price distortions (low capital and foreign-exchange costs), unsuitable capital-intensive technologies, unrealistic job aspirations by school graduates, bias toward urban amenities, and wage pressures from food price rises.

Japan had faster food output growth and more stable food prices than today's LDCs because of rapid technical progress in agriculture during the Meiji period and cheap food from colonies during the early twentieth century. LDC food supply problems often result from urban bias in investment and amenities, agricultural price disincentives, and bureaucratic mismanagement in supplying farm inputs. But LDC food demand has risen relatively fast because of high income elasticities of demand for food resulting from rapid population growth.

In the midst of a large urban wage premium, the flood of urban immigrants is restrained only by high open urban unemployment rates, which keep down expected urban wages (wages times the probability of employment, as in Harris-Todaro) but not actual urban wages. The LFR model's unlimited long-run supply of labor to the industrial sector, roughly valid in Japan from 1868 to 1915, is replaced by relatively high wages in today's LDCs, reducing industrial profits and savings.

IX. Industrial Dualism

Meiji Japan had a dual economy consisting of: (1) a traditional, peasant, agricultural sector, producing primarily for family or village subsistence, with little reproducible capital, using old or intermediate technology, and with a marginal productivity of labor lower than the wage (together with semisubsistence agriculture, petty trade, and cottage industry); and (2) capital-intensive modern manufacturing and processing operations, mineral extraction, and commercial agriculture, producing for the market, using reproducible capital and new technology, experiencing high and growing labor productivity, and hiring labor commercially. This dualism was exacerbated by Japan's continuing rapid growth, especially in technology.

As implied above, the modern-sector wage was more than the traditional-sector wage for identical labor skills from 1868 to 1915. After World War I, these wage differentials widened, as demand increased especially for skilled labor, which large firms tried to keep through rationalization, lifetime employment policies, seniority preference, and fringe benefits. The large firms' price-controlling power in product markets and credit rationing in the capital market made higher wages possible. Additionally, large firms economized on unskilled labor by hiring temporary workers, contributing to greater labor-market dualism. By 1955, in the midst of the labor shortage of the postwar economic boom, the dual market for similar labor disappeared (although there were still wage differentials for different levels of skills and experience).

In this section, I go beyond industrial-agricultural dualism to discuss dualism within the industrial sector, including regional dualism. Due to geographical labor immobility, a labor market usually consisted of a village or no more than a few districts. Moreover, poor transport provided natural protection for regions with high wage costs.

Japan has not stressed large leaps to the most advanced state of industrial technology available, but step by step improvements in technology and capital as ministries, regions, industries, firms, and work units learn by doing. In the early Meiji period, this meant technical and management assistance and credit facilities to improve and increase the scale of small workshops, handicraft producers, and cottage industry left from before 1868, causing less social disruption, as small industry's environment was not alien. The 1884 plan emphasized improving traditional technology through applied science and favored postponing massive foreign large-scale factory transplantation until traditional enterprises could utilize new techniques. Factory enterprises in Japan developed faster than in India, but they were less destructive of cottage and workshop industry than in India.

Large industry evolved, after state assistance and two wars (1894-1895 and 1904-1905), into zaibatsu concentration by 1910, but small industry, encouraged by government to take cooperative action, was retained, even in the leading manufacturing industry, textiles. Large-scale enterprises created external economies in the supply of raw materials, working capital, and markets. Additionally, these enterprises could not manufacture every item needed and found it cheaper to buy parts and components from independently-run small workshops, to which the large firms provided technical advice, scarce inputs, credit, and, where needed, access to a large international trading company (*sogo shosha*), which economized on the scarce language skills of both Japanese and foreigners. Small industry (establishments with less than 50 workers) increased its real output (though not output share) from 1884 to 1930, contributing 65% to 75% of Japan's employment and 45% to 50% of her gross manufacturing output in 1934. But many small firms were not independent, being dominated by major banks, industrial companies, and trading corporations.

Many LDCs use training, extension, credit, and industrial estate programs to encourage small-scale manufacturing establishments. Since 1958, China has had a policy of "walking on two legs," with large urban manufacturing augmented by a "second leg," small- and medium-size industry on the rural communes. Since the 1950s, India has limited the expansion of large firms and provided subsidies for the establishment of small-scale industry, especially in nonmetropolitan areas.

But few contemporary LDCs have had as well-developed a small-scale manufacturing sector as post-1868 Japan. Many LDCs, trying to modernize industry, have emphasized capital-intensive technology representing the most advanced state of the arts in rich countries, allowing small industry to decline. These countries have not stressed gradual technical improvement and learning from experience among existing ministries and industries, together with dissemination of technology consistent with local factor endowment and culture. Creating small industry from scratch is not as effective as maintaining and upgrading workshop, handicraft, and cottage industry left from an earlier stage of development. Once small industry has been disrupted or destroyed, it is difficult to reconstruct.

To be sure, the technological gap between DCs and LDCs is greater today than during the Meiji period. But contemporary third-world countries still have many alternatives to best-practice capital-intensive techniques.

X. Export Expansion and Import Substitution

From 1868 to World War II, the Japanese had a policy (first forced and later chosen) of multilateral, nondiscriminatory foreign trade outside their empire (1904-1945). This trade policy contributed to rapid growth, even though it would be a mistake to regard Japan's drive for foreign markets as the motor force of her industrialization.

Even though nineteenth-century Meiji Japan partially circumvented Western tariff limitations by providing protection through subsidies and state undertakings, it was more open to international trade than most contemporary LDCs. While foreign trade was modest by Western standards during the Meiji government's first 25 years, its influence stimulated technological learning. The large domestic market usually absorbed most of the products of this new technology. Subsequently, as the Japanese mastered and modified innovations, they often began exporting, as with textiles, the leading export from 1874 to 1940; other light manufactures like consumer goods and simple machines that replaced primary-product exports in second place at the turn of the twentieth century; and the leading sector after World War II, heavy and chemical manufactures (especially electronics, vehicles, and sophisticated consumer goods in the 1970s and 1980s).

Unlike today's LDCs, Japan did not discriminate against exports. Increased tariff protection in the first quarter of the twentieth century reduced the price of foreign exchange, but government export promotion through a bank to finance trade, exhibiting Japanese products overseas, sales bureaus abroad, chambers of commerce and commodity guilds for cooperative export activity, merchant-marine subsidies, and business privilege in the new empire brought export inducements near that of the equilibrium exchange rate through 1937 (except for the 1920s). Japan's annual real average growth rates in exports were 8.4% between

1880 and 1913 (compared to 3.2% for the world as a whole, 2.6% for Britain, and 4.2% for the U.S.), and 5.2% between 1913 and 1937 (compared to 1.4% for the world, 0.4% for Britain, and 1.4% for the U.S.). Today, many LDCs overvalue their domestic currency relative to foreign currency, discouraging domestic producers from exporting and substituting imports unless protected by massive subsidies.

Studies by Krueger, Lary, Monson, and Akrasenee (1981) and Krueger (1978) indicate that the Japanese approach—an emphasis on foreign-exchange rate equilibrium and export promotion—is generally more effective than import substitution in expanding output and employment in contemporary LDCs. As an example, Chile, in the 1960s and 1970s, provided outlandish incentives for import substitutes and implicitly discouraged export development. During the same period, South Korea, on the other hand, generally pursued a policy consistent with the Japanese model, providing few incentives for import substitution while heavily encouraging export activity through capital subsidies, depreciation allowances, import duty exemptions, and exchange rates near equilibrium. From 1960 to 1980, Chile's real annual growth rates were 2.5% in industry and 1.6% overall, compared to Korea's rates of 16.3% and 7.0%—spurred by scale economies, international competition, price flexibility, and no agricultural and foreign-exchange shortages associated with export promotion.

Meiji Japan's exports also benefitted from favorable international economic conditions. From 1868-1897, the yen chronically depreciated vis-a-vis the U.S. dollar. In 1882-1897, the yen was on a de facto silver standard, as silver declined relative to gold. While Chinese indemnities after 1897 (which strengthened the yen) and the military expenses of the 1904-1905 Russo-Japanese War strained the international balance of trade, World War I's export demand spurred a large trade surplus. Although the immediate postwar and early Great Depression trade balance was in deficit due to slow growth of exports, they grew well after 1931, when Japan went off the gold standard.

Today's international economic conditions are not as favorable to LDC export expansion. The most rapidly expanding LDC manufactured exports during the 1970s and early 1980s were textiles, clothing, footwear, and simple consumer goods requiring labor-intensive technology widely available. But the competition from other aspiring, newly industrial exporting countries is more severe than it was for Meiji Japan.

XI. Conclusion

How applicable is the Japanese development model (1868-1939) to present-day LDCs? First, although the Japanese experience indicates the advantages of self-directed development, many small countries are limited in their options of reducing dependence on DC trade and capital movements. But the JDM does underline the importance of LDC governments' controlling the employment of DC personnel introducing technology into the LDC. This is especially important since the technological distance between today's DCs and LDCs is large, making it less likely that foreign experts will adapt technology to local conditions and indigenous production without LDC administrative direction. Second, Meiji Japan's emphasis on primary, vocational, and scientific education provides a model for today's LDCs, but not for those that want education to promote democracy and human rights. Third, Japanese-type "guided capitalism" is limited in today's LDCs, because of inadequate government capability to spur private business and because of political elite and populist opposition to large business subsidies, high industrial concentration, high income inequality between businessmen and others, and favorable legal and labor policies for business. Fourth, Japanese economic history demonstrates the importance of a governmental role in creating and regulating financial institutions, without tolerating growing concentration of private financial institutions. Fifth, many of today's low-income countries, like Meiji Japan, have tried to transfer large amounts of agricultural income to industry for investment capital, but, like Japan, some have sacrificed rural incomes and nutritional levels and spurred agrarian discontent. Sixth, high labor-supply elasticities resulting from vast reserves from the agricultural and informal industrial sectors, together with low industrial wage premiums, kept Japanese unskilled industrial wage rates relatively low before World War I, increasing business profits and reducing urban unemployment. However, today's LDCs, because of minimum wage legislation, trade union strength, unsuitable technologies, and high food prices, have relatively high wages, reducing profits and savings. Seventh, Meiji Japan exemplifies the importance of improving capital and technology step by step, utilizing existing small industry, rather than making substantial leaps to the most advanced technologies available. Eighth, although today's international economic conditions are less favorable to LDCs than those of the late nineteenth century were to Japan, LDCs could still benefit from the Japanese approach of using international competition and market-clearing exchange rates to spur rapid export expansion.

While a contemporary LDC can learn useful lessons from the Japanese development model, these lessons are limited because of Meiji Japan's historically specific conditions, and because some aspects of the Japanese approach also contributed to pathologies of growth, such as zaibatsu concentration, income inequality, labor union repression, militarism, and imperialism. These pathologies were not reduced until military defeat was followed by the democratic reforms of an occupational government, a series of events not to be recommended, nor likely to improve income equality, accelerate economic growth, and democratize the political economy in developing countries as it did in Japan.

Notes

1. Department of Economics, Kansas State University (KSU), Manhattan, KS 66506, USA. This paper was presented to a joint American Economic Association/Committee on Asian Economic Studies panel in Dallas, December 29, 1984. I thank the International University of Japan (IUJ) and KSU for funds, and Hiroshi Kitamura, Ichirou Inukai, Sadasumi Hara, Yujiro Hayami, Shigeru Ishikawa, Ryoshin Minami, Kazushi Ohkawa, John Power, Patrick Gormely, Herbert Bix, Seiji Naya, and IUJ and University of Hawaii scholars for criticisms, but they are not responsible for errors.

2. This excludes high-income capital-surplus oil exporters like the United Arab Emirates, Kuwait, Saudi Arabia, and Libya.

3. My computations from the World Bank, 1984, pp. 218-19, indicate that 43 of the 53 noncommunist low-income and lower-middle income countries ranking the lowest in GNP per capita are from sub-Saharan Africa and south and southeast Asia.

4. Scholars have usually rejected concepts of abrupt historical thresholds like Rostow's takeoff or Engels's industrial revolution (see Nafziger, 1984, pp. 153-55). Even Simon Kuznets's modern economic growth, a rapid, sustained increase in real per capita GNP associated with capital accumulation and rapid technical change under private or state capitalism, begins so gradually that its start cannot be dated by a given year or decade. In Japan, we cannot pinpoint the beginnings of modern (or capitalist) growth more precisely than the Meiji reform era of the late nineteenth-century period.

5. In contrast, independent Siam, which in 1868 faced initial conditions somewhat comparable to Japan, did not establish government factories or provide assistance to private industrial entrepreneurs in the latter part of the nineteenth century (Yasuba and Dhiravegin, 1985, pp. 25-26).

References

Dore, Ronald P., *Education in Tokugawa Japan* (Berkeley and Los Angeles: University of California Press, 1965).

Dore, Ronald P., "Land Reform and Japan's Economic Development," *Developing Economies* 3(4) (December 1965), pp. 487-496.

Dore, Ronald P., *Land Reform in Japan* (London: Oxford University Press, 1959).
Dower, John W., ed., *Origins of the Modern Japanese State: Selected Writings of E.H. Norman* (New York: Pantheon, 1975).
Goldsmith, Raymond W., *The Financial Development of India, Japan, and the United States: A Trilateral Institutional, Statistical, and Analytical Comparison* (New Haven: Yale University Press, 1983).
Griffin, Keith, and Azizur Rahman Khan, eds., *Growth and Inequality in Pakistan* (London: Macmillan, 1972).
Hayami, Yujiro, *A Century of Agricultural Growth in Japan: Its Relevance to Asian Development* (Tokyo: University of Tokyo Press, 1975).
Hayami, Yujiro, and Vernon W. Ruttan, *Agricultural Development: An International Perspective* (Baltimore: Johns Hopkins University Press, 1971).
Hirschmeier, Johannes, *The Origins of Entrepreneurship in Meiji Japan* (Cambridge, MA: Harvard University Press, 1964).
International Development Center of Japan (Kazushi Ohkawa, team leader), "Japan's Development Experience and the Development Strategy for the Contemporary Developing Countries," Tokyo, March 1980.
International Development Center of Japan, "Japan's Historical Development Experience and the Contemporary Developing Countries: Issues for Comparative Analysis," Tokyo, February 1982.
Inukai, Ichirou, "Experience in Transfer of Technology from the West: Lessons from False Starts," in Haruo Nagamine, ed., *Nation-building and Regional Development: The Japanese Experience* (Hong Kong: Maruzen Asia, 1981), UN Centre for Regional Development Vol. 10, pp. 76-98.
Inukai, Ichirou, "The Kogyo Iken: Japan's Ten Year Plan, 1884," *Kyoto Sangyo University Economic and Business Review* (May 1979): pp. 1-100.
Ishikawa, Shigeru, *Essays on Technology, Employment, and Institutions in Economic Development: Comparative Asian Experience* (Tokyo: Kinokuniya, 1981).
Ishikawa, Shigeru, "Relevance of the Experiences of Japan to Contemporary Economic Development," *The Philippine Review of Economics and Business*, 19 (1982), pp. 255-79.
Krueger, Anne O., *Foreign Trade Regimes and Economic Development: Liberalization Attempts and Consequences* (Cambridge: Ballinger, 1978).
Krueger, Anne O., Hal B. Lary, Terry Monson, and Narongchai Akrasenee, eds., *Trade and Employment in Developing Countries*, vol. I, *Individual Studies* (Chicago: University of Chicago Press, 1981).
Kuznets, Simon, *Modern Economic Growth: Rate, Structure, and Spread* (New Haven: Yale University Press, 1966).
Kuznets, Simon, "Quantitative Aspects of the Economic Growth of Nations: I. Levels and Variability of Rates of Growth," *Economic Development and Cultural Change*, 5 (October 1956), pp. 5-94.
Lee, Teng-hui, *Intersectoral Capital Flows in the Economic Development of Taiwan, 1895-1960* (Ithaca: Cornell University Press, 1971).
Lipton, Michael, *Why Poor People Stay Poor: A Study of Urban Bias in World Development* (London: Maurice Temple Smith, 1977).
Lockwood, William W., *The Economic Development of Japan: Growth and Structural Change, 1868-1938* (Princeton: Princeton University Press, 1954).
Mahajan, V.S., *Development Planning: Lessons from the Japanese Model*

(Calcutta: Minerva Associates, 1976).'
Minami, Ryoshin, *The Economic Development of Japan* (London: Macmillan, 1985).
Minami, Ryoshin, "The Introduction of Electric Power and its Impact on the Manufacturing Industries: With Special Reference to Smaller Scale Plants," in Patrick, 1976, pp. 299-325.
Minami, Ryoshin, *The Turning Point in Economic Development: Japan's Experience* (Tokyo: Kinokuniya, 1973).
Mody, Ashoka, Sudipto Mundle, and K.N. Raj, "Resource Flows from Agriculture: Japan and India," in Ohkawa and Ranis, 1985.
Munakata, Seiya, "The Course and Problems of National Education," *Developing Economies*, 3 (December 1965), pp. 540- 59.
Mundle, Sudipto, *Surplus Flows and Growth Imbalances* (New Delhi: Allied Publishers, 1981).
Nafziger, E. Wayne, *The Economics of Developing Countries* (Belmont, CA: Wadsworth, 1984).
Nafziger, E. Wayne, *The Economics of Political Instability* (Boulder, CO: Westview, 1983).
Nakamura, Takafusa, *Economic Growth in Prewar Japan,* translated by Robert A. Feldman (New Haven: Yale University Press, 1983).
Ohkawa, Kazushi, "Japan's Development: A Model for Less-Developed Countries?" *Asian Development Review* 1(2) (1983), pp. 45-57.
Ohkawa, Kazushi, and Gustav Ranis, eds., *Japan and the Developing Countries: A Comparative Analysis* (Oxford: Basil Blackwell, 1985).
Ohkawa, Kazushi, and Henry Rosovsky, *Japanese Economic Growth: Trend Acceleration in the Twentieth Century* (Stanford: Stanford University Press, 1973).
Ohkawa, Kazushi, Yutaka Shimizu, and Nobukiyo Takamatsu, "Agricultural Surplus in Japan's Case: Implication for Various Possible Patterns in the Initial Phase of Development," International Development Center of Japan Working Paper No. 19, March 1982.
Ohkawa, Kazushi, and Miyohei Shinohara, eds., *Patterns of Japanese Economic Development: A Quantitative Appraisal* (New Haven: Yale University Press, 1979).
Ohkawa, Kazushi, Miyohei Shinohara, M. Umemura, M. Ito and T. Noda, *The Growth Rate of the Japanese Economy Since 1878* (Tokyo: Kinokuniya, 1957).
Oshima, Harry T., "Meiji Fiscal Policy and Agricultural Progress," in William W. Lockwood, ed., *The State and Economic Enterprise in Japan: Essays in the Political Economy of Growth* (Princeton: Princeton University Press, 1965), pp. 353-89.
Patrick, Hugh T., "Japan, 1868-1914," in Rondo Cameron, *Banking in the Early Stages of Industrialization: A Study in Comparative Economic History* (New York: Oxford University Press, 1967), pp. 239-89.
Patrick, Hugh T., ed., *Japanese Industrialization and its Social Consequences* (Berkeley: University of California Press, 1976).
Power, John H., "Trade Trends in Asia," *Asia Pacific Community,* (Fall 1979), pp. 45-55.
Ranis, Gustave, "The Community-centered Entrepreneur in Japanese Development," *Explorations in Entrepreneurial History,* 8, no. 2 (1955), pp. 80-98.

Saxonhouse, Gary R., "Country Girls and Communication among Competitors in the Japanese Cotton-spinning Industry," in Patrick, 1976, pp. 97-125.

Shinohara, Miyohei, *Structural Changes in Japan's Economic Development* (Tokyo: Kinokuniya, 1970).

Shishido, Toshio, "Japanese Industrial Development and Policies for Science and Technology," *Science,* 219 (21 January 1983), pp. 259-64.

Sumiya, Mikio, and Koji Taira, eds., *An Outline of Japanese Economic History, 1603-1940: Major Works and Research Findings* (Tokyo: University of Tokyo Press, 1979).

Tachi, Minoru, and Yoichi Okazaki, "Economic Development and Population Growth—with Special Reference to Southeast Asia," *Developing Economies* 3(4) (December 1965), pp. 497-515.

Takeda, Takao, "The Financial Policy of the Meiji Government," *Developing Economies,* 3 (December 1965), pp. 427-49.

World Bank, *World Development Report, 1979* (Washington, 1979).

World Bank, *World Development Report, 1980* (Washington, 1980).

World Bank, *World Development Report, 1983* (New York: Oxford University Press, 1983).

World Bank, *World Development Report, 1984* (New York: Oxford University Press, 1984).

Yasuba, Yasukichi, "The Evolution of Dualistic Wage Structure," in Patrick, 1976, pp. 249-298.

Yasuba, Yasukichi, and Likhit Dhiravegin, "Initial Conditions, Instituional Changes, Policy and their Consequences: Siam and Japan, 1850-1914," in Ohkawa and Ranis, 1985.

Yamamura, Kozo, "A Re-examination of Entrepreneurship in Meiji Japan (1868-1912)," *Economic History Review,* 21 (February 1968), pp. 148-58.

The Family Farm: A Success Story With Global Implications

by

Orville Freeman

The family farm is a practical manifestation—down to earth in the most complete meaning of that much abused metaphor —of how high technology and human freedom can be melded— indeed must be melded—for optimum results.

Beyond that, the family farm is almost a classic case history of what I think of as the Rohatyn Proposition, namely, that "societies and economies are successful to the degree that they can forgo satisfaction of the moment if that is necessary to make provision for the future." Putting this into language that every family farmer recognizes as basic reality: a successful farmer cannot eat his seed corn.

Finally, the family farm answers unequivocally the intriguing question of whether technology is neutral in the deepest sense, that is, the motives that inspire and the values that infuse society. In that context, it is an incontrovertible demonstration of the fact that in all societies, whatever the cultural context, technology is a response to human need. And if you accept the fact, as I do, that meeting human need is a desirable undertaking, and as such profoundly moral, technology is *not* neutral. It is a positive force.

Some Definitions

Having placed the family farm in these transcendental dimensions, let me now put it into more practical perspective by offering some definitions of what the family farm is and what it is not.

Some seductive myth-making and romantic nostalgia not-

Orville L. Freeman is a former U.S. Secretary of Agriculture, now practices law in Washington, D.C.

withstanding, the family farm is *not* a pastoral, idyllic arrangement in which people are made better by communing with nature and being close to the soil and the elements. Family farmers can be as parochial and irrational, self-centered and passionately wrongheaded as any other segment of the population. What is true about the family farm in the socio-political context is that it constitutes a solid base to measure, test, and evaluate social and political phenomena in a framework that assumes free choice and that recognizes that choice is most free when the object chosen is directed to the benefit of the individual or to the benefit of someone with whom he has close bonds.

Family Farm and Small Farm Are *Not* Synonyms

Another popular notion that needs to be dispelled is that a family farm is the same as a small farm. Far too often, farm discussion and farm programs idealize the small farmer and express regret that the traditional American farm, defined as forty acres and a mule, is no more. This is not to say that farm units of this size no longer exist—even in the U.S.—and that they or the people who work on them do not warrant concern. But it is important to realize that the family farm has an economic definition that is clear and concise even though, like other successful economic units, it varies in magnitude. A definition of the family farm that is meaningful in both economic and social terms and that applies anywhere in the world is a farm that is operated by one family with no more than 1.5 man years of outside labor and that utilizes the agricultural technology necessary to become an effective economic unit that can earn its way in the world's competitive marketplace.

In the United States today a family farm is a fairly large unit, and the size has grown over the years. The "forty acres and the mule" definition passed into history with the nineteenth century. In 1920, a U.S. farm constituted roughly 180 acres. In 1980, it was closer to 450 acres. And these are broadbrush averages. Today a family farm, in the economic, operational definition, can vary from 10 acres for a truck or vegetable farm to 2,500 acres for a wheat farm. But it is these economically determined family farms that make up the overwhelming percentage of agricultural productivity in the United States, a productivity that constitutes the miracle of American agriculture, which has not been matched anywhere on the globe or anytime in history.

The Fabulous Record

It is a miracle that can be measured. Only 100 years ago, U.S.

agriculture was subsistence agriculture, with 80% of all Americans living on the land. Today, 2.2 million farm families, totaling 6 million persons, feed the American people better and cheaper than any other people on the planet and feed, in addition, millions of others in the rest of the world. Food from America's family farms has reached hungry people under a wide variety of programs, including, on a global scale, the Food for Peace program and, domestically, such programs as food for school lunches, food stamps for the needy, food for shut-ins, and for pregnant women and young children. The fact that some of these programs are under attack today for inequities and inefficiencies that have perhaps distorted their original intention does not change the fact that they have made an important contribution—and continue to make such a contribution—to the welfare of mankind.

In another measure of the phenomenal story of the success of the American family farm, as late as 1940, each American farm family fed 10 persons. Today, the average American farm family feeds 77 persons.

Farming Is a Sophisticated Operation

One other widely held and thoroughly erroneous notion about the family farm requires correction. It is a mirage that constitutes the other side of the rosily romantic, bucolic existence. In that mirage, the family farmer is an unsophisticated rube, with limited intellectual horizons, pursuing an essentially simple and simple-minded task. People who view the family farm in this light believe that agriculture is a primitive process where you dig a hole, throw some seed into the ground, sprinkle a little fertilizer on it, and get results. This is not only untrue: it is a dangerous misconception. The truth of the matter is that agriculture is incredibly complex and difficult. It is also subject to complex political, emotional, sociological and anthropological forces that vary with the traditions of areas, countries, localities, and tribes.

Indeed, today, from a production process point of view of agriculture, we need to think in terms of systems of engineering. The system must include land, reasonably knowledgeable people, credit and inputs such as seeds, fertilizer, chemicals, water, and a suitable climate. You have to be able to harvest the crop within sharp time dimensions. You have to be able to store it so that it doesn't deteriorate. You then have to move the overwhelming segment of production you then have to move to processing so it can become food, because agriculture and grain are not food. And then you have to move it to market. It is a long, complicated, involved, convoluted chain.

The "High Tech" of Agriculture

In addition, agriculture today is at the forefront of technological advance. Biogenetics and allied technologies have the potential of changing human lives and improving human welfare, not only in the United States but around the globe, in a manner and at a pace that parallels the role and effect of computers. Richard Critchfield, a sensitive and knowledgeable expert on rural development worldwide, argues, and I concur, that "one can now confidently say that a quiet agricultural revolution has begun that is likely to have more dramatic effects on more human beings than any revolution that has gone before."

Critchfield also notes, and again I can confirm this from personal experience and observation, that "biological technology is a chapter just begun." This is true in the U.S., but, as important from a planetary perspective, it is also true in the Third World, where the overwhelming majority of the planet's people live. Critchfield points out—and, once more I can corroborate this from my own firsthand experience that

> the best-informed sources on the Third World in the 1980s, I find, are agricultural scientists: the agronomists, plant breeders, soil men and such who have been quietly changing the face of world agriculture the past 15 years. Most of them are connected with the new international network linking 13 agricultural research centers, eight of them set up since 1971. Scientists in national programs in 130 developing countries are participating. Since the Chinese became actively involved during the late 1970s, this network has been pooling knowledge and genetic material on every crop grown on the planet, plus livestock breeding, plant and animal diseases and cropping systems.
>
> These scientists know what is happening because they are making it happen.

Labor-Intensive Technology

And what they make happen has yet another dimension—of very great importance and often overlooked. That dimension has to do with the fact that biotechnology, unlike mechanical technology, does not demand the same substitution of capital for labor. Critchfield reports from the field: "Large-scale experience in Asia during the 1970s shows that it is more labor-intensive, not less."

The Staggering Potential

Let me add to Critchfield's deeply meaningful observations my own vision of the enormous potential that agriculture holds for all of us on this planet. Not long ago in *The New York Times*, there was an interesting article by the eminent scientist and ecologist Rene Dubos, who was then a professor at Rockefeller

University. Dubos pointed out that only about one-half of the usable land in the world today is actually being used. Only one-half.

Two Illustrations

To illustrate what can be done not only with this empty space crying out for action, but even beyond it, he cites two areas in the world where land that historically did not exist has literally been created and is now notably productive.

I am familiar with both and can confirm Dubos's assertion from personal observation.

One is the area around Brasilia, the capital of Brazil. Built 50 miles into the hinterlands twenty years ago, Brasilia today is a city of a couple of million people. The area surrounding it, millions of acres, was scrub forest land, totally unproductive. Today that land is intensively cultivated and profitably so. There are probably 400 million acres of such land in Brazil—more than all the land under cultivation in the U.S.

On the other side of the world, in Australia, is an area that was 90 miles of desert but has, in a comparable way, with the addition of soil nutrients and other available technologies, also become highly productive.

There are hundreds of millions of acres in Africa that have the potential to become equally productive. The Sudan alone has as much land not under the plow as the land used for agricultural production in the U.S. The problem is that there are no railroads, no storage, no people, and no know-how. But the potential is there.

As a matter of fact, regarding the combined potential of land not in use and the agricultural technology that exists and is not used, Roger Lavell, an eminent American scientist, wrote recently in the *Scientific American,* "If the level of technology and resources were applied to land around the world and employed at levels comparable to the usage of a typical Iowa corn farmer in the U.S., enough food could be produced to sustain 38-40 billion people."

The Desperate Need

Given the cutting-edge technology we now have, plus the demonstrated productivity of the family farm, what can be done in this vital area is almost commensurate with what needs to be done. The needs are clear and staggering. The Presidential Commission on World Hunger, which was constituted in the fall of 1979 and of which I was a member, has defined these needs in starkly realistic terms. I cite them here:

- Approximately 25% of the world's people are hungry or undernourished.
- Malnutrition affects over 500 million persons.
- Twelve to thirteen million small children die each year, the majority from malnutrition-associated causes.
- Approximately one out of three children born into the world will die before reaching the age of five, mostly from malnutrition-related causes.
- Between 50,000 and 100,000 children throughout the world become blind every year due to Vitamin A deficiency.
- The majority of hungry people exist in well-defined geographic areas, concentrated on the Indian subcontinent, Southeast Asia, sub-Saharan Africa, with pockets in the Middle East and Latin America.
- Hunger is a major health problem for some half billion individuals, an ethical, moral and human rights problem for the rest of the world, and a world order problem if the alarming spread of hunger is allowed to continue.

Fortunately, we do not have to head into that dark night. The point I want to make emphatically is that alternatives exist. Positive solutions are possible. And the key to them is the family farm.

The Magnitude of Possible Solutions

It is estimated—obviously a rough estimate—that there are about 1 billion farm families in developing countries around the world, owning and working less than five hectares of land. If these 1 billion farm families, cultivating one to five hectares, were helped to increase their net income by only $100 a year, the global impact would be enormous. Not only would their own lives and the lives of their families and communities improve measurably, the additional purchasing power would provide a tremendous stimulus to the economies of their villages and their countries.

Further, the impact on the growth and expansion of the world economy would be significant. These 1 billion farmers constitute a gigantic new market. Many of the problems the global economy struggles with today would find a solution that is both quick and sound. The world economy would surge dramatically. It would spell the end of the stagflation that has haunted us for the past decade. And it would lay a foundation for a sane and sustainable global economic order for all.

Another important result would be to reverse the massive migration of impoverished people from the countryside to horrible, putrid city slums that is taking place all over the world.

The vital question then becomes how the miraculous dynamics of the family farm can be sustained at home and propagated abroad. I am convinced that it requires a working partnership between the private and public sectors, shaped to the social, political and cultural givens of the respective societies.

What Does Not Work . . .

In reviewing agricultural production worldwide, two facts seem incontrovertible. One is that large production units and collectivism as a social and economic structure usually do not work well. The latest example of this is East Germany, where the regime merged 800,000 farming units, mostly farms, into 4,000 "agricultural factories" averaging 5,000 hectares. This was done in 1955, with the result that today the GDR imports up to 4 million tons of grain a year, mainly from the U.S., since the USSR has none to spare. The imports eat up 20% of East Germany's hard currency earnings and have prompted GDR Chairman Erich Honecker to declare, in July 1982: "Today, one can compare the grain problem with the oil problem in terms of priority."

The second incontrovertible fact seems to be that something about the agricultural producer and his relation to the land is *sui generis*.

. . . And What Does Work

But the farmer and his land, however strong the bond between them, do not constitute an economic or social island. Fair market conditions and access to technology, credit, the appropriate chemical inputs, the required physical infrastructure—in all of which government attitudes and policies inevitably play a role—are part of the system in which the individual producer can get the desired results. Where such a system is in place, where the combination of access to supplies and to the market exist, where government policies recognize the importance of stable and reasonable prices, the individual producer, whose reward is clearly the product of his own effort, has demonstrated initiative and creativity that have delivered results unmatched by any other approach.

This is true not only in the United States, but also in countries with cultures and traditions as different as Taiwan, South Korea and Israel. In each case, however, the basic component of success was the same: a private sector encouraged by sensitive and effective government support to stimulate productivity.

The question then becomes, how can the success story of the

American family farm be "exported"? How can small-holders in the developing countries, families that cultivate 1-5 hectares (which, for the present, is a working definition of the family farm in these countries), be organized and energized to increase their productivity?

A Novel Hybrid

I am convinced that the answer is a novel hybrid that I have seen successfully introduced over the past decade in Latin American, Asia and Africa. The hybrid I refer to is not a generic one. It is structural. It is, in fact, an integrated system in which a corporate core serves to move individual farmers from subsistence agriculture into the market economy.

In this system, private-sector companies, processors, and/or marketers of foodstuffs and industrial crops develop an integrated operation in areas of potential productivity. They reach agreement with small producers, guaranteeing a market at a fair price, providing credit, technology, inputs such as fertilizers, herbicides and seeds, assistance in soil preparation, harvesting, storage and, finally, services in moving the product to processing and market. In some parts of the world, where land is abundant, small-holders who participate in such a scheme develop the know-how to move out of their mini-plots and learn to manage larger tracts of land, graduating into larger family-size farmers. This is not a process that takes place overnight. It requires long-term planning, infrastructure in place, and dependable government support so that investments made by the private sector and responsibly carried forward are protected for the long haul. If it is to succeed, it requires, in addition, the involvement and support of the entire rural community.

The key is a holistic approach, with a broad involvement of people, particularly women, who do an estimated 78% of the farming in most developing countries and whose willingness and capacity to make necessary changes has been demonstrated time and again when they have been properly approached and mobilized. Once increased production brings money into the pockets of small producers, production techniques spread rapidly throughout the community, stimulating a host of related economic activities that, in turn, provide jobs for the landless and build new markets. The process can multiply wealth rapidly, creating a win/win situation with four dimensions:

1. A substantial increase in the living standard of small-holders;

2. An important contribution to the sound development of the host country;

3. A profitable undertaking for the core company; and

4. An input into meeting the basic human needs for nutrition around the world.

Some Guidelines

Global experience with this hybrid, which I and some of my colleagues have researched in depth, on-site, makes it possible to produce a set of guidelines that can constitute a framework for action that combines the proven potential of the family farm with the demonstrated dynamic of a corporate core.

Let me lay them out here:

In the operational area, to achieve a successful symbiosis between a corporate core and a network of small-holder farmers, the following conditions are mandatory:

1. A firm, clear agreement between the family farmers and the company. Under this agreement, the farm family must commit itself to adopt the company's techniques and practices to grow the product. They must commit themselves as well to prompt harvesting and delivery to the processing facility to make possible a continuous flow of product to the processing facility.

The company, for its part, must contract for the product at a fair and equitable price level and make a dependable commitment to provide credit, inputs, and technical assistance. The details of such agreements inevitably vary, depending on crop, conditions, country and culture, but the contract must conform as far as possible to local practices and customs.

2. An efficient and specialized advisory service that constantly reviews the training and supervision of the farmers, as well as the corporate staff, in the production, processing, and marketing facets of the operation. Such an advisory service can also interpret the organization to the community and can communicate to all parties the importance of performance and the advantages that will result to participants in the enterprise from performance. Conversely, it can advise the company on people problems and community problems that may arise.

3. Efficient management of the operation from soil preparation to marketing of the final product is, and must be seen to be, the responsibility of the company. Management is critical and, historically, has been the most serious shortfall in carrying such satellite farming programs forward successfully. Companies must make top-level managers available to run these enterprises.

4. A comprehensive research facility that can explore the latest technology and instruct and assist farmers in the application of the best production practices. This is a vital ingredient in boosting both farmer income and corporate responsibility.

In the systemic area, there are four important conditions:

1. The most important systemic element for success is market orientation. The needs of the market must be rigorously identified and measured before a project is launched. There are many distressing examples where decision makers have concentrated on production capacity without identifying and defining the market. A project won't work if the cart gets before the horse, which is what happens when production takes priority over the market. Both production capacity and market capacity must be established at the outset of any project.

2. Overall management, including allocation and coordination of all inputs, whether for production, processing, marketing, social or infrastructure purposes, must be in the hands of a single authority.

3. A long-term orientation is required from all participants. For the company, this means a stretching-out of profit expectations; for the farmer, it means accepting instruction and guidance for a protracted period.

4. A balanced approach to local culture and traditions is often the crux of a successful operation. Management must recognize and address this dimension from the outset. Failure to do so will haunt the enterprise and can threaten its viability in the long term.

In the policy area, industrial country aid programs that focus on agriculture should secure maximum participation from the private sector to assure the most dynamic approach and the most effective results. The system of family farms grouped around a corporate core has great potential. The experience of companies that have successfully implemented this system can be made available to other firms to enlist their interest and abbreviate their learning curve.

Governments of industrialized countries with aid programs designed for the agricultural sector should approach agricultural and agribusiness companies with demonstrated records of knowhow and performance; the government should make clear to these companies that they assign high priority to effective agricultural undertakings in the developing world and are prepared to undergird this priority with credit facilities and perhaps also with insurance and other mechanisms that ameliorate the corporate risk in such long-term and often politically vulnerable undertakings.

Specifically, the governments of industrialized countries should make clear to companies prepared to take the risk that the home government will do its best to see to it that host governments honor their commitments. In the U.S., the Bureau of Private

Enterprise in the AID agency is giving serious consideration to providing this kind of support to companies prepared to launch agricultural undertakings based on the family farm system. Other industrialized countries should adopt the same policy.

In addition to mobilizing and supporting their own private sector companies willing to undertake agricultural projects in developing countries, the industrialized nations should also support the host countries that welcome these enterprises. Such support could take the form of assistance to the host government for farm-to-market roads, irrigation, and social and educational services in the rural areas. It could include support of training for the agricultural sector at educational institutions and perhaps even for on-site training provided by the companies under a special contract.

International institutions, particularly development banks, which have credit, prestige, and experience, should put their considerable muscle behind such undertakings. The World Bank, for example, can be a powerful force, with great influence on the host country in facilitating the necessary follow-through on commitments made and in resisting the inevitable political meddling that occurs in developing countries when real change takes place.

Host country policies are, of course, basic. Today, the political leadership in most of the developing countries recognizes that food production is a key to progress and that a healthy agricultural sector is basic to sound economic development. The recognition was long in coming and, in too many cases, the gap is still wide between rhetoric and action. It will be necessary to bridge this gap in the developing countries in order to get companies with production and processing know-how and marketing expertise to commit themselves to the substantial risks involved in such agricultural enterprises, with all their complexities and long-term payouts.

And Some Fundamentals

Finally, I want to offer five keys to understanding the full meaning and impact of agriculture and the way in which agricultural effort can be made optimally successful, essentially by using and adapting the superb success record of the family farm in the U.S. They are:

1. Agriculture is the key to economic development. No country, with the exception of a few city-states, has ever prospered and built a sound economy without a solid agricultural base.

2. Agriculture is different. The forces with which agriculture must contend and which it must mold and master are quite dif-

ferent from the forces affecting industry. Agriculture is subject to outside, uncontrollable elements: weather, diseases, pests, to name a few. Also, farmers, like other raw-material producers, have a relatively weak bargaining position, falling short of the return that processors and marketers of raw materials get from the marketplace. Management in agriculture is difficult. It is much easier to manage and produce efficiently using 10,000 men in a factory on one acre of land than it is to manage 1,000 people on 10,000 acres of land. This is why large-scale producing units are extremely difficult to operate efficiently and profitably. The family farm, with a land holding adequate to apply modern technology effectively, is the most productive size. The incentive that results when the producer benefits directly from his efforts cannot be duplicated by large holdings whether they are privately held, communal, cooperative, or state-owned. Results from the factory-size organization of state farms and large collectives in the USSR are dramatic demonstrations of how not to organize agriculture.

3. Sound agricultural policies are difficult to develop and carry out. The time span required to put into place an appropriate land/people balance, to make available credit and necessary inputs to the grower, and to construct storage, processing, and marketing capacity is longer than the usual time span of a political officeholder. In addition, carrying out a sound, meaningful agricultural policy calls for changes that, by their very nature, shake up traditional patterns, with the result that they are fiercely resisted.

4. A system whereby the producer on the soil benefits directly from his efforts is the single most important element in increasing productivity. In most places in the world, this means producer ownership and requires egalitarian land policies, adequately supported by the government. Taiwan, Japan and Korea are examples of success where this principle has been applied.

5. Concentration on the family farm is the key to success both in increasing productivity everywhere in the world and in creating a sociopolitical base for a society in which self-reliance, enterprise, and commitment to cohesive family relationships are important and enduring values.

The Economic Impact of the Emerging Global Information Economy on Lesser Developed Nations

by

Kenneth B. Taylor

Until the recent past, human economic history has been structured around three basic paradigms: hunting, agriculture, and industry. Rapid change in the underlying configuration of technology within each paradigm became the central force in the transformation of a society into the next paradigm. A repetitive pattern can be characterized concerning this process. First, many diverse technological innovations and inventions come together to represent a unique technological complex. Second, the new technology complex spreads through the society and gradually displaces the old paradigm. Third, this period entails sociological, psychological, and political displacement as well as economic growth. Many people have argued that the rapid technological changes that have emerged in the telecommunications and commuter fields represent a new axial force that will transform the industrial paradigm into an information paradigm.

Daniel Bell's *The Coming of Post-Industrial Society* was published in 1973 and represents a landmark in the articulation of projected change in the framework of Western society. In his treatise, Bell conceives of the post-industrial society as a "knowledge society":

The major source of structural change in society—change in the modes

---

Kenneth B. Taylor is chairman and assistant professor of economics and management, Chatham College, Pittsburg, Pennsylvania.

of innovation in the relation of science to technology and in public policy—is the change in the character of knowledge: the exponential growth and branching of science, the rise of the new intellectual technology, the creation of systematic research through R&D budgets, and, as the calyx of all this, the codification of theoretical knowledge.[1]

With time comes a clearer understanding of the evolutionary process affecting our socioeconomic systems. A recent book by Yoneji Masuda stresses the role of information technology in the post-industrial society. In this book, Masuda asserts, "Unlike the vague term 'post-industrial society,' the term 'information society' as used here will describe in concrete terms the character and the structure of this future society."[2] He goes on to say: "In the information society, 'computer technology' will be the innovational technology that will constitute the development core, and its fundamental function will be to substitute for and amplify the mental labor of man."[3] Some students of economic development have estimated that between 60% to 90% of economic growth has been derived from technological change.[4] The continued rise in the standard of living in the More Developed Nations (MDNs) may very well rest on the technological developments and applications in the computer and telecommunications industries.

Since discussion of the emergence of a new information era began, students of the subject have suggested that the new paradigm will be the key to freeing the Less Developed Countries (LDCs) from their cycles of poverty and subservience to the MDNs of the world.

In the book *The Next 200 Years*, Herman Kahn argued that the current widening income gap between MDNs and developing nations will actually create rapid, sustained growth in the LDCs. Kahn stated that, by the year 2000, it is possible that in excess of two-thirds of mankind will have passed the $1,000 level of per capita income.[5] This assertion set off a controversy that continues to this day as to the feasibility and the means of attaining this goal. Several students of the subject have indicated that the revolution in telecommunications and computer technologies holds the key to future growth in the LDCs. The French journalist-author Servan-Schreiber specifically suggested in *The World Challenge* that the future of LDCs does not rest in low-cost labor but in the systemic integration of information technology.[6] Two specialists in the new information technologies, Charles Gould and C.R. Gerber, have recently written that: "By the year 2000, a new system of communicating via space will distribute the benefits of the information revolution around the globe, making productivity jumps possible even in isolated areas of the Third World."[7] Hope springs eternal, and there is little doubt that the economic generating power of the new technologies offers an attractive potential solution to the economic problems of LDCs. A short inquiry into the history of attempts to deal with their problems will help to place this potential solution in perspective.

The two decades after World War II saw the emergence of independent nations from Europe's former colonies. Encouraged by the success of the Marshall Plan and using it as a model, the United States took the initiative in trying to help these newly emerged nations develop by providing capital in the form of foreign aid. Over time, the size, composition, and participants of aid programs changed. The motives of the MDNs in promoting these programs ranged from generous to selfish. Regardless of the motive, the rationale for aid was essentially to foster economic development. Much controversy still rages over the effectiveness of the billions spent for foreign programs. What is indisputable is the fact that the spectacular performance of the Marshall Plan concept has not been observed outside of Europe.

The reasons for this nonduplication lie with certain circumstances unique to the modern LDC. The idea behind "vicious circles of poverty" is simply that it is easier for rich nations to save and invest than poor ones. To break the vicious circle, either more savings must be extracted out of poor people, or external funds for investments must be found. Since developing nations are too poor to save for themselves, foreign aid was conceived as the only logical means to achieve sustained economic progress. As was stated above, foreign-aid programs have proven less than totally effective. Still, the "vicious circle of poverty" argument is only a partial explanation as to why LDCs remain LDCs. The size of markets in developing countries is small precisely because incomes are low in such countries; yet this limited extent of the market makes the employment of many of the most efficient modern technologies inappropriate. Small, fragmented markets, in conjunction with an incomplete infrastructure, hinder the move to developing status. In addition, over time the role of government in development has risen to the point where growth is highly unlikely without active government involvement. If the government cannot create and maintain a stable environment for modern enterprises, or if the stability is not oriented toward promoting genuine local development, any growth begun will not be sustained. Pursuit of economic development involves difficult choices, and the transition phase from non-growth to sustained growth is full of inequities and sociocultural contradictions. The attitude and policies of the government are crucial during the transition and have often ended up presenting a hindrance to, rather than a support for, development. Finally, many economists argue that the main barriers to development today lie with conditions external to the developing world. It is argued that the existence of already rich and industrialized nations creates international pressures that hamper the growth efforts of LDCs. While almost everyone acknowledges that developing countries are in a position to learn from the experience of already-advanced nations, many have argued that the potential to learn is seldom realized in practice because the advanced nations create trade and financial barriers to the progress of poor nations. What we need to ask ourselves is: Will the new information society help with the development of LDCs, or will the computer and telecommunications equipment that is pouring into their countries be tomorrow's equivalent of yesterday's rusting tractors sitting in Third World fields?

The fountainhead of the emerging information paradigm is the telecommunication and computer industries. An examination of the global state of these industries will provide a picture of the current state of this important global force and put us in the position to begin to evaluate its potential impact on LDCs.

The Global Telecommunications Market

The driving force underlying the information paradigm is the rapid creation of information technologies. Two primary technologies can be identified as being central to the process: the semiconductor chip and the satellite. Technological improvements in launch vehicles and power sources have aided users of satellites by lowering the costs associated with placing a payload into orbit and extending the useful life of the satellites once they are placed in orbit. More importantly, the technological developments with regard to transponders (the relay components for transmissions within the satellites) have significantly reduced the cost of information transmission over great, and in some instances small, distances. Technological improvements in the semiconductor chip are paving the way toward digital communications and low-cost computing. The information-processing capabilities of a semiconductor chip have been increasing by a factor of ten almost every five years.[8] This has led to a sustained decline in size and cost of semiconductor technology. The new information economics can be "summed up by an unrelenting year-after-year 30%-40% improvement in cost performance of circuity and mass storage, with steady smaller cost performance improvements in telecommunications."[9]

An amorphous, new industry is vigorously emerging from the joining of computers and telecommunications. This new industry, the fountainhead of the emerging information paradigm, has many distinctive functional characteristics: it provides the hardware and services to allow users to interact directly with one or more computers, one or more individuals, data bases, and problem-solving software. All this can be accomplished over a distance, using the existing telecommunications infrastructure. All of this gives almost-instantaneous access to relevant information and the tools for analyzing and transforming that information into usable forms.

The information power and decreasing costs of this "network information goods and services"[10] industry have given a financial incentive to business to switch to the new system. Not only are the new technologies transforming the system for gathering, transmitting, analyzing, and storing information, they are also leading to a transformation in the structure of the production process. Information can be likened to a natural resource. In the analysis of production, traditional economics includes information under the general headings of labor and entrepreneurial ability. Developments over the past two decades call for factoring information out of these two broad factors of production for more detailed study. Information has always been an important input to the productive process. Years ago, archaeologists uncovered a wealth of inscribed clay tablets in the ruins of ancient Assyria and Babylonia. Upon deciphering the cuniform inscriptions, the archaeologists found not lost religious texts but rather invoices, receipts, contracts, and accounts. The need for information is as ancient as mankind. What has changed over time is the needed types and details of information, as well as the technology of information.

If today we were only seeing the improved ability to do what we were already doing, there would be little significance to the current events. The fact is that the new technologies described above are opening up new production opportunities and altering the existing cost relationships. This can be articulated by examining information as a separate factor input. As manufacturing and service industries shift to production structures that emphasize robotics and other automatic data processing equipment, the production function is altered. All of the new technologies place a greater reliance on information flows, and the marginal product of information is affected. Figure 1 illustrates that, as the productive function shifts toward information-intensive technologies, the marginal product curve of information shifts from MP_I1 to MP_I2. Not only will the production system's demand for information increase, the marginal product of each "byte" of information will correspondingly increase. This shift to MP_I2 will take place gradually over time, and there are limits to how far the marginal product curve will shift up. The important points here are that the new production systems are more information intensive and that both the internal and external demand for information inputs will increase. Increased demand will fuel the growth of the network information goods and services industry. Production conversion integrating the new technologies has been occurring for the past decade and a half, and the market for these technologies has grown substantially. We turn now to a discussion of this emerging industry.

Figure 1

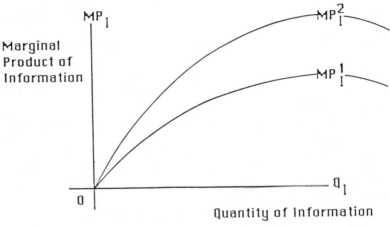

With regard to output and employment in the MDNs, the telecommunications and computer-equipment industries are relatively small when compared to other industries. Nevertheless, the rapid growth of the industries' output, in conjunction with its projected future growth, clearly indicates the emergence of a network information goods and services industry that may dominate many nations' economies and international trade as early as the turn of the century. In 1982, the worldwide trade in telecommunications and computer equipment reached 58 billion U.S. dollars.[11] Demand for telecommunications and computer equipment is ultimately derived from the demand for information services. The growth potential for these equipment industries stems mainly from these industries' impact on the range and quality of information services offered. During the remainder of the century, the growth of these industries will lead to a rapid diffusion of a number of related technologies (i.e., fiber optics, satellites, demodulators, the semiconductor chip, videotex systems, etc.). Diffusion of these technologies will facilitate the development of a more integrated information-processing infrastructure for individual nations as well as the global economy. The new generations of equipment are currently having their greatest impact on high-technology manufacturing industries and on the services industries that are heavily dependent on information systems (i.e., the mass media, finance, etc.). Augmenting the cost savings derived from the advancement in the technologies themselves, the growth of the network information goods and services industry will engender substantial economies to scale. This new industry's growth, along with the discussed cost reduction associated with technological improvement, will increase the accessibility and usage of such goods and services. An overall increase in employment, output, and living standards will be the net result for the MDNs.

Many LDCs fear that they will be left out of this new information revolution—as, to a large degree, they have been from the industrial revolution. We can divide the international information flows that have been increasing in such great volumes during the past few years into three basic categories:

(1) Data base—financial, insurance, accounting, and marketing information.

(2) Cultural—films, television, radio, books, newspapers, etc.

(3) Knowledge—educational services provided by government agencies (both international and national), institutions of higher learning, multinationals, etc.[12]

The production, storage, distribution, and usage of these information types are intricately linked to the emerging global network goods and services industry. Each of these international data flows is heterogeneous and represents distinctive challenges and promises to the governments of LDCs. Each is directly related to the utilization of network information goods and become more pervasive as imports of these products increase. The growth of international trade in network information goods and services has touched LDCs' economies, politics, and cultures with a speed and intensity unparalleled in the modern era.

International demand for these goods and services are driven by the following three forces:

(1) Many nations have realized that they cannot compete in the development of the information industries without good telecommunications technology.

(2) The convergence of computer and communications technologies has created the possibility of growth into each other's territory.

(3) Multinational corporate operations require worldwide, round-the-clock communications and global networks for banking, air traffic control, travel reservation, news, and trade.[13]

One important implication of these facts is that the emergence of the information economy is reinforcing the emergence of a global economy. LDCs have not sat idly by as these developments have unfolded. They have had strong vocal reactions, we explore next.

Reactions and Involvement of LDCs

The LDCs' call for a New International Economic Order (NIEO) is an attempt to alter the framework of rules and institutions governing the relations between nations. They have made this call since they perceive the old rules and institutions as locking them into a subervient role in the global economy. The three essential goals of the NIEO are to reduce economic dependence on MDNs, accelerate development of the economies of developing countries, and establish control over domestic resources. Through the collective call for a NIEO, LDCs are expressing their rejection of the socioeconomic ideas of the MDNs and endorsing the formulation of institutions and policies of development based on their own socioeconomic realities.

At a time when LDCs are vocally expressing their independence, the rapid developments in the network information goods and services industry appear to be undermining, rather than enhancing, their efforts. Currently, developing countries are being almost totally relegated to the status of mere consumers of information. Multinational corporations of the MDNs have a near monopoly on world advertising, originate 80% of the world news flow, produce and distribute almost all films and television shows, and, in many instances, control the media in LDCs through direct investment.[14] One result is that the transnational media inadvertently imposes the MND's way of seeing the world on the LDCs and erodes the unique cultural values of developing countries.

In addition to cultural imports of information, there is another less conspicuous information flow that has LDC leaders even more concerned. This is the transnational flow of data base information. The transportation of information across national frontiers is not a new phenomenon. What differs in the 1980s is the speed and scale of the process. With the rise of the network information goods and services industry comes the ability to collect, process, and store vast quantities of information on people and the socioeconomic environment in which they live. This enhances the ability of multinational corporations to compete with domestic firms in developing markets and raises the policy issue of protection of privacy. LDC officials are encountering situations where foreigners know more about their local economy than they do. They are coming to "view the processing of information outside of their countries as creating a dependence on foreign sources that threatens their economies and cultural sovereignty and compromises their national security."[15] A common pattern is displayed by the following example. P. Catala of the University of Paris cited an instance where "legal data which had been collected in France was subsequently processed in Korea, exported to the U.S., and finally sold back to France."[16] The Canadian government estimates that 90% of its exported data are generated by foreign multinational subsidiaries.[17] Given that nearly 90% of the world's information market is controlled by MDNs, this gives these nations the power to control access by LDCs and increases dependence. If this represents a pattern that can be generalized to other nations, then data base information is by far the largest of the three aforementioned data flows. In reaction to these developments, over 60 countries are considering or have passed legislation related to transborder data flows.[18] Among LDCs, Brazil has most vigorously introduced policies and passed laws dealing with information goods, and services. Brazilian industrialization policy is directed toward absorption of the network information goods, not merely their transfer. Their belief is that only by absorbing these technologies will the opportunity be provided to be competitive in world markets and to lay a sound foundation for continued development. In regard to transborder data flows, Brazilian law specifies that account must be taken of the impact on domestic employment and markets before permission is given to establish international data links.[19] The law also specifies that multinational corporations must keep duplicate copies of data bases in Brazil and, whenever possible, purchase software from Brazilian sources.[20] Acceptance of the principle that data flowing out of the country hurts the Brazilian economy has resulted in little foreign processing of Brazilian data.

The Importance of Telecommunication Goods and Services by LDCs

The author began the paper by making the observation that many researchers have indicated that the technological revolution occurring in the developed countries would be the factor allowing the LDCs to begin to accelerate the economic growth process. Since the technological revolution of which we speak has been occurring for over a decade, there should be some indication in current statistics to answer the question of whether or not these technologies are being employed in such a way that LDCs' surplus-generating capacity is being enhanced.

The approach that will be taken is to attempt to determine what is creating demand for automatic data processing and telecommunications equipment within LDCs. A cross-sectional study of 18 developing countries for the year 1981 was conducted using the following regression specification:[21]

1. $MC/T = a + b_1 NDPI + b_2 X + b_3 GDI + b_4 gnp + b_5 XC/T$

Where:
MC/T = imports of information-related equipment
NDPI = net direct private investment
X = goods and nonfactor services
GDI = gross domestic investment
gnp = per capita gross national product
XC/T = the export of information-related equipment

Imports and exports of information-related equipment (MC/T and XC/T) were derived from summing the following four United Nations commodity categories: automatic data processing equipment; office automatic data processing parts and accessories; telecommunications equipment, parts, and accessories; and switchgear and related parts. All other explanatory variables were obtained from World Bank data sources. Net direct private investment (NDPI) reflects the net amount invested or reinvested by nonresidents in enterprises in which they or other nonresidents exercise significant managerial control. Inclusion of NDPI as an explanatory variable was made to measure the degree to which foreigners influenced the decision to import information equipment in the target period. The author's preference was to use the stock of foreign direct investment in the sample LDCs in place of NDPI, yet these statistics were not available. One argument sighted above for the increased flow of information-goods imports to LDCs was the realization that, to compete with the MDNs, use of the most up-to-date technology is a prerequisite. Exports of goods and nonfactor services (X) were included to capture to what extent the imports of information goods are related to the exports of those goods that directly compete with MDNs' products. Net direct private investment was netted out of gross domestic investment to measure the degree to which outlays for addition to the fixed assets of the economy originating from the indigeneous population were fueling the importation of information goods. Finally, per capita gross national product was included to reflect the effect of the relative standard of living of a nation on the imports of information goods. Millions of 1981

U.S. dollars were used as the standard of measurement.

The results of this regression are summarized in the following equation:

2. MC/T = 184 + .0402NDPI + .00767X + .00169GDI - 10618gnp + .682XC/T (1.59) (.59) (1.08) (.36) (.35) (2.31)

The regression had an R-squared of 65.9%, or 51.7% once adjusted for degrees of freedom. Net direct private investment did not prove to be a significant variable. This may be due to the use of a flow rather than a stock variable, yet we can still say that the current investment decisions of foreigners in LDCs do not influence current import decisions on computer and telecommunications hardware. The export of goods and nonfactor services looks to be more significant, yet it fails the standard tests of significance. The author views this variable as a borderline case and will not venture an interpretation at this time. Neither gross domestic investment nor the level of per capita GNP proved to be important explanatory variables. Gross domestic investments failing to be significant casts doubt on the notion that, in general, LDCs are incorporating the new information technologies in their new domestic investments. It is tempting to speculate on the negative sign of the per capita variable, but the coefficient's lack of significance only tells us that the standard of living in an LDC does not drive the demand for these goods. Finally, the importation of computer and telecommunication equipment is significantly related to the exportation of these same goods. A couple of explanations are possible. It may be that some of the LDCs in the data set are importing intermediate computer and telecommunications products and using them in producing final products to be exported. Another possibility is that the larger the importation of these products, the more developed the nation, and the more likely we are to encounter an emerging domestic information goods industry that competes both domestically and in world markets (thus, the higher exports of these goods). The answer to this question is not clear from the data at the disposal of the author.

Both the small cross-sectional sample size and the lack of time-series data hampered the efforts to completely answer the question of what is driving the demand for information goods to LDCs. This current study clearly points to the exportation of information goods as being linked to the importation of this same classification of goods, yet this is an empirical link with the causal explanation unknown. The study hints that the exportation of goods and nonfactor services may be linked to the importation of information goods. If this is true, it would reflect the general awareness in

LDCs of the need for using these goods in order to remain competitive in world markets. Finally, outside of export industries, there is no evidence in this study that LDCs are making a fundamental shift in their economies to incorporate these new technologies.

The Use of Information in LDCs

Dividing of the world into neatly defined economic categories is not easy. Developing countries are a heterogeneous lot where there exists a whole spectrum of developmental situations. Even if we limit our attention to the definitely poorer countries of the world, each of these nations faces a unique economic environment. Some possess rich endowments of natural resources, others none; some are relatively underpopulated, while others stagger under heavy burdens of overpopulation; some have governments that are democratic and oriented toward fostering development, others governments that are brutally dictatorial with policies antithetical to growth. In short, the problem of economic development is not one of a single situation with a single cure, but of a whole complex of different situations calling for various solutions. To state that the revolution in information technologies is the great economic hope for these nations is to misunderstand the nature of the problem and to set the stage to repeat the failures of the past.

Development economists agree on several facts concerning the modern underdeveloped nations. Poverty is not a new phenomenon: in most cases, LDCs have been poor since the dawn of history. What has changed is that people living in LDCs have become aware of being poor, due in large part to cultural transborder flows of information, and there has ensued an increasing demand to do something about it. The insistence on rapid progress has been hampered by four fundamental problems. Each must be considered in evaluating the potential impact of the network information goods and services on development prospects.

The first problem is that of utilizing Western technology. It must be remembered that this information technology has evolved in relation to the distinctive conditions within the nations that created it. Network information goods use little labor and a larger proportion of capital. Therefore, their use depends on the existence of a reservoir of skilled labor, technically trained personnel, and capital. Since, for most LDCs, skilled labor and capital are scarce, this technology is, on the whole, inappropriate. In E.F. Schumacher's book *Small is Beautiful,* he argues that developing countries should not use most modern Western technology but rather an "intermediate" technology that consists of an adaptation of modern methods to the special conditions of the host LDC. A less-developed country importing the latest Western technologies to aid development will find that it faces acute shortages in support capital and trained personnel, while it has idle surpluses of unskilled workers.

The second problem is that the seeds of development have brought increasing rates of population growth and, in many cases, high population density in relation to land and other resources. Part of the attraction of network information goods and services in MDNs is that they are capital and information intensive rather than labor intensive. This is the basic nature of these products, and it is difficult to imagine an intermediate form that is labor intensive. Advocates of information technologies in development will point out that it is not the initial use of these goods that will enhance employment but rather the subsequent investment of the additional surplus generated by the initial use. This is the "trickle-down" theory in another form, and there are many historic cases where this theory has failed in LDCs. One recurrent theme is where the wealthy few bring in the new technologies and methods only to direct whatever surplus is generated away from the local economy toward opulent, nonproductive consumption or to investments in the MDNs. This does not imply that the "trickle-down" theory fails in all cases, but rather that the theory rests on the collective attitude of those in control of the new technologies within the developing nation.

Even if it can be demonstrated that the above "trickle-down" scenario is valid, a third problem is likely to be encountered: lack of the necessary socioeconomic environment for an industrial, or information, revolution. In general, the lack of prior preparation for economic change means that their agricultural and commercial sectors have not developed to the point where they can easily sustain rapid economic progress. It also means that there has been little time for institutions and value systems to adapt themselves to the demands of economic growth. It is true that network information goods and services can replace the traditional high-cost telecommunications component of a nation's infrastructure with one that is relatively low cost, more encompassing, and more efficient. Still, this is only one component in the highly interdependent infrastructure needed for development, and information technology is no less demanding on established institutions and value systems than the old technologies.

Finally, the international context has presented an unfavorable obstacle to development in the past and shows no signs of immediate change. Private investors in the economically advanced nations have been more willing to provide capital to MDNs than to LDCs. Also, MDNs and multinational corporations (MNCs) have acted in a variety of ways to limit access of enterprises located in developing nations to the markets of the MDNs. According to the World Bank, the international debt of developing countries rose to $810 billion at the end of 1983. This enormous debt, coupled with adverse developments in the world's economy, placed a strain on many LDCs in servicing their debt. In the early 1980s, most of the surplus generated by the economies of debtor LDCs was immediately siphoned off to service external debt rather than being reinvested domestically to foster growth. One consequence of this complex situation has been an increasing reluctance of many private lenders to continue to extend new credit to developing nations. Data released in the middle of 1984 by the International Monetary Fund indicated that inflation in developing countries accelerated sharply in 1983. Inflation in the non-oil developing nations rose to a weighted average rate of 54.1% in 1983, compared with 34.3% in 1982.[22] The increase in inflation appears to be closely related to rates of growth in their money supplies, which has been a common response of government to the fiscal squeeze resulting from the international debt crisis. All of this has created a situation of high uncertainty surrounding foreign investment in many LDCs and, in effect, has reduced the near-term growth potential of many LDCs, regardless of the technologies being integrated into their systems. This comes at a crucial time in the formation of the global network information goods and services industry, and LDCs may be frozen out of participating in the production end of this lucrative industry. The global telecommunications market alone is forecasted to grow to an $88-billion market by the end of 1987. The giant telecommunications MNCs are positioning for dominance in this market and establishing joint venture among themselves at a rapid pace. If the economies to scale for this industry are as vast as many forecasters predict, once the global economic climate eases for LDCs, they will have difficulties amassing the capital necessary to catch up and compete in this market. Remaining mere consumers of information may continue to be the norm with LDCs for decades to come.

A backlash to this situation may be the restriction of transborder flows of all information emanating from developing nations. Data-protection laws, licensing requirements, international communication tariffs, and regulations on data processing are some of the ways a government in a developing country may maintain control of information within its border. These restrictions will add costs to the operations for MNCs, but their economic impact on the LDCs that employ them is harder to assess. Up to a point, it could be argued that information restrictions will enhance the performance and competitiveness of domestic enterprises and, therefore, the growth of the domestic economy. This argument must be tempered by considering the types and extent of restrictions in each case and in comparison to other LDCs. Governments making decisions on restricting transborder data flows must also consider potential reactions of MNCs to increased constraints. Overregulation and taxation of information may induce many MNCs to close down their operations in such countries, as they have in the past when confronted with economic restrictions.

Assessing the potential developments in, and future impacts of, the information technologies is exciting. To be alive during a time when the rare occurrence of a social paradigm shift is underway is awe inspiring. To translate this excitement and awe into a utopian vision of the world's future is to misunderstand the fundamental nature of socioeconomic change. The economic processes that have been unleashed in the world since the beginning of the industrial revolution tend to accentuate the gap between the haves and the have nots. Given the present global political and economic structure, the current revolution in the information technologies shows every indication of accelerating the rate at which this gap widens. All of this is not to say that network information goods and services will not help LDCs in their effort to grow. It is true that there are numerous applications of these goods and services in developing nations that will enhance efficiency and encourage growth. By the very nature of the new information technologies, a far greater income-generating potential lies in their application in the labor-expensive, service-industry heavy economies of the MDNs. Benefits to LDCs will be directly proportional to the degree of awareness of the problems outlined in this paper and to the extent that all nations genuinely participate in international efforts to reduce economic barriers and foster growth in the lesser-developed regions of the world.

Notes

1. Jones, T., *Options for the Future: A Comparative Analysis of Policy-Oriented Forecasts,* Praeger, 1980, pp. 114-115.

2. Masuda, Y., *The Information Society as Post Industrial Society,* World Future Society, 1980, p. 29.

3. Ibid, p. 31.

4. Harman, W., *An Incomplete Guide to the Future,* W.W. Norton & Co., 1979, p. 124.

5. Jones, 1980, p. 282.

6. Dordick, H., "The Emerging World Information Business," *Columbia Journal of World Business,* Spring 1983, p. 69.
7. *Global Solutions: Innovative Approaches to World Problems,* Edward Cornish, editor, World Future Society, 1984, p. 85.
8. Dordick, 1983, p. 74.
9. Derived from commodity tables of the *Yearbook of International Trade Statistics,* New York: Department of International Economic and Social Affairs, Statistical Office, 1983.
10. Porat, M., "Global Implications of the Information Society," *Journal of Communication,* Winter 1978, p. 73.
11. Dordick, 1983, p. 70.
12. Smith-Hobson, S., "New World Information Order," *Freedomways,* 1981, pp. 110-111.
13. "The Threat to International Data Flows," *Ideas and Trends,* August 3, 1981.
14. Williamson, J., "Confab Mulls International Movement of Information—Second World Conference on Transborder Data Flow Policy," *Telephony,* July 23, 1984.
15. Samiee, S., "Transnational Data Flow Constraints: A New Challenge for Multinational Corporations," *Journal of International Business Studies,* Spring/Summer 1984, p. 145.
16. Ibid, p. 147.
17. Ibid, p. 141.
18. Ibid, p. 146.
19. Sample was drawn from those countries the World Bank classifies as low, lower middle, and upper middle income for which there existed a complete data set.
20. *International Letter,* Federal Reserve Bank of Chicago, #530, July 13, 1984.
21. "Telecommunications: The Global Battle," *Business Week,* October 24, 1983, p. 83.

References

Adams, F., N. Glickman, *Modeling the Multinational Economic System,* Lexington Books, 1980.

Batton, D., *Spatial Analysis of Interacting Economies: The Role of Entropy and Information Theory in Spatial Input-Output Modeling,* Rbuwer-Nyhoff Pub., London, 1983.

Bell, D., *The Coming of Post-Industrial Society: A Venture in Social Forecasting,* Basic Books, Inc., 1973.

Benjamin, R., "Information Technology: A Strategic Opportunity" *Sloan Management Review,* Spring 1984, pp. 3-10.

Bert, Hickman, editor, *Global International Economic Models,* North-Holland, 1983.

Contractor, F., "Technology Importations Policies in Developing Countries: Some Implications of Recent Theoretical and Empirical Evidence," *Journal of Development Areas,* July 1983, pp. 499-519.

Dadaian, "The Potential Uses of Forecasting and Analysis of a Balance of the Flows of Gross World Output between Regions," *Matekon*, Winter, 7: 4, pp. 3-23, 1983.
Dordick, Herbert, "The Emerging World Information Business," *Columbia Journal of World Business*, 18:69-76, Spring 1983.
Gillis, M., D. Perkins, M. Roemer, D. Snodgrass, *Economics of Development*, W.W. Norton & Co., 1983.
Global Solutions: Innovative Approaches to World Problems, Edward Cornish, editor, World Future Society, 1984.
Gribiches, "Interindustry Technology Flows and Productivity Growth: A Re-examination," *Recent Economic Statistics*, May 1984, pp. 324-29.
Hamilton, "Efficiency and Distributional Implication of Global Restrictions on Labor Mobility," *Journal of Developmental Economics*, Jan.-Feb. 1984.
Harman, W., *An Incomplete Guide to the Future*, W. W. Norton & Co., 1979.
Hope, K., "Basic Needs and Technology Transfer Issues in the 'New Economic Order,'" *American Journal of Economics and Sociology*, Vol. 42, No. 4, October 1983.
Jones, T., *Options for the Future: A Comparative Analysis of Policy-Oriented Forecasts*, Praeger, 1980.
Lipton, M., "Urban Bias Revisited," *Journal of Developmental Studies*, 41:4, pp. 139-66.
Masuda, Y., *The Information Society as Post-Industrial Society*, World Future Society, 1980.
McCall, J., *The Economics of Uncertainty*, The University of Chicago Press, A Conference Report Universities—National Bureau Committee for Economic Research, #32, 1982.
McGraw, H.W., Jr., "The Information Industry: The Principles that Endure," *Computing People*, 32:7-10+, May-June 1983.
Momigliano, "New Trends in Internationalization: Processes and Theories," *Economic Notes*, 1983, (3), pp. 42-68.
Porat, M., "Global Implications of the Information Society," *Journal of Communication*, Vol. 21, No. 1, Winter 1978.
Rubin, M., *Information Economies and Policy in the U.S.*, Libraries Unlimited, Littleton, CO, 1983.
Ruttan, "Toward a Theory of Induced Institutional Innovation," *Journal of Developmental Studies*, May 1984.
Samiee, S., "Transnational Data Flow Constraints: A New Challenge for Multinational Corporations," *Journal of International Business Studies*, Spring/Summer 1984.
Schumacher, E., *Small Is Beautiful: Economics as if People Mattered*, Harper & Row, 1973.
Smith-Hobson, S., "New World Information Order," *Freedomways*, 21, no. 2, pp. 106-13, 1981.
Telecommunications: Pressures and Policies for Change, OECD, 1983.
"Telecommunications: The Global Battle," *Business Week*, October 24, 1983.
"The Threat to International Data Flows, *Ideas and Trends*, August 3, 1981.
Weiss, E.O., "Transborder Data Flows and Telecommunications," *Telephony*, 206:71-72+, June 25, 1984.
Williamson, J., "Confab Mulls International Movement of Information—Second World Conference of Transborder Data Flow Policy," *Telephony*, 207:94-5 July 23, 1984.

Debt and World Trade

Latin American Debt: Lessons and Pending Issues

by

Eduardo Wiesner

The Fiscal Origin of the Debt Crisis
No other set of factors explains more of the debt crisis than the fiscal deficits incurred by most of the major countries in the Western Hemisphere. Although there were other factors which were relevant, I have no doubt that the main problem was excessive public—and private—spending which was financed by both easy domestic credit policies and by ample resources from abroad. The world recession and high real rates of interest in international markets aggravated the crisis but I do not believe they created it. What actually happened was that previous domestic macroeconomic policies had made economies more vulnerable to exogenous factors.

The figures for the period 1979-82 cannot be more eloquent. In only four years, the three largest countries of the region—Argentina, Brazil, and Mexico—more than doubled the size of their nonfinancial public sector deficits, which rose from the already high levels of around 6% of gross domestic product (GDP) to well over 15%. Behind these growing fiscal deficits were strong political pressures for higher public spending. As long as external financing permitted total absorption to exceed domestic income, it was possible to accommodate those demands. But as the world recession worsened and as it became evident that the additional financing from abroad was not being accompanied by a corresponding increase in exports or in domestic capital formation, capital inflows dropped substantially and the fiscal imbalance

---

Eduardo Wiesner is director of the Western Hemisphere Department of the International Monetary Fund. The opinions expressed here are those of the author and do not necessarily reflect the views of the International Monetary Fund.

became an exchange rate and a debt crisis. In brief, the debt crisis can be traced back to a fiscal disequilibrium and ultimately to an unresolved political struggle between competing groups which wanted to have a larger share of income.

This view of the debt crisis as a fiscal manifestation of a political struggle may explain why it is still so difficult to resolve some of the most severe problems of the adjustment process. The intractability would arise because at the bottom of the adjustment process still lies partially unsettled the equity and political question of who is going to pay for that portion of absorption which was not covered by taxes, has not become a productive investment within the debtor country, was presumably and to some extent a creditor risk, and by now may be gone forever. Under peremptory, abrupt adjustment, these political questions are resolved without delay by force of circumstances. But under managed adjustment, which is clearly preferable, the attempt to control the process may also allow, in some cases, for postponement of at least part of the most difficult political decisions, and thus it runs the risk of prolonging uncertainty and making recovery more elusive. This is a delicate political issue. Its importance lies in that it may explain why sometimes the gradual approach to adjustment does not seem to work.

The Absorption of Foreign Financing

The combined external debt of Argentina, Brazil, Chile, Mexico, Peru, and Venezuela more than doubled between 1978 and 1982. This huge inflow of external resources was, of course, largely the other face of the large fiscal and current account deficits. External financing was allowing these countries to sustain absorption levels higher than national income. Since most of the external financing came from private international banks, it was widely believed then that these countries were creditworthy and were effectively utilizing external savings. In some instances, the external financing was even allowing—if not inducing—real appreciation of the exchange rate and was luring policy-makers into believing that a new era of low inflation, high growth, and exchange rate stability was about to begin. Kavalsky and Squire (1984) point out that in countries like Peru, Argentina, and Mexico, real exchange rates actually appreciated. We now know that not much of this proved to be a reality. Unfortunately, debt accumulation was not, according to Dornbusch and Fisher (1984), "financing investment that was productive by the test of net dollar earnings." After the initial appreciation of local currencies capital inflows turned into capital outflows (Harberger, 1984), precipitating sharp depreciations of the real exchange rate.

While the flows of external financing were pouring into the countries, two fundamental developments were taking place. The first one, domestic savings as a proportion of GDP, was not increasing and, in most cases, was actually declining. Furthermore, gross domestic investment actually declined as a percentage of GDP. Countries, (Ffrench-Davis, 1983) were absorbing external resources but they were not using all of them to increase investment but rather to allow for more consumption. Since the accumulation of external debt was growing at a faster pace than the accumulation of productive investment,[1] a debt crisis was just a question of time, which would prove shorter in the event of external monetary disturbances.

Table 1

Savings and Investment
(As percent of GDP)

	1980	1981	1982	1983
Argentina				
Gross domestic investment	25.7	20.0	18.1	17.1
National savings	22.6	16.2	13.0	13.3
External savings	3.1	3.8	5.0	3.8
Brazil				
Gross domestic investment	21.1	19.2	18.4	15.0
National savings	16.0	15.1	12.9	12.0
External savings	5.1	4.1	5.5	3.0
Mexico				
Gross domestic investment	28.1	29.0	21.2	16.5
National savings	24.0	23.2	17.8	20.2
External savings	4.1	5.8	3.4	-3.7

Source: International Monetary Fund

The second very important development that was taking place had to do with the weakening, (de Vries, 1983), of the link between external financing and specific project investment evaluation. Since most of the additional external financing came from international commercial banks and since the debtors generally were public sectors, the importance of the economic feasibility of investment projects was diluted. This meant that the global quality of the investment programs deteriorated and that many projects were initiated not because they were economically sound but because they had found external commercial financing that, directly or indirectly, was guaranteed by a sovereign debtor. And as Swoboda (1985) has pointed out, banks are "willing to acquire assets at rates of return lower than the riskiness of these assets" if there is a guarantee. This development contrasted sharply with the traditional external financing for specific investment projects provided by multilateral agencies like the World Bank or the Inter-American Development Bank.

The lessons from this are not novel in my view, and yet the recent experience would suggest that they need to be emphasized. To begin with, developing countries do not have an unlimited capacity to absorb external resources because their absorptive investment capacity sets a limit to the volume of resources that they can utilize efficiently.[2] There are limits to the taxing capacity of developing countries' public sectors. Higher fiscal deficits may end up being financed by external savings, but this does not necessarily mean that all of these savings (McDonald, 1982) become investments in the debtor countries or that the margin created by those additional external resources is used to increase investment.

The Role of Risk Revisited

Although the debt crisis can be explained mostly in terms of fiscal deficits and inadequate economic policies in the debtor countries, it could also be explained by the wrong perceptions that debtors and creditors had about the real risks they were taking. If they had had perfect foresight about these risks, no major crisis could have developed. A serious crisis can only result from a cumulative process. In the case of the current debt crisis, fiscal deficits and external debt accumulated because the risk factor did not play *ex ante,* in the early stages, its crisis-defusing role.

The experience of this debt crisis teaches that at least two of the fundamental risk assumptions which guided international lending and borrowing were wrong. In the first place, international banks assumed that a sovereign risk was a small risk because public sectors normally do not default. As a result, they did not pay sufficient attention to the quality of economic policies in the debtor countries, nor did they worry about the economic feasibility of the investment projects they were, directly or indirectly, financing. Apparently, they thought that an official guarantee, implicit or explicit, was all that was needed to circumvent risk. Perhaps it was considered that high spreads were sufficient to cover for any possible extra risk incurred. Finally, it is not clear what the risk perception of international banks was with regard to their lending to private banks or enterprises in the debtor countries.

Secondly, governments understood that if private flows were freely coming in to finance their expenditures then, their macroeconomic policies could not be all that bad and their exchange rates could not be much out of line with long-term equilibrium rates. In fact, they often found it difficult to control expenditure and to follow more prudent macroeconomic policies simply because the external financing was there. On the other hand, public sectors thought they were not taking any risks in the case of private external lending to their private sectors. Thus, they did not establish adequate controls or precise conditionality for the modality of international financing. The model[3] of international lending held that these transactions could not pose a risk to public sectors, since, according to Congdon (1982), "there is no such a thing as a balance of payments problem between consenting adults."

Well, we now have relearned that public sectors of borrowing countries can find themselves unable to service their debts and that, in some cases, debtor countries have been unable to resist pressures to guarantee private loans or to provide some form of exchange rate guarantee. This has converted a private risk into a fiscal burden. When I say that now we know the obvious, I am, of course, speaking within the context of what, above, I have called the investment absorption capacity of less developed countries. Nothing very original. It used to be almost an axiom a few years ago when few, if anybody, thought that developing countries could absorb massive doses of financial resources. They did not have an infinite amount of economically feasible investment projects nor could they hope to have instant improvement in the quality of their macroeconomic policies. These realities, which meant risks, were temporarily forgotten.

Risk is a stabilizing factor in the functioning of markets. The insurance or guarantee of loans against risk may actually increase willingness to incur risk.[4] This is the so-called moral hazard problem. Attempting to interfere with the role of risk is a very risky exercise, as the current crisis has confirmed. The process of delinking risk from the economic feasibility of investment projects and from the capacity of debtor countries to rapidly adopt all of the right macroeconomic policies in the face of abundant external financing is one of the most underestimated causes of the debt crisis. In brief, both debtors and creditors made wrong decisions on the basis of wrong perceptions of their respective risks.

One basic question emerges out of the previous analysis. If both debtors and creditors share responsibility in the formation of the debt crisis, how are the costs of the resolution of that crisis going to be apportioned?

In principle, strict adherence to the role of risk would mean that the market would distribute the costs of resolving the crisis. In essence, this would mean that creditors would sell their claims in the market—and thus absorb in losses the reduced value of these claims—and divorce themselves from their debtors. For the debtors, the market solution would mean instant adjustment without financing and according to Eaton and Gersovitz (1981), "an embargo on future loans." These hypothetical scenarios surely have been considered by both debtors and creditors since they would be the consequence of not providing any rescheduling or new money, on the one hand, and of defaulting, on the other hand. The answer that both debtors and creditors have decided to give to the debt crisis is to manage jointly the resolution of their conflicting interests. The fact that both parties have chosen or resigned themselves to this route can be interpreted as an ad hoc market solution in which they have carefully assessed the risks of all alternatives and have come to the conclusion that their losses are minimized under this alternative.

Choices and Issues

At this juncture, critical choices are being made in at least the following two main areas: (a) international borrowing and lending, and (b) the openness and efficiency of the economies of the Latin American countries. The first choice concerns the question of what to do about borrowing. While it is true, as Cline (1984) has said, that "these countries have erred on the side of excessive borrowing in the last decade," the question now is how to reduce the rate and, if possible, the level of indebtedness—which is the desirable thing to do—if at the same time there is a need to mitigate the tribulations of adjustment. This is a formidable dilemma. More financing alleviates adjustment, but simultaneously it adds to the debt service. There is no simple solution to this predicament. At the bottom of the circularity involved there lies, once again, the question of how should the costs of the resolution of the crisis be apportioned. Until now both parties have opted for negotiations rather than confrontation. While it is not possible to predict what will be the final outcome, it could be said that the answer will largely depend on what happens to the world economic recovery and to the export earnings of indebted countries. In the words of Simonsen (1984), "a growing economy with expanding exports hardly would seek confrontation with its creditors."

The second area where difficult choices have to be made concerns the degree of openness and of economic efficiency of the region. The issue here is how to preserve long-term efficiency when short-term and urgent pressures make it attractive to reduce openness and to seek economic reactivation through protectionism. The prospects in this area are not encouraging. Unfortunately, it seems that one of the most costly consequences of the debt crisis is that at the end some Latin American countries will be more closed and less efficient. At this juncture it seems that some policy makers of the region are striving to avoid a repetition of the crisis of 1982 and 1983. Apparently, they find it preferable to accumulate international reserves than to increase imports and to open up trade; they find it less destabilizing—and more fiscally productive—to raise import tariffs than to promote exports through the exchange rate. And in the future, they may feel less vulnerable if they regulate or control international capital flows than if they open up and let market risk, once again, be the final arbiter. Unfortunately, on the basis of the recent experience, some policymakers are apprehensive about what to expect from the free play of the market forces.

Notes

1. Kharas, (1984) holds that "the critical relationship in debt analysis is that between the accumulation of productive capital relative to external debt."

2. Alexander (1952) in his celebrated article did not imply that investment necessarily increased when external financing was available. His assertion was that both investment and consumption taken together could be higher than national income.

3. See Corden (1979) for an interesting discussion on the distinction "between private problems and public problems" in the area of balance of payments.

4. See Wallich (1984) for an excellent discussion of the risks and advantages of insurance on bank lending.

References

Alexander, Sidney, "Effects of a Devaluation on a Trade Balance," *Staff Papers,* International Monetary Fund, April 1952, p. 265.

Cline, William R., *International Debt: Systematic and Policy Response,* Institute for International Economics, Washington, D.C. 1984, p. 178

Congdon, Tim, "A New Approach to the Balance of Payments," *Lloyd's Bank Review,* October 1982, p. 5.

Corden, A.W., *Inflation Exchange Rates and the World Economy,* The University of Chicago Press, 1977, p. 45.

de Vries, B., "International Ramifications of the External Debt Situation," *Amex Bank Review,* Special Papers, November 1983, p. 10.

Dornbusch, R., and S. Fischer, "The World Debt Problem," Report to the Group of Twenty-Four, UNDP/UNCTAD, September 1984, p. 4.

Eaton, Jonathan, and Mark Gersovitz, "Debt with Potential Repudiation: Theoretical and Empirical Analysis," *Review of Economic Studies,* April 1981, p. 290.

Ffrench-Davis, Ricardo, "Que Paso con la Economia Chilena?" *Estudios Publicos,* Santiago, Chile, No. 11, 1983, p. 25.

Harberger, Arnold C., "Lessons for Debtor Country Managers and Policymakers." Forthcoming in J.T. Cuddington, and G.W. Smith, *International Debt and the Developing Countries,* Washington, D.C., July 1984, p. 13.

Kavalsky, B. and Squire, L., et al., "Debt and Adjustment in Selected Developing Countries," unpublished paper. World Bank, Washington, D.C., July 1984, p. 13.

Kharas, H.J., "The Long-Run Creditworthiness of Developing Countries: Theory and Practice," *The Quarterly Journal of Economics,* August 1984, p. 419.

McDonald, Donough, "Debt Capacity and Developing Country Borrowing: A Survey of the Literature," Staff Papers, International Monetary Fund, December 1982, p. 610.

Sachs, Jeffrey, "Theoretical Issues in International Borrowing," *Princeton Studies in International Finance,* No. 54, July 1984, p. 1.

Swoboda, Alexander, "Debt and the Efficiency and Stability of the International Financial System," forthcoming in *International Debt and the Developing Countries,* edited by Cuddington, J.T. and Smith, G.W., Washington, D.C., World Bank, 1985, p. 24.

Simonsen, Mario, "The Developing Country Debt Problem," unpublished paper, Getulio Vargas Foundation, June 1984, p. 68.

Wallich, Henry, "Insurance of Bank Lending to Developing Countries," Group of Thirty, Occasional Paper No. 15, New York, 1984.

The United States as the World's Largest Debtor: Implications for the International Trade Environment

by

Richard L. Drobnick

Which nation will be leading the "International Debt Derby" by the end of 1985? Will the early leaders, Brazil and Mexico, remain in front, or will an unrecognized entry—the United States of America—streak into the lead? Using a somewhat broader concept of debt than is normally used by journalists, it is certain that the United States will find itself in the winner's circle!

By the end of 1985, the United States will have captured the dubious distinction of being the world's largest net user of foreign savings. Foreigners will have deposited substantially more money in American banks, purchased more American stocks and bonds and made more direct investments in factories and real estate in the United States than Americans have made abroad. The remarkable thing about this situation is that within just a three-year period, from 1983 to 1985, America's post-World War I tradition of being a net supplier of savings to the world will have been reversed. The net international investment position of the United States will have plummeted from its 1982 peak of $150 billion to a 1985 official value that will approach minus $100 billion!

What are the implications of the United States' becoming a net capital importer? First, the good news: The large trade deficits

---

Richard L. Drobnick is director of the International Business Education and Research (IBEAR) Program at the University of Southern California's Graduate School of Business and has written numerous articles on international economic issues.

that accompany America's capital importer status enable debtor nations to at least repay the interest on their international loans. Thus, in the short run, America's trade deficits and capital imports help stabilize the international financial system. Such trade deficits also directly affect the U.S. economy in many important ways: Americans can consume more than they produce; consumer choice is enhanced; inflationary pressures are reduced; U.S. firms and workers that compete with imports and are compelled to become more efficient; and U.S. firms that utilize imported components can become more competitive.

And now the bad news: First, such large trade deficits mean that American firms, on balance, will continue to lose sales to foreign competitors. Lost profits and jobs of the magnitudes currently expected in trade-sensitive industries will encourage business, labor and local government coalitions to create new trade barriers. Second, by attracting investment capital to the United States, this process retards economic growth and job formation in Europe and in the Less Developed Countries (LDCs). This could initiate a "vicious circle" of political instability and further impoverization, additional constraints on American exports, and more capital flight to the U.S. Third, the American government's choice of fiscal and monetary policy will be constrained as a result of its sensitivity to the interests of America's creditors. Creditors—both foreign and domestic—are much more concerned about continuing to receive high real rates of return on their dollar-denominated assets than they are about the demise of trade and interest-sensitive sectors of the U.S. economy. When creditors feel that their investment returns are not sufficient to offset their potential losses from the depreciation of the dollar's exchange rate, they will move their money. And every year this becomes easier to do as world financial markets continue to become ever more integrated. Fourth, by becoming a net debtor, America is mortgaging its future.[1]

When foreign creditors want repayment, America will have only three choices: (1) to consume less than it produces, (2) to sell its assets, or (3) to repudiate its debts. To follow the first choice, the U.S. would have to achieve a trade surplus. Aside from the economic and administrative difficulties of accomplishing this, it means that Americans must reduce their living standards. To some extent, the U.S. is already following the second option of selling its assets to foreigners. One consequence of this will be a deterioration of the services export account. The third choice of repudiation—if it was to be taken—would most likely be accomplished by creating a period of sustained inflation. However, this would require a reversal of Federal Reserve Chairman

Volcker's monetary policy of the past five years, as well as create a major source of political stress on the fabric of American society.

America's situation will be similar to that which is imposed by the International Monetary Fund (IMF) on debtors like Mexico and Brazil. To a debtor, the IMF's "conditionality requirements" are bitter medicine because the debtors are forced to choose among three evils: (1) implement austerity programs to create a trade surplus[2] (2) sell foreign and domestic assets; (3) weigh the consequences of outright repudiation. There is, however, one principal difference between the U.S. and other international debtors. As the creator of the international reserve currency, the U.S. does not have to request loans to finance its trade deficits. It can, within limits, create the "foreign exchange" it needs to finance its trade deficits.

In attempting to explore the implications for the international trade environment if the United States becomes the world's largest debtor, this paper addresses four broad questions. First, in what sense is the United States becoming a net debtor nation? Second, what were the contributing factors in the 1970s and early 1980s that set the stage for America to reverse its 70-year-long tradition of being a net capital exporter? Third, what are the implications of the United States becoming a net capital importer? Fourth, what is the likely future of the international economic environment?

Reversal of a 70-Year Tradition:
The U.S. Becomes an International Debtor[3]

Trading Patterns and Current Account Balances

Since 1982, Americans have not been "paying-their-own-way" in the world. The standard of living enjoyed by Americans was increasingly supported by foreigners in 1982, 1983, and 1984. America was able to "consume" more than it produced because its trading partners wanted to "consume" less than they produced. America purchased more goods and services than it sold in the international marketplace.

In brief, the United States substantially changed the nature of its economic relations with the world in 1982.[4] Instead of continuing to sell as much as it purchased from its trading partners (in terms of its multilateral balance), the United States joined the world's debtor countries, running current account deficits of $9 billion, $42 billion, and $102 billion from 1982 to 1984.[5] This anomalous situation, of the world's richest country borrowing from poorer countries, is expected to continue in 1985, probably recording a four-year deficit in excess of $250 billion!

In the final analysis, international credit can only be provided by nations that consume less than they produce, i.e., nations that are presently or have previously generated an export surplus. Today, there is only one nation generating substantial current account surpluses and thus becoming the world's principal source of capital—that is Japan. Between 1982 and 1985 alone, Japan will record a current account surplus of about $100 billion. Other major international creditors include the "Low Absorber" OPEC nations (i.e., Saudi Arabia, Kuwait, Libya and the United Arab Emirates) and Germany. OPEC's cumulative surplus (since 1973) peaked at about $410 billion in 1981, declined to $375 billion by 1984, and OPEC is expected to maintain its consumption patterns by selling some of its previously acquired financial assets. Germany's cumulative surplus (since 1973) is about $35 billion and is expected to continue to grow slowly and steadily.

A question of monumental political and economic importance is whether or not Japan has permanently replaced the United States as the source of international capital—as the U.S. once replaced Britain. Unless the U.S. federal deficit is quickly eliminated or unless political changes force a major realignment of established patterns of international trade, it appears that a recurring deficit in America's current account has become a structural feature of its economy, as has a recurring surplus for Japan.[6]

Financing Current Account Deficits

Current account deficits of LDCs such as Brazil and Mexico are financed quite differently from that of the United States. To a large extent, Brazil and Mexico relied upon bank loans—which they have been unable to service. In contrast, the United States financed its current account deficit by inducing foreigners (ultimately Saudi Arabians, Japanese, and Germans) to exchange some of the goods and services they sold in the international marketplace for claims on assets located in the United States. These claims took the form of dollar-denominated savings accounts, stocks, bonds, and direct investments in factories, equipment, and real estate.

Since 1982, foreigners have been acquiring American assets much faster than Americans have been acquiring foreign assets. The net international investment position of the United States plummeted from its 1982 peak value of $150 billion, to $106 billion in 1983. A projection of this trend, based on the $104 billion current account deficit in 1984 and a similar forecast for 1985, puts the U.S. net international investment position at minus $100 billion by the end of 1985.

Furthermore, the official data on which this statement is based understates the amount of foreign savings being utilized in the United States, perhaps by as much as $80 to $100 billion.[7] Also, the composition of the U.S. net international investment balance has deteriorated substantially in the past few years. In 1979 the net U.S. position in direct and portfolio investments reached its peak of $130 billion and accounted for 70% of America's foreign investment portfolio, while foreign loans provided the other 30%. By 1983, America's net portfolio and direct investment position had fallen to $67 billion and only accounted for 30% of America's foreign investment, while bank loans had climbed to 70%!

In order to set the stage for exploring the policy implications of America's role reversal, the next sections briefly review the contributing factors: OPEC's revolution and Reagan's revolution.

The 1970s: OPEC's Decade of Wealth and Power Set the Stage for Stagnant 1980s

During the 1970s, four fundamental changes occurred in the international environment. First, in 1971, the United States repudiated its obligation to redeem U.S. dollars with gold. The removal of the "golden discipline" from U.S. monetary policy contributed to numerous financial changes, including the replacement of fixed exchange rates with floating exchange rates, the vast expansion of unregulated Eurodollar lending, a worldwide inflationary explosion, and a 24% collapse in the value of the U.S. dollar between 1970 and 1979. Second, the relative importance of fuel trade increased dramatically as a result of OPEC price hikes. Its importance peaked in 1980 when fuel exports accounted for 25% of the dollar value of total world exports, as compared to only 9% in 1970 (by 1983, fuel's importance had declined to 19%). Third, many advanced countries were seriously threatened by competition from the newly industrializing countries. The combination of a low-wage, skilled work force with modern technology appears to give nations such as Taiwan, South Korea, and Brazil insurmountable cost advantages over the developed nations that are members of the Organization for Economic Cooperation and Development (OECD). Fourth, the petroleum efficiency of the OECD nations (in terms of oil consumption per dollar of real GNP) increased by about 25 percent between 1973 and 1980.

OPEC's two oil shocks substantially reduced the rate of growth of world trade and world economic product. The 1973-74 oil price hikes caused world trade growth (in inflation-adjusted terms) to be cut almost in half—from 9.3% to 4.8% per year; world product growth (inflation-adjusted) fell from 4.7% to 3.4% per year. After the 1979-80 oil price hike, world trade growth collapsed to 2.2% per year and world product growth dropped to 2.2% per year (1980-84) average).

As the decade of the 1970s closed, the trade system was showing serious signs of strain. Efforts by oil-deficit nations to offset astronomically higher oil import bills stimulated protectionist "trade offensives" that subsidized exports and inhibited non-oil imports. Domestic content, export requirements, and countertrade practices became commonplace. An important philosophical departure from the concept of multilateral free trade towards the concept of bilateral balance had begun.

The 1980s: An International System Infected by Debt and Protectionism Responds to the Reagan Revolution

Japan and Germany "won" their trade battles and achieved positive current account balances. Most other nations "lost" and had to borrow heavily to finance their trade deficits. This resulted in a mountain of international debt (estimated to be $805 billion for just the Less Developed Countries), which could only be serviced if the debtors launched IMF-designed "trade offensives." In turn, this stimulated protectionist policies by their trading partners, thus reducing the LDCs' ability to service their debts.

Today's "vicious circle" between debt and trade policy is a fundamental dilemma that reminds one of the "transfer problem" debate initiated by John Maynard Keynes with his 1919 essay, *The Economic Consequences of the Peace*. The issue that dominated international policies in the 1920s was whether or not German reparation payments could be transferred to the Allies without severely damaging the sales and profits of Allied industries. Non-resolution of German indebtedness, and the consequent transfer problem, dominated the interwar period and probably contributed to the enactment of "beggar-thy-neighbor" trade policies and the onset of the Great Depression.

In essence, the LDC debt problem can be condensed into three questions. Are the debtors able to pay? Are the debtors willing to pay? Are the creditors willing to receive payment?[8] According to IMF data, LDC borrowers need to achieve $130 to $150 billion balance of trade surpluses for the foreseeable future.[9] If the LDC economies are able and the LDC governments are willing to generate export surpluses to meet debt obligations, are some nations willing to receive the net imports of goods? Quite clearly, the ultimate creditor nations—Saudi Arabia, Japan, and Germany—

are not. Which nation(s) is willing to run the offsetting trade deficits?

Since 1982, the United States has more or less inadvertently fulfilled the role of the "willing" importer. To a large extent, this is a result of the revolutionary—even though unintentional—impact of the Reagan Administration's domestic initiatives on international economic affairs. First, consider the continuation of Federal Reserve Chairman Volcker's long-lasting campaign against inflation. To the amazement of its critics, this policy achieved the desired effect of slashing U.S. inflation from its 1980 level of 12.4% to 4% in 1984. Nevertheless, this policy precipitated the global recession and the international commodity price deflation of 1981-82. In turn, this exacerbated the LDC debt crisis and stimulated their trade offensives. Second, consider the combination of loose fiscal and tight monetary policy pursued by the Reagan Administration. While this policy set the stage for the remarkable non-inflationary recovery of 1983-84, it also caused unprecedented high real interest rates and a 30% appreciation of the dollar (70% since 1980). In turn, this dramatically increased the burden of LDC debt repayments, attracted foreign capital into the U.S., and contributed to massive American trade deficits. Third, consider how reducing taxes, eliminating regulations, and privatizing parts of the public sector have helped promote robust economic growth in the United States and high profit potential for the private sector. In turn, this provided strong attractions for an influx of foreign capital. Furthermore, the U.S. Treasury has tried to attract even more foreign capital by repealing the 30% withholding tax on foreign investors and by allowing foreigners to anonymously purchase its debt. Fourth, consider how this administration's ideological commitment to "free markets" makes it an enemy of protectionist concepts and practices—even though on numerous occasions it has succumbed to intense lobbying efforts for help against "unfair" foreign competition. This ideological stance views a massive trade deficit and the consequent capital imports with relative equanimity.[10]

The United States as a Capital Importer

Implications

Foreign nations are trying to achieve trade surpluses and their business men are trying to transfer capital to the United States for a variety of reasons that include: to repay debts, to earn high real rates of return, to avoid political instability, and to avoid protectionist restrictions on their exports to the U.S. The extremely strong U.S. dollar facilitates the ability of other nations to achieve an export surplus with the U.S., while at the same time making it more expensive for them to acquire dollar-denominated assets.

Notwithstanding the wishes of America's trading partners, it is neither desirable nor feasible to continue this process for much longer. Some of the reasons include:

1. LDC borrowers need to generate a trade surplus of $130 to $150 billion per year for at least the rest of the decade in order to maintain their already rescheduled principal and interest payments. If the U.S. continues to be the recipient of this export surplus, it will result in the decimation of large segments of the American economy. In fact, the manufacturing sector reversed its traditional trade surplus in 1982, experiencing deficits of $4 billion, $30 billion, and $80 billion from 1982 to 1984.

2. As America approaches the status of a net debtor, the customary surplus on its international service account balance will disappear as the payments of profits and interest to foreigners begin to exceed the investment receipts of Americans, thus putting the U.S. deeper in debt.

3. At some point in the creation of America's massive cumulative current account deficit, there will be flight from dollars by foreign and domestic investors trying to avoid what they perceive as the impending depreciation of the dollar. When this occurs, the United States will be faced with a dilemma. Its options will all be unpalatable: (1) accept the stagflationary consequences of a steep enough depreciation to correct the current account deficit; (2) raise interest rates to attract and retain capital inflows; (3) impose exchange controls to restrict capital exports as well as merchandise imports; (4) repudiate the debt by inflating it away; or (5) adopt some combination of the above.

4. To the extent that America becomes a net debtor, it will be mortgaging its future income in order to maintain present consumption standards. Rather than relying on foreign savings America should reduce its consumption and increase its savings. Alternatively, America could reduce investment or government spending. But to do so would undermine the basis of future economic growth, undercut the defense buildup, or weaken social programs.

5. The capital imports that accompany America's massive trade deficits are likely to stifle economic growth in Europe and the LDCs. In addition to straining political stability and worsening the poverty of these nations, this process will reduce markets for American exports.

Policy Prescriptions

If it is desirable for the United States to have a diversified, robust economy and a governing structure that has a healthy independence from the strategems of foreign competitors, then the President and the Congress need to realistically design domestic policies that are appropriate for the uncharted international environment in which we are living.[11] Six policies that would help address today's problems are discussed below:

1. Establishing International Goals. The U.S. should explicitly determine a strategy regarding the internationalization of the economy. The strategy should be consistent with the fulfillment of America's domestic policy goals—such as promoting social welfare, environmental safety, urban vitality, technological leadership, national defense, high living standards, etc. This strategy needs to address such questions as: To what extent, and under what conditions, should foreigners have access to U.S. markets, technology, and capital? To what extent, and under what conditions should the U.S. economy be dependent on export markets and foreign credit? Should the U.S. promote nondiscriminatory, multilateral relationships, or should it develop a web of preferential, bilateral relationships?

2. International Impact Statements. Macroeconomic policy alternatives must be evaluated in terms of their international, as well as their domestic implications. An "International Impact Statement" should be a requirement for all major policy changes.

3. Increase Savings and Eliminate Budget Deficits. The U.S. should increase savings, as well as slash budget deficits. The consequent drop in interest rates will substantially reduce debt repayment problems, as well as permit the investments America needs to increase productivity and promote long-term growth.

4. Fair Trade and Reciprocity. The U.S. should expect and require its major trading partners to follow roughly equivalent rules for managing their international trade and capital flows.[12]

5. Current Account Balance. The balancing of the current accounts should become a policy objective so that the United States is, once again, living off of its own income and not mortgaging its future.

6. Formally Acknowledge the Realities of the International Debt Situation. In concert with the ultimate world creditors— Saudi Arabia, Japan, and Germany—the United States should reassess the LDC situation. This creditor bloc should acknowledge the obvious and make the appropriate institutional arrangements to "write-down" the debts to a level where they become repayable—from the point of view of both the debtor and creditor nations. Although the banks should participate in these discussions, the international policy decisions as to how the "write-offs" are to be distributed should be decided by the governments of the creditor nations. As part of the bargain, debtor nations should transfer some of their assets to their creditors in order to reduce their debt obligations.

It is extremely unlikely that the policy prescriptions discussed above will be implemented in the near future. Since this is the case, what might happen to the international trading environment in the next few years?

One Possible Future: Debt Problems, Trade Offensives, and Protectionism

Will the world slowly and steadily become both more interdependent and more prosperous? Alternatively, might the world experience robust economic growth without increasing its interdependence? Or, will an era of reduced, or unchanging, interdependence lead to slow, or even negative, economic growth? In an attempt to address these questions, one possible scenario, as it might be described by a historian in the year 1990, is sketched below.

This scenario postulates the collapse of the multilateral free trade system and the emergence of preferential trading blocs. It is characterized by reduced interdependence, slower economic growth, and the philosophical acceptance of regions of prosperity and promise coexisting alongside regions of poverty and despair. There are two reasons for describing this scenario. First, it is a plausible outgrowth of today's deteriorating international economic environment.[13] Second, this scenario, which contrasts so sharply with the conventional wisdom, needs to be considered so that actions might be taken today to prevent its emergence tomorrow.

The Present-1990. In 1990, the international environment is dominated by American, European, and Japanese preferential trading blocs. As can be seen from Table 1, each trading bloc contains a complementary balance of industrial capacity, raw materials, and scientific expertise. China, the Latin American nations, and most of the Third and Fourth World nations are not yet strongly affiliated with any of the principal trading blocs. However, the unaffiliated nations that are rich in essential raw materials are being eagerly sought and competed for by the various trade blocs. Resource-poor LDCs are stuck on the periphery of the main trade channels and are forced to struggle towards national self-sufficiency without much external assistance.

Table I

Preferential Trade Blocs of the 1990s

Trade Bloc	Member Nations
1. American	United States, Canada, Mexico, Central American and Caribbean Nations, Korea, Taiwan, Israel, and Saudi Arabia
2. European	European Economic Community with expanding ties to resource rich former colonies
3. Japanese	Japan, ASEAN (Indonesia, Malaysia, Philippines, Singapore, and Thailand), Australia, New Zealand, and Iran
4. Russian	Soviet Union, East European members of COMECON, and India
5. Unaffiliated	China, the Latin American nations, and other Third and Fourth World nations

Trade flows are once again growing in the aftermath of the "beggar-thy-neighbor" trade wars of the late 1980s. However, most of this activity occurs within the confines of the preferential trading blocs. It is organized and facilitated by aid and investment flows directed by the blocs' dominant partner(s). Trade between blocs is also occurring, but primarily on the basis of balanced bilateral accounts; otherwise, commodity-based international reserves are exchanged. There is virtually no credit available for balancing interregional trade accounts, nor are there any substantial flows of interregional investments or aid. The multinational corporations that survived the trade wars are in the process of reorganizing their operations so as to concentrate on the opportunities within their primary trade bloc.

How did this radically different international trading environment arise? The most important factors that contributed to the breakdown of the old environment and the emergence of this new one are described below:

The Past—1973-90. The post-World War II international economic system was fundamentally changed in a haphazard and unplanned manner by the OPEC and Reagan Revolutions. In brief, the OPEC Revolution resulted in an inegalitarian shift in international income and wealth, the creation of an enormous amount of unrepayable debt, and a substantial slowdown in the growth of world prosperity and trade. To a great extent, the processes initiated by OPEC in the 1970s set the stage for its demise in the 1980s.

The Reagan Revolution, with its emphasis on promoting noninflationary growth in the United States, helped drive the nails into OPEC's coffin—primarily as a result of its contractionary policies that reduced the worldwide demand for oil. However, by creating conditions that curtailed credit expansion at home and abroad, the Reagan Administration inadvertently promoted "trade offensives" by the heavily indebted LDCs, strengthened the U.S. dollar, and presided over a series of unprecedented trade and current account deficits. While Europeans and Japanese paid lip service to multilateral free trade goals, the Americans actually allowed whole sections of their high- and low-technology industries to be overwhelmed by imports.

The reasons for America's acquiescence in the decimation of its industry are complex, but they appear to include: (1) fears of retaliation by America's trading partners, (2) fears of a political backlash from American users of imports (consumers and producers alike), (3) fears of a collapse of the international financial system if the LDCs could not export their products (4) nonrecognition of the long-term consequences of America's becoming a net debtor, and (5) an ideological bias against developing a trade policy concept that competes with the prevailing "free trade" paradigm.

From 1985 to 1987, international economic conditions became even more difficult: the trade offensives of debtor nations increased as they found themselves more restricted in European and (to a lesser extent) U.S. markets; trade frictions between Japan and the U.S. and between Japan and Europe increased (in spite of more frequent consultations); the international financial system became more unstable as a result of the need to continuously restructure LDC debts; U.S. monetary policy became extremely erratic as efforts were made to combat sporadic "runs" on the dollar. In this environment, it became apparent that the U.S. economy was bearing politically unacceptable burdens to support a free trade dogma that, for the most part, was used as a subterfuge by America's trading partners.

These conditions spawned a further proliferation of trade barriers, which in turn, further impaired the ability of LDCs to service their debts. As loan losses by the commercial banks continued to grow, central banks prevented the complete collapse of their banking system by "nationalizing" their money-center banks in a fashion similar to the rescue of the Continental Illinois bank in 1984. The subsequent credit contraction had a strong deflationary impact on the world economy. International trade almost came to a halt as nations and companies were forced to structure complex barter transactions for essentials.

Economic dislocations occurred throughout the world as employment, income, and profits that were dependent on international trade fell precipitously. Nations and businesses that were most dependent on foreign markets or resources naturally suffered the greatest disruptions. In some cases, this led to food riots, urban unrest, and the virtual shutdown of industrial sectors that ran out of markets of raw materials. Throughout these tumultuous years, America, Europe, and Japan were all attempting to initiate or strengthen preferential trade relationships. By the close of 1987, the United States had formally given up on the concept of multilateral trade as a means of resolving its problems. It established "Internationalization Goals" that set limits to foreign access to U.S. markets and to U.S. dependence on foreign credit. The U.S. had concluded Free Trade Agreements with Canada, Israel, and Mexico and had also initiated a round of bilateral discussions with Korea, Taiwan, and Saudi Arabia about the possibilities of establishing preferential trade relationships.

Ultimately, the governments that survived the economic and political disruptions reoriented their national economic structures towards greater self-sufficiency and closer ties with the members of their emerging preferential trading bloc. The objectives of these trading blocs were to ensure that long-term political goals—such as stable economic growth and internal stability—would guide and control short-term market opportunities and threats. That is, the member nations were willing to forego some freedom of choice and economic growth potential in order to reduce their vulnerability to the types of disruptions they had experienced for the past five years.

Conclusion

The dynamics of the present international situation suggest that a continuation of the trading relationships of the early-1980s is not probable. Yet the political, business, and academic leaders of the OECD nations continue to speak and act as if it is. Most likely, this simply reflects wishful thinking on their part. Although they admit that today's international system needs some marginal adjustments—regarding debts, protectionism, and the value of the U.S. dollar—they do not recognize any fundamental flaws in the structure.

In order to achieve the preferred future of the OECD's leaders—a revival of the post-World War II "norm" where international prosperity is propelled by an expanding regime of multilateral free trade—three problems that are presently undermining their goal must be resolved.

1. Unrepayable International Debts. Unrepayable international debts would need to be reduced in an "equitable" manner. The U.S. and the ultimate lenders—Saudi Arabia, Japan, Germany—should take the leading role in doing this in order to avoid the debilitating effects of perpetual trade offensives and the ever-present possibility of an avalanche of defaults.

2. **Protectionism.** Protectionist practices would need to be reversed.

3. **Unstable International Currency.** The United States would need to follow a macroeconomic policy that would enable American businesses and America's trading partners to anticipate the dollar's value.

In today's interdependent world, none of these problems can be solved unilaterally by one nation. Cooperation among the principal trading nations is imperative. However, this cooperation is difficult to achieve because all the necessary remedies are known to harm particular stakeholders in the near-term, without providing any guarantee of relief to the affected stakeholders in the long-term. Nonetheless, if the major trading nations cannot cooperate successfully, the problems plaguing the international system will still be resolved. However, this resolution may entail the type of breakdown of the existing system described in the scenario above.

The widespread pessimism that permeates non-official discussions of future international conditions stems from recognition of three things: (1) the difficulty of coordinating the macroeconomic and trade policies of the major trading nations, (2) the failure of the credit and aid-dependent development programs of many of the world's nations, and (3) the difficulty of managing the international debt situation. Although this pessimism reflects the precarious state of current international conditions (as contrasted with the optimism of official spokesmen), a continuation of these conditions is not inevitable, i.e., trend is not destiny.

Hopefully, this article will motivate official spokesmen, as well as others, to re-examine their assumptions about the "inevitability" of their particular visions of the future international environment. Such feelings of inevitability are damaging because they stifle actions—actions that can influence the course of the future trade system, as well as actions that can change the impact upon particular individuals or institutions of whatever trade system evolves.

Notes

1. For similar views, see Paul Volcker, "Monetary Policy Objectives for 1984," Washington, D. C.: Federal Reserve Board, July 25, 1984, p. 3, and Paula Stern (Chairwoman, U.S. International Trade Commission), "Macro Policy, Economic Health, and the International Order," a speech to the Group of Thirty, New York, December 17, 1984.

2. Even in the third year of the international economic recovery, IMF austerity measures are still creating tremendous political pressures in the debtor nations. The most obvious recent victim was the government of President Jaafar Numeiri of the Sudan, which was deposed on April 6, 1985.

3. Because the U.S. can sell its previously acquired large inventory of international assets, there is not a one-for-one correspondence between its current account balance and its net creditor or debtor status.

4. For Japanese perspectives on the inherent fragility of U.S. economic policy, see Kenjiro Hayashi, "U.S. Growth Raises an International Storm," *Economic Eye,* Tokyo: Kezai Koho Center, Vol. 5, No. 4, December 1984, pp. 12-15, and Yoshihide Ishiyama, "Yen Internationalization as Part of the Yen-Dollar Issue," *The Wheel Extended,* Vol. XIV, No. 4, Tokyo: Toyota Motor Corporation, 1984, pp. 30-33.

5. The current account balance summarizes a nation's international behavior in terms of its net sales of goods and services, as well as its foreign aid and remittance flows. Data on current account balances for the U.S. and other countries is reported in the *International Monetary Fund, World Economic Outlook 1985* and *Council of Economic Advisors, Economic Report of the President 1985.*

6. For Japanese perspectives on the magnitude and future prospects of Japan's current account surplus, see Kunio Miyamoto, "Japan's Massive Current Account Surplus," *Economic Eye,* Tokyo: Kezai Koho Center Vol. 5, No. 4, December 1984, pp. 4-7, and Isamu Miyazaki, "Taking Stock of the Japanese Economy," *Journal of Japanese Trade & Industry,* Vol. 4, No. 1, Jan./Feb. 1985, pp. 12-15.

7. The sum of unreported dollar inflows (the official statistical discrepancy) between 1970 and 1983 was about $126 billion. A substantial portion of this represents unreported capital inflows.

8. One study of the reparations problem suggests that Germany was able but unwilling to pay and that the Allies were ambivalent about their willingness to receive payment (as well as in disagreement about Germany's ability to pay). See Marc Trachtenberg, *Reparations in World Politics,* New York: Columbia University Press, 1980.

9. International Monetary Fund, *World Economic Outlook* 1985, p. 262.

10. See for instance, Council of Economic Advisors, "The United States in the World Economy," (Chapter 3), *Economic Report of the President 1985,* Washington, D.C.: Government Printing Office, February 1985. Most American academic trade specialists also have an almost religious-like fascination with the free trade paradigm. At a major conference, titled "U.S. Trade Policies in a Changing World Economy," that was sponsored by the Institute of Public Policy Studies at the University of Michigan (March 28-29, 1985), most speakers reiterated the benefits of free trade and condemned interventionist practices; see Deardoff and Stern, *Current Issues in U.S. Trade Policies: An Overview;* Dornbusch and Frankel, *Macroeconomic Performance*

and Policies: Impacts on U.S. International Trade and Trade Policies; Corden, *Designing Rules for the International Trading System for the Year 2000 and Beyond.* A minority felt the U.S. should engage in strategic negotiation tariffs; see Dixit, *How Should the U.S. Respond to Other Countries' Trade Policies?* and Branson and Pearce, *The Case for an Import Surcharge.* A cogent view against the logic, as well as the results, of the free trade paradigm is made by Robert Kuttner, *The Economic Illusion: False Choices Between Prosperity, and Social Justice.* Raston: Houghton-Mifflin, 1984.

11. A recent report recognizes the critical need for America to develop a trade strategy, see The Report of the President's Commission on Industrial Competitiveness, *Global Competition: The New Reality,* Washington, D.C.: Government Printing Office, January 1985.

12. For a judicious balance of "official" opinion, see United States-Japan Advisory Commission, *Challenges and Opportunities in United States-Japan Relations,* Washington, D.C.: Department of State, September 1984. For a journalistic perspective on fair trade and reciprocity, see "Collision Course: Can the U.S. Avert a Trade War With Japan?" *Business Week,* April 8, 1985 (cover story).

13. In radical departures from customary free trade positions, protectionist proposals have emerged in 1985 from such diverse sources as Senator John Danforth, Congressman John Dingell, Motorola Chairman Robert Galvin, and even the Morgan Guaranty Bank with its proposal for a 20% surcharge on Japanese imports. Another departure, was the U.S. efforts to negotiate bilateral free trade agreements (FTAs). The rationale for doing so is described in the *Economic Report of the President 1985,* pp. 125-27. For a discussion of the recently negotiated U.S.- Israel Free Trade Agreement (FTA), America's efforts to develop a FTA with Canada, and its interest in opening FTA discussions with ASEAN, see Gary Brower, "Key Executives Explain Free Trade Agreements with Israel, Canada," *Daily Commercial News and Shipping Guide,* Los Angeles, March 15, 1985, p. 1.

Asian-Pacific
Economic Developments

Japan and Asian-Pacific Economic Integration

by

Hiroshi Kitamura

The merits of any scheme of regional economic integration will, in the final analysis, be judged in the light of potential or actual contributions that can be expected or realized from such a scheme to solving substantial policy problems of the particular geographical area. The importance of this viewpoint of problem-solving in discussing the institutional arrangements for Asian-Pacific economic cooperation has recently been elevated to a level of official recognition in the practical work program, when the first reports of separate task forces established in the previous year were submitted to the third session of the Pacific Economic Cooperation Conference (PECC), held at Bali in November 1983.

One of the task forces, which dealt with trade in manufactured goods, concluded—noting that changes in the structure of comparative advantage seem to have progressed smoothly—that "these changes in the structure of comparative advantage among the Pacific Basin countries indicate that the regional developing countries are in the process of 'catching up' to the developed countries in industrial development." It was then suggested that "the 'catch up' by the developing countries means that intra-regional trade will have to rely increasingly on intra-industrial trade in the future" (Pacific Economic Cooperation Conference, 1983, p. 38).

The implication of the above statement is that the possibility of intra-industry specialization opens up significantly new per-

---

Hiroshi Kitamura is professor of international economics, Graduate School of International Relations, International University of Japan, Niigata, Japan.

spectives for the structural patterns of economic interactions among the countries of the Asian-Pacific region. Linking to the statement of the task force, then, the present paper intends to examine the relevance of these perspectives and relate them to the demand for fundamental reforms of the world trading system. For, at the present stage of changing patterns of international division of labor, these developments seem to pose quite new challenges to Japanese trade policy making. That is, if the emergence of a closely knit regional system of interdependent industrial economies becomes a reality for the first time in history in this region, this may provide a new possibility of trade strategy that may in fact lead to superior results as compared with the present system of compromised free trade and ad hoc protectionism. This paper will draw heavily upon a series of significant statistical analyses that have recently been undertaken by various authors in the field.[1]

The Increasing Economic Interdependence in a Growth Region

The recent economic performance of the countries in the Asian-Pacific region continues to reinforce the widespread view that special importance must be attached to what is happening in this particular area in gauging the future prospects of the world economy. Indeed, the region has been characterized during the past decade by the spectacular speed of economic growth and structural change in overall terms. Up to the early 1970s, it was Japan's phenomenal growth record, called a "miracle," that attracted world attention. When Japan's long-term growth rates were halved after the first oil crisis, the Asian Newly Industrializing Countries (NICs) continued to maintain the growth impetus of 8% to 10% per year, and a number of Southeast Asian countries soon followed the footsteps of the NICs, even accelerating the past decade's growth. Today, the Asian-Pacific region is without doubt one of the fastest-growing poles of the world economy, suggesting in the view of the OECD Interfutures group that an area taking shape in the Far East "might, in the second quarter of the twenty-first century, become a center of the world economy" (OECD, 1979, p. 399).

This process of rapid change has obviously transformed the Asian-Pacific region into a closely integrated economic group of increasingly interdependent countries. How close the trade relationship between two countries is can be measured by the trade intensity index, defined as the share of one country's trade with another country divided by the latter's share of world trade. The bilateral indices of trade intensity among the countries within the region now average two, which indicates that the regional countries trade with each other about twice as intensively as would be expected given the partner country's importance in world trade (Anderson, 1983, p. 377). Since the degree of trade integration of the countries of North America with the western Pacific countries is relatively low as compared with intra-western Pacific trade, the exclusion of the North American developed countries from Anderson's table would raise the average intensity of the regional trade to a figure close to three. The recent intensification of trade relations among the Pacific countries was obviously somewhat biased towards the western side of the Pacific, centering around three distinct groups of countries: Japan, the Asian NICs (Singapore, Hong Kong, South Korea, and Taiwan), and the other ASEAN countries (or ASEAN-4, namely, Indonesia, Malaysia, the Philippines, and Thailand). It is for this reason that in considering the future prospects for regional trade in manufactured goods, particular emphasis will sometimes be placed on the interactions among these three groups of countries in the western Pacific region.

In focusing on the mutual relationship between the dynamic growth processes of the three groups of East Asian countries, it will probably not be beside the mark to describe the process as a sequential pageant of continual pursuit of one group by another: while Japan was first catching up with the level of capital accumulation and technological progress of the Western advanced countries, the Asian NICs were soon pursuing Japan's development path, with the other ASEAN countries following the NICs' footsteps from relatively short distances. The increased flows of capital goods and technology in the form of direct foreign investment among the Asian-Pacific economies allowed the regional scene of sequential economic growth to be compressed within a very short span of time. Thus, the rapid shift of industrial development from one group of countries to another in the neighboring region proved, in fact, to be essential ingredients of the phenomenal level of overall growth rates, reflecting the unprecedented dynamism of the Asian-Pacific region.

A resource-poor developing country, when embarking upon exports of manufactured goods, will have a comparative advantage in unskilled labor-intensive products. This comparative advantage will be felt with particular strength in the producing country's relations with the traditional high-wage countries, whose factor endowments show conceivably the largest difference from those of the producing developing country. Incidentally, this partly explains why exports of labor-intensive manufactured goods from the Asian NICs and ASEAN countries tend to find proportionately greater outlets in the developed-country markets of North America and Western Europe rather than in the Japanese market.

With internal capital accumulation and technological improvements, the country's real wage level will tend to rise, and comparative advantage will have to shift away from unskilled labor-intensive products towards more skill- or capital- and technology-intensive production lines. This means that the developing country has attained the level of the NICs or more advanced developing countries, accepting increasing imports of unskilled labor-intensive products from less developed countries. But a smooth transition to a shifting trade pattern in the country can be realized without friction only if the industrial structure of the more advanced countries can be adjusted so as to allow free market outlet for the country's products of new comparative advantage. It is obvious that the successful evolution of the shifting patterns of specialization is conditional on smooth industrial adjustments, particularly in the industrially developed countries.

This shifting pattern of specialization can be exemplified in the case of the textile industry in the Asian-Pacific region. Within the textile industry, there are a spectrum of shifting factor proportions in different product categories. There are more capital- and technology-intensive products such as synthetic fibers upstream on the one hand, and more labor-intensive products such as textiles, fabrics, and clothing downstream on the other. In the former categories, Japan still boasts of its one-fifth share of the world exports, maintaining comparative advantage over the other two groups of Asian countries, although both of the latter countries are actually gaining in the market share with considerable speed. In textile fabrics and clothing, however, the revealed comparative advantage index of the Asian NICs and the ASEAN-4 countries already surpasses that of Japan; moreover, we may even detect in these labor-intensive categories the trend of the ASEAN-4 countries to slowly replace the NICs in terms of comparative advantage in the world market.

Now, while speaking of the textile industry in the Asian-Pacific region, it would be most appropriate to add that a potentially very important supplier has recently made an appearance on the scene along with the other ASEAN countries, at least in so far as unskilled labor-intensive textile products are concerned. That is China, a developing country with a remarkable growth record in recent times; the recent value of textile exports from China is at a level comparable with some of the Asian NICs. Thus, the dynamic sequential catching-up process should be interpreted as involving a continuous chasing of more advanced countries by newcomers, extending beyond the three groups of Asian countries in terms of geographical coverage as well as in terms of shifting factor proportions. All the more urgently will the industrially developed countries be required to facilitate this dynamic transition by keeping their own markets open to the products of latecomer nations through continued adjustments in their industrial structures.

The network of ever closer interactions among groups of Asian countries at different levels of economic development has generated greater growth effects just because the increased competition between the groups also implied equally important complementary relations. The need for investment and growth of rapidly industrializing Asian countries means that they must import an increasing quantity of capital and investment goods from more advanced countries on the development ladder, and the existence of Japan as a supply center of capital goods in the neighboring region of East Asia has been an important element facilitating the rapid process of industrialization. A no less important role has been played by increased foreign investment flows originating in Japan, which involve not only transfer of capital and technology, but, more importantly in terms of trade flows in manufactured goods, also extensive transfer of intermediate goods, parts, and accessories as well as capital equipment across national boundaries. In the reverse direction, however, such investment flows may provide an important vehicle for expanding regional exports of final products derived from transnational activities.

In gauging the prospects of world trade development in the future, an important consideration will be differing scopes of relative growth of individual markets. If, as is generally assumed, the relatively low growth of the traditional centers of the world economy limits the expansion of the absorptive capacity of the main extra-regional markets for manufactured exports from the Asian NICs and Southeast Asian countries, a renewed emphasis should be placed on the importance of Japan as a nearby market outlet for manufactured goods from the developing Asian countries. Obviously, an effort to diversify the Asian countries' trade more in the direction of increasing intra-regional transactions is desirable in order to take advantage of faster growing regional markets. The Asian countries will be able to grow economically faster if they join hands than they would otherwise.

It would mean losing sight of balance if we did not dwell upon some important ways in which Japan can make the access to its own market easier for its Asian neighbors. This is clearly the most urgent policy agenda for Japanese trade policy making. We have referred earlier to structural factors favoring an extra-regional orientation for manufactured exports from the Asian countries, such as relative differences in comparative advantage and factor endowments. While at present the Japanese market can be considered as open as the markets of other industrially developed countries (Cline, 1982, pp. 9-12), the fact that the liberalization has been of a recent origin leaves the access to the Japanese market perhaps still less open than might be desirable.

The particular pattern of rapid economic growth of the Asian-Pacific countries has thus contributed to the formation of a closely knit system of international economic interdependence among the countries in the area, even without any conscious attempt to promote or organize integration at the regional level. Increased economic interdependence does not only mean that the economic prospects of one country are increasingly sensitive to what happens in the trading partners in the neighborhood. There is also a kind of interdependence among policies in the sense that the optimal course of action for one country would depend in a decisive way on the actions taken by another. An independent national pursuit of economic objectives in isolation, if explicit account is not taken of what actions other regional countries are taking, will lead to a suboptimal result.

That the past patterns of economic interdependence have been highly beneficial to the developing countries of the region can now be regarded as generally accepted. The exceptionally high growth rates common to these countries testify to the benefits of cooperation. The high degree of regional concentration in trade and investment flows will probably ensure that major benefits of trade expansion in the Asian-Pacific region will primarily accrue to the countries of the region themselves. The fact of regional interdependence itself, however, provides the possibility that such a trade and investment expansion can be organized with greater ease on a regional basis. While the increased interdependence among the regional countries suggests the need for closer policy consultation and coordination, the same circumstances create the conditions for increased regional efforts to ensure successes in coordinated development of the economies of the region.

The Emerging Perspective of Intra-Industry Trade

The rapid process of sequential industrialization has resulted in significant changes in the patterns of shifting division of labor in the Asian-Pacific region. Not only has the shift been greatly compressed in terms of time, but the differences in existing comparative costs have also been enormously reduced, giving rise to a greater possibility of substitution in production. This change has been most pronounced in the case of the Asian NICs: the pattern of manufactured exports from the NICs has rapidly become more similar to that of the advanced industrial countries[2] (Finger and Kreinin, 1979, p. 919). But changes in the same direction, of course to a lesser extent, have also been observed for countries at lower levels of economic development.

The multiple trends of diminishing gaps in factor endowments have opened up very important perspectives of so-called intra-industry trade or specialization, becoming not only characteristics of trade relations among the industrialized countries, but also significant trade channels between the industrialized countries and the less developed countries. As intra-industry trade is interpreted as those parts of exports of an industry that are matched by a corresponding value of imports of the same industry in trade relations between a given pair of countries or groups of countries, the absolute percentage value is obviously dependent on the specifications of "industry," that is, on the level of statistical grouping of an industry. To the extent that an industry is defined in terms of irreversible intensity in factor uses in production, however, the fact that a given industry simultaneously both exports and imports between a given pair of countries or groups of countries is inconsistent with the premises of the static factor proportions theory: the same industry cannot be capital intensive and non-capital intensive at the same time vis-à-vis a given trading partner.

Now, the increasing share of intra-industry trade, regardless of whatever level of specification is used for the calculation of the share, among manufacturing subsectors of advanced industrial countries has been a major element that distinguishes world trade development since World War II from its earlier history. That the postwar trade expansion in the world has been spearheaded by the increasingly intensified trade transactions among the industrialized countries has, indeed, been the reflection of the rising importance of this intra-industry trade. There is general agreement that the extent of intra-industry specialization is positively correlated with the level of economic development: the relative share of intra-industry trade is very high for the industrialized countries, where it generally accounts for 60% to 80% of all trade, compared to the level of 40% to 50% for the NICs, and much lower levels of 10% to 20% for the rest of the developing countries (Havrylyshyn and Civan, 1983, p. 132).

Over the past decade or so, however, it has been the group of so-called Semi-Industrialized or Newly Industrialized Countries that has recorded the largest increase in the extent of intra-industry trade, suggesting that the process of integration of these countries into world trade in the recent past has predominantly assumed the form of increasing two-way dependence on trade of similar goods (Havrylyshyn and Civan, p. 134). It is also interesting to note that, as the intra-industry trading network has been extended to include part of the developing countries, the decade of the 1970s witnessed the reversal of the past trend of increasing shares of world trade being transacted among a small number of highly industrialized countries. In bringing about the new world-trade trend, of course, this structural change has been additional to the effects of the rise in oil prices.

A considerable proportion of the intra-industry trade that has been identified in the Asian-Pacific region, especially in so far as countries at different levels of development are concerned, can be explained by referring to the traditional factor proportion hypothesis, which is well suited to account for inter-industry specialization. It includes important elements of what may called vertical intra-industry specialization, entailing extensive flows of intermediate goods, components, parts and accessories across national boundaries within the same industry or even within the same firm. Such a specialization may assume great importance in the case of international subcontracting, when the production process is internationally divided between the industrial countries and the NICs and other developing countries, or between the more advanced and other developing countries. Even in trade flows in differentiated capital and intermediate goods, the possibility of such a vertical intra-industry specialization is suggested by advantages of economies of scale, due to the length of production run and size of plant, in addition to reaping the benefits of different factor prices (Grubel and Lloyd, 1975, p. 100).

As the factor endowments of the NICs approach more closely those of the industrialized countries, an increasing number of manufacturing industries will show the patterns of specialization that are more easily explained by the quality and taste differentiation of products, principally on the consumer side, economies of scale effects, and other factors that play important roles in "horizontal" trade flows within the same industry among the industrial countries (Schumacher, 1983, p. 105). The fact of intra-industry specialization itself does not provide any indication of greater welfare gains from trade, as compared with the traditional vertical specialization based on different factor proportions as between industries. But, to the extent that some dynamic gains due to economies of scale in differentiated products are involved, these gains are additional to the benefits in the static sense, derived from the factor variation possibilities. Increased intra-industry interdependence can therefore be construed as an important element in the dynamic interactions of the regional growth.

In this process of dynamic interactions in the Asian-Pacific region, the transmission of growth impetus between three groups of countries has been facilitated by an important characteristic of intra-industry specialization: namely, the more the nature of trade between a given pair of countries or groups of countries approaches intra-industry specialization (as opposed to inter-industry specialization), industrial adjustments consequential upon an increase in imports will involve lesser social costs. In the case of horizontal specialization, in particular, firms will be in a position to change their product composition and redirect workers easily within the same firm. The basis for increased trade gains is often, as indicated earlier, economies of scale, due to a longer production run, which made differentiated products possible: Reducing product varieties may increase gains through the use of specialized machinery and learning by doing. Even in the case of vertical intra-industry specialization, adjustment costs will be lower than in the case of vertical inter-industry specialization, because necessary adjustment shifts can be performed within the firm if the same firm produces several parts and components (Balassa, 1983, pp. 272-273).

This aspect of industrial adjustments is an important factor making the prospects of intra-regional trade expansion in this area extremely favorable. Trade expansion is, after all, conditional on the smoothness with which necessary industrial adjustments can be achieved, particularly in the more developed partners in the trade relations. In the Asian-Pacific region, however, as the developing countries diversify their exports through regionally oriented intra-industry trade, new opportunities will be opened up for the more advanced countries in the region to increase exports in the same industry to the developing partners. Whether these opportunities can actually be seized will depend on the countries' trade policy in a given market situation. We have to admit that a high degree of product differentiation tends to involve oligopolistic market structures. This would suggest that a conscious regional effort of consultation and coordination of economic and trade policies among the regional countries would be required to make optimal use of opportunities for intra-industry division of labor (Grubel and Lloyd, 1975, pp. 122-124).

Now, what is the role Japan is expected to play in this process of emerging intra-industry trade patterns in the Asian-Pacific region? Available indications inform us that the share of trade being operated intra-industrially is generally very much lower for Japan than for the other industrially developed countries of the West. The accompanying table consists of two parts: (A) reproduces the estimates of the relevant ratios for the four industrial countries in 1979, made by Bela Balassa on the basis of a 91-industry classification scheme characterized by high substitution elasticities in production. In (B), however, in anticipation of the argument to be presented later, the corresponding figures for the year 1977 for geographically different groups of the NICs have been added, which are derived from the study by Gavelin and Lundberg based on 4-digit ISIC industry groups by the World Bank.

Table 1

Extent of Intra-Industry Specialization of the Four Developed Countries in Trade with Various Country Groups

Trade of	A			B		
with	World	DCs	NICs	Other LDCs	Asian NICs	Southern Europe
Japan	0.275	0.393	0.313	0.087	0.362	0.143
United States	0.568	0.672	0.407	0.250	0.380	0.302
Western Germany	0.666	0.772	0.376	0.167	0.269	0.482
United Kingdom	0.763	0.797	0.386	0.432	0.285	0.473

Notes: The two series of figures are not strictly comparable because of the differences in methodology.

Sources: (A) Balassa, 1983, p., 270. The year is 1979. (B) Gavelin and Lundberg, 1983, p. 181. The year is 1977.

The table confirms that the level of Japan's intra-industry specialization in world trade in manufactured goods has recently been far the lowest among the four industrially developed countries, and that the level has even declined over the past decade, whereas the ratio increased in other countries. The corresponding ratio in Japan's trade with oil-importing developing countries is also substantially lower than in similarly situated countries. Balassa attributes this low level of intra-industry specialization of Japan to the country's long history of protectionism (Balassa, 1983, p. 271). This is not to deny the considerable justification of this point of view; it was argued earlier that, although formal trade liberalization in Japan has by now reached a comparable or even superior level relative to the other industrially developed countries, it has been of relatively recent origin. Since it takes considerable time to adjust the industrial structure to institutional changes, Japan's industrial structure may continue to exhibit much of its traditional characteristics of being less dependent on imports from abroad.

However, there are also other factors relevant to a country's relative share of intra-industry specialization. As far as Japan's trade with the developing countries, including the NICs, is concerned, a relatively smaller difference in the patterns of comparative costs compared with the trade relations involving the other developed countries may account for the lower level of intra-industry trade. But we are inclined to attach greater importance to the factor of economic distance, which is, according to Gavelin and Lundberg, one of the significant determinants of intra-industry specialization (Gavelin and Lundberg, 1983, p. 190). The table (B) indicates that Japan's share of intra-industry trade with the NICs, the more advanced developing countries, was concentrated on East and Southeast Asia, whereas the Western European countries operated intra-industry trade mainly with the NICs in southern Europe, with relatively small shares being devoted to intra-industry trade with the Asian NICs.

It may not be entirely out of place to refer to an earlier econometric study that emphasized the importance of distance in explaining the trade patterns. Characterizing Japan as a badly situated country with long distances to the major markets of world trade, in contrast with smaller Western European countries like the Netherlands and Belgium in the "ideal" foreign-trade location, Hans Linnemann concluded that "the effort involved in realizing a certain volume of foreign trade is about six times greater (for Japan than for the Western European countries)" (Linnemann, 1966, p. 187). The implication was that, in the absence of important industrial-country markets in the neighborhood, Japan had to attempt to industrialize under very serious handicaps. Now, the emergence of a regional network of intra-industry specialization in East and Southeast Asia means for Japan that, for the first time in history, a growing market of manufactured products is forming in its neighborhood.

Indeed, the recent increase in the importance of Japan's intra-industry trade with the Asian NICs has been fairly impressive: the strongest growth in the number of manufactured items with substantial intra-industry specialization between 1970 and 1975 was recorded in Japan among industrially developed countries, in addition to the Netherlands (Tharakan, 1983, p. 14). This provided Japan for the first time with the possibility to aim at a balanced industrial structure by increasing imports of manufactured goods from neighboring countries, thus avoiding the heavy handicaps of location under which it had to attempt to industrialize earlier. But such a possibility does not become automatically realized as the share of intra-industry trade rises.

Japan will be called upon to deliberately increase imports of manufactured products from those countries that are rapidly growing into close trading partners in intra-industry specialization. In this respect, economic rationality dictates that Japan should give a much higher priority to meeting the trade demands coming from the Asian NICs and the other ASEAN countries than the demands originating from the trade frictions with other developed countries. If Japan attempts to satisfy the former demands to the fullest extent, this will serve to strengthen emerging industries in the region: the policy action will be along the lines of comparative advantage. By contrast, the trade conflicts with other developed countries often derive from pressures to prevent the disappearance of declining industries: such actions working against the postulates of shifting comparative advantage should be minimized. In other words, the formation of the regional network of intra-industry specialization provides a unique chance for transforming Japan's traditional "self-sufficient" industrial structure into a more balanced and mature shape. This, in turn, will possibly lead to the development of a highly balanced and self-contained economic community of nations in the Asian-Pacific region.

Towards a New Regional Economic Order

We have seen that the Asian-Pacific region has recently been building up one of the most integrated high-growth systems of increasingly interdependent nations. That system has been characterized by an increasing share of regional trade taking the form of intra-industry specialization, which opens up the possibility of developing a well-balanced, self-contained, and stable grouping of highly efficient economies in the area. What remains for us to do is simply to relate these regional developments to the concept of international economic order or its fundamental reforms by putting the problems of trade expansion into the historic and world policy perspective, in order to identify Japan's policy agenda towards the economic integration in the Asian-Pacific region.

As economic interdependence among countries becomes more intensive, the problem of managing the international trade relations will have to be seen in quite a different light from the angle of the traditional international relations. The premises of the present trading order as incorporated in the General Agreement on Tariffs and Trade (GATT) were, first, that there are clear dividing lines separating the sphere of domestic policy concerns from the international trade policy. From this, it followed, second, that the trading order can be maintained by a purely negative approach of reducing trade barriers though negotiations among independent nation states, limited strictly to the international trading norms as distinct from domestic policy objectives. These premises of the GATT system appear today to be increasingly questioned in theory and in practice.

The dividing lines between the spheres of domestic and foreign economic policy concerns are in many cases irreparably blurred, because major domestic objectives cannot be achieved without explicit account being taken of impacts of foreign policy actions, on the one hand, and international trading norms are increasingly affected by what is subject to domestic policy regulations within each nation, on the other. A number of non-tariff barriers are nothing but domestic government measures pursued for their own legitimate objectives, which, however, cannot help affecting international trade flows in important ways. Trade negotiations cannot, therefore, be confined any more to foreign aspects only, without looking at the domestic roots of barriers. It is obvious that most of these restrictions cannot be eliminated simply through agreeing on a timetable of mutual reduction, without attempting to harmonize underlying objectives and policies. In an effort to accommodate to increasing economic interdependence, therefore, the increasing need will be felt for continuing consultation and, if possible, coordination and harmonization of internal economic policies among interdependent nations.

In the context of intra-industry specialization in particular, international consultation will tend to include more and more domestic policy issues within the purview of trade negotiation, for intra-industry specialization typically provides increasing room for domestic government policy to shape comparative advantage within a given industry. This is the case of what is called "arbitrary comparative advantage," (Cline, 1982, p. 9), in which the pattern of trade specialization for a whole range of manufactured products is determined by government actions or by uncompetitive firm behavior rather than by objective circumstances such as factor endowments and factor prices. Then it would appear almost accidental, from the point of view of the static theory of division of labor, which country prevails in the market of a given differentiated product, because economies of scale primarily depend on the firm's decision or the government's incentive policies affecting the choice of product varieties.

However, the importance of domestic policy issues in international negotiations is not limited to the intra-industry portion of trade. As the willingness and capacity of the industrially advanced societies to adjust to changing conditions has visibly declined over time, a country's commitment to free trade in general depends on the extent of industrial adjustment that can be absorbed by the society concerned without intolerable social costs. This means that any international negotiation aimed at moving in the direction of free trade will have to include a great deal of consultations and arrangements on the domestic questions of what is generally called "industrial policy," namely, on what shifts in production should be permitted to take place in each nation and at what rate. It has been a conventional wisdom of economic theory that a system of domestic subsidies and taxation can be equivalent to a system of trade interference through tariffs. The logical consequence of this argument is that extensive consultations and agreements on domestic policies for regulating and encouraging industrial development are now an essential ingredient of any successful trade negotiation (Ahearn, 1982, p. 27).

In view of the essentially domestic orientation of these policies, we are faced with a kind of dilemma if we are to aim at keeping the world trading system virtually open. In the absence of the minimum agreement on necessary institutional arrangements to ensure supranational decision-making, we would not be able to endorse very strongly the primacy of international trading objectives over any conflicting domestic options. Unless the trade effects of these domestic policies are effectively brought under control, however, the basic premises of a liberal trading system are seriously threatened. In these circumstances, efforts to maintain the international trading order essentially open will increasingly necessitate political bargaining and compromises, often on a bilateral or some restricted grouping basis—a pragmatic approach that may aim at some degree of limited harmony, rather than at optimum solutions for the world as a whole.

In this context, a regional approach such as in the form discussed in the present paper, focusing on the Asian-Pacific area, assumes an added importance. If consultation and coordination on policies in depth are aimed at, there must be a limit in the number and scope of countries to be included in the negotiation. Such a policy coordination can be successfully achieved only within a group of a limited number of countries sharing a similar political outlook and common cultural and historical traditions. Very probably, such countries will be found in the same geographical region.

It should be noted that such an attempt to solve the international trading problems on a regional or a limited grouping basis may embody a new form of conditional most-favored-nation treatment, though sanctioned by Article XXIV of the GATT—as distinct from the first principle of the GATT, that of unconditional nondiscrimination (Camps, 1974, pp. 49-50). I am not prepared to deny the validity of the principle of conditional most-favored-nation treatment entirely, because it still serves an important function in defending the rights of weaker nations in trade negotiations. But, in actual fact, the GATT's principle of unconditional nondiscrimination is honored more in breach than in observance, as exemplified by import restrictions directed at individual countries, bilaterally negotiated and imposed "voluntary export restraints," and sectorally negotiated "systems of industrial protection," such as the MFA. To the extent that import restrictions take the form of bilateral pressurizing, a regional attempt to liberalize trade within a group of countries, within which at least trade obligations are supposed to match trade rights, will undoubtedly represent a positive step forward toward "multilaterality" (Tumlir, 1974, p. 266).

The erosion of the principle of nondiscrimination has recently gone so far that even the commercial diplomacy of the United States appears to have radically departed from the traditional platform in the omnibus trade bill with strong elements of "reciprocity." The concept of reciprocity as a weapon in trade negotiations implies unilateral judgments on the part of the United States about market access in a foreign country, which will be the condition for granting equal market access (Weiss, 1983, p. 165). The principle of reciprocity is something basically different from the traditional liberal principle of national treatment, as the national treatment in a foreign country itself is made subject to international negotiations in the light of the customs and value system of the leading country. The principle of conditional most-favored-nation treatment also underlies the U.S. administration's proposal for a new North-South trade talk involving the establishment of a new most-favored-nation category of duty rates conditional on "graduation" of some more advanced developing countries. Anybody who has taken President Reagan's Caribbean Basin Initiative (Samolis, 1983, pp. 135, 140) seriously will not be able to withdraw effective support; David Sicip demanded that the first step towards Asian-Pacific economic integration should be a "Pacific Economic Community Initiative, providing for duty-free entry into developed country markets of the region of the products of the region's developing countries for a specified period of time" (submission by David Sicip, Pacific Economic Cooperation Conference, 1983, Appendix, pp. 78-80).

On the positive side, however, an intensified attempt at solving urgent economic problems on a regional basis will make important contributions to the management of growing world interdependence. Depending on the nature of particular problems, a more differentiated and flexible approach taking the specific circumstances of a given region into account will be required to organize effective consultation and cooperation in the changing environment of the world economy. A regional approach should therefore be regarded as supplementary to and supportive of a genuine global solution of the world trade problems. Emphasis is here on the progressive nature of any open regionalism, considering that the real alternative to regionalism is not global free trade as the first best solution, but rather prevailing ad hoc pressures for bilateral trade restrictions. It is in this context of uncoordinated national policies and unilateral or bilateral trade restrictions that a regional-multilateral approach appears a significant step forward toward global multilateralism.

Whether Japan can effectively contribute to making the Asian-Pacific region the dynamic basis from which expansionary influences will widely spread all over the world trade depends on its capacity to reorient its trade policy in adaptation to the development requirements of the region. A dynamic group of interdependent economies is already emerging in its neighborhood in East and Southeast Asia. They are prepared to play constructive roles in an expanding network of regional intra-industry specialization. Since Japan is already in a unique position as a major supplier of capital goods and savings for the region, the only requirement for Japan will be to give the highest priority to the trade demands of the region's developing countries for increases of imports of manufactured goods from them. This will provide Japan with the best opportunity to transform its structure of industrial production in the more balanced direction. A more balanced Japanese economy in this sense will be an indispensable element in the future well-balanced and stable system of growing economies that is expected to emerge in the Asian-Pacific region.

Notes

1. An important research project under the leadership of Professor I. Yamazawa is now in progress at the Institute of Developing Economies in Tokyo on the structural changes in patterns of trade in manufactured goods in the Asian-Pacific region. The research, partly linked with the international inter-industry analysis developed for the first time for this region, is focused on the policy agenda of industrial adjustment. The special issue of *The Developing Economies* (December 1983) on trends and structural changes in Pacific Asian countries included papers by some members of the group: Yamazawa et al., 1983, and Tanaka et al., 1983. The same issue also included a paper by K. Anderson, 1983. Reference is made to Aoki, Takeshi,

1983. In October 1984, the Japanese Economic Research Institute, Tokyo, issued a report entitled "Progress of Intra-Industry Specialization in Asia and Japan's Agenda" (in Japanese) (Japan Economic Research Institute, 1984).

2. It is interesting to note that the index of export similarity between the semi-industrial LDCs (NICs) and Japan is slightly higher than that between the semi-industrial LDCs and the United States or the old EEC.

References

Ahearn, Raymond J., "An Overview of the International Trading Environment," Rubin, Seymour J. and Thomas R. Graham (eds.), *Managing Trade Relations in the 1980s: Issues Involved in the GATT Ministerial Meeting, 1982,* Totowa, NJ: Rowman & Allanheld, 1983.

Anderson, K., "Prospects for Trade Growth Among Pacific Basin Countries," *The Developing Economies,* December 1983, Vol. XXI, No. 4.

Aoki, Takeshi, *Sengo Sekai Booeki no Hatten to Koozoo Henka* (The Development and Structural Changes in the Postwar World Trade) (in Japanese), Tokyo: Tanizawa Shoboo, 1983.

Balassa, Bela, "Industrial Prospects and Policies in the Developing Countries," in Machlup, Fritz, Gerhard Fels, and Hubertus Muller-Groeling (eds.), *Reflections on a Troubled World Economy: Essays in Honor of Herbert Giersch,* London: Macmillan, for the Trade Policy Research Center, 1983.

Camps, Miriam, *The Management of Interdependence—A Preliminary View,* New York: Council on Foreign Relations, Inc., 1974.

Cline, William R., *'Reciprocity': A New Approach to World Trade Policy,* Washington, D.C.: Institute of International Economics, 1982.

Finger, J.M., and M.E. Kreinin, "A Measure of 'Export Similarity' and Its Possible Use," *The Economic Journal,* December 1979, Vol. 89, No. 356.

Gavelin, L., and L. Lundberg, "Determinants of Intra-Industry Trade: Testing Some Hypotheses on Swedish Trade Data," in Tharakan, P.K.M. (ed.), *Intra-Industry Trade—Empirical and Methodological Aspects,* Amsterdam: North-Holland, 1983.

Grubel, Herbert G., and P.J. Lloyd, *Intra-Industry Trade; The Theory and Measurement of International Trade in Differentiated Products,* London: Macmillan, 1975.

Havrylyshyn, O., and E. Civan, "Intra-Industry Trade and the Stage of Development: A Regression Analysis of Industrial and Developing Countries," Tharakan, P.K.M. (ed.), *Intra-Industry Trade—Empirical and Methodological Aspects,* Amsterdam, North- Holland, 1983.

Japan Economic Research Institute, *Ajia Sangyonai Bungyoo no Shinten to Nihon no Kadai* (The Progress of Intra-Industry Specialization in Asia and Japan's Agenda) (in Japanese), October 1984.

Linnemann, Hans, *An Econometric Study of International Trade,* Amsterdam: North-Holland, 1966.

OECD, *Interfutures: Facing the Future—Mastering the Probable and Managing the Unpredictable,* Paris, 1979.

Pacific Economic Cooperation Conference, 1983, in Bali, November 1983. *Issues for Pacifice Economic Cooperation: A Report by the Task Forces,* Jakarta: Center for Strategic and International Studies, 1983.

Samolis, Frank R., "SOS for the CBI: Lessons of the Caribbean Basin Initiative," in Rubin, Seymour J., and Thomas R. Graham (eds.), *Managing Trade Relations in the 1980s: Issues Involved in the GATT Ministerial Meeting, 1982,* Totowa, NJ: Rowman & Allanheld, 1983.

Schumacher, D., "Intra-Industry Trade Between the Federal Republic of Germany and Developing Countries: Extent and Some Characteristics," in Tharakan, P.K.M. (ed.), *Intra-Industry Trade—Empirical and Methodological Aspects,* Amersterdam: North-Holland, 1983.

Tanaka, T., H. Osada, and K. Onoda, "Economic Development and the Structural Change of Trade in the Pacific Asian Region," *The Developing Economies,* December 1983, Vol. XXI, No 4.

Tharakan, P.K.M., "The Economics of Intra-Industry Trade: A Survey," in Tharakan, P.K.M. (ed.), *Intra-Industry Trade—Empirical and Methodological Aspects,* Amsterdam: North-Holland, 1983.

Tumlir, Jan, "Emergency Protection Against Sharp Increases in Imports," in Corbet, Hugh, and Robert Jackson (eds.), *In Search of a New World Economic Order,* London: Croom Helm, 1974.

Watanabe, T., and H. Kajiwara, "Pacific Manufactured Trade and Japan's Option," *The Developing Economies,* December 1983, Vol. XXI, No. 4.

Weiss, Leonard, "Reciprocity," in Rubin, Seymour J., and Thomas R. Graham (eds.), *Managing Trade Relations in the 1980s: Issues Involved in the GATT Ministerial Meeting 1982,* Totowa, NJ: Rowman & Allanheld, 1983.

Yamazawa, I., K. Taniguchi and A. Hirata, "Trade and Industrial Adjustment in Pacific Asian Countries," *The Developing Economies,* December 1983, Vol. XXI, No. 4.

Decision of the Central Committee of the Communist Party of China on Reform of the Economic Structure

The Third Plenary Session of the 12th Central Committee of the Communist Party of China, having analyzed the current economic and political situation in China and summed up the experience, both positive and negative, in socialist construction, and particularly that of reform of the economic structure in the urban and rural areas over the past few years, holds the consensus view that, proceeding from the overall need to build socialism with Chinese characteristics by integrating the basic tenets of Marxism with actual conditions in China, we must go a step further with the policy of invigorating the domestic economy and opening to the outside world and accelerate the restructuring of the national economy as a whole, with the focus on the urban economy, so as to create a new, better situation for our socialist modernization.

I. Reform Is a Pressing Necessity in the Current Developments in China

China has prepared and practiced reform of its economic structure for several years. The Third Plenary Session of the Party's 11th Central Committee, in deciding to shift the focus of the work of the whole Party to economic construction, stressed the imperative need to reform the economic structure for China's socialist modernization. The Party made tremendous efforts after that session to set things to rights and readjust the national economy, and carried out reform mainly in the rural areas. The 12th Congress, basing itself on the historic change consequent upon the rectification of the guiding ideology of the Party, set the explicit task of reforming the economic structure systematically. It

(Adopted by the 12th Central Committee of the Communist Party of China at Its Third Plenary Session on October 20, 1984)

pointed out that this reform would provide an important guarantee for keeping to the socialist road and achieving socialist modernization. In the past two years, and particularly since the beginning of this year, the Party Central Committee and the State Council have taken a number of policy decisions and issued major directives, stimulating reform in various fields in depth and breadth.

Our economic restructuring scored great achievements first in the countryside. Agricultural production, which worried us for so long, has been enabled to develop vigorously in a very short time, displaying the great vitality of our socialist agriculture. This is due fundamentally to a bold break with "Left" ideas. We have changed the structure of China's rural economy that was incompatible with the development of the forces of production in agriculture and introduced across the countryside the system of contracted responsibility for production with remuneration linked to output, bringing into play the enormous initiative of the 800 million peasants for building socialism. The rural reform is going forward and the rural economy is moving towards specialization, large-scale commodity production, and modernization. Therefore, there is an urgent need to unclog the channels of circulation between town and country, expand the market for the increasing amount of agricultural products, and satisfy the rising needs of the peasants for manufactured goods and science and technology, as well as culture and education. Our successes in rural reform and the demands on the cities by the growing rural economy provide highly favorable conditions for restructuring China's entire national economy, focusing on the urban economy.

Such restructuring has been repeatedly explored and tested in recent years, and a number of important measures have been taken. This has yielded marked results and important experience, and economic life has been invigorated to an extent unknown for many years. Our urban reform is only in the initial stage, however, and defects in the urban economic structure that seriously hinder the expansion of the forces of production are yet to be eradicated. The economic effectiveness of our urban enterprises is still very low, the huge potential of our urban economy is far from being fully tapped, and there is serious loss and waste in production, construction, and circulation. Expediting reform is a prerequisite for the growth of the urban economy. The cities are economic, political, scientific, technological, cultural, and educational centers where modern industry and members of the working class are concentrated and they play the leading role in socialist modernization. Firm, systematic reform is the only way that the cities will play their due leading role of invigorating the urban economy and enlivening the domestic economy, as well as opening to the outside world and promoting a healthier and faster development of the national economy as a whole.

It should also be noted that emerging on a global scale is a new technological revolution that presents both new opportunities and new challenges to our economic growth. This means that our economic structure must become better able to utilize the latest scientific and technological achievements, promoting scientific and technological advancement and generating new forces of production. Reform, therefore, is all the more imperative.

Political unity and stability in China are ever more consolidated; major successes have been achieved in economic readjustment; the economy has been growing steadily; the major targets of the Sixth Five-Year Plan (1981-85) have been fulfilled ahead of schedule; and the country's financial situation has improved gradually. This has made all comrades in the Party and the people of all nationalities much more confident about socialist modernization. Their wish to speed up reform of the economic structure is much stronger. In particular, the sound all-around consolidation of Party organizations at the central, the provincial, and the autonomous regional and municipal levels has set, or is setting, to rights the ideas guiding all fields of work in modernization and has given, or is giving, the reform a clear orientation. Conditions are now ripe for all-around reform of the economic structure. We both can and must raise and expound, in a rather systematic way, a number of major issues related to the reform so as to achieve unity of thinking and enhance it among all comrades in the Party (particularly among leading Party cadres). We must make the reform more effective and give fuller play to the superiority of socialism. The Central Committee hopes and is confident that the Third Plenary Session of the 12th Central Committee will play a historic role in drawing up a blueprint for an all-around reform, quickening its tempo, and stimulating the restructuring of the entire national economy with the urban economy as the focus, just as the Third Plenary Session of the 11th Central Committee did in setting things to rights and raising the task of restructuring the economy and promoting rural reform.

II. Reform is Aimed at Establishing a Dynamic Socialist Economic Structure

The founding of the People's Republic of China and the establishment of the socialist system marked the end of the century-old history of our people's misery in a semifeudal and semicolonial society. The system of exploitation was abolished and the people of all nationalities became real masters of their country. The people of the whole country, led by the Chinese Communist Party, have established an independent and fairly comprehensive industrial as well as national economic system through arduous efforts and have scored tremendous successes inconceivable in the old China, thus laying the indispensable material foundation for building China into a powerful and prosperous modern socialist country with a high level of democracy and civilization. The people of all our nationalities have come to realize through long historical experience that only socialism can save China.

The founders of Marxism predicted that by eliminating the exploitation of man by man, socialism would make possible a higher rate of labor productivity and a faster expansion of the forces of production. The profound changes that have taken place in the 35 years since the founding of the People's Republic are an initial demonstration of the superiority of the socialist system. But this superiority, it must be pointed out, has yet to be brought into full play. Apart from historical, political, and ideological causes, a major economic cause for this is a rigid economic structure that cannot meet the needs of the growing forces of production. Following are the major defects of this structure: No clear distinction has been drawn between the functions of the government and those of the enterprise; barriers exist between different departments or regions; the state has exercised excessive and rigid control over enterprises; no adequate importance has been given to commodity production, the law of value, and the regulatory role of the market; and there is absolute equalitarianism in distribution. This has resulted in enterprises lacking necessary decision-making power and the practice of "eating from the same big pot" prevailing in the relations of the enterprises to the state and in those of the workers and staff members to their enterprises. The enthusiasm, initiative, and creativeness of enterprises and workers and staff members have, as a result, been seriously dampened, and the socialist economy is bereft of much of the vitality it should possess.

China gradually established a unified and centralized economic structure on a nationwide scale in the early post- liberation days and during the First Five-Year Plan (1953-57) when the country faced the heavy tasks of unifying its financial and other economic work, carrying out socialist transformation of capitalist industry and commerce, and undertaking large-scale, planned economic construction. However, control then was not very rigid in many aspects, and the measures and steps we took for socialist transformation were based on China's actual conditions and were highly creative. But with the basic completion of socialist transformation and the ever-growing scale of economic construction, the measures taken to restrict and transform capitalist industry and commerce no longer suited the new situation. The defect of excessive and rigid control gradually became manifest in some aspects of the economic structure. The Central Committee and especially the comrades in overall charge of economic work, at the Eighth National Congress of the Party in 1956, as well as before and after, perceived this problem and raised some suggestions for correction. However, our Party was, after all, inexperienced in guiding socialist construction. Certain rigid concepts about socialism developed over the years that were not in keeping with the actual conditions in China. The influence of the "Left"-deviationist errors in the Party's guiding ideology after 1957, in particular, resulted in the various correct measures aimed at enlivening enterprises and developing socialist commodity economy being regarded as "capitalist." As a result of all these, the problem of overconcentration in the economic structure long remained unsolved and, what is more, became more and more serious. It is true that we tried to delegate power to lower levels on a number of occasions. But this was limited solely to readjusting the administrative power of the central and local authorities and of the different departments and regions. The critical issue of giving enterprises decision-making power was not dealt with. We therefore failed to break with outmoded conventions.

To bring about a radical change in the economic structure that hinders development of the forces of production, we must conscientiously sum up China's historical experience and study the concrete conditions and requirements for economic growth. In addition, we must draw on the world's advanced methods of management, including those of developed capitalist countries, that conform to the laws of modern, socialized production. In line with the Party's consistent principle of integrating the fundamental tenets of Marxism with China's actual conditions and the principle of adopting a correct approach towards foreign experience, the Central Committee holds that we must emancipate our minds more, follow our own road, and build a socialist economic structure with Chinese characteristics that is full of vigor and vitality so as to promote the growth of the forces of production. This is the fundamental objective of our present reform.

The basic contradiction in socialist society remains that between the relations of production and the forces of production, between the superstructure and the economic base. Reform of China's economic structure means reforming, on the premise of adherence to the socialist system, a series of interrelated links and aspects of the relations of production and the superstructure that are not suited to the development of the forces of production.

As a form of self-improvement and development of the socialist system, this reform is to be carried out under Party and government leadership in a planned, systematic, and methodical way. It should serve to advance, and not to impair, social stability, expansion of production, improvement of the people's living standards, and the growth of state revenue. The essential task of socialism is to develop the forces of production, create ever more social wealth, and meet the people's growing material and cultural needs. Socialism does not mean pauperism, for it aims at the elimination of poverty. We must, with firm determination and maximum tenacity, concentrate on economic development and modernize China's industry, agriculture, national defense, and science and technology. This is the inevitable trend of history and the wish of the people. In carrying out reform, all Party comrades must unfailingly grasp the above-mentioned basic concept of Marxism and set whether the reform facilitates this task as the most important criterion for assessing the success or failure of all reforms.

III. Invigorating Enterprises Is the Key to Restructuring the National Economy

The chief and direct responsibility for industrial production and construction and commodity circulation falls on urban enterprises. They constitute the main force spurring the growth of the forces of production and encouraging economic and technological progress. China now has over one million urban industrial, building, transport, commercial, and service enterprises, with a total work force of more than 80 million. The taxes and profits delivered by urban industrial enterprises alone account for over 80% of the state's revenue. This means that the enthusiasm, initiative, and creativity of the urban enterprises for production and operation, as well as their 80 million workers and staff members, must be brought into full play; in other words, the urban enterprises must have great vitality. This has a vital bearing on basic improvement of the national economy as a whole and of the state's financial and economic situation and on quadrupling China's annual industrial and agricultural output value by the end of the century, a task set by the Party's 12th National Congress. Socialism with Chinese characteristics should, first and foremost, be able to instill vitality into the enterprises. In essence, the drawbacks of our present economic structure are precisely the lack of vitality in our enterprises. Therefore, the key to reconstructing the national economy, with the focus on the urban economy, is invigoration of enterprises, particularly the large and medium-sized enterprises owned by the whole people.

With this key in mind, we must handle two types of relationships satisfactorily. That means we should extend the decision-making power of enterprises owned by the whole people by establishing a correct relationship between them and the state, and safeguard the status of the workers and staff members as masters of the enterprises by establishing correct relationships between them and their enterprises.

One of the main reasons why the state exercised excessive and rigid control over enterprises in the past was to equate the concept of their ownership by the whole people with the concept of their direct operation by the state institutions. As Marxist theory and the practice of socialism have shown, ownership can be duly separated from the power of operation. To make the economic activities of all enterprises conform to the overall requirement of economic growth, the socialist state institutions must manage, inspect, guide, and regulate the activities of the enterprises, as is necessary, through planning and by economic, administrative, and legal means; it must use taxation and other means to concentrate in its treasury that part of enterprises' net income that should be used by the state in a unified way; it must designate, appoint, and remove the principal leading members of the enterprises or approve their employment and election; and it must decide on the establishment of enterprises, their removal to other places, their switching over to other lines of products, their merger with others, suspension of operations, or closing down. However, since social demand is very complex and in a state of constant flux, since the conditions in enterprises differ in a thousand and one ways, and since the economic links between enterprises are complicated, no state institution can know the whole situation fully and cope with everything in good time. If the state institutions were to directly administer and manage various kinds of enterprises owned by the whole people, it would be very hard to avoid serious subjectivism and bureaucratism, with a consequent suppression of enterprise vitality. Therefore, on the premise of following the state plans and subjecting itself to state control, the enterprise has the power to adopt flexible and diversified forms of operation; plan its production, supply, and marketing; keep and budget funds it is entitled to retain; appoint, remove, employ, or elect its own personnel according to relevant regulations; decide on how to recruit and use its work force, and on wages and rewards; set the prices of its products within the limits prescribed by the state; and so on. In short, the enterprise should be truly made a relatively independent economic entity and should become a producer and operator of socialist commodity production that is independent and responsible for its own profit and loss and capable of transforming and developing itself and that acts as a legal person with certain rights and duties. This is the way to ensure both overall unity of the growth of the national economy as a whole and the diversity and flexibility of individual enterprises in production and management, as well as their desire to make progress. Instead of weakening socialist ownership by the whole people, this will contribute to consolidating and improving it.

The wellspring of vitality of the enterprise lies in the initiative, wisdom, and creativeness of its workers by hand and brain. When the status of the working people as masters of their own enterprise is guaranteed by its rules and regulations and when their labor is closely linked with their own material benefits, their initiative, wisdom, and creativeness can be brought into full play. This has been vividly and convincingly proved by our experience in rural reform. In restructuring the urban economy, it is imperative to handle correctly the relationship of the workers and staff to their enterprise so that they are its real masters and can work as such at their jobs. This will arouse their deep interest in the operation and effectiveness of their enterprise, so that their performance is closely linked with their social prestige and material benefits. Modern enterprise calls for centralized and unified leadership and direction of production and strict labor discipline. Because ours are socialist modern enterprises, in carrying out such centralized leadership and strict discipline, we must resolutely ensure the workers and staff and their elected representatives the right to participate in democratic management of the enterprise. Under socialism, there is unity between the authority of the enterprise's leadership and the status of the working people as masters of the enterprise and their initiative and creativity. This unity is a prerequisite for the proper, effective exercise of their initiative.

Correct relations between the state and the enterprise and between an enterprise and its workers and staff are the essence and basic requirement of the restructuring of the national economy as a whole with focus on the cities. Fulfillment of this basic requirement inevitably calls for reform of every aspect of the entire economic structure. This involves a whole range of reforms including planning, pricing, economic management by state institutions, and the labor and wage system. The Central Committee is of the opinion that these reforms should be carried out step by step in harmony with the inherent connections between the various links of the national economy, according to the degree of ripening of the subjective and objective conditions and in the right order of importance, urgency, and feasibility, and that they should basically be accomplished in about five years. Specific plans will be drawn up separately to this end.

IV. Establish a Planning System Under Which the Law of Value Is Consciously Applied for Developing a Socialist Commodity Economy

Socialist society practices a planned economy on the basis of public ownership of the means of production. It can thus avoid the anarchy of production and cyclical crises characteristic of capitalist society and ensure that production constantly meets the growing material and cultural needs of the people. This is one of the fundamental indicators of the superiority of a socialist economy over a capitalist economy. Since the founding of the People's Republic, we have practiced a planned economy and concentrated vast financial, material, and human resources on large-scale socialist economic construction, with tremendous achievements to our credit. At the same time, historical experience shows that the socialist planning system should be one that combines uniformity and flexibility. We must take into account China's vast territory and large population, the difficulty of drastically improving in a short period its poor transport conditions, its inadequate information facilities, and the obviously uneven economic and cultural development of its various regions; and we must realize that because of China's rather undeveloped commodity production at the present stage, it is necessary to stimulate commodity production and exchange. In view of all this, it is all the more urgent for us to institute this planning system. If the actual conditions of our country are ignored and if we try to incorporate all economic activities into the plans and implement them by administrative orders alone, in disregard of the importance of the economic levers and the market, then there will unavoidably be a discrepancy between the subjective guidelines for planning and objective conditions, with the plans seriously out of step with reality. After the October Revolution, Lenin expressed the idea when working out Russia's plan for electrification that "a complete, integrated, real plan for us at present--'a bureaucratic utopia.'" "Don't chase it,"[1] he added. Although China's conditions today are vastly different from those of Russia at that time when its economy was in extreme difficulties, our practical experience has proved that this idea of Lenin's was not only applicable to the Russia of that day, it is also of lasting significance. We must be realistic and admit that for a considerably long time to come, our national economic plans on the whole can only be rough and elastic and that we can do no more than, by striking an overall balance in planning and through regulation by economic means, exercise effective control over major issues while allowing flexibility on minor ones. In this way, we will be able to ensure the appropriate proportions between the major economic branches and, in general, the proportionate and coordinated growth of the national economy.

In the reform of the planning system, it is necessary, first of all, to discard the traditional idea of pitting the planned economy against the commodity economy. We should clearly understand that the socialist planned economy is a planned commodity economy based on public ownership, in which the law of value must be consciously followed and applied. The full development of a commodity economy is an indispensable stage in the economic growth of society and a prerequisite for our economic modernization. It is the only way to invigorate our economy and prompt enterprises to raise their efficiency, carry out flexible operations, and promptly adapt themselves to complex and changing social demands. This cannot be achieved by relying only on administrative means and mandatory plans. Meanwhile, we must also realize that the extensive growth of a socialist commodity economy may also lead to certain disorder in production, and there have to be guidance, regulation, and administrative control through planning. This can be achieved under socialist conditions. Therefore, a planned economy by no means excludes the application of the law of value and the growth of commodity economy; they in fact form a unity. It would be wrong to pose one against the other. The difference between socialist and capitalist economy, as far as a commodity economy and the law of value are concerned, lies not in whether these are still functioning, but the difference in ownership, in whether there is an exploiting class and whether the working people are masters of the state, in the different purposes of the production, in whether the law of value can be consciously applied throughout society, and in the different scopes of commodity relations. Under our socialist conditions, neither labor power nor land, mines, banks, railways, and all other state-owned enterprises and resources are commodities.

In the light of historical experience and the practice since the Third Plenary Session of the 11th Party Central Committee, the basic characteristics of our planning system can be further summed up as follows: First, ours is on the whole a planned economy, that is, a planned commodity economy, not a market economy that is entirely subject to market regulation. Second, production and exchange completely subject to market regulation are confined mainly to certain farm and sideline products, small articles of daily use, and labor services in the service and repair trades, all of which play a supplementary but indispensable role in the national economy. Third, our planned economy does not necessarily mean the predominance of mandatory planning, both mandatory and guidance planning being its specific forms. Fourth, guidance plans are fulfilled mainly by use of economic levers; mandatory plans have to be implemented, but even then the law of value must be observed. To reform our present planning system in accordance with the above points, it is necessary, step by step and to an appropriate extent, to reduce the scope of mandatory planning and extend guidance planning. Mandatory planning will be applied to major products that have a direct bearing on the national economy and the people's livelihood and that have to be allocated and distributed by the state, as well as major economic activities that affect the overall situation. Other products and economic activities that are far more numerous should either come under guidance planning or be left entirely to the operation of the market, as the case may require. The focus of planning will be shifted to medium and long-term planning, and annual plans will be appropriately simplified. There should be a corresponding reform of the methods of planning. Full attention should be paid to economic information and forecasting so as to raise the scientific level of planning.

V. Establish a Rational Price System and Pay Full Attention to Economic Levers

Because the law of value was long neglected and because of various other historical reasons, there is much confusion in our present system of pricing. The prices of many commodities reflect neither their value nor the relation of supply to demand. This irrational price system has to be reformed. Otherwise, it will be impossible to assess correctly the performance of enterprises, ensure the smooth circulation of goods between urban and rural areas, promote technological advances, and rationalize the production mix and consumption patterns. This will result in an enormous waste of social labor and seriously hamper application of the principle of distribution according to work. As the decision-making power of enterprises grows, pricing will be increasingly important in regulating their production and operation. It is, therefore, all the more urgent to establish a rational system of pricing. The various aspects of the reform in economic structure, including planning and wage systems, depend to a large extent on reform of the price system. Pricing is a most effective means of regulation, and rational prices constitute an important condition for ensuring a dynamic yet not chaotic economy. Therefore, reform of the price system is the key to reform of the entire economic structure.

Our present irrational price system finds expression mainly in the following: inadequate price differentials for a given product with diverse quality, irrational price ratios between different commodities, particularly the relatively low prices for some mineral products and raw and semifinished materials; and the retail price of major farm and sideline products being lower than their state purchasing price. From now on, we must gradually redress this irrational situation.

The irrational system of pricing is closely related to the irrational system of price control. In readjusting prices, we must reform the overcentralized system of price control, gradually reducing the scope of uniform prices set by the state and appropriately enlarging the scope of floating prices within certain limits and of free prices. Thus, prices will respond rather quickly to changes in labor productivity and the relation between market supply and demand and better meet the needs of national economic development.

As the reform of the price system affects every household and the national economy as a whole, we must be extremely prudent, formulate a well-conceived, feasible program based on the growth of production and the capability of state finances and on the premise that the people's real income will gradually be increased, and then carry it out in a planned and systematic way. The principles guiding the reform are: First, we should readjust irrational price ratios on the basis of the exchange of equal values and changes in the relation between supply and demand, lowering or raising prices as the case may be. Second, when the prices of some mineral products and raw and semifinished materials are raised, the processing enterprises must substantially cut down consumption so that the increased production cost resulting from the higher prices of such products and materials can be basically offset within the enterprises, with only a small part of the increase being borne by the state through tax reductions and exemptions. This will avoid a consequent rise in market sales prices of manufactured consumer goods. Third, in solving the problem of the states purchasing farm and sideline products at prices higher than their selling prices and in readjusting the prices of consumer goods, we must adopt effective measures to ensure that the real income of urban and rural inhabitants does not go down as a result of price readjustments. Instead, with the growth of production and improvement in economic results, the pay of workers and staff members will have to be raised gradually. It must be widely publicized among the people that on the condition of developed production and ever greater abundance of goods, the reform of the price system and readjustment of various irrational price ratios carried out on our own initiative will never bring about a general and spiralling price rise. Such a reform is the urgent need for further developing production and accords with the fundamental interests of the consumers. All enterprises should achieve better economic results through efforts to improve management and operation and should never try to increase their income by price increases. It is absolutely impermissible for any unit or person to boost prices at will by taking advantage of the reform, deliberately generating a tendency towards a general rise in prices, disrupting the socialist market, and harming the interest of the state and the consumers.

While reforming the price system, we should further improve the tax system and reform the financial and banking systems. The more the economy is enlivened, the more attention we should pay to macroeconomic regulation and the more we should try to have timely grasp of economic trends so as to use pricing, taxation, credit, and other economic levers better. This will help regulate such major proportional relations as those between aggregate social supply and aggregate social demand and between accumulation and consumption, regulate the direction of the flow of financial, material, and human resources, regulate the industrial setups and the distribution of the forces of production, regulate external economic exchange and so on. We have fallen into the habit of using administrative means to keep the economy functioning and have long neglected the use of economic levers for regulation. Economic departments at various levels, especially the departments in charge of comprehensive economic management, must take it as an important task to learn to use the economic levers and make this aspect the focus of our leadership over economic work.

VI. Separate Government Functions from Enterprise Functions so That Government Organs Can Properly Perform Their Function of Managing the Economy

After the proletariat and the whole people take state power in their hands, it becomes a basic function of the state organs to lead and organize economic construction. Over the past 30 years or more since the founding of New China, our state organs have, on the whole, played a significant role in performing this function. But how the state organs, especially government departments, can better lead and organize economic construction to meet the needs of the national economy and social development still remains a question calling for effective solution. The functions of government for a long time were not separated from those of enterprises, that in fact became appendages of administrative organs, and the central and local governments took responsibility for many matters which were not really theirs and at the same time did not do well what they ought to have done. This, plus the barriers between different departments or regions and the practice of endless wrangles, increased the difficulties in running enterprises. If this state of affairs were not changed, the enthusiasm of the enterprises and other grass-roots units could not be aroused; cooperation, association, and competition between enterprises could not develop; and a unified socialist market would not grow. Moreover, the role that government organs should play in managing the economy would be seriously weakened. So there is a pressing need to conduct reform in line with the principle of separating the functions of government and enterprises, streamlining administration and instituting decentralization in order to invigorate the enterprises and the national economy as a whole.

Practical experience over the years shows the following to be the principal functions of government organs in managing the economy: They should formulate the strategy, plans, principles, and policies for economic and social development; work out plans for the exploitation of natural resources, for technological transformation, and for the development of intellectual resources; coordinate the development plans of localities, departments, or enterprises and the economic relations among them; arrange for the construction of key projects, especially those in energy, transports, and the raw and semifinished materials industries; collect and disseminate economic information, learn to utilize economic means of regulation; work out economic regulations and ordinances and supervise their execution; appoint and remove cadres within a prescribed scope; administer matters related to external economic and technological exchanges and cooperation; etc. The performance of these functions requires immense efforts on the part of the governments at various levels. In the past, some of the functions were not performed well and others not performed at all. As far as the relations between governments and enterprises are concerned, from now on government departments at various levels will, in principle, not manage or operate enterprises directly. As for the small number of government economic departments that have been entrusted by the state with direct operations and management of enterprise, they must also correctly handle their relations with the enterprises under them through simpler administration and decentralization so as to enhance the capacity of enterprises and other grass-roots units for independent management and avoid drawbacks that may arise from overcentralization. The national and local corporations are economic associations set up for better economic development and mutual benefit of enterprises concerned. They must be enterprises and not administrative organs, and must not follow old practices, but should master modern methods of scientific management.

After the functions of government and enterprises are separated, the central role of cities must be brought into full play, and open and interconnected economic zones of various sizes must gradually be formed with support from cities, the large and medium-sized cities in particular. In this reform, it is necessary to call the attention of all leading urban comrades to the need for the city governments to separate their functions from those of enterprises and achieve simpler and decentralized administration, and not to repeat the past practice of mainly depending on administrative means to control enterprises so as to avoid creating new barriers between departments or regions. City governments should concentrate on urban planning, construction, and management; building public facilities; carrying out comprehensive ecological improvement; guiding and promoting the specialized cooperation of enterprises, their reorganization, association and technical transformation, and the modernization of their management and operation; guiding and promoting a rational circulation of materials and commodities; improving cultural, educational, public health, and social-welfare work, and various services; promoting the building of a civilization with a high cultural and ideological level, and the fostering of better social conduct; and maintaining public order. Moreover, they should also work out satisfactory medium- and long-term plans for economic and social development based on the general requirements of developing the national economy and on local conditions.

   The relationship between socialist enterprises is first of all one of cooperation and mutual support, but this by no means excludes competition. For a long time, people used to consider competition peculiar to capitalism. As a matter of fact, where there is commodity production, there is bound to be competition. The point is that the purposes, nature, scope, and means of competition vary under different social systems. Competition between socialist enterprises is fundamentally different from that under capitalism, where the law of the jungle prevails. On the basis of public ownership and subject to the control of state planning and laws, and for the purpose of serving socialist modernization, our enterprises are put to the test of direct judgment by consumers in the marketplace so that only the best survive. This will help to break the blockade and monopoly hampering the growth of production, lay bare the defects of enterprises quickly, and stimulate enterprises to improve technology, operation, and management. It will stimulate the economy as a whole and benefit socialism. As for some undesirable trends and unlawful acts that may appear in the course of competition, the relevant leading organs at various levels should keep a clear head and strengthen education and control and tackle such problems in real earnest.

More and more norms guiding economic relations and activities will have to be framed in the form of law in the restructuring of the economy and national economic development. State legislative bodies must produce economic legislation faster, the courts should make greater efforts to try economic cases, the procuratorates should strengthen their work in dealing with economic crimes, and the judicial departments should offer active legal services for economic construction.

The separation of the functions of government and enterprises as well as simpler and decentralized administration constitute a deep-going transformation of the socialist superstructure. When the structure changes, the organization and the style of thinking and work should also change. We must unhesitatingly change the working style of government departments in accordance with the principles of serving the people and of streamlining, of unifying and increasing efficiency and raising the competence of their functionaries. We must end the long-standing practice of leading organs making enterprises and units completely dependent on them, instead of serving the enterprises and other grass-roots units, and eliminate such bureaucratic maladies as organizational overlapping, overstaffing, vague delimitation of functions, and endless wrangling. The leading organs at various levels will thus be able to orient their work towards promoting production, serving the enterprises and other grass-roots units, and helping build a strong and prosperous country and bring prosperity and happiness to the people.

VII. Establish Various Forms of Economic Responsibility System and Conscientiously Implement the Principle of Distribution According to Work

Experimental urban reforms in the past few years have amply demonstrated that the basic experience of the system for contracted responsibility in the rural areas is also applicable in the cities. Enterprises must specify in explicit terms the requirements for each work post and the duties of each worker and staff member and must establish various forms of the economic responsibility system with contracted jobs as the main content so as to invigorate the urban enterprises, raise the sense of responsibility of the workers and staff members, and bring into full play their initiative, enthusiasm, and creativeness. The basic principles of this responsibility system are a combination of responsibility, authority, and benefit; the unity of the interests of the state, the collectives, and the individuals; and the linking of the income of workers and staff members with their job performance. In applying rural experience to urban areas, we must take into account the characteristics of urban enterprises. It is neither feasible nor necessary to transplant mechanically the specific measures of the rural areas. As the nature of trades and the size and production conditions of enterprises differ from one another, urban enterprises cannot follow a single model of responsibility system. Our comrades, leading comrades of enterprises in particular, should always proceed from reality and in the course of practice gradually work out concrete forms of the responsibility system suited to their specific conditions. Then the contracted responsibility system will take root, blossom, and bear fruit in the cities.

Modern enterprises have a minute division of labor, a high degree of continuity in production, strict technological requirements, and complex relations of cooperation. It is therefore necessary to establish a unified, authoritative, and highly efficient system to direct production and conduct operations and management. This calls for a system of the director or manager assuming full responsibility. Party organizations in enterprises should actively support directors in exercising their authority in giving unified direction to production and operations, guarantee and supervise the implementation of the principles and policies of the Party and the state, strengthen the Party's ideological and organizational work in enterprises, improve their leadership over the trade unions and Communist Youth League organizations, and do effective ideological and political work among the workers and staff members. While the director assumes full responsibility, we must improve the system of congresses of workers and staff members and other systems of democratic management and give play to the authority and role of the trade union organizations and workers' and staff members' deputies in examining and discussing major decisions to be taken by the enterprise, supervising administrative leadership, and safeguarding the legitimate rights and interests of the workers and staff members. All of this expresses the status of the working people as masters of the enterprise. Their status is determined by the nature of the socialist enterprise and must in no way be neglected or weakened.

With the general replacement of profit delivery by taxes and the widespread establishment of various forms of economic responsibility in enterprises, the socialist principle of distribution according to work will be implemented more fully. An important step already taken in this respect is that enterprises decide on the amount of bonuses for their workers and staff members according to the results of enterprise operation, while the state only collects an appropriate amount of tax on the above-norm bonus from enterprises. In the future, adequate measures will be taken to better link wages and bonuses with the improved enterprise performance. In the enterprises, the difference between the wages of various trades and jobs should be widened so as to apply fully the principle of rewarding the diligent and good and punishing the lazy and bad and of giving more pay for more work and less pay for less work, as well as to fully reflect the differences between mental and manual, complex and simple, skilled and unskilled, and heavy and light work. In particular, it is necessary to change the present remuneration for mental work, which is relatively low. We should also reform the wage system in state institutions and public organizations in accordance with the principle of linking wages with responsibilities and achievements. While reform of the wage system in enterprises, state institutions and public organizations is under way, the reform of the labor system will be speeded up.

There has long been a misunderstanding about the distribution of consumer goods under socialism, as if it meant equalitarianism. If some members of society got higher wages through their labor, resulting in wide gaps in income, it was considered polarization and a deviation from socialism. This equalitarian thinking is utterly incompatible with scientific, Marxist views on socialism. History has shown that equalitarian thinking is a serious obstacle to implementing the principle of distribution according to work and that if it is unchecked, the forces of production will inevitably be undermined. Naturally, a socialist society must guarantee its members a gradual improvement in material and cultural life and their common prosperity. But common prosperity cannot and will never mean absolute equalitarianism or that all members of society become better off simultaneously at the same speed. If common prosperity were understood as absolute equalitarianism and simultaneous prosperity, not only would this be impossible, but such thinking would lead to common poverty. Only when some regions, enterprises, and individuals are allowed and encouraged to get better off first through diligent work can there be a strong attraction and inspiration to the majority of the people. More and more people will be prompted to take the road of prosperity, one group after another. At the same time, we must provide social relief for the old, weak, sick, disabled, and for widows, widowers, orphans, and childless elders who cannot support themselves. We must aid those who have not yet become well-off and adopt special and preferential policies towards some old revolutionary-base areas, minority nationality, and remote and other areas where the economy is still very backward and give them the necessary material and technical assistance. The difference arising from the prosperity of some people before others is a difference in speed, with all members of society advancing on the road to common prosperity. It is certainly not polarization, which means that a handful of people become exploiters while the vast majority fall into poverty. The policy of encouraging some people to get better off earlier accords with the law of socialist development and is the only road to prosperity for the whole of society.

We must never discard the fine tradition of working hard and building the country through diligence and thrift that was developed during the long period of our revolution and construction. In the new historical period, this tradition chiefly means the spirit of working hard and defying all difficulties in dedication to the motherland and the people, practice of strict economy in production and construction, opposition to any act that squanders state materials and funds, and avoidance of erroneous policy decisions that result in waste. It should not be misconstrued as overlooking due growth in the people's level of consumption. According to the basic tenets of Marxism, production is the starting point and the predominant factor of all economic activities and determines consumption; but consumption also determines production in that the growth of consumption gives a strong impetus to creation of new social demands, opens up vast markets, and encourages production. We must gradually bring about substantial increases in the pay of workers and staff members and in the people's level of consumption. This should be based on increased production, better economic results, a steady increase in state revenue, and a correct proportion of accumulation and consumption. It is incorrect to put forward demands for consumption in excess of the capacity of current production. But it is likewise incorrect not to appropriately increase but keep restricting consumption that is well within the capacity of current production.

VIII. Work to Develop Diverse Economic Forms and Continue to Expand Foreign and Domestic Economic and Technological Exchanges

We must mobilize all positive factors if we are to achieve rapid growth in all fields of production and construction and make our country strong and prosperous and our people rich and happy at a fairly fast pace. Under the guidance of state policies and planning, the initiative of the state, the collective, and the individual should all be encouraged. We must work to develop diversified economic forms and various methods of management. And we must actively expand foreign economic cooperation and technological exchange on the basis of independence, self-reliance, equality and mutual benefit, and mutual good faith.

Enterprises owned by the whole people constitute the leading force in China's socialist economy and are decisive in ensuring our socialist orientation and the steady growth of our entire national economy. But their consolidation and development should not be predicated on restriction and exclusion of other economic forms and other methods of management. The collective economy is an important component of the socialist economy, and we can give the collectives a free hand in running enterprises in many areas of production and construction. The individual economy now found in China is linked with socialist public ownership and differs from the individual economy linked with capitalist private ownership. It plays an irreplaceable role in expanding production, meeting the people's daily needs, and providing employment. It is a necessary and valuable adjunct to the socialist economy and is subordinate to it. At present, we should try to remove obstacles in the way of the collective economy and individual economy in cities and rural towns and create conditions for their development and give them the protection of the law. We should promote individual economy, particularly in those economic fields mainly based on labor services and where decentralized operation is suitable. Meanwhile, we should, on the basis of voluntary participation and mutual benefit, extensively encourage diverse and flexible forms of cooperative management and economic association among the state, collective, and individual sectors of the economy. Some small state-owned enterprises can be leased to collectives or individuals, or run by them on a contract basis. It is our long-term policy and the need of socialist development to promote diversified economic forms and various methods of operation simultaneously. This is not retrogression to the new-democratic economy of the early period of the People's Republic when the socialist public ownership was not yet predominant in town and country. Far from undermining China's socialist economic system, the new policy will help consolidate and develop it.

Marx and Engels pointed out long ago in the *Manifesto of the Communist Party* that with the exploitation of the world market due to the growth of capitalism, the old local and national seclusion and self-sufficiency had given place to intercourse between nations in every direction, and production and consumption in every country had become cosmopolitan in character. The productive forces including science and technology in our times are developing ever faster. Although international relations are complex and ridden with contradictions, international economic and technological ties are, generally speaking, very close, and national seclusion cannot lead to modernization. Since the Third Plenary Session of the 11th Central Committee, we have taken opening to the outside world to be our long-term, basic state policy, a strategic measure for accelerating socialist modernization. Practice has already yielded marked results. We must continue to pursue flexible policies and reform our foreign trade structure in line with the principle of both arousing the enthusiasm of all quarters and developing a unified approach in our external dealings. We will work to expand economic and technological exchanges and cooperation with other countries, strive for the success of the special economic zones, and open more coastal cities. Using foreign funds and attracting foreign businessmen for joint ventures, cooperative management, or exclusive investment in enterprises are also a necessary and beneficial complement to China's socialist economy. We must make the best use of both domestic and foreign resources and both the domestic and foreign markets, and learn both to organize domestic construction and develop foreign economic relations.

As we open to the outside world, we shall open up even more between different areas within China itself. We should smash blockades and open doors in the relations between economically more developed and less developed areas, coastal areas and interior and border areas, cities and countryside, and between all trades and enterprises. We must act in conformity with the principle of making the best possible use of favorable conditions and avoiding the effects of unfavorable ones, developing diversity of forms, offering mutual benefit, and achieving common progress, and strive to develop economic relations among enterprises and regions; promote appropriate exchanges of funds, equipment, technology, and qualified personnel; introduce diverse forms of economic and technological cooperation; and run joint economic enterprises. This will speed up the rationalization of our economic setup and of the geographical distribution of our enterprises and accelerate modernization.

IX. Promote a New Generation of Cadres and Create a Mighty Contingent of Managerial Personnel for the Socialist Economy

Reform of our economic structure and the development of our national economy badly need a large contingent of managerial and administrative personnel, and especially managers, who are both knowledgeable in modern economics and technology and imbued with a creative, innovative spirit and who are capable of bringing about a new situation in whatever they do. The point now is that our contingent of managerial personnel falls far short of the above requirements. We have large numbers of veteran comrades in this contingent who, in the long period of hard struggle, have made great contribution to our socialist economic construction. Their good work style, managerial ability, and steadfastness in observing the rules of inner-Party life had an educational influence on many young and middle-aged cadres. But they are getting up in years, and we can no longer ask them to continue in arduous leading posts. Our present urgent task is to promote boldly thousands upon thousands of young and middle-aged managerial personnel and take steps to train them.

Large numbers of talented persons have come to the fore in economic construction, especially in the course of Party consolidation and the reform of the economic structure. Party committees at all levels must take pains to discover and assess them and must not be fettered by outdated ideas and conventions. They must not fault-find and demand perfection and must guard against the influence of factionalism and gossip. When we act in this manner, we can discover large numbers of excellent cadres. Of course, young and middle-aged cadres lack experience in giving leadership. But they can gain experience through tempering in practical work and will gradually do so. Under no circumstances should we use lack of experience as an excuse for holding back young cadres. We have to be analytical in our attitude to experience. Our comrades accumulated rich experience, both positive and negative, in the course of revolution and construction. This is very valuable. Generally speaking, however, all our cadres—old, middle-aged, or young—are facing brand-new tasks in the new historical period and all lack the new knowledge and experience necessary for modernization. All of them will have to reevaluate their capabilities and make new efforts to learn. It would be wrong to hang on to the outmoded and rest complacent about experience that is no longer applicable.

The Central Committee calls for completion of the reshuffling of leadership in enterprises, especially key enterprises, before the end of 1985. In addition, plans should be drawn up and effective measures taken to train fairly soon large numbers of the following: directors (managers) who can successfully organize and direct enterprise production and operations; of chief engineers who can strengthen technical management and promote technological progress; chief economic managers who can improve business operations for better economic results; chief accountants who can strictly uphold financial and economic discipline, do careful budgeting, and exploit new sources of revenue, and Party secretaries who can keep to a correct political orientation and unite the workers and staff members of the enterprises. This is how to create a mighty contingent of managerial and technical cadres for the socialist economy. This contingent should consist of qualified personnel in all trades and occupations for the whole chain of enterprise management.

The Central Committee has pointed out on many occasions that in our drive for socialist modernization, we must respect knowledge and talented people. We must combat all ideas and practices that belittle science and technology, the cultivation of intellectual resources, and the role of intellectuals. We must take resolute action to redress cases of discrimination against intellectuals which still exist in many localities and to raise the social standing of intellectuals and improve their working and living conditions. All our reforms must lead to progress in science and technology, to greater initiative of the localities, departments, units, and individuals in making effective use of intellectual resources, and must enable our vast numbers of young people, as well as workers, peasants, and intellectuals, to raise their cultural and technical levels quickly. Those who have made important inventions and innovations or other outstanding contributions should be amply rewarded.

Science, technology, and education are extremely important in developing our national economy. Advances in reforming the economic structure pose as a matter of increasingly urgent strategic importance the reform of our scientific, technical, and educational setups. The Central Committee will hold special discussions on these issues and take relevant decisions.

X. Strengthen Party Leadership to Ensure the Success of Reforms

Reform of China's economic structure will be carried out over a fairly broad area and in a fairly deep-going way. It will have a direct bearing on the nation's future and affect the vital interests of millions upon millions of workers, peasants, and intellectuals. All Party comrades should stand in the forefront of the reform, which represents the trend of our times. This reform is an exploratory and innovative undertaking by the masses, and it is very complex. We are generally now at the stage of accumulating experience in the reform of the entire economic structure that focuses on cities, and the vast number of cadres are not familiar with this work. Leading Party and government functionaries at all levels have to be sober-minded and give meticulous guidance. They should emancipate their minds, seek truth from facts and proceed from reality and carry out Party policies creatively by integrating them with the actual situation in each locality, department, and unit. Full consideration should be given to the particularities of the regions concerned in reforming the economic structure in minority nationality regions. All moves in the reform have to be tested in practice, through which new experience will be acquired. Errors can hardly be avoided, but we should make every effort to prevent them whenever possible. Once an error does occur, we must try to discover it promptly, resolutely correct it, draw the lessons, and continue to go ahead. We should take active but prudent steps in carrying out reforms. We should carry them out firmly where we are sure of success, make reforms one by one when the conditions are ripe, and make experiments when we are not sure of success. We must not try to accomplish the whole task at one stroke. All major reforms that affect the whole country will be arranged by the State Council under a unified plan. All localities, departments, and units should be encouraged to conduct exploratory and pilot reforms. Nevertheless, any reform involving the overall situation or one that is extensive in scope must first be approved by the State Council.

Party organizations in numerous localities and enterprises will undergo consolidation next year. Reform should be closely linked with this. Party consolidation should promote economic growth, which is an indicator of how successful it is. While carrying out the reform, we must strengthen the leadership over Party consolidation, making sure that the consolidation will not become a mere formality. The more we enliven the economy and invigorate enterprises, the more we must pay attention to combating the corrosive influence of capitalist ideas, eliminating the decadent practice of seeking personal gain by abusing one's position and authority and preventing any action that seriously harms the interests of the state and the consumers, and the more we should strengthen the building of a fine Party style and sense of discipline and maintain healthy inner-Party political life. In ideological and organizational work in the new historical period, we must firmly carry out the Party's guiding principle that such work should help fulfill the general task and reach the general goal set by the Party and be closely linked with economic construction and reform of the economic structure. We should actively support cadres and the masses who are keen on reforms. When errors or deviations appear in the course of reform, apart from those seriously violating the law and discipline that must be dealt with according to law, we should adopt a policy of persuasion, criticism, and education towards the persons concerned and must not stick political labels on them. People with different views and approaches about reforms may discuss their differences. We must not divide the cadres and masses by calling some people "reformers" and others "conservatives." We should have faith in comrades who fall behind the development situation for a time, confident that they will understand things better in the course of reform. In the past five years of rural reform, many comrades who had doubts about it have been convinced by the facts and have changed their views. The Central Committee has adhered to the principle of patient education in guiding rural reform, thereby ensuring its smooth progress. This is a valuable experience in solving ideological problems inside the Party on the question of major policies, and we should keep to this principle in the future. By citing the facts about reform, we should provide Party members and the masses with lively education in the theory and policies of the reform. This will help them realize that socialism with Chinese characteristics should be full of vitality, different from the rigid pattern of the past and fundamentally different from the capitalist system. This will deepen their understanding of scientific socialism so that they devote themselves to making reforms.

The reform of economic structure will lead to tremendous changes not only in people's economic life, but also in their mental outlook and way of life. We should build socialist civilization with both a high material level and high cultural and ideological level. This is our Party's unswerving principle. While trying to create a socialist economic structure full of vigor, we should work to create a cultured, healthy, and scientific way of life for the whole society that meets the requirements of expanding the modern forces of production and social progress, and eliminate backward and decadent ideas and ignorance. We should foster throughout society an active, forward-looking, and enterprising attitude and overcome such forces of habit as complacency, mental sluggishness, fear of change, and conventionality. Such an approach to life and such an attitude are important aspects of a socialist civilization that has a high cultural and ideological level. They give great impetus to reform of the economic structure and the building of a socialist civilization with a high material level. Comrade Mao Zedong said, "Mankind makes constant progress and nature undergoes constant change; they never remain at the same level. Therefore, man has constantly to sum up experience and go on discovering, inventing, creating, and advancing. Ideas of stagnation, pessimism, inertia, and complacency are all wrong. They are wrong because they agree neither with the historical facts of social development nor with the historical facts of nature so far known to us."[2] This statement is a graphic expression of one of the fundamental points of view of the Marxist world outlook and conception of history. The Chinese Communists take the constant promotion of social development and progress as their historical mission. Our Party led the masses of the people under reactionary rule in the past in making revolution to overthrow the old order. Under the socialist system with the people as masters of the country, our Party has been leading the masses in conscientiously carrying out reforms and building China into a modern, powerful socialist country with a high level of culture and democracy.

The current situation is very favorable to reform. The people are highly creative in this endeavor. By relying on their wisdom and strength and adhering to the four cardinal principles,[3] we will certainly succeed in our reform and fulfill the general task and reach the general goal set by the Party's 12th National Congress.

NOTES

1. V.I. Lenin, *Collected Works,* Eng. ed., Progress Publishers. Moscow, 1966, Vol. 35, p. 475.

2. Quoted in "Premier Zhou Enlai's Report on the Work of the Government to the First Session of the Third National People's Congress of the People's Republic of China" (December 21-22, 1964).

3. This means keeping to the socialist road, upholding the people's democratic dictatorship, upholding leadership by the Communist Party, and upholding Marxism-Leninism and Mao Zedong Thought.

Formulas for Productivity Growth

Productivity Standard: For a Healthier Global Economy

by

Christos N. Athanasopoulos

Simply put, a productivity standard means tying wage and salary raises to productivity gains but neither at the departmental or functional level (as piece rates for blue collar workers only) nor at the national level (with uniform rates and terms across whole diverse industries as labor-management contracts are drawn up now). Ideally, the productivity standard should be applied at the company level. It can also be applied at the divisional or as far down as the plant level.

We need a flexible form of productivity standard as an instrument of connecting domestic prices with domestic costs and prices in the American economy with prices in other economies with which we are in competition. We need the productivity standard to keep wages tied to productivity gains and, therefore, to prevent the costs and prices of American goods from making them unable to compete in world markets. Furthermore, we need the productivity standard to prevent the further loss of millions of American jobs to foreign competitors who are able to supply the American market with products of higher quality at lower prices. For shoes, textiles, steel, machinery, automobiles, and tires, foreign competitors have acquired between 20% and 50% of the American market, the world's largest. If we do not find viable answers for the steel and auto industries of today, other industries will join them tomorrow. How long, for instance, will it take the Japanese to do the same thing to the American computer industry as they did to the American auto industry?

Christos N. Athanasopoulos is an associate professor of management at Western New England College, Springfield, Massachusetts.

Diagram A illustrates the need for a productivity standard and a way to smooth out the steep ups and downs in both the productivity rate and the inflation rate. Therefore, the formulation: tie wage rates to productivity gains to avoid the very negative effects of prices' going up and down with the frequency of one inflation surge every four or five years (we have had three cyclical rounds between 1968 and 1983).

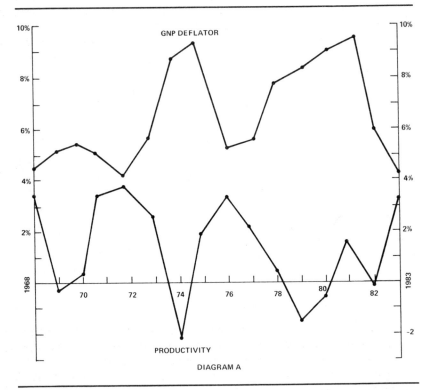

DIAGRAM A

Does the application of the productivity standard mean lower wages for everyone? Not at all. Industries with rising productivity can have rising wage rates without fueling inflation on the one hand and without risking declines in sales and employment on the other. *The crucial point is that wage increases do not outpace productivity gains.* The behavioral sequel to this is that if employees have a contractual agreement with their employer (a productivity standard agreement), then they will be more cooperative, perhaps even very cooperative, with management on ways to improve productivity. This would lead to labor contracts based on economic realities rather than wage increases obtained through political means—the threat of a strike. If steel workers had increased their productivity enough between 1972 and 1982, they would still have made $16.35 an hour and possibly more in 1982 (without benefits). Further, they would not have caused the influx of steel imports that resulted in the loss of one million jobs in basic steel and metal product industries.

The cyclical pattern of productivity and inflation is shown in a more abstract way in Diagram B. Productivity and inflation each follow an S-shaped curve lying sideways to and mirroring each other (ignoring the fact that productivity usually leads inflation). The 1972-1976 period best shows this symmetric pattern. One is tempted to call it the "productivity-inflation roller coaster."

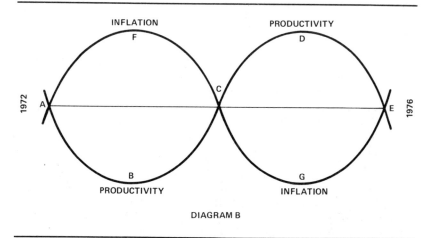

DIAGRAM B

With productivity-standard contracts between labor and management, there will be no drop in productivity at the cyclical booms because there will be no "booms" as we know them today. And there will be no "troughs" as we know them today. The powerful brake of tying wages to productivity will keep the economy going at a much steadier pace. This will eliminate hasty accelerations upward and hectic slides downward.

It is human nature to delay taking action until or unless we are forced to do so. Inflation was well below 10% in the early 1970s, and no massive layoffs had occurred yet in the steel and motor-vehicles industries. Double-digit inflation came in 1974, followed by massive layoffs in these industries five years later. Then, in 1980, conditions were ripe and compelling for the productivity standard. If we are willing to focus our attention on and debate openly the connection between productivity and inflation in 1984, we are moving rather swiftly to lay the groundwork for the acceptance of new concepts. My participation in the White

House Conference on Productivity during 1983 triggered and inspired my thinking on the productivity standard as the surest way to fight worldwide stagflation.

The application of the productivity standard can bring about a significant and critical measure of anti-inflation defense that is not envisioned by the monetary and fiscal tools of the Keynesian megatheory or the monetarist "counterrevolution." Those tools gave us only hand brakes. They never gave us the power brakes that we need to keep our modern economic systems going at a steady speed with the assurance that we can come to a stop without overturning our economic vehicles at regular intervals as we do today. Milton Friedman's 20-year-old argument that you can have full employment with price stability by simply managing money supply better has proved as impotent as pure Keynesian tools have. Trying to control an economy by the monetarist tools is like trying to control a steaming boiler by applying pressure on the lid from above rather than slowing down the fuel pressure from below. The productivity standard does just that. It regulates the "energy pressure" from below (wages are tied to productivity) so you don't have to deal with a steaming boiler every four or five years.

Besides, unlike the Keynesian or monetarist tools that rely exclusively on the government bureaucrats in Washington or Paris or London for their administration, the productivity standard can and should be administered independently by each economic organization (public or private) in cooperation with its employees (with or without a union). This is tantamount to installing a thermostat at every point where costs, wages, and prices are decided every day rather than waiting for the cumbersome political machinery in each modern economy to take corrective measures based on its own political mega-thermostat that almost always leans toward political expediencies rather than economic necessities. And in terms of economic ideology, the productivity standard is both more "progressive" than Keynesian tools and more "conservative" than monetarist tools. Its implications in terms of greater economic freedom and greater industrial democracy are staggering.

Existing tools are mono-directional. They can fight unemployment at the expense of fueling inflation (Keynesian) or they can fight inflation at the expense of higher unemployment (monetarist). The productivity standard is a multidirectional tool. It has a two-pronged effect. It is both anti-inflationary and anti-unemployment at the same time (see discussion of the Chrysler case below).

Movements like the "quality circles" and employee-participation groups that are already flourishing can complement the broader concept of the productivity standard. The advent of a limited American version of what the Europeans and the Japanese call "industrial policy" would also be a synergistic supplement to the more universal instrument of the productivity standard.

The basic premise of the productivity standard rests on the fact that almost 70% of U.S. GNP is received as compensation by those who work for somebody else, that is, as income of "employees." This means that the cost of every good or service that is exchanged consists on the average of 70% "labor costs," that is, compensation of those who are paid to invent, design, produce, advertise, market, sell, deliver or service it.

If the basis of arriving at how much each "contributor" to the final product will receive becomes part of an economic process rather than remains part of a political process as it is today, then the productivity standard method is the most effective tool to advance not only the competitiveness and survival of the producing organization (corporation) but the effective instrument that will make the objectives of the organization and the objectives of its individual members one and the same.

First Application: ABC

A hypothetical example follows. Assume that we are Company ABC and want to explore the potential of the productivity standard. We like the idea of applying it at the company level, so we want a method for determining how much we could offer in the form of annual raises next year to our 1,000 employees without having to raise prices due to higher labor costs.

Predictably, the first step is to compute a productivity index for ABC this year. This will show whether ABC did better this year than the previous one in converting raw materials and human talents into useful products or services. Computing the productivity index at the company level has the substantive advantage of dealing with a homogeneous measuring "rod," the dollar, rather than the units of toasters produced by Department A, refrigerators produced by Department B, and perhaps meters of copper wire made by Department C. It also accepts the impossibility of measuring and separating the contribution of the janitors or the members of the board to the company's net output.

Let's assume that ABC had net sales of $100 million this year and $90 million the year before. Let's assume further that there was no change in the total hours worked or in the total number of ABC employees between this year and the year before (1,000 persons). Assume also that ABC bought raw materials and other parts or services (inputs) worth $60 million in 1983 and $55 million in 1982. The difference between net sales (outputs) and outside purchase (inputs) is what economists call "value added." I call it "gross corporate product."

In Table 1 we have:

Table 1
Company ABC

Fiscal Year	1983	1982
Net sales (Outputs)	$100M	$90M
Less Outside Purchases (Inputs)	$60M	55M
Gross Corporate Product	$40M	$35M
Number of employees	1,000	1,000
GCP per employee	$40,000	$35,000
Human Productivity Index	114	100

Each employee of ABC contributed on the average $40,000 to the U.S. economy in 1983 as compared to $35,000 in 1982. The entire company ABC contributed $40 million in 1983 and $35 million in 1982 to the country's GNP (assuming no overseas operations). Therefore, total annual "productivity" per employee increased from $35,000 last year to $40,000 this year or by 14% in current dollars (human productivity index: 114).

How many U.S. companies come up with this simple but powerful type of computation each year? How many American companies know how much they contribute each year to the nation's GNP and how they fare in overall productivity comparisons with their competitors here and abroad? How many U.S. companies plan on the basis of how much they need to raise their productivity index in order to avoid raising prices? Not very many. More companies abroad use this method than in the United States. In fact, it was in Europe that I learned how to compute productivity indices at the company level myself. Indeed, I was advising companies on how much they had to raise productivity in order to absorb government-imposed wage increases without raising their prices.

We have computed the human productivity index of ABC. It stood at 114 for 1983, which means 14%-higher total productivity per person than the year before. We said this is in current dollars, which means we have to take off inflation before we arrive at the figure that we need. Assuming that inflation was 4% in 1983, we subtract it from our human productivity index in "current" dollars

(114) to arrive at the index of 110 for 1983 in "constant" dollars. This is as close as one can come to measuring productivity at the company level. For the purpose of applying our productivity standard, we do not need anything more and we should not settle for anything less.

Therefore, ABC can give an average wage and salary raise of 10% this year without raising prices and still have a "buffer" of 4% against inflation. This sharp measuring tool could advance the state of the art in corporate and financial reporting by fifty years.

If everyone at ABC would accept an across-the-board raise of 10%, we would be done with the application of our productivity standard in a manner that would not fuel inflation on ABC's part at all. From now on, it is up to the particular company's management and union to proceed. Do they want to vary the annual raises from 5% to 15%? They certainly can, provided the total bill for wages, salaries, and benefits does not exceed 10% of what it was the year before. Does this method give the employees all the gains from higher productivity? Of course not. If employment costs accounted for, say, 50% of GCP last year, then the employees get 50% of the additional GCP due to productivity gains. The other 50% goes to the stockholders and to the company.

Second Application: Chrysler

The following illustration (Table 2) is a perfect example of a real and known company that could have avoided reaching the brink of bankruptcy in 1979 by the use of the productivity standard. Let's do for Chrysler, then, what we did before for the hypothetical ABC.

As can be seen from the Chrysler table (see Table 2—actual figures computed from its respective annual reports), the task of figuring out gross corporate product (value added) is considerably more complicated here. Because Chrysler, like the great majority of corporations, does not disclose figures for its outside purchases (inputs), we have to come up with its gross corporate product indirectly by adding up the "shares" of the six recipients of its GCP. We have to locate items #1 through #6 in its annual report. Their sum constitutes Chrysler's GCP for the respective years. (Fortunately, Chrysler like GM and Ford, reports the items in line 6—wages, salaries, benefits—which the majority of the Fortune 500 companies do not report yet).

Please note that for the years 1979 and 1980, employee wages, salaries, and benefits (line 6) amounted to more than the total difference between net sales and outside purchases (gross corpo-

Table 2
Chrysler Corporation

Fiscal Year	1982	1981	1980	1979	1978
1 Income Taxes	1	17	40	-5	81
2 Interest expense	338	406	333	275	166
3 Dividends (total)	—	—	—	34	66
4 Depreciation, depletion	433	451	567	401	352
5 Retained earnings	170	-476	-1,710	-1,133	-270
6 Wages, salaries, benefits	1,796	2,080	2,353	2,901	3,285
7 Gross Corporate Product	2,738	2,478	1,583	2,473	3,679
8 Average employment (number)	73,715	87,825	92,595	133,810	157,960
9 GCP per employee	$37,145	28,215	17,095	18,480	23,290
10 Payroll costs per employee	$24,365	23,685	25,410	21,680	20,795
11 Difference (#9 − #10)	12,780	5,530	-8,135	-3,200	2,495
12 Human Productivity Index	103	85	60	60	75
13 GCP as % of sales	27%	23%	17%	21%	23%
14 Payroll costs as % of sales	18%	19%	26%	24%	20%
15 GCP Margin (#13 − #14)	9%	4%	-9%	-3%	3%
16 Index of GCP growth (1978 = 100)	159	121	73	79	100
17 Index of Payroll cost/employee	117	114	122	104	100
18 Net Sales*	10,045	10,822	9,225	12,002	16,341

* millions of dollars.

Source: *Corporate Productivity Atlas* (Delphi Research Center), 1983 edition, pp. A-74 and A-76, and 1981 edition, p. A-123.

rate product). This means that in 1979 and 1980 Chrysler had to dip into its accumulated retained earnings, not only to pay for such items above as interest expense (bankers and lenders in general do not usually wait to be paid later) but also to pay the difference in payroll costs not covered by Chrysler's total contribution to the country's GNP, its gross corporate product.

One can easily write a whole book on Table 2 that may revolutionize corporate reporting in the future (i.e., connecting and comparing each corporation's gross corporate product to the nation's gross national product). If you compare the figures in lines 9 and 10, you will see that the average Chrysler employee cost the company more than the total contribution per employee (line 9) in 1979 and 1980. In 1980, for instance, Chrysler paid for each employee $8,315 more than each employee contributed to Chrysler's GCP and the nation's GNP. Nothing is left for dividends, or depreciation or interest expense, not to mention any contribution to keeping the government of the country going by its share of the burden known as "taxes" (line 1).

Human productivity index (line 12) is not how Chrysler compares with itself but rather how it compares with its industry (motor vehicles and parts). It stood 25% below in 1978 (75)—an early warning if GCP measures were in use then. In 1979, it stood 40% below the industry average (60) and it remained the same in 1980 (60), but it was only 15% below its industry in 1981 (85) and finally 3% above its industry in 1982.

The figures in lines 13 and 14 and their difference in line 15 are very critical. Chrysler had GCP as 23% of sales in 1978, 21% in 1979, and only 17% in 1980, when payroll costs alone amounted to 26% of 1980 GCP—a shortfall of 9%. No company can make a profit with less than 10% GCP margin (line 15), and no company can escape bankruptcy with a negative GCP margin. Chrysler had a GCP margin of minus 9% in 1980. So, no one doubted the inevitability of bankruptcy without the $1.5 billion government bailout (1980).

The most crucial question now arises: What if Chrysler were operating under the proposed productivity standard in 1978 (and after)? No one can tell what specific form the productivity standard agreement between Chrysler and UAW could have taken. But we can safely assume that it would have had certain boundaries or outer limits. In no case, for instance, would a company under the productivity standard pay to its employees more than the total difference between net sales and outside purchases (the company's entire GCP). That provision alone would have meant that in 1979 Chrysler would have paid $428 million less in payroll costs. That would have meant $18,480 in payroll costs per employee instead of $21,680. In 1980 the total difference in payroll costs would have been $770 million less or $17,095 instead of $25,410 per employee. This is equivalent to a 15% pay and benefits cut in 1979 and a 33% cut in 1980.

How many of the 84,000 Chrysler employees (both blue collar and white collar) who lost their jobs between 1978 and 1982 would have said no to these cuts if they were realistically informed about the consequences? Put another way, how many of those 84,000 out of jobs and out of unemployment benefits by now would be willing to return to their jobs at Chrysler at 33% pay cuts? Very many, I believe! That's exactly what the employees of Braniff Airlines did in March 1984 when their reorganized company started operations again. They accepted not 33% but 50% pay cuts as a precondition for putting the company back in operation. Other airline employees have entered into "productivity standard" type agreements like the above (i.e., Eastern Airlines). When we propose, then, a productivity standard, we are not proposing something unknown—only that we should be applying it before bankruptcy becomes inevitable or the loss of thousands of jobs unavoidable.

Chrysler would have saved at least $428 million in 1979 and $770 million in 1980 if it had invoked not a 50% cut in payroll costs but only a 15% cut in 1979 and a 33% cut in 1980. A typical productivity standard agreement would most likely have provided for it. This type of agreement between Chrysler and UAW would have made unnecessary the painful bailout but most importantly would have saved most of the jobs lost at Chrysler between 1978 and 1982. This is what we meant earlier when we stated that the implementation of the productivity standard would bring about simultaneously two very needed economic results: an effective defense against inflation (that destabilizes the whole economy) and an equally needed defense against the unnecessary loss of American jobs.

A halfhearted attempt to adopt a form of productivity standard was made during the Kennedy Administration in the early 1960s (when it was not really needed—so much so that UAW gained a 3% annual "productivity" salary raise without either side ever bothering to tie the two!). We could have started it preventively in 1971. We did not think of the productivity standard in 1974 when inflation went through the roof (double digit) for the first time in the entire postwar period. We needed it badly in 1980

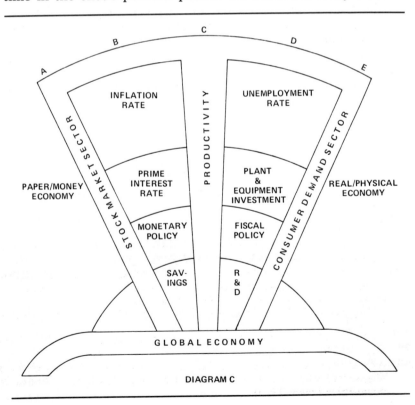

DIAGRAM C

when inflation (13.5%) plus unemployment (7.2%) exceeded 20%. We need it in 1985 if we want to avoid the next vicious spiral of high prices and high unemployment.

It will take all of our "doctors of economy" and all the business leadership of the auto makers and all the union leadership of UAW in Detroit to leave behind the adversarian attitudes of the past and start sitting at the same bargaining table ("cooperation table" would be better) at least once a year (rather than every three years). This alone can and should change the course of economic history in this country.

The gradual adoption of the productivity standard is not only the means of making better products at a lower cost, it is the means of building better societies and better citizens as well. And here is where North America and Western Europe still hold a decisive lead over the Japanese or any other society that has mastered quickly the secret of making sturdier products at a lower cost. We have all the resources needed to do that and still retain our lead in the quality of life and equality of opportunity in general. We lack only the will to do it.

Diagram C shows that productivity is the economic force that ultimately balances the physical and money sectors of every economy domestically. National productivity is also the major economic force that connects each national economy with the global economy. It ultimately determines the relative standing and competitiveness of each national economy within the global economic system.

Notes

Abernathy, William J., and Alan M. Kantrow, *Industrial Rennaissance* (Harper & Row, 1981).

Athanasopoulos, C.N., *Corporate Productivity Atlas,* (Delphi Research Center, 1983) pp. 13-14.

Blumenthal, Sidney, "Drafting A Democratic Industrial Plan," *The New York Times Magazine,* August 28, 1983, p. 31.

"Computer Conference on Productivity: A Final Report on the White House Conference on Productivity" (American Productivity Center, 1983).

"The Decline of Europe," *Newsweek,* April 9, 1984, p. 44.

Drucker, Peter F., *Toward the Next Economics and Other Essays* (Harper & Row, New York, 1981).

Gale, Bradley T., "Can More Capital Buy Higher Productivity?" *HBR,* July-August 1980.

Goodwin, Craufurd D., editor, "Exhortation & Controls: The Search for a Wage-Price Policy, 1945-1971" (The Brookings Institution/Studies in Wage-Price Policy, 1975).

"The Halloween Party," *Road & Track,* February 1984, p. 60.
Hayes, Robert H., and William J. Abernathy, "Managing Our Way to Economic Decline," *HBR,* July-August 1980.
Henrici, Stanley B., "How Deadly is the Productivity Disease?," *HBR,* Nov.-Dec. 1981.
Kendrick, John W., *Improving Company Productivity: Handbook with Case Studies* (The Johns Hopkins University Press, 1984).
"The Labor Showdown of the Decade," *Fortune,* April 16, 1984, p. 128.
Leone, Robert A. and Stephen P. Bradley, "Toward an Effective Industrial Policy," *Harvard Business Review,* November/December 1981.
Malkiel, Burton G., "Productivity—the Problem Behind the Headlines," *HBR,* May-June 1979.
McConnell, Campbell R., "Why Is U.S. Productivity Slowing Down?" *HBR,* March/April 1979.
Olson, Mancur, *The Rise and Decline of Nations* (Yale University Press, 1982).
Reich, Robert B., "Why the U.S. Needs an Industrial Policy" *(Harvard Business Review,* January-February 1982).
"The Revival of Productivity," *Business Week,* February 13, 1984, p. 92.
Scobel, Donald N., "Business and Labor—From Adversaries to Allies," *HBR,* November-December 1982.
"A Surprising Surge in Productivity," *Newsweek,* February 6, 1984, p. 62.
"Taming Britain's Unions," *Fortune,* April 16, 1984, p. 134.
U.S. Industrial Outlook (Washington, D.C.: U.S. Department of Commerce, 1983 edition).
Wilson, Ian H., "Business Management and the Winds of Change," *Journal of Contemporary Business* (Winter 1978): pp. 45-55.

The Global Economy Requires Greater U.S. Productivity

by

Charles W. McMillion

The "global economy" has come of age in the United States. It has moved from the classroom to the boardroom and now, a decade after the 1973 oil crisis exposed U.S. international economic vulnerability, the global economy is beginning to reshape government economic policy. A recent Presidential Commission on Industrial Competitiveness has declared "the new reality of global competition" is the American economic challenge of the next decade.[1] How well we understand and cope with this fundamentally new situation will determine whether we can improve or even sustain our standard of living into the future.

Gone are the days when discussions of the world economy—if they occurred at all—generally evoked images of a peaceful and plentiful "global village" and focused primarily on abstract philosophical or mathematical models of world order. Today the focus is on unemployment rates, which as Table 1 demonstrates, have risen constantly in every U.S. administration since World War II, and on the apparent shrinking of middle-class jobs and product markets.[2] Driven by jet engines and communications technologies, the careful pursuit of and competition for raw materials, markets, and investment opportunities worldwide have created opportunities and fundamental problems never imagined even a few years ago.

As Gerard Adams of Wharton Econometrics notes, today's open, global economy is "altogether different" from that of the past.[3] Traditional Keynesian economic orthodoxy prescribes that when demand falls off, government pumps it back up through deficit spending. This renewed demand is supposed to rekindle new

---

Charles W. McMillion has lived and worked in Europe, Latin America and Africa. He is currently the Senior Economist for U.S. Senator Donald Riegle, Democrat of Michigan.

Table 1

**Average Unemployment Rates
Under Recent American Presidents**

Truman (1946-52)	4.2
Eisenhower (1953-60)	4.9
Kennedy/Johnson (1961-68)	4.9
Nixon/Ford (1969-76)	5.8
Carter (1977-80)	6.5
Reagan (1981-84)	8.5

Source: Clair Brown, *Industrial Relations:* Spring, 1983.

investment, which adds jobs and tax revenues. With an open, global economy, however, additional demand in the U.S. does not require additional production in the U.S., as our current trade deficit of more than $10 billion per month demonstrates. In the global economy, demand is one thing; production (or supply) is another. Certain recent critics of too much emphasis on the demand side have some justification. Their equally orthodox trickle-down remedies, unfortunately, have only made a serious problem much worse.

How can U.S. small businesses and workers successfully compete, and how can multinational corporations justify employment and production in the U.S.? In the highly competitive global economy, there is at least the appearance of a strong incentive for most production to be transferred abroad. Compared with the U.S., comparable wage rates (at 1985 exchange rates) in most of Europe and Japan are 50% of U.S. levels, and in Mexico, South Korea, and Taiwan, they are less than 10%. Many of the other factors of lifestyle and affluence (health and safety standards, environmental concerns) that make the U.S. such a wonderful place to live and to sell your goods or services, make it an extremely noncompetitive economic structure in which to employ workers and to produce.

Locating or relocating a major facility can take years, of course, whether in Birmingham or Barcelona. The strictly technical capabilities now exist, however, to transfer state-of-the-art process and product technology, capital and managerial expertise virtually anywhere in the world in a matter of minutes or hours. Foreign workers are often as well trained as Americans at all but the most senior technical levels, and, particularly in Asia, their discipline can border on the maniacal. According to the U.S. Department of Labor, national productivity as measured by real gross domestic product per employed person, increased by 1.2% per year in the U.S.from 1960 to 1983, compared with 5.9% for

Japan, 5.3% for South Korea, 3.7%for France, and 3.4% for West Germany. This, combined with the real or potential availability of synthetic substitutes for natural resources and the global organizational abilities of multinational corporations, has destroyed the concept of inherent international comparative advantage.

Government policies and political risks, of course, distort purely technical market capabilities beyond any recognition. Otherwise, the equilibrating function of the global economy would reduce world living standards to the lowest common denominator—as in the 16¢-per-hour sweatshops in Bangladesh and elsewhere. The micro-logic (and competitive necessity) for each firm to produce cheaply abroad and export to affluent consumer markets ultimately would become a macro-fallacy. Consumers can live on accumulating debt for a time, but finally they must produce and earn incomes commensurate with their consumption. The interplay between public policy and the new global economy therefore affects every aspect of our standard of living, from job security to consumer prices and mortgage interest rates. The new situation requires that careful reconsideration be given to government economic policy.

The United States and most of the other 167 unique, sovereign countries of the world have been slow to adjust to the new global economy. There are two broadly distinct aspects of needed adjustment. One, which is unfortunately outside the scope of this article, involves reformulating and enforcing the cooperative and competitive relationships between nations. The second aspect, and the one that I emphasize here for the United States, pertains to the necessary adaptation of domestic policy to respond to the new competitive global economic reality. Following a brief overview of the new environment, I will discuss some of the difficulties now posed for U.S. economic policies and the need for a major change toward more focused, cost-effective public policies.

Two basic and related points, however, should be stated clearly at the outset: A) our national well-being is directly tied to the productivity and international competitiveness of our firms and industries, but B) there are important differences between our national economic interests and the interests of individual firms or industries. That is, the U.S. needs a competitive electronics industry, but the facilitating of foreign sources of electronic components, while it may serve the interests of the industry or particular firms, may or may not serve the interests of the U.S. economy. These important points will be discussed below.

Adjustment problems in the United States are severe. Present trends cannot be allowed to persist. The 1983 trade deficit of

$69.4 billion was unprecedented in world history. The 1984 trade deficit, however, was $123.3 billion, and the Commerce Department expects 1985 to be worse. To offset these enormous trade and current account deficits, U.S. foreign borrowing in 1984 totalled $101.6 billion—substantially more than the total foreign debt accumulated by Mexico or Brazil over their entire histories. In early 1985, the U.S. became a net debtor nation for the first time since 1914, and it will become the world's largest debtor nation by the end of 1985. It is estimated that if present policies and the current accelerating trend continue, the U.S. could be a net debtor of more than $1 trillion by 1990. A quite reasonable 15% annual return on these foreign obligations would require an outflow from the U.S. of $150 billion by 1990—and substantially more in subsequent years.

These incomprehensible numbers represent the grudging loss to American firms and workers of enormous markets both here and abroad, as well as enormous future obligations. Markets take years to develop and, once lost, are very difficult to win back for new high-technology products and services, as well as for basic industries and agriculture. Under these circumstances, servicing—much less repaying—rapidly accumulating foreign debt obligations poses an enormous challenge to our economy and standard of living.

U.S. competitive difficulties in traditional "smokestack" industries such as steel and autos have received considerable attention in recent years. Even with a strict "Voluntary Restraint Agreement" limiting the importation of Japanese cars, the U.S. was a net importer of nearly $35 billion in automotive products and parts in 1984. It has been reported that even excluding automotive products, the U.S. became a net importer of capital goods in 1984, with a strong trend toward a widening deficit.[4] Table 2 illustrates the broad trend of import penetration into the U.S. domestic market. It should be noted that with the removal of the VRA, imported passenger cars are expected to gain 30% of the U.S. market in 1986.

This decline in the competitiveness of traditional U.S. industries was until recently believed to be the inevitable and unimportant consequence of the product cycle. That is, as older products matured and began to decline in the U.S., the technology to mass produce them became standardized and easy to transfer abroad where the markets for these products were still growing. It has become apparent, however, that today foreign products and production technologies are often on a par with, or even exceed, the best in the United States. A midsize car which takes approximately 120 labor hours to produce in the U.S. is produced in

Table 2

Foreign Import Share of U.S. Markets: 1970-1984 in percent

	Total Goods Purchases	Capital Equipment*	Consumer Durables*	Passenger Cars
1970	9.3	8.2	10.2	—
1974	10.5	10.2	10.6	—
1977	10.7	11.7	11.4	18.8
1980	11.5	15.6	13.1	25.9
1981	11.7	17.4	14.2	27.5
1982	12.1	19.5	14.5	27.8
1983	12.7	20.2	14.9	26.0
1984	14.6	25.9	17.4	23.6

*Nonautomotive. Price-adjusted data. Passenger car share based on unit sales.

Source: Department of Commerce, *Business America*, March 4, 1985

about 60 hours in Japan.

The U.S. position in high tech trade has worsened dramatically in recent years as the dollar has become badly overvalued, but as with more traditional goods, the trend has been clear for many years. Table 3 illustrates the U.S. loss of world market shares for technology from 1965 to 1980. In high-tech trade, the U.S. has gone from a trade surplus of about $7.5 billion in 1980 to a $1.5 million surplus in 1983 to a $7 billion deficit in 1984. The U.S. ran a deficit in communications-equipment trade for the first time in 1984. We have run a deficit in semiconductors and components since 1982. We run major deficits in consumer electronics and office machines. The U.S. still has an apparent surplus in computing equipment and scientific instruments, but even this is eroding. The IBM PC, for example, is mostly produced abroad. Of the total manufacturing cost of $860, $625 is produced overseas. (Of this, $230 is accounted for by U.S.-owned firms.) The keyboard ($50) is from Japan; the floppy disk drives are produced in Singapore ($165) with $25 worth of U.S. assembly; the monochrome monitor ($85) is from Korea; the graphics printer ($160) is from Japan; the power supply ($60) is from Japan; the semiconductors are from Japan ($105) and from the U.S. ($105); and the case and final assembly ($105) are done in the U.S.[5]

Finally, it is sometimes argued that the competitive decline in U.S. manufacturing can be offset by trade in services. Tradeable services, however, largely "service" goods-producing industries. As more and more goods are produced overseas, more of those services are provided there—whether by U.S. corporations abroad or by their own home-grown firms. The U.S. barely broke even in services trading in 1984 (excluding income on foreign investments). The U.S. will probably begin running deficits in tradeable services in 1985. As noted above, when the effects of becoming a debtor nation begin to be felt, our still substantial net inflow on investment earnings will be reversed, greatly compounding the trade deficit's pressure on our current accounts. Current trends suggest that if nothing were done, the U.S. could face annual current-account deficits in five years in the $400-$500 billion range. Foreign borrowing required to offset this deficit would send interest rates ever higher and would create unsustainable world financial pressure.

Table 3

United States Shares of World High-Technology Exports, 1965 and 1980:

Percentages	0	10	20	30	40	50	60
Aircraft and parts							
Office, Computing Accounting Machines							
Engines and Turbines							
Agricultural Chemicals							
Professional and Scientific Instruments							
Electrical Equipment and Components							
Optical and Medical Instruments							
Drugs and Medicines							
Plastic and Synthetic Material							
Industrial Chemicals							

1965 • • • • • •
1980 ———

Source: U.S. Department of Commerce

To avert this growing crisis in U.S. competitiveness each individual must take up the challenge, get smarter, and work smarter. It requires government action to A) reduce the proliferation of unfair foreign trading practices, B) assure a reasonable and stable exchange rate, and especially, C) assist the private sector in massively improving productivity. Jacques De Larosiere, managing director of the International Monetary Fund, recently estimated that whereas products subject to one kind of trade restriction or other accounted for about 20% of total consumption of manufactured goods in the U.S. and Europe in 1980, the figure is now well above 30%.

The U.S. must be much more aggressive in demanding elimination of trade barriers imposed by developed countries such as Japan and by some of the more advanced developing countries such as South Korea. When necessary, and before massive damage is done to an industry, the U.S. must be willing and able to effectively threaten and to carry out well-targeted retaliation.

However, as important as the problem of unfair trading practices is, the explosion in the price of the dollar has done more to undermine American competitiveness than all the subsidies and trade barriers in all the countries in the world put together. The exchange rate is central to the process of national integration into the global economy. Except with reference to the trade or current account balance, there is no longer any reliable method of determining what a currency's value "should" be. There is general belief that the dollar was undervalued in the late 1970s. However, according to the Federal Reserve's trade weighted index, from its low point in July 1980 to mid-February 1985, the dollar appreciated by more than 85% against foreign currencies. Overpricing the dollar by even 40% effectively imposes a 40% tax on goods produced in the U.S. and provides a 40% subsidy to foreign imports. Certainly, this has been a major factor in the rapid decline of our international competitive position in recent years.

Twelve years ago, when the Bretton Woods system of fixed exchange rates was abandoned, economists hoped domestic economic policy would maintain discipline and international cooperation freed from the past constraints of maintaining a fixed rate. Experience has shown this not to be the case, with the consequence that exchange-rate volatility has increased dramatically and misalignments have become substantial.

The perception of the U.S as a safe haven for capital and the austerity and slow growth in much of the world has contributed to the recent appreciation of the dollar. However, the differential between extraordinarily high U.S. interest rates and rates abroad has been the major force driving up the dollar's price.[6] There is no substitute for sound fiscal and monetary policies. The U.S. must reduce its federal budget deficit to allow for a more expansionary monetary policy and lower interest rates. In addition, we must cooperate more closely with the central banks of our allies and other appropriate institutions to reduce currency misalignments while ensuring noninflationary monetary policy. Greater stability for exchange rates is in every nation's interests.[7]

The most complex and important challenge facing the U.S. in adjusting to the global economy is the need to drastically improve productivity growth. Although much of the responsibility lies with the private sector, major adjustments are also required of government policy. Again, the importance of sound and consistent fiscal and monetary policy must be emphasized. As with the individual who occasionally borrows long-term for a house, a car, an education, etc., the government should certainly not be bound to an annual balanced budget. But the current rate of government debt accumulation and its unending—indeed, compounding—nature is unsustainable and destabilizing to the entire economy. The federal budget deficit is a reflection, however, of the difficulties we face paying for our standard of living in the new global economy. It dramatizes the need for productivity growth and more effective public policy in at least four major areas: 1) taxes, 2) technology, 3) human and information resources, and 4) the general economic climate.

The U.S. tax code has developed over our history as a nation without any conscious design or overall planning. Despite literally tons of descriptive pages, no one fully understands the "whats"— much less the "whys"—of the tax code. Federal tax breaks to business and individuals in 1986 alone are estimated by the Congressional Joint Tax Committee to exceed $400 billion. These breaks, or loopholes, affect everything from hog farming and race horse breeding to charitable deductions. The most recent statistics from the Treasury Department indicate that 9,000 people with a 1983 income over $250,000 legally paid no federal income tax. Table 4 lists the 65 major profitable U.S. corporations that legally paid no federal income tax for the three year period of 1981, 1982, and 1983. In fact, most of these companies—led by General Electric which (net) received $283 million from the federal government over the three years—were actually net recipients of funds.

Our pervasive and uncoordinated tax system replaces market incentives with tax benefits and undermines competition between industries as well as between firms and individuals. Table 5 demonstrates the enormously different effective tax rates paid by various industries. The important point is not that these disparities exist, but that they exist for no well-defined reason. Since tax provisions do not have to weather the grueling annual budget process, they tend to persist far beyond their initial justification. There are more cost-effective, direct means of providing assistance to specific individuals, firms, or industries if they can demonstrate a specific national need. This is the goal behind the various "flat tax" proposals that are currently receiving considerable attention. Economic decisions must be driven by productivity concerns, not by obsolete and inefficient tax preferences.

Major American Companies Paying a Total of Zero or Less in Total Federal Income Taxes, 1981-1983 (in millions of dollars)

Company	Profit	Tax	% Rate
General Electric	$6,527.0	$-283.0	-4.3
Boeing Co.	1,530.0	-267.0	-17.5
Dow Chemical Co.	776.0	-223.0	-28.7
Tenneco	2,678.0	-189.0	-7.0
Santa Fe Southern Pacific Corp.	1,579.0	-141.7	-9.0
Weyerhaeuser Co.	640.7	-138.6	-21.6
DuPont	2,591.0	-132.0	-5.1
St. Regis Corp.	123.9	-121.3	-97.9
Georgia-Pacific Corp.	400.0	-99.0	-24.8
Columbia Gas System	886.7	-94.6	-10.7
Martin Marietta Corp.	490.2	-94.3	-19.2
Transamerica Corp.	584.9	-86.4	-14.8
General Dynamics	930.8	-70.6	-7.6
Union Carbide	613.0	-70.0	-11.4
Continental Group	462.0	-69.0	-14.9
Dun & Bradstreet Corp.	595.7	-64.0	-10.7
RCA	514.2	-60.9	-11.8
Texaco	1,699.0	-58.0	-3.4
IC Industries	322.9	-56.0	-17.3
U.S. Home	54.3	-53.6	-98.7
International Minerals & Chemical	260.5	-50.6	-19.4
Jim Walter Corp.	211.3	-48.2	-22.8
Celanese Corp.	296.0	-45.0	-15.2
Northrup Corp.	177.4	-42.5	-24.0
Greyhound Corp.	290.8	-42.1	-14.5
Amerada Hess	336.7	-41.7	-12.4
Mitchell Energy & Development Corp.	402.8	-41.1	-10.2
International Paper Company	1,028.4	-39.4	-3.8
Ohio Edison Company	1,027.7	-37.6	-3.7
Burlington Northern	1,724.3	-37.6	-2.2
Mellon National Corp.	402.2	-35.3	-8.8
Ashland Oil	346.9	-33.4	-9.6
Philadelphia Electric Co.	1,270.9	-33.4	-2.6
Piedmont Aviation	78.9	-29.6	-37.5
Panhandle Eastern Corp.	938.0	-28.8	-3.1
Arizona Public Service Co.	862.0	-28.7	-3.3
Ogden Corp.	192.5	-27.4	-14.2
Pacific Power & Light Co.	598.1	-22.2	-3.7
Northern Indiana PSC	549.1	-22.0	-4.0
Tesoro Petroleum	100.9	-16.5	-16.4
CSX Corp.	1,755.3	-15.2	-0.9
Air Products and Chemicals	294.0	-13.6	-4.6
Superior Oil	1,083.8	-13.2	-1.2
Singer Co.	104.6	-12.5	-12.0
Grace (W.R.) & Co.	684.1	-12.5	-1.8
Florida Power & Light Co.	1,337.7	-12.2	-0.9
Centrex Corp.	194.2	-11.7	-6.0
Pennsylvania Power & Light Co.	920.8	-10.4	-1.1
Champion International Corp.	167.0	-7.8	-4.7
Southwest Airlines Co.	145.2	-7.2	-5.0
Allied Corp.	404.0	-7.0	-1.7
American Cyanamid Co.	298.7	-6.2	-2.1
Rio Grande Industries	132.5	-4.7	-3.5
St. Paul Industries	440.5	-4.0	-0.9
Tyson Foods	36.4	-3.6	-9.9
Commonwealth Edison Co.	2,425.6	-3.5	-0.1
Comerica	75.2	-3.2	-4.3
Xerox	1,051.2	-2.7	-0.3
Citizens & Southern Ga. Corp.	173.8	-2.0	-1.2
American Financial Corp.	426.9	-1.9	-0.4
American Standard	78.5	-1.6	-2.0
Combined International Corp.	297.6	-0.6	-0.2
First Executive Corp.	312.2	0.0	0.0
Grumman Corp.	474.5	0.0	0.0
Lockheed Corp.	1,085.0	0.0	0.0
Totals (65 Companies):	49,503.0	-3,232.4	-6.5
Totals, 25 Biggest Benefits:	25,244.3	-2,600.4	-10.3
Totals, 10 Biggest Benefits:	17,741.3	-1,689.2	-9.5

Source: "Corporate Income Taxes in the Reagan Years: A Study of Three Years of Legalized Tax Avoidance" by Robert S. McIntyre and Robert Folen, *Citizens for Tax Justice*, 2020 K Street, N.W., #200, Washington, D.C.; (202) 293-5340.

Table 5

Comparison of Effective Federal Income Tax Rates by Industry (in percent)

Industry	1980	1981	1982	1983
Aerospace	16.4	6.8	(0.6)	14.0
Beverages	28.0	28.8	20.5	18.7
Chemicals	13.7	5.0	(17.7)	(1.0)
Computers and office equipment	24.9	25.3	26.4	26.3
Electronics and appliances	24.5	17.1	14.3	7.4
Financial institutions	5.8	2.7	(3.8)	6.4
Food processors	35.6	26.8	31.6	25.9
Instrument companies	37.1	26.6	21.9	32.8
Paper and wood products	(1.4)	(14.2)	36.1	(0.5)
Petroleum*	31.1	21.7	18.2	21.3
Pharmaceuticals	39.2	35.9	32.7	27.2
Retailing	34.1	22.3	20.4	20.0
Tobacco	31.4	31.3	36.3	33.8
Transportation:				
Railroads	10.7	(7.5)	(4.1)	3.3
Trucking	37.5	46.1	36.9	34.5
Utilities (electric and gas, only)	10.9	10.3	15.6	7.1

*company base not strictly comparable, 1980 and 1983
( ) signifies negative tax.

Source: Joint Committee on Taxation.

Advances in technology have long been viewed as almost synonymous with productivity growth. New product and process technologies create new markets and are an essential element in sustaining our ability to compete in the global economy. The U.S. currently spends approximately as much on research and development as Japan, West Germany, France and Great Britain combined and somewhat more than any of these as a percentage of gross national product. More than half of U.S. spending for R&D is done by the federal government, however, where two-thirds of the funding is for defense and space related projects that may or may not have commercial applications.

According to the National Science Foundation, West Germany devotes 14% of its government research budget to activities "promoting industrial growth." Japan spends 13 percent, France 8%, Great Britain 4%, and the U.S. only 1% of government R&D funds to support industrial growth. Civilian R&D expenditures in the U.S., as a percent of GNP, lag far behind Japan and West Germany. Numerous new products and production technologies first developed in the U.S., such as VCRs, robotics, and computer-assisted manufacturing, have been more quickly and effectively commercialized abroad with the help of a government-business partnership.

This public/private partnership not only confronts U.S. political culture but, even more importantly, the actual capabilities of the public sector. Government has to be made capable of becoming a productive and efficient partner before it can actually become one. This goes to the very heart of the global economic challenge. Making government a more responsible partner in productivity growth is not an isolated philosophical choice but an economic necessity required by international competition.

There is currently no coherence and considerable overlapping in the many agencies, organizations, and more than 700 federal laboratories that conduct government supported R&D. These efforts need to be coordinated with much more attention to industrial competitiveness. The private sector should have a much greater role in identifying the productive areas for government's basic research and commercialization, as well as developing effective means for the widest and most rapid dissemination of new technologies throughout the U.S. economy. Currently, there are many worthwhile proposals to begin to address this problem by establishing a cabinet-level Department of Science and Technology or an independent Advanced Technologies Foundation. The fruits of U.S. taxpayer supported R&D must support U.S. competitive interests, however, and must not be immediately exported for foreign production—whether by U.S. or foreign firms.

Closely related to technological hardware and even more important to productivity are the men and women who put them to use. Adam Smith was not the first to recognize that of a nation's resources, its human resources are the most important. The universal system of education in the U.S. has long been seen as a major national strength, and we have been slow to recognize severe problems. Some 23 million American adults are functionally illiterate by the simplest test of everyday reading, writing, and comprehension. The National Commission on Excellence in Education found that only 20% of all 17-year-olds can write a persuasive essay, and only one-third can solve a math problem requiring several steps. The U.S. Chamber of Commerce has found that 35% of firms surveyed had to provide remedial basic-skills training to new employees.

In every major international comparison with students in other major industrial countries, the U.S. loses. Furthermore, since 1972, the United States has produced a declining number of Ph.D. graduates in many engineering disciplines, and about 40% of recent Ph.D.'s are foreign students. One South Korean company that will soon begin exporting automobiles to the U.S. advertises the education of their employees in U.S. magazines. Pictured are three Koreans in sweatshirts from the University of Texas, the University of Michigan, and the University of Wisconsin. Under each employee is his name and the engineering field in which he received his American Ph.D. The caption reads, "Our workers are smart for the same reasons your workers are smart."

The U.S. can no longer be complacent that superior education and training gives our work force an international competitive advantage. Unemployment and underemployment among the college-educated young are staggering throughout the world. Technical skills are rarely in short supply, and when they are, they can usually be quickly imported. As indicated above, foreign workers—especially those without a humanistic tradition or democratic government—are often exceptionally disciplined and productive.

There is growing recognition of the challenge facing U.S. education, and there has been progress in recent years. The unbroken decline of scores on the Scholastic Aptitude Tests (SAT) has been reversed since 1981 as stricter standards have been imposed on both students and teachers and more emphasis has been placed on basic skills, math, and sciences. For the first time, business schools are offering courses on production technology. Government must increase funding, however, to attract the best and the brightest to careers in education, and equally important, to maintain the most modern equipment.

Recently, only 56% of all engineering programs that were evaluated received full accreditation. In most cases, obsolete equipment was a principal reason for failure to receive accreditation. This is crucial because in today's global economy with its rapidly changing technologies, education is not something that is gained once and for all. It is truly a lifelong process where the competitive edge is gained, lost, or retained every day through facility with the most modern equipment and data. The U.S. government has the unique capability—and the responsibility—to assist its citizens in gaining and retaining this edge. Within the limits of proprietary rights and in partnership with the private sector and professional educators, the government should provide an ongoing stream of the most modern equipment on which men and women of all ages can continuously train and retrain.

The U.S. economy and labor markets must be the most productive and the quickest to adapt to new technologies and new product markets. We need a single, well-organized facility for the broad dissemination of commercial information and education modeled after the universally admired Agricultural Extension

Service. The facility, the Productivity Extension Service, would dramatically increase the role of the federal government in the dissemination of the wide range of information that the government already collects on domestic and foreign markets, technologies, government procurements, etc., and would gradually improve the quality and timeliness and enlarge the scope of government data collection. Data would be automated and accessible by home computers and in all public libraries.

The Productivity Extension Service would be established as an independent informational and educational agency, based in colleges and university departments of engineering, management, and business. The service would maximize state and county autonomy in defining specific educational objectives and target clientele. Broad program guidelines, however, would include the full range of business education and training, including:

- Managerial excellence and innovation.
- Production process and technologies.
- Marketing.
- Product development.
- Tax and finance.

Activities would be addressed to current and potential businessmen and businesswomen, as well as consumer-information programs and youth programs. As we become increasingly a world society driven by the power of information, the U.S. has the human and technical potential to excel. We must have the political will to create our national advantages.

Much attention has been given to the potential of the American entrepreneurial spirit. The government has a vitally important role to play in nourishing that spirit, in creating employment and opportunities, and in sustaining our standard of living. We must work to fully utilize our rich diversity and not slam the door on a permanent underclass, nor on immigrants, nor on trade. The U.S. must be sustained within the global economy as the world's beacon of hope and opportunity—and the economic locomotive that pulls the rest of the world to new heights of prosperity.

Notes

1. President's Commission on Industrial Competitiveness, *Global Competition: The New Reality* (Washington, D.C.: USGPO, 1985). As early as 1977, the position of the Carter Administration was: "... international and domestic economic policies cannot be separated organizationally. Rather, nearly every economic issue has major international and domestic dimensions which must be considered simultaneously." The National Advisory Council on International Monetary and Financial Policies, *Annual Report for 1977* (Washington, D.C.: USGPO, 1978), p. 4.

2. See, for example, Barry Bluestone, Bennett Harrison, and Lucy Gorham, *Storm Clouds on the Horizons: Labor Market Crisis and Industrial Policy* (Brookline, MA: The Economic Education Project, 1984).

3. F. Gerard Adams, "The Open Economy and Economic Policy," in *Wharton Economic News Perspectives,* November 12, 1984.

4. The Machinery and Allied Products Institute, *Capital Goods Review,* #122, October 1984, Washington, D.C.

5. *Business Week,* March 11, 1985, p. 60.

6. It is sometimes on the basis of an aggregated (and curiously trade-weighted) index that interest-rate differentials have narrowed or disappeared even as the dollar continued to appreciate. See the *Economic Report of the President* (Washington, D.C.: USGPO, 1985), p. 104. Investment decisions are not made on the basis of aggregated data, however, but on the basis of specific comparisons such as the 2-3 percentage point differential between U.S. rates and those in Japan, Germany, and Switzerland in early 1985.

7. These were the findings and recommendations of a year-long investigation by senior officials of each Economic Summit member. See Philippe Jurgensen, *Report of the Working Group on Exchange Market Intervention* (Washington, D.C.: Department of the Treasury, 1983).

Oil: Past and Future

Economic Growth Before and After the Oil Crisis and the Possibility of Deindustrialization

by

Yoshihiro Kogane

In 1972, the Club of Rome report on *The Limits of Growth* predicted that further growth of the population and economy of the world would become impossible due to the physical constraints on energy, food, and the environment. The oil crisis that took place the next year gave a shock to the growth of the world economy so as to decelerate it to nearly zero growth in 1982. The growth of the world population, the fluctuation of which is naturally far smaller than that of economic growth, has become substantially lower than what was expected 10 years ago. Has the prophecy of the Club of Rome been realized after only 10 years?

Indeed, production of crude oil in the free world has been reduced from 45.8 million barrels/day in 1973 to 38.5 million barrels/day in 1982.[1] But the drop in oil production has not necessarily caused reduced economic growth. On the contrary, the slowdown of economic growth must have caused the reduction of demand for oil that is reflected in the decline of oil production.

The purpose of this paper is to examine how the "mechanism of high economic growth" appeared and disappeared and then, based on those findings, conjecture the future development paths of industrial society.[2]

The Basic Way of Thinking

Contradictory Development

Today's world is heterogeneous, composed of various parts di-

---

Yoshihiro Kogane is associated with the Nikko Research Center, Ltd., Tokyo, Japan.

vided by several axes. To discriminate industrialized societies and nonindustrialized ones may be possible by utilizing the North-South axis. Societies run by a centrally planned economy system and by a market economy system may be distinguished by the East-West axis. Societies are also identified by the axis dividing traditional culture, which assures the continuity and coherence of individual societies, e.g., American, British, Japanese, Indian, and Chinese society.

The problem of today seems to be that the traits of various societies classified in such a way tend to change and interact together without any consistency. Until the end of high economic growth, a more unitarian view of the future of the world seemed to be feasible. For example, the societies of developing countries would be industrialized; East-West confrontation would be ended either by the victory of one side or by the convergence to a hybrid of both systems; with respect to culture, a certain kind of world culture would prevail so as to reduce the difference of tradition between various societies. Since then, the development in such a direction has actually taken place, but it is accompanied simultaneously with the inverse trends, so that the world has become more confused than before. Contradictions such as the coexistence of progress and retrogression, integration accompanied with segmentation, etc., may not be false descriptions of today's situation of the world.

Advanced Industrial Countries (AICs)

Let us see the situation of the group of advanced industrial countries (AICs) with a market economy system. While the techno-economic interdependence between the three poles of the AICs— i.e., the United States, Western Europe, and Japan—is increasing, economic competition is exacerbating sociopolitical friction. The U.S. economy seems to have overcome the comparative slack during the high-growth period so as to recover its predominance over the world economy. However, it is not certain that the present extraordinary situation of the strong dollar under the huge deficit of the government sector and of current balance of payments will last long. As for the Japanese and European economies, they have had to rely so far on the increase of exports to the United States and of private investment, which anticipates the durability of the favorable trend of exports.

So far, the entry of newly industrializing countries (NICs) to this group has been a disturbing factor rather than a stimulating one, since their growth is led by exports to AICs rather than oriented to their internal demand.

In this connection, neither the economies of the East nor those of less-developed countries (LDCs) have shown the possibility of substituting the three poles of the AICs as the leading power of the world economy. Therefore, one has to expect much of them in spite of the problems mentioned before, but one should be careful, since unfeasible expectations often lead to a wrong choice of the people concerned. What is important in this sense will be to identify the feasible development paths of these AICs.

Development in the AICs

In order to make the problems clearer, we may split up the development of these AICs into three components: development as the industrial society, development as the transition to deindustrialized society, and development as the transformation of the traditional culture of each society.

(a) Development as the Industrial Society

This component is concerned with the trends that accompany ordinary economic growth, such as technological progress, change of industrial structure and lifestyles, and so on. Mid- and long-term evolution of economic variables such as rate of economic growth, unemployment ratio, balance of payments, and rate of inflation would indicate the macroeconomic aspect of this component of development. The basis for considering the future of this development could be the intertemporal and intercountry comparisons of economic growth of the United States, Western Europe, and Japan.

(b) Development as the Deindustrialization of AICs

It is said that human society will enter the transition process to post-industrial society or information society when the development as industrial society has reached a certain stage. So far, it is not known whether this transition has already begun or will take place in the long-term future. However, we may conjecture the traits of deindustrialized society and think about the possible transition process on the basis of comparison between industrial society and two other types of human society, i.e., hunting-gathering and agricultural societies. The most important question concerning this task may be: What are the intrinsic needs of human beings and how are they to be satisfied? The reason why this metaphysical problem is important is that the stability of a certain form of society would depend on its capability to respond to the needs of its members, i.e., human beings.

(c) Development as the Evolution of Traditional Culture

In general, cultural evolution will not take place spontaneously, since the culture of a certain society is the product of its accumulated past development and, hence, very stable. Cultural evolution is usually caused by an encounter with a different culture that sometimes gives a great shock to the core of the society. In this sense, the expected increase in the international exchange of goods, peoples, and information would increase the probability of change of traditional culture in each society. But the forecast of cultural changes is neither an easy task nor the major concern of this paper.

Differences of Economic Growth in the AICs

A Statistical Puzzle

Considering that the two oil crises and inflation as the aftereffects of postwar high economic growth have ended, we now have several samples of economic growth to be analyzed. That is, a number of sets of statistical data of long-term economic growth by period and by country have become available on the basis of more or less common concepts and, hence, in comparable form, intertemporarily and internationally.

Table 1 shows the rates of economic growth in real terms of the United States, Western Europe, and Japan for the periods of (a) before World War I, (b) before World War II, (c) after World War II, and (d) after the oil crisis. The first set of data is too old and internationally uncomparable because of time differences; the fourth set may be too short compared to the others, but the

Table 1

Rates of Economic Growth of AICs
(average annual percentage changes)

	Before 1913	1922-1937	1953-1973	1973-1979
United States	3.9 (a)	2.1	3.6	3.3
Western Europe	2.0 (b)	2.5	4.8	2.4
Japan	2.7 (c)	3.9	9.5	4.4

(a) 1890-1913
(b) 1870-1913
(c) 1886-1913

Sources:
   United States: before 1913 and 1922-1937, *Long Term Economic Growth 1860-1970*, Social and Economic Statistics Administration, U.S. Department of Commerce, June 1973, p. 105. 1953-1973 and 1973-1979, International Financial Statistics, IMF.
   Western Europe: *The European Economy: Growth and Crisis*, edited by Andrea Boltho, Oxford University Press, 1982, p. 410.
   Japan: before 1913 and 1922-1937, calculated from *Kokumin Shotoku Binran* (Handbook of National Income), Economic Research Institute, Economic Planning Agency, June 1975, p. 139 and p. 145. 1953-1973 and 1973-1979, International Financial Statistics, IMF.

trends shown in it seem to be more or less continuing to the present. Thus, the number of samples becomes 3 x 3 = 9.

Here we are faced with a puzzle composed of three questions that stem from Table 1. That is:

(a) In all countries, the rates of economic growth are remarkably higher in the postwar period than in the prewar period. Why?
(b) Both in prewar and postwar periods, Japan's rate of growth is particularly high, Europe's is the second, and America's is the lowest. Why?
(c) In all countries, the rates of growth after the oil crisis seem to have been reduced to those of the prewar period. Provided that this is not due to the restriction of supply of oil, then why?

Boltho's Solution

This puzzle will not be solved without a set of hypotheses explaining the mechanism of economic growth. Andrea Boltho proposes a solution that seems plausible with respect to European countries (and Japan, too).[3]

He does not rely on the production-function approach that splits up the increase of GNP in real terms into the volume and productivity of inputs.

> It could be argued that European growth in the postwar period was rapid because employment, capital, and technological progress all grew more rapidly than in earlier years. Yet this is, of course, only a proximate and very insufficient explanation. None of these factors is necessarily exogenous to the growth process itself. In fact, they may all three be at least partly endogenous, in which case the search for a real explanation has not yet begun.[4]

According to him, the cheap and abundant supply of technology from the United States and of labor from the underdeveloped (mostly agricultural) sector allowed the postwar European economy to grow rapidly, but the technological gap and excess labor existed already in the prewar period, so they could not be considered the initiating factors of the postwar supergrowth. The remarkable difference between before and after the war is the sharp upward shift in investment propensities, which, according to Boltho's interpretation, is closely related to the confidence held by entrepreneurs. In this sense, great importance should be attached to the reliability of the institutional framework in which economic policies and business activities are carried out.

> A major reason which might account for such greater optimism and for more favorable expectations could have been the new economic policies put into effect in the late 1940s and early 1950s ... at the international level, the establishment of a new economic order which facilitated reconstruction in the 1940s and growth in the 1950s and 1960s ... at the domestic level, the adoption of a new array of policy

instruments which generated a belief that cyclical fluctuations could be controlled by demand management.[5]

This explanation seems not only plausible with respect to the postwar supergrowth of the Japanese economy but also valid, when inversely applied, for the slack growth of Europe and Japan after the oil crisis. That is, as the economic growth of Western Europe and Japan was far more rapid than that of the United States, the Bretton Woods system, which relied on the predominance of the U.S. economy, collapsed in the beginning of the 1970s. In the meantime, the welfare state as the coproduct of Keynesian—or demand-creating—policy instruments and persistent full employment became too enlarged and rigid for the AIC governments to control. The oil crisis and resulting hyperinflation pulled the trigger to destroy the institutional framework of high economic growth, the basis of which had already become fragile because of the successful workings of the system itself.

Thus, questions (a) and (c) may have plausible answers at least with respect to the prewar, postwar and post-oil-crisis economic growth of Western Europe and Japan. As for question (b), Boltho proposes a general law that an economy with lower productivity and standard of living would initially grow faster than others, a view supported by statistical evidence for the growth of European countries. As it is obvious that Japan's GNP per capita was the lowest and America's was the highest among AICs at the beginning of the growth race in each time period, the result of the race may be considered inevitable, due to the general law of growth.

The Missing Piece

The above explanation would be insufficient if we were not to find a solution to the puzzle of economic growth of industrial society in general, i.e. valid for the United States, Western Europe, and Japan as a whole. More specifically, Boltho's solution leaves three problems unanswered.

First, the mechanism of growth of the U.S. economy is not very clear. As far as the figures of the table are concerned, the United States is so big and mature a country with little potential for growth, that it always seems to be a loser in the growth race. But this may not be compatible with the recent changes in the situation, especially after 1983.

Second, the "general law of economic growth," with respect to the relation between the levels and growth rates, tells nothing about the possible development after the follower has caught up with the forerunner. The possible outcome must be one of the three: (i) it becomes impossible to distinguish between the forerunner and the follower; (ii) the latter outruns the former;

(iii) the former regains predominance. If there were no cause for the difference in growth rates other than that of the level at the starting point, neither (ii) nor (iii) could happen. But it is doubtful that this type of simplistic argument would hold.

Third, Boltho considers it impossible to evaluate the influence of the differences and changes of attitudes of workers/consumers on the rate of growth and, hence, ignores that influence, in spite of the importance of this kind of social factor.[6] This does not seem to have caused a big problem, as he dealt with the growth of European countries during the same (i.e., postwar) period, when such a sociocultural difference or change is not remarkable. But, if we were to deal with the intertemporal and/or intercountry differences of economic growth such as those between Japan and Western countries, between the prewar period and postwar period of AICs, and so on, Boltho's solution could miss the most important determinant of growth. In such a case, the difference or change of people's attitudes toward work and consumption is so great that it must exert considerable influence on the growth of the economy concerned. Even with respect to the confidence of entrepreneurs or the effectiveness of economic policies, the traits of this kind of social factor must be taken into account, since any decision of an enterprise or a government should be based on reasonable expectations about the attitude of workers/consumers with respect to the willingness to work, to purchase, to save, etc., if it is to attain its goal.

In order to solve the above three problems, it would be necessary to elucidate the mechanism of growth of the U.S. economy. And, in order to do so, it would be useful to compare the growth of the U.S. economy during World War II with that before and after the war. In other words, the missing piece of this puzzle is the growth of the U.S. economy during the war, since the wartime was the only period in which the U.S. economy displayed its real ability.

America's Supergrowth during the War

The reason why the long-term growth potential of the U.S. economy seems to be very low is that the data during the War are not included in the foregoing table of rates of growth.

The rate of growth of the U.S. economy from the 1920s to the postwar period fluctuated as follows:[7]

The U.S. economy continued to grow very rapidly after the recovery from the Great Depression until the end of World War II, the average annual rate of growth during 1933-1944 being 8.9%. In the meantime, the period of 1937-1944 was one of minus

Table 2

Average Annual Percentage Changes

1922-1929	4.7	postwar boom
1929-1933	-8.6 - 2.1(mean)	Great Depression
1933-1937	9.5	recovery
1937-1944	8.6	war economy
1944-1949	-2.1 - 1.5(mean)	postwar recession
1949-1953	6.2	recovery, Korean War
1953-1973	3.6	postwar high growth

growth for Western Europe and Japan; in particular, Japan's GNP in real terms was reduced by half (the case for Germany was probably the same).

Needless to say, such a big difference was the product of a noneconomic factor, i.e., the war. But war is not an incident like a natural disaster or a change of climate. To the contrary, the fact that the United States, Germany, and Japan fought this war with their full economic capacities may mean that the result reflects that of the race of economic growth between the United States, Europe, and Japan, (although it should be taken into account that the Allied Forces of Europe collaborated with the United States). If so, the American victory could have been the result of U.S. growth potential, which was higher than that of its enemies at the beginning of the war.

Why was the rate of growth of the U.S. economy the lowest during the period of 1922-1937, in spite of its very high growth potential? Why was the rate of growth of Japan's economy the highest during the same period, in spite of its having the lowest growth potential? In order to answer these questions, it seems necessary to examine the "quality" of economic growth during the prewar, war, and postwar periods of the United States, Europe, and Japan.

Qualitative Differences of Economic Growth

New/Old Product and New/Old Productive System

Here I shall deal with the increase of productivity per worker or level of consumption on the average so as to eliminate the difference stemming from the change of demographic factors. This is mainly because I am concerned with the "efficiency" of satisfaction of demand, which is the major concern of industrial society itself.

Then, in order to identify the difference of quality of the growth of production or consumption per capita, I shall split up the macroeconomic product into "old" product and "new" product, both of which shall be divided into what is produced by the "old" productive system and by the "new" productive system. The "product" here includes both material goods and human services, and producer goods as well as consumer goods.

Over a period of 20 to 30 years, in the economic growth of a certain industrial society, a set of "new" products and a "new" productive system appear, replace "old" ones, and eventually become "old" themselves. The distinction between new and old differs from country to country and from period to period: the tempo of alternation between old and new is not uniform.

When the old product continues to be produced by the old productive system, productivity may increase due to certain improved techniques and/or instruments or a more intensive use of such inputs. But progress slows spontaneously because the marginal cost of improving or increasing inputs would steadily increase so as to equal the declining marginal utility of increasing productivity. However, when a new productive system is introduced to produce an old product—e.g., the appearance of the factory with spinning and weaving machines—the increase of productivity is so revolutionary and discontinuous that the limits of growth do not appear on the supply side; instead, problems arise on the demand side. For awhile, of course, the cheap and abundant supply of an old product creates its own demand, but eventually, markets become saturated. For example, ordinary people do not need so many clothes: they may desire luxury clothes but these must not be produced in large quantities because that would reduce their prestige. As a result, the producer with a new productive system is compelled either to find export markets or to lay off workers in order to restrict the volume of production.

When a new product is invented, only those who are especially rich and/or curious demand it. Ordinary people who have to sacrifice a substantial part of their purchasing power in order to purchase it do not find that worth doing. When a new product appears, moreover, it has to be produced by the old productive system, which is not necessarily suitable for its production and, hence, tends to make the production cost very high. In this case, an increase in productivity is possible but limited, as in the case of an old product.

A remarkable reduction of the production cost—and subsequent diffusion to the populace—of a new product is only possible when a new productive system is invented and installed. However, this takes much time and capital, and adding to the cost of the new productive system is uncertainty about the future demand for the new product.

Once the new product is accepted by the society and begins to be produced by a new productive system, its production and consumption will increase very rapidly, since it will not only create new demand through the reduction of cost and price but also begin to replace the old products that were responding to more or less the same need in people's lives. Furthermore, the new product can be utilized for constructing a new productive system for new and old products.

Combinations of Product and Productive System

The above argument may lead to the following table of combinations of product and productive systems. Each box denotes, schematically, the quality of growth as well as its change from the initial to the matured stage.

Table 3

Combinations of Product and Productive Systems

Productive system \ Product	Old	New
Old	O-O (balanced slow growth spontaneous levelling off)	N-O (shortage of supply - balanced slow growth)
New	O-N (balanced rapid growth - unemployment or export surplus)	N-N (shortage of demand - balanced rapid growth)

Application of the Model to the PreWar Period

Let us assume that the typical new products before the war were mainly durable goods such as motor cars and various electric appliances, capital goods such as airplanes, and so on; typical old products at that time were textiles, light durables such as electric bulbs and bicycles, capital goods such as steel ships and locomotives, and so on. The example of a new productive system is a factory with a conveyor system or assembly lines, which was developed for the production of the Model T Ford in the United States. The old productive system was like a factory of the traditional type where the productive equipment did not move, so that workers had to move around with heavy materials and semifinished goods, etc.

We may classify the pattern of economic growth of the United States, Europe, and Japan during the prewar period according to the combination of the kind of product and productive system.

United States: O-N (old product-new system)
 N-N (new product-new system)

The United States had already developed the mass production system of new products that were applicable to old products, too, resulting in the accumulation of a huge amount of productive potential. As for the demand side, the demand for new products was increasing so as to expand the new American way of life to the entire country, but it was not enough to absorb the increase of productive potential: the tradition of Protestant asceticism was still alive, and the consumers' credit system and social security system were still undeveloped, so that the purchase of new products by low-income people was restricted by a shortage of money or fear of such a shortage.

The demand for old products had been saturated domestically, and their producers preferred to reduce employment rather than increase exports. The Great Depression attacked the U.S. economy at that time, accompanied by grave mistakes of demand management by the government.

Europe: O-N (old product-new system)
 N-O (new product-old system)

Europe was able to produce new products, but its production was still dependent on the old productive system. The cultural paradigm of mass production and mass consumption that developed in the United States was not yet accepted by this older society, where the demand for new products was supposed to arise only from the upper class. It may be said that the necessity or desirability of establishing a new productive system for new products was not recognized in prewar Europe.

With respect to old products, however, a new productive system was actively introduced, which saturated the demand for them and caused serious unemployment. The producers tried to find an outlet for excess production in exports, but this ended in the escalation of protectionist measures and the collapse of the foreign market.

Japan: O-O (old product-old system)
 O-N (old product-new system)

As Japan had very little capacity for producing new products, she had to import most of them from the United States and Europe and also had to establish new industries in order to catch up. The construction of new industries also necessitated a substantial import of new products from advanced countries. So she had a handicap, on one hand, and she had the advantage of being a follower, on the other hand.

It was easy to increase the productivity of old products with the old productive system simply through improving and/or increasing technological and capital inputs. Moreover, there was a large margin for increasing consumption of old products: the demand-supply relationship was far better than in the advanced countries because the level of consumption per capita of industrial products was substantially lower.

The Japanese economy was damaged seriously by the worldwide depression and the mistakes of restrictive policies of the Japanese government at that time, but the increase of exports of industrial products contributed greatly to the quick recovery from the depression. Her export surplus was criticized by the advanced industrial countries as social dumping, but the competitiveness of Japanese industry at that time was supported by a rapid increase in productivity due to the strength of domestic demand.

The Growth Rate during Wartime

If we assume that the United States, Europe (mainly Germany), and Japan entered the war under the conditions outlined above, it is easy to explain the result of the economic growth race during the war.

The United States had been prepared to produce both old and new products by a new productive system during the prewar period, the very low growth rate having resulted from a lack of demand, exacerbated by protectionist policies in the early 1930s.

The outbreak of the war, which followed the recovery from the depression, increased the demand for both old and new products tremendously. Responding to such an increase of demand, the American productive system expanded production and created a huge amount of worker income, which resulted in a demand for new products. Thus, the combination of O-N (old product-new system) and N-N (new product-new system), combined with full-scale demand, brought forth explosive economic growth.

Europe scarcely had a new productive system for new products. And World War II was decided by the quantity of new weapons, mainly produced by the productive system for consumer durables.

The Germans could develop super-new weapons such as rockets to bombard London directly, but they could not exceed Americans in the number of tanks, airplanes, and other ordinary weapons produced by the new productive system.

It is no wonder that Japan was defeated in the growth race when the import of new products was impossible: she had very little capacity for producing new products even by the old system. Japanese production of new weapons had to depend on producers who had never supplied new durable goods to domestic consumers.

At the beginning of the war, Japan obtained control of a huge amount of natural resources from which she could have produced a large quantity of new weapons, but they were useless due to the lack of a productive system in the Japanese economy.

Postwar High Economic Growth

The situation changed drastically after the war. The combinations of product and productive system, as well as the demand-supply relationship, changed everywhere.

United States: O-O (old product-old system)
                 N-O (new product-old system)

As a result of high economic growth during the war, most of the new products before the war had become "old" ones in the United States immediately after the war. The same was true with respect to the productive system.

The new products for the United States were those produced by new technologies such as electronics, electric communication, space technology, nuclear technology, moleculur biology, and so on. As the users of these products were not the American people in general but mainly specialists in the government, big enterprises, research institutes, etc., what was important was the development of new products rather than the invention of a new productive system. With respect to the productive system of old products such as consumer durables, no fundamental change took place.

Thus, the quality of growth of the U.S. economy changed from the prewar combination of O-N and N-N to the postwar combination of O-O and N-O. As mentioned before, production by the old productive system does not necessarily mean a slower growth than with production by a new productive system. It depends on the margin of increasing productivity through improving or increasing inputs on the supply side; on the demand side, it is affected by the cultural and/or institutional frameworks that shape people's attitudes toward consumption.

After the war, the productivity of old products—mainly composed of services such as education, medical care, leisure, and housing—could increase substantially in the United States thanks to the improvement and increase of inputs of material instruments. At the same time, government policies aiming at full employment and improved welfare constantly created a demand for consumer durables and services.

We may summarize the above as follows: the fact that the

increase of production centered on old products such as services made the rate of growth (3.6% during 1953-1973) lower than in Europe (4.8%) and Japan (9.5%) during the same period; the existence of intentional creation of consumers' demand made the rate of growth higher than in the prewar United States, i.e., 2.1% in 1922-1937.

Europe: O-N (old product–new system)
         N-N (new product–new system)

In postwar Europe, as a result of negative or zero growth during the war, the relation between new and old product, as well as between the new and old productive systems, remained the same as before the war. This means that, at least in the first half of the period of high economic growth after the war, many of the "old" products and productive systems for Americans were supposed "new" ones for Europeans.

Immediately after the war—that is, during the reconstruction period—the demand for old products increased very rapidly in order to recover the level of consumption before the war in Europe. The productive system was mostly "new," particularly in Continental Europe where war damage was very serious. Thus, the new productive system for old products, enjoying a very high operation ratio, created a huge amount of worker income, which was recycled to the producers of new products.

Unlike the prewar period, this time there was no obstacle to the adoption of a new productive system for new products. The American way of life had been accepted by most Europeans as an agreeable model, so a cheap and abundant supply of consumer durables became a social goal. Individuals were willing to work in the new productive system to get the high labor income to purchase new products. The government policies were directed toward full employment and perfection of a social security system that would protect the consumption level of workers from economic hazards.

The producers of new products with the new productive system were thus freed from the fear of persistent shortages or a sudden decline of domestic demand thanks to the sociocultural and/or institutional changes that took place after the war. The remaining problem was related to the international economy and taken care of by the establishment of the Bretton Woods system; that is, Europe in the 1950s and early 1960s tended to suffer from balance of payments deficit: it needed foreign currency, mainly dollars, to import goods and services in order to equip its productive system, but its exports were insufficient to finance all imports. The Bretton Woods system assured that the European countries could borrow the necessary amount of foreign currency at a constant exchange rate so as to respond to the demand of their peoples.

After the late 1960s, the former "new" products became "old" in Europe, too, but the resulting excess capacity was directed toward export to the United States and LDCs. It was also utilized for increasing or improving the inputs to production of services, which became the main engine of economic growth as in the United States. Thus, the utility of the Bretton Woods system—along with the predominance of the U.S. economy to support it—disappeared, and the pressure of cost-push inflation began to rise with the increase in the amount of old products produced by the old productive system, i.e., services.

Japan: O-N (old product–new system)
        N-N (new product–new system)

The situation of postwar Japan was fundamentally the same as that of Europe.

Admiration for the American way of life and the eagerness for "modernization" were very strong in postwar Japan. In place of the ideal of European welfare society, which pursues individual material welfare through collective policy measures, there was a national consensus that Japan should catch up with Western countries in income and wealth. This may have arisen from the ascetic or altruistic values of the traditional culture, but the predominant attitude exerted the same sort of influence on economic growth as that of the ideal of European welfare society as far as the adoption of demand-stimulating policies is concerned. The international context of postwar Japanese economic growth and the increased importance of services may be said to be completely the same as in Europe.

Japan's growth rate was far larger than Europe's. Even in the prewar period, Japan's growth rate was twice Europe's. Comparing Japan's intertemporal change of combinations of product and productive system with Europe's, we find that Japan, which had not been producing new products before the war, began to produce them after the war by a "new" productive system. But the composition of the product did not change in Europe. Thus, change could be more fundamental in Japan than in Europe. Even if the increase of demand for old products had been rapid in prewar Japan, it could not have been comparable with that for new products such as consumer durables in postwar Japan.

Therefore, the problem for postwar Japan centered on the supply side: that is, is it possible to introduce a new productive system for new products so as to keep up with the increase of demand? As it was possible for Japan, she realized a high rate of economic growth, unparallelled in peacetime. Many LDCs failed to achieve that, bringing forth instead destructive inflation and/or a deficit in their balance of payments. Some NICs now seem on the verge of breaking postwar Japan's record for peacetime growth.

New Products And New Productive System Today

Chronology of Industrial Society

It may be concluded from the above that the period from the 1920s to the 1970s constitutes one development cycle for the AICs in which a new productive system was born in the United States, diffused to Western Europe and Japan (and the East and NICs), and became "old" at least among the market economy AICs. So it is useful to review the past development of industrial society with respect to the alternation of new productive systems before trying to analyze the present situation and forecast future developments.

Table 4 **History of Industrial Development**

Era	Actor	New Productive System	Remarks
1770s - 1820s	Britain	factories and mines with machines driven by energy extracted from mineral fuels	U.S. independence French Revolution *Wealth of Nations* (1776)
1820s - 1870s	Europe U.S.	the above production units integrated by railway networks	Civil War formation of German Empire Meiji Restoration *Das Kapital* (1867)
1870s - 1920s	Europe U.S. Japan	essentially the same but electric power came into use	Germany and the U.S. catch up with Britain World War I Russian Revolution
1920s - 1970s	U.S. Europe Japan NICs	production units with conveyor system (automated)	World War II Japan catches up with Europe independence of ex-colonies

The Dilemma of New Products Today

As mentioned before, the successive appearance of new products is a cumulative and continuous development process of industrial society, which has been intensified along with the strengthening tie between scientific development and technological progress. In the old days when "necessity was the mother of invention," to invent a certain instrument—e.g., a machine that can fly with persons or that washes clothes—was an extraordinary task, responding to a demand that had existed through human history. Today, however, the situation has changed.

It is now not so difficult to create a new thing that may serve a certain objective. But the flood of products, mostly consumer durables, during the 1920s through the 1970s seems to have made it possible to satisfy almost all human needs, at least in market-economy AICs. Thus, the problem for the producers has become and will be to invent new "demands," not in the sense of economics but in that of intrinsic human needs.

Among the postwar "new" products in the United States, only those produced by biotechnology have little problem on the demand side, since they can be directly utilized for improving people's health. The utility of most others is simply to make the existing instruments more efficient, convenient, cheap, comfortable, and the like; that is, they do not offer a completely new instrument for satisfying "old"—hence, instrinsic—human demands. Furthermore, it is difficult for the new products to compete with old products, due to development costs.

New products must substitute for "old" products,[8] at least to some extent, in order to diffuse throughout the society: e.g. electric appliances for housekeeping, in TV programs for chatting with family members, etc. If the product mix were to disseminate all over the AICs, demand for the products of "natural" human beings could eventually disappear. That is, the new products may become the rival of human beings.

The Potential of the New Productive System Today

The new productive system that appeared in the United States during the 1970s and is expected to diffuse all over the AICs is closely related to "informatization." The trend toward integrating satellites, microwaves, laser beams, host computers and personal computers, various new materials and softwares and the like has made it possible to construct a huge network for accumulating, processing, transmitting, and distributing information. Unlike the traditional information network, the new system can deal with voice, image, and data simultaneously and reciprocally.

This network is not itself a system for material production, but it could revolutionize the efficiency of the productive system if applied. It could also increase tremendously the efficiency of the productive system for old products such as consumer durables, if it were applied to their production. Thus, the new productive system of today may be comparable to that in the period of the 1820s-1870s when the emerging railway networks connected factories, mines, farms, harbors, and residences of workers/consumers, resulting in a revolutionary and discontinuous increase of productivity of European and American industries.

In assuming that the "informatized" productive system could become the engine of economic growth of AICs in the period of the post-1970s, the next question is concerned with the "actors" who would build and drive that machine. The foregoing analysis of economic growth in the history of industrial society suggests that any revolutionary increase of productivity would never take place in a society which lacks either the demand for new products or the ability to create or absorb the knowhow for constructing the new productive system.

From the above point of view, the candidates for the bearers of new economic growth may be selected from the group consisting of the United States, Western Europe, Japan, and the NICs (Eastern Europe could be included in this group, but lack of information about that society has made the author give up examining it as a possibility). The situation of these countries or country groups concerning the introduction of the new productive system of a new era may be summarized as follows.

United States. Up to now, the United States has left all the other competitors far behind in both constructing and utilizing the new productive system. The present flux of foreign capital to the United States and resultant strong dollar in spite of huge deficits in the government's budget and the nation's international trade balance may not be explained without referring to expectations about its future predominance in the world economy when the new productive system comes into full-scale operation.

Europe. Europe seems to be reluctant to introduce the new productive system. This attitude may be related to its attitude toward new products, which was observable in the prewar period. What is different from the prewar period is that Europeans do not seem interested in the adoption of the new system even for the production of "old" products. If such an attitude continues, Europe could become the depressed area in the AICs in the near future.

Japan. In contrast to Europe, Japan is very eager to introduce the new productive system for the production of both new and old products. The problem here may be the shortage of capacity for constructing the new productive system. It seems to arise from the fact that the United States has become cautious in protecting her interest as the inventor and that Japan has come too close to the United States to be the imitator that she was in the beginning of the high-growth period. Furthermore, it is doubtful whether or not Japanese research and development investment would bring forth new products to replace human activities effectively, except for simple work tasks.

NICs. The situation of the NICs for the time being may be

comparable to that of Japan in the first half of the 1920s-1970s; that is, they are able to produce old products such as consumer durables but not new products. However, they may be eager to introduce the new productive system in order to produce old products.

Evaluation of Present Situation

Let us compare the post-1970s' period with the preceding periods which, more or less, coincide with Kondratieff cycles and may be called as the first, second, third, and fourth cycles of industrial society. We now are at the beginning of the fifth cycle. Although it is not certain that the present cycle will continue for 50 years, two things may be pointed out.

First, the new productive system in the present cycle resembles that in the second cycle, (1820s-1970s) in depending on the expansion of an emerging network connecting producers and consumers. As the railway network in the second cycle exerted a strong influence on the spread of changes occurring in the core of economic growth, i.e., the British society, the information network in the present cycle could also give a similar impact on the countries outside the AICs.

Second, the new products in the present cycle are not, as individual products, of a kind that could change people's lives discontinuously. This sharply constrasts with the third cycle (1870s-1920s), which involved many "big"inventions such as the electric light, phonograph, telephone, radio, automobile, movie, and airplane. The nature of the new productive system of the third cycle, however, was not revolutionary, so the worldwide dissemination of these products had to be postponed to the next cycle.

In other words, the present cycle of industrialized society could have the power to spread the changes through the AICs, but the contents of those changes do not seem very attractive to outsiders. Therefore, the future demand for new products depends on whether or not the new productive system—which means here the information network—diffuses through the AICs; that will also be affected by people's attitudes toward the new products. So far, there are two countries where the number of people who feel comfortable living with computer terminals has been increasing. They are the United States and Japan. But the situation is more difficult than in the prewar United States for new lifestyles to become prevalent. New products in the old days were useful for both working life and non-working life: for example, the automobile was remarkably useful both for commuting or transporting and for shopping, amusements, and so on. Today, products supplied through home computers are particularly useful for working at home but not so much for the other purposes: there are traditional—and usually cheaper—options for the users of home-shopping, home-banking, and amusement services. One might have an automobile even though one commutes by train, but one would not have a home computer simply for shopping, banking, and amusement.

In fact, most personal computers in U.S. homes are owned by professionals who need access to information services; in Japan, most computers are used as business equipment in workplaces. If the integration of working life and non-working life proceeds, the obstacle to the expansion of the information network—i.e., the shortage of demand for terminals and circuits—would disappear. But this would also mean the disappearance of an important trait of industrial society—the separation of producer and consumer.

Options for Contemporary Industrial Society

Societal Changes and Human Needs

Industrialized society has a history of about two hundred years: the Industrial Revolution began in Great Britain and has expanded from the Western Hemisphere to Japan and non-Western NICs. It should not be overlooked that Western Europe and Japan had hundreds of years of preparation before the Industrial Revolution and the Meiji Restoration. During this period, these societies underwent societal changes within an agricultural economy. Most of today's LDCs, which have been trying in vain to industrialize, have lacked such a preparatory period.

The history of agricultural society may be about 2000 years, or about ten times as long as that of industrial society. Almost all civilizations in today's world are the heirs of that society or those developed from it. It is impossible to estimate the length of the history of hunting-gathering society due to the lack of record, but, considering that mankind appeared on the earth millions of years ago, we may conjecture that it lasted for at least tens of thousands of years.

If we were to compare people's daily life in industrial society or its physical appearance with those of hunting-gathering society, we should be struck by the large differences between them. But this does not mean at all that the physical entity called man has changed. On the contrary, the physiological as well as psychological needs of human beings have not changed fundamentally from those millions of years ago. What has changed is the set of tools for responding to these needs. As the tools have changed, the behavior and related feelings of man have changed.

Technology, Institutions, and Values

The tools for responding to human needs can be divided into three categories of technology, institutions, and values so as to clarify the traits of the above three types of society by the differences in each category.[9]

Hunting-Gathering Society

The technology of hunting-gathering society is mainly composed of hunting and fishing technology as well as that for producing the instruments for such activities, e.g., bows and arrows, knives, fishing hooks and lines, and the like. The institutions of that society are generally composed of single and scattered groups headed by a leader assisted by a subleader (or subleaders) and having men and women for production, reproduction, care for children, battles, etc. The central values must be bravery and self-sacrifice, since this society is surrounded by wild beasts, severe climate, and hunger.

In the beginning, probably most of these tools were invented in order to respond to people's physical needs. In such a society, the members are all well acquainted with each other and can understand what their comrades are doing, so the emotional ties between individuals are strong and there is no need for inventing special tools for improving or increasing them.

Agricultural Society

The central technology of agricultural society aims at controlling and utilizing plants and animals: for instance, through plows, harnesses, carriages, and the like. As for institutions, it becomes possible to identify kinship so that groups integrating individuals with blood or quasi-blood relationships develop: e.g., family, clan, tribe. Regional communites are also shaped by kinship ties.

The invention of money results in the formation of a market where the buyers and sellers of material goods satisfy their needs even if the people belong to different groups. With respect to values, abstract and globalistic or universal values such as truth, beauty, and benevolence are invented and accepted by the people across the barrier of different communities.

The people who have developed particularly well these tools shape complex societies such as ancient empires and feudal states and then expand them to "undeveloped" areas. In such big and complex societies, people tend to be divided into upper and lower classes that often take the form of different castes. The shift from hunting-gathering society to agricultural society usually accompanies the eradication of old ethnic groups or at least their traditional culture, but the old tools can survive as long as they are compatible with and useful to the new tools.

Although it becomes easier to satisfy people's physical needs than in a hunting-gathering society, the ramshackle structure of the new society arising from the above-mentioned development process has little coherence among its various parts and tends to frustrate its members. People have ceased to live in a single monolithic and unified group and are put in a situation that is more unreasonable than before, from an individual point of view. To mitigate such frustration is a new mental need that cannot be dealt with by the means available in the old society.

Therefore, things previously used to meet physical needs begin to be diverted to provide mental satisfaction: for example, one may eat too much or wear too much simply to be respected and envied by one's peers. From a macro point of view, such an "abuse" of physical resources by individuals is dangerous, since such demands may sacrifice resources that should be conserved for the production of plants and animals. People, therefore, need to invent various ascetic values to impose on themselves; otherwise, those resources would perish.

Industrial Society

The technology of industrial society is mainly concerned with the control and utilization of inanimate (material) things and can be applied to the production of the means for any kind of human activity. The reason why this technology could make remarkable progress is that it was supported by natural science, which explained natural phenomena such as movement, heat, light, electricity, and so on.

The market becomes the core of industrial society, and most productive and distributive functions shift to enterprises that are supposed to obey only market rules. Some products are produced or distributed through the medium of the welfare state, which has developed to supplement the role of the market.[10] Only small families with the simplest structure are left.

Value neutrality is the basic principle of this society. In other words, the improvement of efficiency of producing and distributing the means for human activities becomes the central value of this society. Individualistic values such as freedom, equality, fairness, etc., would have little meaning, if people were not to pursue maximum economic gains through market competition.

Assuming that the people of industrial society have mental needs to be met by mental inputs, let us infer how they could meet such needs. In the early stage of industrialization, simply becoming freed from old ascetic values could bring forth mental satisfaction, since the frustrations in agricultural society diminish. At the same time, the regional communities and extended families still remain so that people can get mental inputs within such groups. Furthermore, the increase of physical outputs could be converted to that of mental inputs as in the case of agricultural society, but on a larger scale.

These merits do not last long, as the removal of traditional taboos happens only once: the emotional tie within the old groups disappears, along with the decline of old institutions and values. The joy of having or controlling something new diminishes when it becomes available to everybody. In industrial society, people are supposed to obtain physical resources in the market, distribute them to family members, and get mental satisfactions from them. But, in order for mental satisfactions to last long, it is necessary to do that reciprocally. Thus, the artificial separation between work (production) and leisure (consumption) or between rationality and emotionality in industrial society has brought forth a new frustration that has been mostly, so far, taken care of by the successive supply of new products. This results in environmental pollution and the destruction of human relations in the workplace and family.

The Persistence of Industrial Society

Some people might argue that the world has entered a completely new era, judging from the recent development of computation-communication technology, bio-technology, and the like. But is the change more fundamental than what was observed in the development of railway networks in the 1820s-1870s, or the invention of the epoch-making new products such as electric power, the automobile, and the airplane in the 1870s-1920s, or the appearance of mass production and mass consumption in the 1920s-1970s?

The core of present technological progress has been shifting from the production of material goods to that of human services, from the transformation and transmission of material and energy to that of information, from standardized production of homogeneous products to a differentiated supply of products that combine various goods and services. It is certainly different from the technological progress that arises from the tradition of industrial society. But, looking from a longer-term point of view, one may find that such a revolutionary change itself is one of the traits of the technology of industrial society.

Every 50 years, the old paradigm was abandoned and a new one appeared so as to create revolutionary new products and a new productive system.[11] Considering that, one may not conclude that the nature of technology in the contemporary AICs has changed from that of industrial society simply because it is undergoing revolutionary changes.

As for institutions and values, there have been continuous protests against the failure of the market and the destructive character of the value-emptiness of the philosophy of industrial society. Nevertheless, none of the new initiatives such as economic planning, the welfare state, government intervention in the market to manage demand, the protection of consumers or the natural environment, etc., has brought forth alternative institutions and values to substitute for those of industrial society. The main thrust now is toward deregulation and small government.

The Crisis to Come

We may now speculate that the present economic growth of AICs is destined to conclude the fifth Kondratieff cycle, which would extend, roughly speaking, from the 1970s to the 2020s. And one important fact is that there has never been a cycle (among the four) that did not involve "crises."

Aside from the first three cycles, nobody would deny that the crisis in the 1920s-1970s appeared in the period from the Great Depression (1930-1933) to World War II (1937-1945, including the Sino-Japanese War). Concern about the coming of a crisis in the present cycle is neither a groundless fear nor a Marxist threat foretelling the doom of the capitalist world. The nature of the crisis to come—probably in the next decade—could be conjectured by combining an analysis of prewar experience and current trends.

The United States is now investing heavily in research and development (R&D) and infrastructure that would eventually connect up the computer terminals of professionals all over the AICs through the medium of satellites. This investment is forecast to shape a new productive system with an extremely high efficiency within 10 years. And, if it were fully utilized for the production of old products—e.g., consumer durables, education, leisure, and commerce—a huge amount of unemployment would appear. The diffusion of completely automated factories, offices, shops, play parks, schools, hospitals and the like, connected with each other and data centers, would replace most of the jobs of ordinary workers and even managers and engineers (by means of artificial intelligence).

Americans will probably not do that. Instead, they will try to utilize the new system to produce new products, just as they did in the prewar period. But they will probably fail because of the reasons mentioned earlier. In the 1990s, how then might the excess productive capacity be used? If economic policy measures follow the classical school of economics, the combination of deregulation and small government would reproduce the Great Depression of the 1930s. If they follow the Keynesian school, a huge amount of surplus dollars would flow out of the United States so as to raise the prices of natural resources, land, space, and so on all over the world. There could be no alternative other than depression or stagflation.

Western Europe and Japan, which are currently dependent on the strong demand of the U.S. economy, would be seriously damaged by a decline in U.S. demand, even without offensive exports from the United States: As it is difficult to find sufficient internal demand for new products, Europe and Japan must depend on the demand for old products. Once they begin to produce old products by the new productive system, supply would become excessive immediately. The only means for protecting employment is to increase exports: in this case, Western Europe would probably give up competing with Japan and rely on protectionist measures. The position of the NICs is relatively advantageous, as in the case of prewar Japan, and they would become tough competitors against Japan.

Three Options

What would be the feasible and desirable solution of the problem of demand-supply discrepancy that seems likely to appear in the 1990s? Three options are conceivable.

The first one is to discharge the excess productive potential by means of war. The second is to freeze the excess potential so as to contain the crisis until the end of this cycle, i.e., around the 2020s. The third one to deindustrialize the AICs, maintaining the desirable features of industrial society.

Option A: War
Some people may interpret an East-West war as helping to discharge the excess productive potential as well as reducing the internal frictions of the West, since the necessity of solidarity would be strongly felt. This option is, of course, very undesirable for the peoples of the AICs.

Option B: Containment
Since the goal of this option is to restrain the new productive system so as to keep its capacity from being used, worldwide cooperation of rival producers or workers is indispensable. The spread of international informatization would provide favorable conditions for establishing an oligopolistic network of world enterprises. Japanese enterprises that were always the disturbing factor in the world market would become civilized, along with the strengthening of the tie with foreigners. This type of concertedness may be against the spirit of pure capitalism but could be

the sign of maturity of industrial society. However, it would create two problems, the first being the polarization of the peoples of AICs: a few elites who are equipped with fully automated facilities would enjoy high productivity and income. But, in order to keep the output per capita at a low level artificially, the majority would have to work as auxiliary or part-time workers. Frustrations would prevail among both the privileged workers, who would face extremely intensive work and severe competition for jobs, and the unprivileged workers, who would have poor incomes and little opportunity to realize their productive potential.

The second problem is the discontent of the LDCs. The restrictive strategy of the AICs would certainly jeopardize efforts to increase industrial production of the LDCs. Consequently, an overwhelmingly large part of the world population would be left in a mentally frustrated and politically unstable condition that would threaten the security of the populace of the AICs as a whole.

Option C: Deindustrialization

The LDCs could rapidly increase their production of "new" products such as consumer durables—which are "old" for AICs but not for LDCs (and, hence, irrelevant with saturation of demand). Of course, they may also increase the production of old products such as foods and textiles, if domestically needed, especially in the case of the least-developed countries. They could do that either by improving inputs in the old productive system or by establishing a new (for them) productive system.

The task of the AICs is to utilize their "new" products such as mentioned to help the economic growth of LDCs. These products are utilized domestically for responding to the psychic needs of the peoples of AICs. As a large part of the productive potential of the new productive system is utilized for the production of new products that meet appropriate demands, underemployment of human capacity can be avoided. Among the AICs, their cooperation is organized through the information network.

Strictly speaking, this option is not available now, even though its seeds may be in existence already. The traits of the products and producers of industrial society are not such as to allow such a way of utilizing their capacity. Consequently, this could happen only if the contemporary AICs are deindustrialized. And, if the deindustrialization of AICs were to start in the 1990s, the Kondratieff cycle itself could disappear in the next century.

Conditions for Desirable Deindustrialization

The shortage of material goods in today's LDCs could not occur if the method of choosing the combination of productive system and inputs to it were adequate, that is, based on an appropriate recognition of the needs and capacity of their populace. The physical and intellectual capability that mankind has accumulated must be sufficient for providing necessary conditions for that. The reason why the experiences of many countries have been contrary to this expectation seems to be that traditional institutions and values have collapsed due to disturbances brought about by the invasion of different kinds of institutions and values.

At the same time, it cannot be overlooked that the transfer of technology from AICs that was supposed to help LDCs has often exerted destructive effects on LDCs' technology. As mentioned before, the technology in hunting-gathering society or agricultural society was composed of techniques for raising the efficiency of human activities and producing the instruments for them. But the technology of industrial society concentrates on the latter, i.e., the production of means in general. Moreover, even the production of material goods cannot be the central concern of advanced technology in contemporary AICs, which has deviated from the pursuit of specific human demands so much that it is difficult to tell what the objective of technological superiority is.

When the LDCs try to replace their traditional technology with such an "advanced" one, the probability that they fail and lose both is very high. It has been argued already that such a nature of technological progress has arrived at a stage where it tends to increase difficulties as it tries to increase comfort, even in the AICs. Thus, the following question arises: what is the efficient way of pursuing satisfaction of human beings by utilizing one's own body and brain for the sake of helping the group or society to which they belong?

The importance of this question is based on the inference that the satisfaction of individual persons' needs would be inseparably interdependent with what they do themselves and particularly, from a macro point of view, what they do for each other: the program of mental and physical functioning of human beings must have been made as that of a social animal. This is not to revive the ascetic or altruistic values of the old days, when physical means for controlling nature were so limited that individual persons had to train themselves for getting necessary resources as well as refrain from pursuing the satisfaction of their needs irrespective of the ways determined by the nature and amount of instruments available for the group to which they belonged.

In today's AICs, on the contrary, an abundant supply of technologies often leads to their abuse, which results in underemployment of human potentials, environmental destruction, unemployment, frustrations, and so on. The availability of physical means is no longer the absolute exogenous factor to which the way and degree of satisfaction of human needs have to be obedient—but, of course, this does not mean that they are a panacea or infinitely available. The relationship between the two should be an interdependence in which the technology could play an important role.

The human race after industrial society would have to develop the technology for exploiting and controlling itself, taking into consideration the existence of various options about the combination between self-production and use of instruments. Such a technology would need adequate knowledge about human beings, especially the behavioral characteristics of human groups, just as the technology of pre-industrial societies needed knowledge about the behavioral characteristics of plants and animals as the object of exploitation and control.

The observations of social phenomena informed and stored as news, histories, legends, etc., of various nations would supply abundant raw materials for developing human science, which is the system of knowledge as mentioned above. The problem is how to comprehend them consistently: simply to juxtapose various "facts" as in the Baconian natural histories would not bring forth a dynamic development of human science. In this sense, the existing metaphysics and social sciences are weak tools for dealing with such raw materials.

As for ways to assist technology in extracting and managing human potentials, there seems to be a promising candidate: that is, the "new" products that are being developed in contemporary AICs. These kinds of new products would be highly efficient if utilized for productive purposes, that is, for making contributions to other nations. The efficiency of the human race in managing itself could rise substantially if it is aided by these new products. They may also be exported to assist the LDCs in increasing the efficiency of the management of their societies.

Lastly, deindustrialization would not be completed only by technological development based on human science and the full utilization of new products. It would need institutions and values that differ from those of industrial society; otherwise, the technology in the new era could exacerbate the evils of industrial society. However, the knowledge of human science could also be useful for shaping new institutions and values suitable for new society. A collaboration of thinkers including historians and social scientists is desirable in this connection. In considering the difficulty involved in creating new technology, institutions, and values, a period of ten years (i.e., from now to 1990s) for commencing the dynamic development of this science may be too short. The gigantic gear of technological progress based on natural science has already begun to move toward a new revolution, irrespective of whether or not human science will be able to follow.

Notes

1. *Oil and Gas Journal.*
2. The Report of INTERFUTURES, "Facing the Future: Mastering the Probable and Managing the Unpredictable" (O.E.C.D., Paris), which was published in 1979, proposed several alternative scenarios about the possible development paths of the world economy. It perceives the long-term economic and social trends to be generated by interactions of people's activities and resistances that also take physical constraints into account. The author shares basically the same worldview and, hence, has made it the foundation of the arguments in this paper.
3. Andrea Boltho, "Growth," in *The European Economy: Growth and Crisis* (edited by A. Boltho), Oxford University Press, 1982.
4. Ibid., p. 12.
5. Ibid., p. 16.
6. Ibid., p. 35.
7. The figures for 1922-1953 were obtained from *Long Term Economic Growth 1860-1970,* U.S. Department of Commerce, June 1973, p. 105. The figures for 1953-1973 were obtained from International Financial Statistics, IMF.
8. Here it is assumed that the productive activities of human beings are not limited to those in the *formal sector,* i.e., the market sector and the welfare state, but carried out also in the *informal sector,* e.g., self, household, and regional community. Thus the definition of products or production is far wider here than that employed in national accounts statistics. See Yoshihiro Kogane, "Changing Value Patterns and Their Impact on Economic Structure;" Y. Kogane, "New Demands and the Development of Advanced Industrial Societies;" Jonathan I. Gershuny, "Goods Replacing Services: Some Implications for Employment," *In Changing Value Patterns and Their Impact on Economic Structure* (edited by Y. Kogane), Tokyo, University of Tokyo Press, 1982.
9. In connection with Daniel Bell's the way of distinguishing social realms one may assign technology to the *techno-economic structure,* institutions to the *polity,* and values to the *culture,* respectively, in Bell's paradigm. See Daniel Bell, *The Cultural Contradictions of Capitalism,* New York, Basic Books, Inc., 1976.
10. With respect to the countries with a centrally planned economy system, this description will have to be modified to some extent, but even they could not eliminate the market system, having to admit that it is an indispensable tool for managing their society.
11. Thomas Kuhn pointed out the necessity of understanding the difference between revolutionary changes and cumulative changes in the history of scientific development. The former are generated by the change of paradigms that are "universally recognized scientific achievements that for a time provide model problems and solutions to a community of practitioners." The same thing could be said concerning the history of technological development and the community of engineers. See Thomas S. Kuhn, *The Structure of Scientific Revolutions,* Chicago, The University of Chicago Press, 1962, 1970.

1995: The Turning Point in Oil Prices

by

Hamid Gholamnezhad

Weak oil prices and today's relative abundance of oil have led many to believe that the oil supply problem has been solved and that plenty of oil will be available from the Organization of Petroleum Exporting Countries (OPEC), Mexico, the North Sea, the Soviet Union, and other sources.

In the past 13 years, we have witnessed major fluctuations in oil prices. The price of a barrel of Arabian light crude went from $2 in 1972 to $34 in 1981. Then, in March 1983, for the first time in its history, OPEC reduced its official price from $34 to $29 per barrel. This decision was made because of a surprisingly low demand for oil. Demand for oil in the noncommunist world dropped 14% from its peak of 50.3 million barrels per day (mbd) in 1979 to 43.4 mbd in 1983 (*Petroleum Economist,* September 1984). Most observers of the international oil market describe the major causes as the recession in the industrialized countries, energy conservation measures by consumers, substitution of alternative energy sources for oil, and a drawdown of oil companies' stockpiles.

Some of these causes will have a permanent effect on the world demand for oil. But, as the economic activities in the industrialized world revive and oil companies begin refilling their stockpiles, demand for oil will rise again.

The dollar value of oil has declined substantially in the past four years, but strengthening of the dollar in the past two years has caused a rise in oil prices in most other countries. For example, oil prices went up by some 10% in Japanese yen, 33% in deutsche marks, and 40% in British pounds (*Petroleum Economist,* March 1985).

Hamid Gholamnezhad is director of the Energy Research Institute, Moorhead State University, Moorhead, Minnesota.

Although oil prices may continue their declining trend in the next two years, most analysts agree that oil prices will rise again, particularly in the 1990s. Projections made by the United States Department of Energy indicate oil prices ranging from $30 a barrel to $55 a barrel for 1995 (1984 dollar value). There have also been a number of other projections by oil companies such as Chevron Corporation (*World Energy Outlook,* July 1984) and Conoco (*World Energy Outlook through 2000,* April 1984). Most of these projections are based on quantitative economic factors such as the rate of economic growth, the demand for oil, and the supply of oil. But the international oil market is complex, and economic factors alone will not predict its future. Rather, political factors play important roles in shaping its future. As we have witnessed in the past 13 years, oil prices can be influenced by wars, revolutions, and other political events. With so many variables to consider, one should not be surprised that different forecasts come up with different answers.

In this paper, using the analytic hierarchy process (AHP), an approach with demonstrated effectiveness for this type of problem, the real price of oil in 1995 will be predicted. It should be emphasized, however, that our approach is a complement to existing methods. It is a systematic and logical synthesis of the information provided by these methods and other qualitative factors.

The Methodology

The analytic hierarchy process is a method of breaking down a complex, unstructured, and fuzzy problem into its component parts; arranging these parts, or variables, into a hierarchic order; assigning numerical values to subjective judgments on the relative importance of each variable; and synthesizing the judgments to determine the overall priorities of the variables (Saaty, 1982). AHP has been applied successfully to a variety of problems: planning, prediction, prioritization, resource allocation, conflict resolution, and decision-making. The process has three major components:

Step 1 The problem is decomposed into factors or elements. Elements are grouped on different levels and form a chain or hierarchy. Each element is, in turn, broken down into another set of elements. The process continues to the lowest level of the hierarchy. The hierarchy does not need to be complete; that is, an element in a given level does not have to function as a criterion for all the elements in the level below. Thus, a hierarchy can be divided into subhierarchies sharing only a common topmost element.

Step 2 The degree of importance of the elements at a particular level over those in the succeeding level is measured by a procedure of paired comparisons. This is done by the decision-maker(s). To quantify our judgments, a scale with values ranging from 1 to 9 is used (see Table 1).

Table 1. The Scale and its Description

Intensity of Importance	Definition
1	E_i and E_j are <u>equally</u> important
3	E_i is <u>moderately</u> more important than E_j
5	E_i is <u>strongly</u> more important than E_j
7	E_i is <u>very strongly</u> more important than E_j
9	E_i is <u>extremely</u> more important than E_j
2, 4, 6, 8	Intermediate values between two adjacent judgments.
Reciprocals:	If activity i has one of the preceding numbers assigned to it when compared with activity j, then j has the reciprocal value when compared with i.

E_i and E_j are the elements of the hierarchy, i.e. criteria, alternatives, etc.

Step 3 To compute the priorities of the elements in each matrix of paired comparisons, we solve the eigenvalue problem of each matrix. This vector is then weighted with the weight of the higher-level element that was used as the criterion in making the pairwise comparisons that constitute the matrix in question. The procedure is repeated by moving downward through the hierarchy, computing the weights of each element at every level, and using these to determine composite weights for succeeding levels.

The most crucial stage of the process is the structuring of the model. If the analyst has a clear understanding of the problem and is familiar with all the relevant factors involved in the problem and their interrelationships, the model could be constructed easily in a relatively short time. A more detailed explanation of the methodology is given in Appendix I.

Factors Affecting Future World Oil Prices

The international oil markets are characterized by many uncertain factors. The most important factors affecting oil price projections include world oil consumption growth rate, world excess oil production capacity, additions to world oil reserves, intensity of the development of alternative energy sources, influence of international financial institutions, and, above all, political factors. These factors are described briefly in the following sections.

a. World Oil Consumption Growth Rate (W_1)

World oil consumption growth rate depends on a number of factors, including the economic growth rates, the consumers' response to higher oil prices, and the availability of replacement fuels.

The share of oil in the world energy mix is projected to decline in the future, but total volume of oil consumption will increase significantly. Free-world oil demand went down by 14% from 50.3 mbd in 1979 to 43.4 mbd in 1983. But oil demand in the developing countries as a whole rose from 9.5 mbd in 1979 to 10.3 mbd in 1983 (*Petroleum Economist,* September 1984). According to a report by the United States Energy Information Administration, free-world oil demand will rise to 53.2 mbd by 1995 (United States Department of Energy, 1983). Most of this increase is expected in the less developed countries (LDCs), especially in OPEC-member countries, where the economic growth will be high and no other competitive substitute will be available. The Soviet bloc and China will also have above-average growth rates. However, in 1983, the industrialized countries of the free world accounted for more than 70% of the total free world's oil demand. Thus, world oil demand in the future will depend greatly on the strategies of these countries regarding energy conservation and fuel substitution.

b. World Excess Production Capacity (W_2)

The world's excess production capacity is today about 14 mbd. More than 7 mbd of this excess capacity is in Saudi Arabia alone, and most of the rest is in OPEC-member countries. Also, at the end of 1983, world stocks were 4.7 billion barrels, or about 101 days of supply (United States Department of Energy, 1983). Thus, between now and 1990, there will be plenty of oil available to meet the world demand, even at the highest levels of projections. However, by 1995, as the demand for oil approaches the available supplies, there will be upward pressures on oil prices.

OPEC's demand for oil, which was 2.5 mbd in 1980, is projected to increase to 3.7 mbd in 1985, 5.3 mbd by 1990, and 6.7 mbd to 16.7 mbd by the year 2000 (Fesharaki and Johnson, 1982). OECD net imports will not change, due to both declines in production and consumption. But non-OPEC LDCs' oil production is expected to increase from 5.7 mbd in 1980 to 9.7 mbd in 1990 and then decline to about 7 mbd in the year 2000. In this same period, their consumption will increase faster than the production, increasing their net imports from 2.5 mbd in 1980 to about 4.7 mbd in the year 2000 (Fesharaki and Hoffman, 1982).

When the level of excess capacity is high, as it is today, only large oil producers can affect oil prices significantly by fluctuating their output. However, when the excess capacity declines substantially, approaching 2 to 3 mbd, even small producers can cause a sudden jump in oil prices by cutting back their production (or large producers by cutting back on a small portion of their production).

c. Additions to Reserves (W_3).

The amount of oil available in the future depends primarily on two factors: the productivity of already discovered reserves, and the amount of recoverable oil reserves left in the ground, including undiscovered reserves.

Before 1970, oil discovery rates were much higher than oil production rates, about 20 to 30 billion barrels per year. Therefore, the volume of the world's discovered reserves was increasing. But, in the 1970s, oil discovery rates declined to about 15 billion barrels per year, while production rates rose continuously. According to the Exxon Corporation, in the future, "finding and developing the world's as yet undiscovered oil and gas resources will be progressively more difficult and costly. The number of unexplored areas where there are chances of finding large fields is steadily diminishing. Furthermore, many of the more promising of these are either in remote, undeveloped locations or involve exceptionally harsh operating environments, such as deep water or the cold of the polar region" (Exxon Corporation, 1982).

There is a wide range of estimates of the remaining oil resources. In the decade before 1974, total world oil reserves rose from 342 billion barrels to 639 barrels. But in the nine years from 1974 to 1983, proved reserves increased by only 5% from 639 to 669 billion barrels. More than 55% of these reserves are in the Middle East.

Since 1974, reserves have decreased by 15% in the United States, by about 25% in the U.S.S.R., and 10% in Western Europe. The largest elsewhere has been in Mexico, where the volume of proved reserves increased from 5 billion barrels in 1970 to 48 billion barrels in 1983. At the current rates of production, proved reserves will last only 9 years in the United States, 14 years in the U.S.S.R., 19 years in Western Europe, and 85 years in the

Middle East (*Petroleum Economist,* October 1983). At the current rate of consumption, the world's total proven oil reserves will last less than 30 years.

d. Intensity of the Development of Alternative Energy Sources (W_4)

A substantial amount of oil could be replaced by synthetic fuels from coal, oil shale, tar sand reserves, and biomass resources. Most of the oil used in the residential and commercial sectors could be replaced by natural gas, electricity, or even coal. In the industrial sector, particularly, for power generation, oil could be substituted by coal (if available). Despite the recent antinuclear movements in the United States, nuclear's share of world energy consumption will increase significantly in the next decade. Solar energy, particularly solar heating, will become more popular in the future. Above all, with appropriate policies of the consuming governments, energy conservation, particularly in the transportation sector, could contribute significantly in reducing demand for oil.

This transition to alternative energy sources will certainly take more than a decade to complete. Because of the technological, environmental, and financial constraints, these alternative resources are not expected to replace more than one mbd of oil by 1995. However, with rising oil prices and appropriate government policies, most of these fuels will become competitive with oil in the late 1990s.

e. Influence of International Financial Institutions (W_5)

Oil price increases of the 1970s created a large transfer of wealth from the oil-importing countries to the oil-exporting countries. OPEC revenues were $90.5 billion in 1974, $279 billion in 1980, and $160 billion in 1983 (*Petroleum Economist,* September 1983). If the funds are circulated properly, they will provide more incentive to oil producers to increase their oil supply beyond their domestic financial needs. Besides, since oil prices are based on the U.S. dollar, the value of the dollar vis-a-vis other currencies and the rate of inflation in the industrialized countries would significantly influence oil-exporters' decisions on the price of oil.

f. Political Factors (W_6)

Oil and politics have never been apart. One may argue that, in the past 13 years, every major price increase was caused by political events. The Arab oil embargo of 1973, the Iranian revolution, the Iran-Iraq war, and the consequent disruptions in world oil supplies have demonstrated the significance of political factors in shaping this most international of businesses. The following is a brief description of these factors.

P_1: Stability of oil-exporting countries. Eight of the major oil-exporting countries are located in the Middle East, three in Latin America, and two in Southeast Asia. All of these areas have been and will continue to be politically unstable. The region that will continue to be of extreme importance in the future supply and prices of oil is the Middle East, particularly the Persian Gulf states. The Persian Gulf is surrounded by a number of major oil-exporting countries such as Saudi Arabia, Iran, Iraq, Kuwait, Qatar, Bahrain, and the United Arab Emirates. These countries, excluding Bahrain, are members of OPEC and altogether account for over 80% of its proved oil reserves or nearly half of the world's total reserves. Currently, almost 20% of the noncommunist world oil supply passes through the narrow Strait of Hormuz in the Persian Gulf.

Stability of the oil-exporting countries itself depends on several other factors, particularly the social strains due to rapid economic development, industrialization, distribution of income, distribution of authority, religious and political movements, and tensions between the individual states, as we are now witnessing between Iran and Iraq and their Arab allies. This conflict could escalate, directly involving other Arab countries.

Although most Arab oil-exporting countries have an interest in the economic well-being of the industrialized world, a change in government could affect their oil production policies. The power struggle between different political groups in Iran or any of the conservative Arab states, a coup d'etat in Iran or Iraq, and political unrest in Mexico are among the possibilities that could lead to the overthrow of the regimes and restrict oil production in these countries. On the other hand, if the Iran- Iraq conflict is resolved, both could boost their oil production and flood the market.

P_2: Intensity of the Arab-Israeli conflict. The Arab- Israeli conflict has been the major source of instability in the Middle East. So far, we have witnessed four wars between the Arabs and the Israelis: the 1948 war that led to the closing of the Iraqi pipeline in Haifa; the 1956 and 1967 wars that led to the closing of the Suez Canal; and finally, the 1973 war that led to the oil embargo and high oil prices. Long delays in resolving the conflict will discourage the major Arab oil producers from cooperating with the industrialized world in meeting its demand for oil. This could lead to the overthrow of moderate regimes, and, consequently, oil prices could rise drastically.

P_3: Increasing Soviet influence in the Middle East. The Soviet Union is now the world's biggest exporter of oil after Saudi Arabia. Its oil exports to the West make up more than 60% of its badly needed hard currency earnings. But its exports are likely to decline, and the Soviet Union will be competing with the West for Middle Eastern oil. Some political observers believe that Soviet intervention in Afghanistan and its assumed assistance to the rebels in Baluchistan are, among other things, for the purpose of providing itself with secure oil- and gas-supply sources in the future by having access to the Persian Gulf.

Increasing Soviet influence in the Middle East will enhance its position in the oil market vis-a-vis the West, and, if it is advantageous, the Soviets would not hesitate to use oil as an economic weapon against the West, particularly the United States. This action would lead to higher payments for oil for the Western countries.

P_4: OPEC pricing behavior. OPEC has managed well for its members in the 1970s. Today, Saudi Arabia, because of its large production capacity and its secure financial status, is dominating OPEC's decisions. But in the future, in a tight market situation, increased radicalization in member nations would reduce Saudi Arabia's power in OPEC and would force prices upward. Moderate members have had a damping effect on price increase, but, in the long run, they would tend to be outnumbered and may gradually lose their influence. In the next decade, OPEC's behavior should be favorable to stable and steady oil price increases. But the actions of the Soviet Union could encourage radicalization, whose dangers are greatest for Saudi Arabia and Kuwait (Saaty and Gholamnezhad, 1981).

P_5: Great power struggle. This factor represents all major economic and military powers as they individually and collectively work to enhance their influence in the world and to secure their domestic economic needs. To do this, some have been known to pay higher prices, thus gradually encouraging their adoption by oil producers. Some of these countries are able to absorb higher prices through increased export.

Computation of Oil Price Increases

The analytic hierarchy process is used to determine oil price increases by 1995. Figure 1 is a hierarchical model representing the factors and their interdependence as they affect the future oil prices. The following steps describe the computation process.

Step 1: Compute relative weights of the major factors (W_1, W_2, ... W_6) according to their influence on the price of oil by 1995. The question asked is: which factor would have *more* influence on the price of oil by 1995? For demonstration purposes, the pairwise comparison matrix of major factors, its largest eigenvalue (λ max), eigenvectors, and consistencies are shown below:

	W_1	W_2	W_3	W_4	W_5	W_6	Weights
W_1	1	1	7	3	5	1/3	.200
W_2	1	1	7	3	5	1/3	.200
W_3	1/7	1/7	1	1/5	1/4	1/9	.026
W_4	1/3	1/3	5	1	3	1/5	.095
W_5	1/5	1/5	4	1/3	1	1/7	.052
W_6	3	3	9	5	5	1	.427

$\lambda_{max} = 6.35$
C.I. = .07
C.R. = .06

The judgments on the relative importance of the elements of the matrices are made by the author. It must be emphasized, however, that the judgments are not arbitrary, but based on my lengthy involvement in the energy field, an exhaustive survey of current research on the international oil market, as well as informed opinions of some of the leading experts in this field. In the following paragraphs, I demonstrate how one makes use of the scale listed in Table 1 to fill in a pairwise comparison matrix.

In the above matrix, when comparing world oil consumption growth rate (W_1) to world excess production capacity (W_2), I assigned a value of 1, which means, in my judgment, they are of "equal importance" in determining the price of oil in 1995. This is because increased oil consumption would reduce excess capacity.

When comparing world oil consumption growth (W_1) to the additions to reserves (W_3), I assigned a value of 7, which means W_1 is "very strongly" more important than W_3 in determining oil prices in 1995. Obviously, additions to reserves is limited and requires long lead times. Therefore, when compared to oil consumption growth, it will not have much effect on oil prices by 1995. However, when comparing oil consumption growth (W_1) to the political factors (W_6), I assigned a value of ⅓, which means political factors (W_6) are "moderately" more important than oil consumption growth (W_1). The importance of political factors has been described in detail in the previous section of this paper. The same process is repeated for the second, third, fourth, and fifth rows.

An important point to consider when filling a pairwise comparison matrix is that, first of all, a good look must be taken at all the factors to be compared. Then, while keeping the "big picture" in the background, a comparison is made of two factors at a time. This approach improves the consistency of judgments and gives more realistic weights for the factors being compared.

The numbers in the lower triangular part of the matrix are simply the inverse of the numbers in the upper triangular part. For example, $W_1/W_3 = 7$, whereas $W_3/W_1 = 1/7$. Both of these numbers show the dominance of W_1 over W_3 as well as the intensity of this dominance. Using a computer program specially designed for this methodology, the largest eigenvalue, eigenvectors, and consistencies are computed. The normalized eigenvectors (the far right column) represent the relative importance of the factors. Political factors ($W_6 = .427$) being the most important and additions to reserves ($W_3 = .026$) being the least important in this analysis. Also, since the consistency ratio (CR = .06) is less than 10%, it indicates a good consistency in my judgments.

Step 2: For world oil consumption growth (W_1) and political factors (W_6), determine relative importance of their subfactors. The subfactors for W_1 are four groups of countries: industrialized countries of the free world (C_1), oil-rich developing countries (C_2), non-oil developing countries (C_3), and centrally planned economies (C_4). The question asked is: which group's oil demand would have more effect on oil prices by 1995?

The subfactors for W_6 are stability of oil-exporting countries (P_1), intensity of the Arab-Israeli conflict (P_2), Soviet influence in the Middle East (P_3), OPEC pricing behavior (P_4), and great power struggle (P_5). The question asked in comparing these factors is: which political factor would have more influence on the price of oil by 1995? The weights of the subfactors are multiplied by the weight of their corresponding factor to compute overall weights (see Tables 2 and 3).

Step 3: The political factor labeled as the stability of oil-exporting countries (P_1) is broken down into five subfactors: stability of the Saudi Arabian government (S_1), stability of the Kuwaiti government (S_2), stability of the Iranian Islamic regime (S_3), stability of the Mexican government (S_4), and tension between individual states in the Persian Gulf (S_5). The question asked here is: which factor would have more influence on the stability of the oil-exporting countries? Again, the relative weights of these factors are multiplied by the weight of P_1 from Table 3 (see Table 4).

Table 2. Relative Weights of Oil-Consuming Groups

Group	Weight	Weight x W_1
C_1: Industrialized countries of the free world	.636	.127
C_2: Oil-rich developing countries	.05	.01
C_3: Non-oil developing countries	.09	.018
C_4: Centrally-planned economies	.224	.045

Table 3. Relative Weights of the Political Factors

Factor	Weight	Weight x W_6
P_1	.482	.206
P_2	.139	.059
P_3	.088	.038
P_4	.249	.106
P_5	.042	.018

Table 4. Relative Weights of the Factors Determining the Stability of Oil-Exporting Countries

Factors	Weight	Weight x P_1
S_1	.491	.101
S_2	.159	.032
S_3	.075	.015
S_4	.041	.008
S_5	.234	.048

Step 4: For each factor C_1, C_2, C_3, C_4, W_2, W_3, W_4, W_5, S_1, S_2, S_3, S_4, S_5, P_2, P_3, P_4, and P_5, compute the relative likelihood of its corresponding subfactors. The questions asked are:

(a) Which of the three levels of oil-consumption growth rate is more likely for each group of countries: .5% per year, 1% per year, or 1.5% per year?

(b) Which of the three levels of excess production capacity is more likely by 1995: 2 mbd, 4 mbd, 8 mbd?

(c) Which of the three rates of additions to reserves is more likely: 5 billion barrels per year, 10 billion barrels per year, or 15 billion barrels per year?

(d) Which of the three levels of development in alternative energy sources is more likely: low, moderate, or high?

(e) Which of the three levels of influence of international financial institutions is more likely: low, moderate, or high?

(f) What is the likelihood of the stability of the governments of Saudi Arabia (S_1), Kuwait (S_2), Iran (S_3), and Mexico: (S_4) unstable, status quo, or stable?

(g) What is the likelihood of tension between individual states in the Persian Gulf (S_5): decrease, status quo, or increase?

(h) What is the likelihood of the Arab-Israeli conflict (P_2): decrease, status quo, or increase?

(i) What is the likelihood of Soviet influence in the Middle East (P_3): decrease, status quo, or increase?

(j) What is the likelihood of OPEC pricing behavior (P_4): unfavorable or favorable?

(k) For great power struggle (P_5), we ask the question: Which of the three levels of intensity is more likely for the period under consideration: low, moderate, or high?

Step 5: Compute the composite weights for each subfactor as was described in the section on methodology. Note that one may eliminate factors with very low weight without having a significant impact on the final outcome (see Table 5).

Step 6: Compute the relative likelihoods for each level of price increase for each subfactor.

Step 7: Compute composite weights of the levels of price increases. The result will be a set of numbers representing the likelihood of each price increase (see Table 6).

Step 8: Compute the expected value of price increase by weighting the percentages by the values of their likelihood and adding. We come up with the equation: 10 x .075 + 20 x .134 + 40 x .241 + 80 x .296 + 160 x .254 = 77.39%

Table 5

Factors		Composite Weights	Factors		Composite Weights
W_1	L M H	.013 .029 .004	S_3	U SQ S	.011 .003 .001
W_2	L M H	.033 .148 .019	S_4	U SQ S	.0008 .005 .002
W_3	L M H	.006 .017 .003	S_5	D SQ I	.003 .013 .031
W_4	L M H	.006 .021 .068	P_2	D SQ I	.012 .035 .012
W_5	L M H	.007 .037 .007	P_3	D SQ I	.004 .010 .024
S_1	U SQ S	.019 .074 .008	P_4	U F	.080 .027
S_2	U SQ S	.003 .023 .006	P_5	L M H	.002 .005 .012

Table 6. Expected Price Increases

Level	Percent (P)	Likelihood (L)
Very Low	10	.075
Low	20	.134
Medium	40	.241
High	80	.296
Very High	160	.254

Conclusions

The international oil market is the most complex trade market in the world today. Its influence is felt not only in the economic affairs of nations, but also reaches out to the technical, social, environmental, and political domains, all continually interacting and affecting one another. Predicting oil prices in such a dynamic and volatile market would be fruitless without the consideration of intangible factors, particularly political influences.

In this paper, using the analytic hierarchy process (AHP), the price of oil for 1995 is predicted. AHP provides a new framework for analyzing the oil market. It allows an analyst to lay out the problem in its complex natural state, but to solve the problem in a rather simple way. The debates that take place in the prioritization process enhance the understanding of the problem. Since the computations are rather simple, the process can be implemented easily without incurring large costs and without using elaborate facilities and other resources. I must caution, however, that this should not be a number-crunching experience. Rather, the process itself must be emphasized.

The prediction made in this paper shows a 77.39% increase in oil prices between 1985 and 1995—or, on the average, about 5.9% per year. Considering the present OPEC-weighted average price of $28.20 per barrel, this percentage amounts to the following real price of oil by 1995 (1985 dollars): $28.20 x 1.7739 = $50.02. Assuming an average annual inflation rate of 6%, the nominal price of a barrel of oil could be as high as $89.90 by 1995.

Recent projections by the United States Department of Energy indicate that the price of crude oil could range from $30 per barrel to $55 per barrel in 1995 (1984 dollars) (United States Department of Energy, 1984).

Considering the increasingly higher costs of producing oil outside OPEC and the costs of alternatives to oil from $40 to more than $70 per barrel of oil equivalent, the results of this prediction are reasonable. According to my estimates, in 1995, oil will be much cheaper than synthetic fuels and most of its alternatives. Higher oil prices will also increase the production costs of alternative energy sources. Thus, this level of oil prices will provide the major oil exporters such as Saudi Arabia and Kuwait with long-term security of demand for their oil.

It should be noted that, in an extreme situation, when a supply crisis is triggered by a political event in the Middle East or elsewhere in the world, we could see skyrocketing prices in the spot market. In that case, at least temporarily, the price of a barrel of oil could reach as much as $100 a barrel before 1995.

Appendix

The Analytic Hierarchy Process

Assume that we are given n stones, $A_1, \ldots, A_n$, whose weights $w_1, \ldots, w_n$, respectively, are known to us. Let us form the matrix of pairwise ratios whose rows give the ratios of the weights of each stone with respect to all others. Thus, we have the matrix:

$$AW = \begin{array}{c} \\ A_1 \\ A_2 \\ \\ \\ \\ A_n \end{array} \begin{array}{cccc} A_1 & A_2 & \cdots & A_n \\ \end{array} \\ \left[\begin{array}{cccc} \dfrac{w_1}{w_1} & \dfrac{w_1}{w_2} & \cdots & \dfrac{w_1}{w_n} \\ \dfrac{w_2}{w_1} & \dfrac{w_2}{w_2} & \cdots & \dfrac{w_2}{w_n} \\ \cdot & \cdot & & \cdot \\ \cdot & \cdot & & \cdot \\ \cdot & \cdot & & \cdot \\ \dfrac{w_n}{w_1} & \dfrac{w_n}{w_2} & \cdots & \dfrac{w_n}{w_n} \end{array} \right] \left[\begin{array}{c} w_1 \\ w_2 \\ \cdot \\ \cdot \\ \cdot \\ w_n \end{array} \right] = n \left[\begin{array}{c} w_1 \\ w_2 \\ \cdot \\ \cdot \\ \cdot \\ w_n \end{array} \right] = nw$$

We have multiplied A on the right by the vector of weights w. The result of this multiplication is nw. Thus, to recover the scale from the matrix of ratios, we must solve the problem $Aw = nw$ or $(A - nI)w = 0$. This is a system of homogeneous linear equations. It has a nontrivial solution if and only if the determinant of $(A - nI)$ vanishes, i.e., n is an eigenvalue of A. Now A has unit rank since every row is a constant multiple of the first row. Thus, all its eigenvalues, except one, are zero. The sum of the eigenvalues of a matrix is equal to its trace, and, in this case, the trace of A is equal to n. Thus, n is an eigenvalue of A, and we have a nontrivial solution. The solution consists of positive entries and is unique to within a multiplicative constant, by the Perron-Frobenius theorem.

To make w unique, we normalize its entries by dividing by

their sum. Thus, given the comparison matrix, we can recover the scale. In this case, the solution is any column of A normalized. Note that, in A, we have aji = 1/aij, the reciprocal property. Thus, also, $a_{ii} = 1$. Also, A is consistent, i.e., its entries satisfy the condition: ajk = aik/aij. Thus, the entire matrix can be constructed from a set of n elements that form a chain across the rows and columns.

In the general case, we cannot give the precise values of wi/wj but estimates of them. For the moment, let us consider an estimate of these values by an expert whom we assume makes small perturbation of the coefficients. This implies small perturbation of the eigenvalues. Our problem now becomes $A'w' = \lambda_{max} w'$ where max is the largest eigenvalue of A'. To simplify the notation, we shall continue to write $Aw = \lambda_{max} w$ where A is the matrix of pairwise comparisons. The problem now is how good is the estimate w. Note that, if we obtain w by solving this problem, the matrix whose entries are wi/wj is a consistent matrix. It is our consistent estimate of the matrix A. A itself need not be consistent. In fact, the entries of A need not even be ordinarily consistent, i.e., A_1 may be preferred to A_2, and A_2 preferred to A_3 but A_3 is preferred to A_1. What we would like is a measure of the error due to inconsistency. It turns out that A is consistent if, *and only if,* $\lambda_{max} = n$ and that we always have $\lambda_{max} \geq n$.

Since small changes in a_{ij} imply a small change in max the deviation of the latter from n is a deviation of consistency. This is represented by (λ_{max}-n)/(n-1), which we call the *consistency index* (C.I.). On calculating the consistency, we compare the result with those of the same index of a randomly generated reciprocal matrix from the scale 1 to 9, with reciprocals forced. We call this index the *random index* (R.I.). The following table gives the order of the matrix (first row) and the average R.I. (second row) determined as described above.

2	3	4	5	6	7	8	9
0.00	0.00	0.58	0.90	1.12	1.24	1.32	1.41	1.45

The ratio of C.I. to the average R.I. for the same order matrix is called the *consistency ratio*. A consistency ratio of 0.10 or less is considered acceptable.

We preserve the relations $a_{ji} = 1/a_{ij}$, $a_{ii} = 1$ in these matrices to improve consistency. The reason for this is that, if one stone is estimated to be k times heavier than another, to preserve sanity one should require that the second stone be estimated to be 1/k times the weight of the first. If the ratio of our index to that from random matrices is significantly small, we accept the estimates. Otherwise, we attempt to improve consistency by obtaining additional information. Contributing to the consistency of our judgment are (1) the homogenity of the elements in a group, i.e., not comparing a grain of sand with a mountain, (2) the number of elements in the group— psychological experiments show that an individual cannot simultaneously compare more than seven objects (plus or minus two) without being confused (Miller, 1963), and (3) the knowledge of the analyst about the problem under study.

In quantifying our judgments, we use a scale with values ranging from one to nine as shown in Table 1. There are several reasons for choosing such a scale (Saaty, 1980):

(1) The quantitative distinctions are meaningful in practice and have an element of precision when the items being compared are of the same order of magnitude or close together with regard to the property used to make the comparison.

(2) We note that our ability to make qualitative distinctions is well represented by five attributes: equal, weak, strong, very strong, and absolute. We can make comparisons between adjacent attributes when greater precision is needed. The totality requires nine values, and they may well be consecutive—the resulting scale would then be validated in practice.

(3) The psychological limit of 7 ± 2 items in a simultaneous comparison suggests that, if we take 7 ± 2 items satisfying the description under (1), and if they are all slightly different from each other, we would need 9 points to distinguish these differences (Miller, 1956).

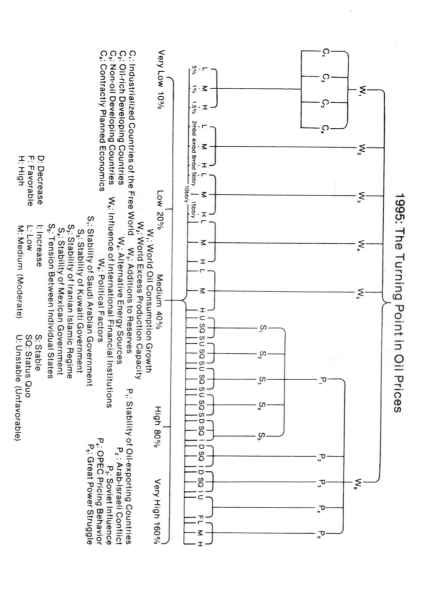

References

Aperjis, Dimitri, *The Oil Market in the 1980s—OPEC Policy and Economic Development,* Ballinger Publishing Co., 1982.

Chevron Corporation, *World Energy Outlook,* Economics Department, San Francisco, July 1984.

Conoco, Inc., *World Energy Outlook through 2000,* Coordinating and Planning Department, Washington, D.C., April 1984.

Exxon Corporation, *How Much Oil and Gas?* Exxon Background Series, New York, May 1982.

Fesharaki, F. and Hoffman, S., "Medium Term and Long Term Outlook for Conventional Oil: Survey and Analysis of the State of the Art," Resource Systems Institute, The East-West Center, Honolulu, Hawaii, May 1982.

Fesharaki, F., and Johnson, T., "Short Term and Medium Term Outlook for Oil: A Review and Analysis of Recent Studies," Resource Systems Institute, The East-West Center, Honolulu, Hawaii, February 1982.

Petroleum Economist, "Hopeful Signs for World Economy," Volume 5I, No. 9, September 10, 1984.

Petroleum Economist, "Costly Quest for New Oil," Volume 51, No. 10, October 1984.

Petroleum Economist, "Oil Prices in Perspective," Volume 52, No.3, March 1985.

Saaty, T.L., *The Analytic Hierarchy Process,* McGraw-Hill, Inc., NY, 1980.

Saaty, T.L., *Decision Making for Leaders,* Lifetime Learning Publications, 1982.

Saaty, T.L., and H. Gholamnezhad, "Oil Prices: 1985 and 1990," *Journal of Energy Systems and Policy,* 5, 1981, pp. 303-318.

United States Department of Energy, Energy Information Administration, *Annual Energy Outlook, 1983, with Projections to 1995,* Washington, D.C., 1984.

United States Department of Energy, Energy Information Administration, *Annual Energy Outlook, 1984.*

Conventional Economic Assumptions Questioned

Post-Economic Policies for Post-Industrial Societies

by

Hazel Henderson

It is hardly news to anyone today that industrial countries are restructuring themselves into various types of post-industrial societies. Trend-watchers feel that the changes leading to these post-industrial societies are accelerating, irreversible, and not well understood by economists who, nonetheless, are still in the policy catbird seat. These restructurings are partially an outcome of the new interactions between the evolving technologies and the value systems of industrial societies and of how those interactions function in specific ecosystems and resource bases. Our current models and theories of economics, being based on equilibrium assumptions, cannot deal with the forces at work in the transformation to post-industrial societies. In particular, they have no capacity to cope with the phenomenon of irreversibility. Furthermore, they consider technology to be a parameter rather than the central dynamic of industrial societies. Because all policy decisions made by our government and financial institutions rely on the recommendations of economists using macroeconomic theory, it is critically important that those theories be applicable to our times. There is ample evidence they are not. In the rest of this paper, I will review the many reasons why current economic theory is now unsuitable as the chief policy tool for managing these societies (spelled out in depth in my *The Politics of the Solar Age* 1981).

Hazel Henderson is an author and a respected futurist, the producer of a public-television talk show series. Her paper was first published in the journal ReVISION *Vol 7 No 2 Winter 84/Spring 85.*

Restructuring: The Symptoms

Societies are facing many painful symptoms in their restructuring: unemployment, industrial dislocation, massive government deficits, shifting demographics, population migrations, crime, addiction, unpredictable political swings, breakup of traditional family and community patterns, historically high real interest rates, bouncing currencies, protectionism, and unruly citizen movements—all within a context of the newly turbulent globalized economy, military confrontations, and a degrading global environment and resource-base. Politicians are increasingly baffled as the old economic formulas and tools become less reliable and often perverse. The simple economic remedies offered by economists of all persuasions, from socialist central planners to monetarists, Keynesians, neo-Keynesians, post-Keynesians, and "supply-siders," consist of little more than stepping on either the gas pedal or the brakes (or even both simultaneously!) using various mixes of fiscal and monetary policies (Figure 1).

Figure 1
THE POLITICS OF THE LAST HURRAH
The Simple World of Economic Remedies
Simultaneous Braking and Accelerating Cancels

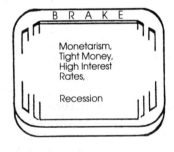 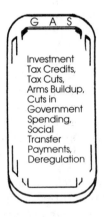

Copyright © 1982
Hazel Henderson

This deflating and reflating, as if society were a hydraulic system, has drastically different effects regionally and across each level of society. It is as if a doctor, using highly aggregated data, prescribes identical medicine (in this case, adrenalin or insulin) to patients with cancer, high blood pressure, and leprosy. Not surprisingly, such simple linear policies lead to the kind of vicious circles politicians must deal with today:

• Each additional increase in real interest adds another $10 billion of interest to the national debt (already the third largest item in the U.S. budget).

- Fighting inflation with tight money and high interest rates sucks in foreign investment, overvalues the currency, leads to balance-of-payments deficits (the U.S. deficit is currently running at an annual rate of approximately $118 billion), which costs jobs and competitiveness and can choke off recovery or lead to higher deficits and eventually more inflation.
- Each additional 1% of unemployment adds some $25 billion to the federal budget deficit (largely in lost taxes and unemployment compensation).
- Federal tax and budget cutting lead to local tax increases, defer needed infrastructure maintenance, and thus incur longer-term costs.
- High real interest rates increase inflationary expectations, squeeze corporate profits, force mergers, increase the cost of government borrowing, all of which pressure the available credit pool, which leads to even higher interest rates (unless the Fed opens up the money supply—which is inflationary).
- Trying to cool the economy with tight money and recessions increases farm-support payments, which adds to federal deficits without lifting farm incomes significantly and leads to farm foreclosures (farm-support outlays in the U.S. in 1983 quadrupled, bringing total farm spending to $22 billion, or 10% of the increase in the federal deficit).

During the "Soaring Sixties," there were two barometers of distress that politicians had to keep within politically manageable limits: inflation and unemployment. The economists' remedies for these worked reasonably well. But during the "Stagflation Seventies," to economists' dismay, both of these barometers marched upward together, a fact not admissible in the economists' model of the Phillips Curve and its supposed tradeoff between them. Now, in the "Orwellian Eighties," we see politicians trying to turn the clock back. In the face of the two new barometers of distress—high real interest rates and ballooning government deficits (Figure 2) —their rhetoric consists of empty slogans about "full employment" and "returning to prosperity." In this new "politics of the last hurrah," trying to hold down one of these barometers of distress merely causes the other three to bounce upward.

Thus, Mr. Reagan focuses on keeping inflation low while explaining away the huge deficit he campaigned to eliminate; Mrs. Thatcher continues to decimate many viable British industries under the banner of monetarism; Mr. Mitterand, France's socialist president, turns out to be the world's last Keynesian. The Eastern industrial countries suffer from all the same problems, from the U.S.S.R.'s sluggish overcentralization and low

Figure 2
THE VICIOUS CIRCLE ECONOMY
OF FAST FEEDBACK LOOPS (Now 4 Barometers of Distress)

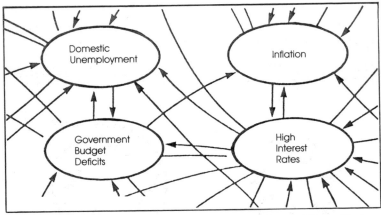

Copyright © 1982 Hazel Henderson

productivity to Poland, whose workers' revolt against the same dinosaur inflexibility has led to a stalemated economy. Even the miracle of Japan's heyday is over, as Mr. Nakasone adjusts to lower growth while paying the long-overdue social and environmental costs overhanging its economy.

This transformation of industrialism to post-industrialism is multidimensional, nonlinear and practically unmodelable because of the intricacy of domestic and global interlinkages. Since energy and resource-use patterns form the foundations of industrial societies, their multiplier effects cannot be mapped in simple economic terms but need new interdisciplinary policy models. Only models from biology—in particular, morphogenetic models as opposed to mechanistic and homeostatic models—can capture these accelerating, interactive changes.

Multidimensional change processes are common in all living systems as morphogenesis. (A good example of morphogenesis is the series of developmental changes a caterpillar goes through as it becomes a butterfly.) Models based on equilibrium or, at best, homeostatic changes no longer serve policy decision-making. In equilibrium models, the overall structure is stabilized by negative feedback, such as in a thermostatic system. Morphogenetic systems, on the other hand, are constantly evolving an unanticipated new structure because they are governed by positive feedback loops, which push many parts of the system over thresholds simultaneously (Figure 3).

Figure 3
SIMPLE DIAGRAMS OF TWO MAJOR TYPES OF CYBERNETIC SYSTEMS

STABLE, EQUILIBRIATING SYSTEM (morphostatic)
(Structurally stable)

e.g., thermostat-controlled mechanical system; early agrarian or small-scale production economies (as conceived in market equilibrium supply-demand theories); reversible components and decisions

System internally dynamic, but stable structure maintained and governed by *negative* feedback loops

UNSTABLE, DIS-EQUILIBRIUM SYSTEM
(morphogenetic) (Evolving new structure)

e.g., living, biological systems, human societies; large-scale socio-technical economic systems; rapid innovation and evolving structurally; many irreversible components and decisions

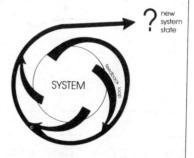

System internally dynamic *and* structurally dynamic, governed by *positive* feedback loops, which can amplify small initial deviations into unpredictably large deviations, which sometimes break through thresholds and push the system to a new structural state.

copyright © 1980
Hazel Henderson

Interactive global systems cannot be managed according to linear models. The displaced and delayed consequences of all such (purely economic) manipulation can be seen in an expanded model (Figure 4). Interactions and mutual causal processes are familiar to all systems analysts and life scientists, but they come as a terrible shock to economists. Voters no longer believe that economic policymakers can deliver on the promises they reiterate at economic summit meetings: that they will simultaneously hold down inflation, unemployment, interest rates, and deficits, and that their economies will pick up and resume growth. The vicious circles and "Catch-22s" created by economists' remedies are simply feedback loops delayed and displaced. They only signal that we are moving to an era of post-economic policy-making, a remapping of our own technologies of mass communications, air travel, and computer-speeded banking.

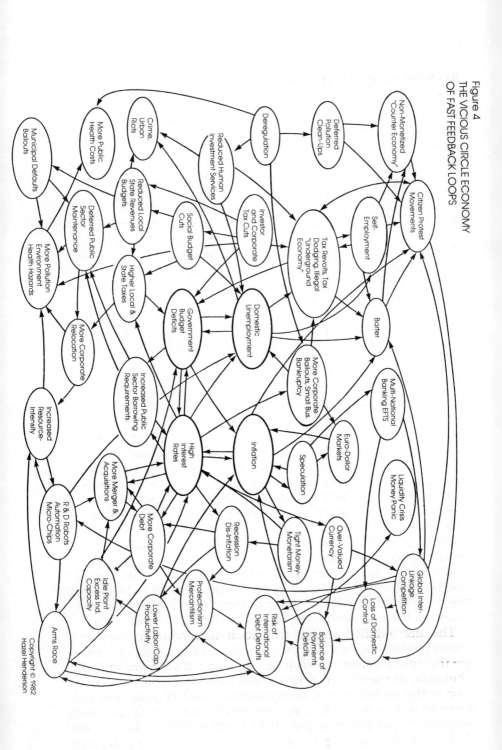

Figure 4
THE VICIOUS CIRCLE ECONOMY
OF FAST FEEDBACK LOOPS

Copyright © 1982
Hazel Henderson

An Emerging Paradigm

What we see emerging today in all the industrial societies are basic value and behavior shifts, new perceptions, and a paradigm that faces up to an awareness of planetary realities. It is confirmed by a post-Cartesian scientific worldview that is based on biological and systemic life sciences, rather than inorganic, mechanistic models. Its principles can be summed up as:
Interconnectedness—at every level.
Redistribution—recycling of all elements and structures.
Heterarchy—networks and webs of intercommunication, not fixed hierarchies; many interactive systems, mutual causality.
Complementarity—replace "either/or" dichotomous logic with "win/win" cooperative games.
Uncertainty—from static, equilibrium models to probalistic, morphogenetic, and "self-organizing" models of living systems.
Change—change as fundamental.

These new worldviews are already generating better policy tools and models outside of economics—in technology assessment, social and job impact studies, environmental impact statements, futures research, cross-impact studies, scenario building, and global modeling and forecasting. At the grassroots level, in academia, and in all our institutions, the politics of reconceptualization has begun. We see it in the new agendas of citizens, from the Nuclear Freeze and antinuclear/antiwar movements, to the emergence of human rights and planetary citizenship movements. These movements all embrace a new world order based on renewable resources and energy, sustainable forms of productivity and per-capita consumption, ecologically based technologies, and equitable sharing of resources. The sharing of resources both within and between countries is the only path to peacekeeping. It necessarily entails redirecting the billions spent on the global arms race.

We have witnessed the many wrenching shifts to sustainable and ecologically viable forms of productivity since the 1960s. But the overall pattern of this great industrial transition has, until recently, been obscured by obsolete analytical and policy tools.

The inevitability of this transition to renewable-resources-based productivity has been evident for decades to those trained in the life sciences, as well as to many thermodynamicists, chemists, engineers, physicists, and systems analysts, not to mention many sociologists, anthropologists, psychologists, and millions of well-rounded citizens and generalists. But as the great industrial societies reached their fossil-fueled zeniths in the 1950s and the "Soaring Sixties," signs of trouble were publicized only by a courageous few. Rachel Carson's warning note in *Silent Spring* was dismissed in 1962 by the celebrants of industrialism's success. So great was the euphoria that ominous social costs, from polluted air and water to deteriorating cities, were ignored. But not only were the social and environmental costs of industrialism ignored—so were its many subsidies unaccounted for in economic models (see Figure 5).

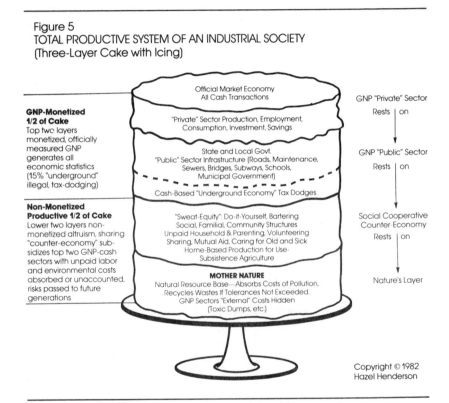

Figure 5
TOTAL PRODUCTIVE SYSTEM OF AN INDUSTRIAL SOCIETY
(Three-Layer Cake with Icing)

A more realistic view of total productivity is now coming into focus. It transcends the economic, money-dominated, GNP-measured view so prevalent today. This view embraces non-monetarized productions: from subsistence agriculture, do-it-yourself building, repairs, and maintenance, to household production, parenting, volunteering, and all the cooperative activities that subsidize the GNP-measured "formal economy." While some economists have embraced this larger view (for example, Kenneth Boulding, the late Barbara Ward [U.K.], Lester Brown, and Orio Giarini [Switzerland]), most economists prefer to stay on safer turf.

Monetarization: The Tyranny

Industrial societies now labor under excessively money-denominated methodological biases. Their tools are quite similar whether devised by Marxist or laissez-faire economists: national income statistics, cost/benefit analyses, etc. I have analyzed this pervasive tyranny of monetarization in my book, *The Politics of the Solar Age*. The underlying assumptions of this monetarized view are:

1. that major policy tools and analyses can be derived from statistical data quantified in money-coefficients.

2. that reliable statistical yardsticks for managing complex, socio-technical/ecological interactions can be derived from accounting only for money-based interactions between people/groups and resources (i.e., production, consumption, maintenance, investment, recycling, etc.).

3. that we can extrapolate from such micro-data gathering of these monetarized activities to simulate larger-scale, regional, national, and international levels of these functions.

In the United States, overreliance on economic policy has produced some interesting variations of the politics of the last hurrah. It has disguised many important policy choices as "technical" issues based on efficiency and has framed them in cost-benefit terms. However, traditional cost-benefit and risk-benefit analyses are too narrow and employ data too highly averaged to illuminate specific social choices, costs, and impacts borne by society and the environment. Such methods also routinely shortchange future generations and incur longer-term costs. Therefore, an expanded framework is needed for all important policy decisions. This framework must include: 1) the global dimension, 2) the ecological dimension, 3) the social dimension (nonmonetarized production, unacccounted social costs and subsidies), and 4) the future dimension (trade-offs between short- and long-term costs and benefits.)

The ideologies and recommendations of laissez-faire economists have proved particularly erratic because of this narrow, short-term framework. In fact, since all price data are historical, these economic models actually tend to back us into the future by looking in the rearview mirror. The unforeseen consequences of knee-jerk deregulation in airlines, communications, and banking; the ill-planned, across-the-board tax cuts; the health effects of hazardous wastes in the workplace; and the dangerous flirting with doctrinaire monetarism have all created great uncertainty and contributed to high real interest rates and deficits. Much of this laissez-faire economic doctrine has proved a triumph of ideology over common sense. It pretends that impersonal market forces determine industrial policy, not owning up to the de facto industrial policy that lies buried in the tax code. It obscures the fact that the Invisible Hand is our own: in the colossal subsidies that led to the overinvestment in nuclear energy, in the bemused economic numbers game by which we compare our military expenditures to those of the Soviets, in the lack of development of low energy and capital-input forms of agriculture and renewable energy technologies.

The world has changed drastically since Adam Smith outlined the conditions needed to permit free markets to allocate resources efficiently, i.e., that millions of small buyers and sellers with equal power and information should meet each other in widely dispersed marketplaces, without visiting unwanted side effects on others. This vision of eighteenth-century England is almost completely inapplicable to today's massive institutions, huge urban complexes, industrialized agricultures, and large-scale technologies, which now all ride together on the global roller coaster of world trade. I have examined elsewhere the great problems in using the price system (even corrected for some of the gross errors) as a *surrogate* for more specific policy decisions (1973). Unfortunately, it's a strategy most economists continually recommend (e.g., incentives, pollution taxes, subsidies, etc.). We don't grasp the nettle of overt political choices and debate them *on the merits,* and this has led to today's crazy quilt of backdoor policies embedded in our tax code: the tax credits, accelerated depreciation, subsidies, "off-budget" tax expenditures, the arbitrary interest rates, and the underwriting of risks for some groups and classes of investments. All of these manipulations of the price system constitute *legislated markets,* and their legitimacy needs to be discussed openly, rather than mystified as "economic laws" or "the workings of the market." Sooner or later, the voters, baffled and furious, catch on to these manipulations by special interests, and widespread tax evasion usually results. It is not a matter of whether any of these policies are good or bad, but that they are *mystified.*

Actually, the device of allocating resources via free markets was a brilliant social invention some 300 years ago. Prior to that time, two other basic principles of allocation were more prevalent in most human societies: reciprocity and redistribution.[1] But, using the price system as a policy directive not only makes citizens suspicious of government, it fosters tax evasion and a burgeoning underground economy. Furthermore, it leads to degrading of the currency and growing speculative manipulation of "funny money." Similarly, as environmentalists have pointed out to economists for decades, effluent taxes and trading the rights to pollute air and water are hardly good public health policy. Nor can economists' calculations of how much a human life is worth (or how much we should pay companies as incentives to desist from "antisocial behavior") stand as credible statistics on which to base economic policies. At some point, it becomes cheaper to *legislate compliance* with social rules.

Similarly, rationing every commodity by price (the doctrinaire market model) can also lead to perverse effects: for example, in the event of another cutoff in Mid-East oil supplies, emergency rationing would keep oil and gas flowing to vital agriculture, rather than having farmers bid up fuel prices against vacationing motorists and other less-essential uses. Another parallel situation involves interest rates. Rationing money by *price* alone (i.e., allowing interest rates to swing in the "free" marketplace) can, under today's distorted market conditions, lead to overuse of credit for mergers and acquisitions and other dubious uses, as well as excessively high real interest rates in today's deregulated banking environment. Such high real interest rates are very sticky, but what's worse, they may have already reached levels where they begin to "metastasize," cancerlike, and push up underlying costs throughout the society, as in the vicious circle model I have described.

To illustrate the danger of these kinds of distortions, let us imagine that the EFTS systems were speeded up to what computer experts call "real time," i.e., with almost no delays in transmission of information. At this point, in the case of EFTS, the velocity of the *information-about-money* flows would lose all relationship with the thermodynamic realities of the actual system (subject to natural cycles of crops, weather, friction, inertia, and human frailties), and the amount of money or capital available at any point in the banking system would tend toward infinity! As the *information-about-money* system became delinked from actual events, all manner of new ventures and schemes might be initiated by false promissory notes signaling capital availability with nothing more than an electronic impulse over a computer terminal.

Another example concerns the newly computerized operations of securities markets where aggressive trading by large institutional investors is blurring the line between investment and speculation.[4] The marriage of computer technology and financial markets has fundamentally altered them and the nature of money itself. For example, in "The Wiring of Wall Street" (*New York Times Magazine,* Oct. 23, 1983), Desmond Smith describes the speedup of transactions and quotes one analyst's view of the ultimate nightmare: the total automation of the whole function of the Stock Exchange with gambling on a worldwide scale and with no pretension to serving any social function. As is well known, some $80 billion in electronically transmitted funds are already floating in the international banking system. During the Iran hostage crisis, when that country's deposits were embargoed by the Carter Administration, automatic computer "lockout" programs were triggered and many bank presidents could not track their own funds for several days.

This speedup effect, noted by former international banker Frank Feather, is made even more pronounced in today's global capital markets where banks and financial services now offer 24-hour asset management, promising to wire customers' funds around the globe to take advantage of interest rate differentials on an almost hourly basis. Yet, as EFTS approaches "real time," it eliminates the very time lags and distances that competing players have always relied on as they sought out such currency and interest-rate spreads. In the market system, competition is the name of the game, but at some point, as all the actors try to maximize their advantage in this global money-as-information system, paper assets and compounded interest multiply unrealistically. Not all can win in the new environment, and excessive short-term maximizing can lead to disaster, breaking the bank for everyone (see "The Peril in Financial Services," *Business Week*, August 20, 1984).

Economic Theory in an Information Society

The most fundamental shortcoming of current economic theory lies in the way it maps the contours of the emerging information-based societies. Economic theory has never handled information adequately, since information is not a material commodity at all. It can be useful and very valuable, but just as frequently it can be destructive (i.e., "dis-information," propaganda, distortion, dishonesty, and untruth, all of which can play havoc with organizations, nations, and individuals, reducing productivity and often precipitating conflicts). When information is accurate, or contains innovative ideas, inventions, etc., it is not only very valuable, but it behaves unlike other valuable commodities: it is not subject to the zero-sum ("I win, you lose"), competitive rules of the marketplace. If one group gives information to another group, both groups then possess this valuable knowledge and both can share it again with others. Thus, the basic assumption of scarcity in economic theory is invalidated. Nowhere is economic theory more damaging to public policy and private investment than in this area of valuing information, education, and investments in people.

Longer-term social values, risks, investments, and policy must thus be remapped beyond the limits of economic theory. We can then clarify our new choices and review our tax codes and current priorities. Our current set of legislated interest rates need reexamination, since as we have seen, interest rates are never set by idealized "free markets." There is nothing revolutionary about setting interest rates by law and allowing preferences for some classes of borrowers and risks on social or environmental or longer-term considerations. Many government-backed loans (e.g., to students, small farmers and business people) can encourage innovation while developing new markets, technology, and knowledge. Today's outdated ideology of the market economic models has obscured the theoretical basis for cooperative economic behavior and the many pragmatic social credit policies prevalent in other countries including Sweden, Canada, Yugoslavia, Iceland, Norway, Denmark, and most Islamic countries. Similarly, in Japan, as William Ouchi points out in his recent book *The M-Form Society,* capital markets are more efficient and provide lower-cost capital through many differentiated, cooperative strategies.

Selflessness and Economic Theory

Economic texts that have tried to deal with altruism reduce it to a mechanistic model of rational, maximizing behavior, or to an unusual "preference." An example is *Altruism, Morality and Economic Theory* (1975), a series of papers from some of the best economists around: Kenneth Arrow (Nobel Memorialist), William Baumol, James Buchanan, Burton Weisbrod, and edited by Edmund S. Phelps of Columbia. Reading the tortured logic of these papers, with their attempts to explain away people's capacity for love, empathy, and unselfishness, is an education in itself. In another more realistic look at altruism, *Economics and Altruism* (1978), David Collard argues from the revolutionary (for economics!) premise that "human beings are not entirely selfish." He adds in the introduction, "It may seem strange to a layman or even to his fellow social scientists that such an assumption should be in any way remarkable or controversial. Yet it is the case that the self-interested economic man dominates the textbooks—rationality and self-interest are often taken as one and the same thing." Collard then looks at real-world behavior, such as charity, voluntary work, voting in favor of welfare payments, donating blood frequently and voluntarily, by describing the famous book of Richard Titmuss, *The Gift Relationship* (1970), which demonstrated that the British system of voluntary blood donation was more truly efficient and healthy than the U.S. money-motivated one.

Much better models of human economic behavior come out of other disciplines. *Human Values and Economic Policy* (1967), philosopher Sidney Hook's edition of symposium papers from a group of economists on the bases of value judgments in economics, is a good example. Some of the contributors, e.g., Kenneth Boulding, are frank about the valuebase of economics, but most hedge and obfuscate. Two other books on ethics, altruism, and economics that are much more forthright are produced by religious groups: *People, Profits, The Ethics of Investment,* edited by Charles Powers and published by the Council on Religion in International Affairs (1972), which covers the responsibility and control of corporations, and *Economics and the Gospel* by Richard K. Taylor, published by United Church Press (1973), which is even more forthright about justice, sharing, etc. *In Search of a Third Way: Is a Morally Principled Political Economy Possible?* by Tom Settle (1976) is a good critique of economics (rejecting the communism vs. capitalism dichotomy) written by a physicist turned Methodist minister. Economics' absurd model of human motivation was summed up by psychologist David McClelland: "Economists use a totally outdated model of human motivation. They haven't even discovered Freud, let alone Abraham Maslow" (personal communication at a conference on steady-state economics, Johnson Foundation, Racine, Wisconsin, 1970).

The Underground Economy vs. the Counter-Economy

Today, the levers of macro-economic management and its statistical indicators—gross-national-product-measured growth, money supply, nationally averaged unemployment and inflation rates—are all becoming discredited as policy tools. A measure of this new skepticism on the part of government officials, tax collectors, businesspeople, workers, and citizens is the growing attention to what is termed the "Underground Economy," described in 1978 by economist Peter Gutman and the subject of *Business Week*'s April 5, 1983 cover story.

The "Underground Economy" is a shady $380-billion annual operation of tax dodging, moonlighting, and cash-based transactions, much of which is illegal. It is based in the drug trade (estimated at $45 billion), prostitution, pimping, stolen goods, Mafia gambling, loan-sharking, fraud, bribery, and pornography. *Business Week* points out rightly that this rapidly growing subterranean economy not only discredits much traditional macroeconomic analysis but also accounts for much of its large error-factor in measuring GNP performance, levels of total employment, rates of saving, investment, and productivity—all of which are significantly understated. Macroeconomists make errors in measuring savings, investment, innovation, employment, and inflation because such statistical indicators are too highly averaged and almost meaningless. They do not fit any specific regions or sectors of the nation's production system.

This new focus on the "Underground Economy" now flourishing in the United States, Italy, Britain, and other industrial countries is a welcome correction of economists' myopia. However, great care must now be taken *not* to confuse it with the "Counter-Economy." The "Counter-Economy" is a society's productive system that is not monetarized, paid, or accounted for in cash, but rather *subsidizes and buttresses* the cash-based, GNP-measured half. To confuse the "Underground Economy" of greed and illegality with the "Counter-Economy" of altruism would be tragic.

This "Counter-Economy" is still invisible to most economists and policymakers. It is based on very different principles: altruism, volunteering, community and family cohesiveness, cooperation, sharing, respect for the environment and the rights of future generations, and conservation of all resources—human and natural. It fosters individual responsibility, mutual aid, local self-reliance, small-scale enterprises, renewable-resource technologies and the decentralization of economic and political power. Not surprisingly, it is most often studied by noneconomists using sociological surveys. It focuses on total productive hours worked, whether paid or not, and quantifies, where possible, social impacts of market activities. This nonmonetarized half of society is also termed the "Informal Economy" by operations researcher James Robertson (Britain), the "Shadow Economy" by Ivan Illich (Mexico), and the "Household Economy" by Scott Burns (U.S.A.), while Germany's Joseph Huber sees it as one half of the "Dual Economy," and Sweden's Lars Ingelstam and Nordal Ackerman study the cooperative local economy in similar approaches. The United Nations International Labor Office (ILO) has studied the predominant role of women in the nonmonetarized sectors of all the nations, subsidizing the GNP sectors with unpaid, indispensable labor: growing food, parenting children, caring for the sick and old, and in volunteer community services. On a global basis, the ILO reports, women work 47% of all the productive hours worked, but they receive only 10% of the world's wages and own only 1% of the property. The most comprehensive look at the world's nonmonetarized sectors is that of futurist/economist Orio Giarini in *Dialogue on Wealth and Wel-*

fare (1980), where he documents that 80% of all the world's capital investment is *not* monetarized.

A very legitimate new role for economics is that of quantifying social costs—to taxpayers, consumers, and even other producers. These costs include treating polluted water, cleaning and repairing pollution damage, collecting throwaway containers, building and providing new community services for incoming factories, police, schools, access roads, fire protection, sanitation services, etc.

It is not surprising that economists also misunderstand the process of development—too often erroneously equating it with per-capita GNP-measured "economic growth." Today, sociologists are constructing new indicators of development and human welfare—indicators such as progress in meeting the basic needs of the most deprived people for food, shelter, education, health care, access to tools, and political participation, such as the BHNI (Basic Human Needs Index) and the PQLI (Physical Quality of Life Index).

Therefore, the paradigm shift in economics entails the end of economics and economic theory as the predominant policy tool for industrial countries (or any country) and the recognition of its proper range of applicability, i.e., for accounting purposes between firms and keeping cash records for individuals and small enterprises. Furthermore, the proper applications need to take into account social and environmental costs *within* the enterprise's accounts, which should be reflected in the prices of products (full-cost pricing). This formula could be applied to alternative businesses and cooperatives, collectives, etc., where the models of maximizing self-interest and competition are relaxed.

It is only by looking at the world in a profoundly different way that we can attempt to solve the complex problems brought about by our social and cultural evolution. There is no realism in relying on models of current economic theory. Examining our complexity with simple cause-effect projections only exacerbates the distortion of our vision. Those people responsible for the economic destiny of millions cannot base their decisions on mechanistically-determined recommendations. The paradigm being thrust upon us by the precariousness of our situation is one that embraces values of a wholly different order. To realize this paradigm in its fullness and to place its values in the forefront demands that self-interest now must be equated with the interests of the whole species: the human family on this small planet. At last, morality has become pragmatic.

NOTES

1. See, for example, Karl Polanyi's *Primitive, Archaic, and Modern Economics* (New York: Doubleday/Anchor, 1968).
2. See, for example, Denis F. Johnston's "Census Concepts as Knowledge Filters for Public Policy Advisors" in *Knowledge Creation, Diffusion, and Utilization* (Sage Publications, 5-1, September 1983).
3. See the "Institute for the Future on the Implications of Computer Modeling and Its Impacts on Public Policy," in *Toward Understanding the Social Impact of Computers,* ed. Roy Amara (1974).
4. See, for example, "Will Money Managers Wreck the Economy?" *Business Week* (August 13, 1984), p. 86.
5. See, for example, Donald Lamberton, *The Economics of Information and Knowledge* (U.K.: Penguin Books, 1971).
6. I described the "Counter Economy" in "Jumping to the Safety-Net Economy," *Christian Science Monitor* (Oct. 10, 1979).

REFERENCES

Collard, D. *Economics and Altruism.* New York: Oxford University Press, 1978.
Feather, F. "Monetronics and Informatics." In *Prospectus 1984,* ed. Ann Mattis. Durham, North Carolina: Duke University Press, 1984.
Giarini, O. *Dialogue on Wealth and Welfare.* London: Pergamon Press, 1980.
Henderson, H. *The Politics of the Solar Age.* New York: Doubleday, 1981.
Hook. S. *Human Values and Economic Policy.* New York: New York University Press, 1967.
Phelps, E.S., ed. *Altruism, Morality, and Economic Theory.* New York: The Russell Sage Foundation, 1975.
Settle, T. *In Search of a Third Way: Is a Morally Principled Political Economy Possible?* Toronto: McClelland & Stewart, 1976.
Titmuss, R. *The Gift Relationship.* Winchester, MA: Allen & Unwin, 1970.

Bioeconomics:
A Realistic Appraisal
of Future Prospects[1]

by

William H. Miernyk

Conventional economics is in a state of disarray. Paul Samuelson, one of its leading practitioners, has said: "The malaise from which the mandarins of economics are suffering is not imaginary. It is genuine."[2] That observation is as apposite today as when it was made in 1977.

The American economy has recovered from the latest recession, and press accounts portray a robust recovery. When Gross National Product is adjusted for price changes and increased employment, however, the recovery is seen to be sluggish. Two years after the upturn, 8.5 million workers are "officially" unemployed. No one knows how many discouraged workers have dropped out of the labor force because the job search has become pointless. There are other problems: adverse trade and payments balances, continuing urban decay, and a depressed agricultural sector, to name only a few.

High levels of unemployment, and lethargic economic performance, are characteristic of most of the older industrialized economies. These result from declining long-term growth rates. Older economies are not the only ones affected. Declining growth in advanced economies has adversely affected the nations we euphemistically refer to as the "less developed countries" (LDCs).

A number of leading economists have been openly critical of the direction their discipline has taken in recent years. Journalists and commentators also have expressed their disenchant-

---

William H. Miernyk is a professor of economics at the West Virginia University and president of Miernyk and Associates, Inc.

ment. The latter might not understand the arcana of economic theory. But they have observed that global economic conditions are getting worse.[3] The effect of this criticism on the profession as a whole, however, has been negligible. Modern economics has drifted from the world of reality to a land of illusion.

One of the illusions of conventional economics is that declining growth rates are temporary; that the world is going through a "difficult transition." There's an analogy in science fiction. It's that of a spaceship going through a "black hole" in outer space. As the ship approaches the hole, it is rocked by turbulence. Everyone aboard becomes disoriented. Once through the hole—like a bubble sucked down a bathtub drain—the ship enters a new "space" of tranquility. Similarly, in the minds of conventional economists, once we're through the terrestrial transition, the world will enter a new era of robust economic growth.

The *fundamental illusion* of conventional economics is that growth is the answer to all economic problems.[4] A corollary is that, for practical purposes, growth can go on forever. No one says this. But it's implicit in the policy prescriptions of conventional economists when they address contemporary problems.

Another illusion is that scarcity, once the centerpiece of economic analysis, is no longer a problem. It has been replaced by the *principle of unlimited substitutability*. The principle of substitution is an integral part of any meaningful economic theory. The ability to substitute one product, process, or resource for another is what makes any economic system work. But when the word "unlimited" is added, the principle takes on a new meaning.

The new principle states that mankind will never run out of anything essential because there will always be a substitute. The process of substitution, the principle asserts, can go on indefinitely.[5]

The principle of unlimited substitutability has one important qualification. It will work only if mankind can find *an unlimited source of cheap energy*. Clearly that won't be fossil fuels. We will never mine the last ton of coal, never pump the last barrel of oil, or extract the last cubic foot of natural gas from the earth. Before we reach those absolute limits it will take several tons of coal to produce an additional ton, and more than a barrel of oil or cubic foot of gas to replace themselves. Some day it will no longer be economically or technically feasible to produce fossil fuels. Before that day is reached, however, those who accept the principle of unlimited substitutability believe a technological breakthrough will provide an unlimited supply of cheap energy.

The inexhaustible supply of cheap energy will be provided,

we're told, by nuclear *fusion*. This means, in nontechnical terms, replicating on our planet conditions that exist at the center of the sun. That would require something other than earthly matter to contain the 100-million-degree temperature which nuclear fusion would generate.

The theory of nuclear fusion is well advanced, and specialists in plasma physics have studied the containment of solar temperatures. But many questions about fusion remain unanswered. The feasibility of controlled fusion remains speculative. And while a sustained fusion reaction is theoretically possible, there's no guarantee that the process will produce cheap energy. Fusion-generated power could, in fact, turn out to be the most expensive source of energy devised by man. No one has any idea at this stage of its development *what the capital costs of fusion power will be.*

The best that can be hoped is that fusion power will break even; that a million BTUs of heat generated by the fusion reactor will produce a like amount. Some other source of energy will have to be used to manufacture fusion reactors. The only sources we know are nuclear and fossil fuels. These fuels will become increasingly costly as their supplies diminish. So will the cost of fusion reactors. Extremists among the wishful thinkers, who believe that nuclear fusion will lead to a utopia, seem to view it as a form of perpetual motion. The laws of physics insure, however, that perpetual motion will elude us forever.

The principle of unlimited substitutability was conceived by physical scientists, not economists. But conventional economists have made it an integral part of their intellectual baggage. Some concept had to replace scarcity, and this one is consistent with the belief that growth will eventually solve mankind's "transitional" problems.

The attraction of the idea of perpetual growth is obvious. If we could have it, the affluent wouldn't have to worry about sharing their bounty with the poor. The poor would get some share of a steadily expanding economic pie. As long as their condition gradually improved, they might not complain too loudly if the affluent also continued to improve their condition.

If there is little or no economic growth, the only way the "have nots" of the world could gain would be at the expense of the affluent. The poor greatly outnumber the well-to-do, however, so redistribution of the world's goods wouldn't help much. It's a time worn cliche, but if everything in the world were evenly distributed now we wouldn't be sharing wealth, we'd be sharing poverty. The cruelest illusion of all is that economic growth will seriously mitigate, if not eliminate, poverty after "the transition."

Illusions breed myths. There's nothing wrong with myths or fables if they're recognized as such. But the myths of conventional economics are not offered as fiction. They are believed by most practitioners. One of the more pervasive myths is that economics has become a "hard" science. It got that way, the mythmakers believe, by becoming increasingly abstract and by making extensive use of mathematics. As a consequence, few articles in today's economics journals make any pretense of dealing with reality. Their authors aren't interested in communicating with the public. They are only interested in the plaudits of their peers.

The myth that efforts to ape the physical sciences represent progress in economics isn't accepted by all economists. Wassily Leontief, the founder of input-output analysis and a Nobel laureate, has warned against the use of mathematics in ways that trivialize economics rather than making it more "scientific." Nicholas Georgescu-Roegen, about whom more will be said later, also has criticized the misuse of mathematics in economic analysis. William Baumol, another leading American economist, once described some efforts to reduce economic issues to arcane symbolism as "illicit intercourse with beautiful models."[6] Leontief, Georgescu-Roegen, and Baumol are themselves skilled mathematicians.

The list could be extended. But the criticism by some of the great minds in economics has had little impact, particularly on some of the younger members of the profession. Economics is becoming more abstract; it deals less than it used to with issues of general concern. The training of economists has become more rigorous than it was in the past. But does that make them more useful? Only in the minds of the mythmakers. Realism and relevance have been sacrificed to rigor. It has been a poor tradeoff.

Another myth is that bad news grabs the headlines, while the truth (which is, of course, that the news is good) is ignored. This myth was advanced by Julian Simon in *Science*.[7] It was elaborated in the *Atlantic Monthly*.[8] Simon listed some headline-grabbing news: that there were many deaths due to drought in the Sahel region between 1968 and 1973; that the danger of famine is increasing; that higher population means lower per capita growth; that urban sprawl is reducing prime land for agricultural and recreational use; that we're running out of resources; that energy is getting scarcer, and so on. These things, Simon says, are not so.

He dismisses the last two assertions because they don't square with the principle of unlimited substitutability, which he accepts without reservation. Simon denies the others on the ground that there is no "hard evidence" to back them up. His own evidence that the world economy is steadily improving is sparse: a few figures here and there, quotations from friendly sources, and some completely outdated facts. It's anything but convincing.

A number of scholars have pointed out Simon's more egregious errors.[9] His proclivity for simple extrapolation has been noted. Simon's approach reminded Professor George Cowgill, of Brandeis University, of the story about a man who leaped from a tall building. As he passed the 20th floor, he was asked how things were going: "Fine," he replied, "so far."[10]

Ignoring his critics, Simon continued his efforts to exorcise the Malthusian specter in a widely publicized book, *The Ultimate Resource*.[11] In it he argued that, instead of having deleterious effects, the major economic consequence of population growth was augmentation of the stock of human knowledge. He also claimed that population growth is positively related to rising per capita income.

Simon's book reheated the controversy started by his *Science* article. Reviews were mixed.[12] Utopians hailed it as a landmark. Even a friendly critic, however, couldn't accept Simon's basic conclusions. D. Gale Johnson, of the University of Chicago, wrote: "There is so very much of value in Mr. Simon's book. It is too bad that it is blemished by the author's excesses."[13]

Do myths such as the one Simon propagates matter? Can they harm anyone? If they're harmless, why not indulge them? There's enough bad news in the world, some might argue, without forever harping about the dismal economic future. Unfortunately, the notion that the world economy is steadily improving, and will continue to do so, is not a harmless myth. It perpetuates rampant consumerism and the profligate use of resources and energy in the industrialized nations of the world and does nothing to help the deprived. If the citizens of affluent nations believe that future economic growth will take care of the problems of poverty elsewhere, why bother to give more than token assistance to the victims of deprivation? The illusions of conventional economics cannot be considered to be harmless.

Is there any hope that economics will abandon those illusions; that it will once again, as it did in the past, deal with reality? Will economists sacrifice some of the rigor and all of the pseudoscientific mumbo jumbo that has trivialized a once useful discipline? It could happen. But it won't as long as economists continue to look inward, to recycle ideas that have little relevance to the world of today, much less that of the future.

The most remarkable scientific advances of the twentieth century have come from hybrid disciplines; amalgams of older sciences formerly kept in separate intellectual compartments. DNA, for example, wouldn't have been discovered if Watson and Crick had remained within the bounds of a single science. And we might still think the atom is infrangible if scientists, mathematicians, and engineers hadn't collaborated on the Manhattan project. There are other examples: bio-statistics, geo-statistics, sociobiology, to name only a few. If progress is to continue, there will be further integration of the sciences.

One major methodological development in economics, some of us believe, is the wave of the future. It fits the mold of a hybrid discipline. This approach, called "bioeconomics," has attracted considerable attention in western Europe. It has been resisted by the "Economics Establishment" in this country. If this approach is valid, much of economics as it is presently taught and written about in the United States would have to be scrapped.

Bioeconomics is not a rehash of older economic ideas. It's an amalgam of economic theory, biology, and physics—especially thermodynamics. The father of this new economic paradigm is Nicholas Georgescu-Roegen, Distinguished Professor of Economics Emeritus at Vanderbilt University.[14]

Why "bioeconomics?" Because Georgescu-Roegen views the economic process as an extension of natural evolution. Surviving species develop *endosomatic* organs which permit them to adapt to a changing environment. The human species is the only one, however, which has been able to develop *exosomatic* organs: tools, weapons, means of transportation, and so forth. This ability has enabled mankind to enjoy the fruits of economic progress. It also is responsible for the economic and ecological problems which growth and development have engendered.

Bioeconomics deals with the economic process, but it does so by going outside the boundaries of the discipline as it has been traditionally defined. The differences between conventional economics and bioeconomics can be highlighted by contrasting their essential features.

Conventional Economics—From the time of David Ricardo (1772-1823), traditional economics has been based on a *mechanistic* model of the economic process. This is illustrated by the circular-flow diagram at the beginning of comprehensive introductory economics textbooks.

The diagram shows goods flowing in one direction and money (broadly defined) going in the other. The important point about this simple model is that *the two flows do not alter the system in any way*. A thoughtful student would observe that it represents a stationary state and that—while time is not introduced explicitly—the diagram represents perpetual motion.

Bioeconomics—The economic process is not a mechanistic one. Economic activity is a biological phenomenon, an extension of the process of evolution. Every activity affects the system *in a cumulative manner*. What happens today will affect tomorrow's economy. Economic systems go through a life cycle. At first, there is slow growth in real output per capita; then there is growth at an increasing rate. Next, the economy enters the range of diminishing returns. Output per capita increases, but at a declining rate. Eventually, the system will reach a state of absolutely diminishing returns in which output per capita declines. This doesn't mean automatic catastrophe. Properly managed, an economic system could last for a very long time under conditions of absolutely diminishing returns.

Conventional Economics—In spite of the increasing use of mathematics and the belief that this has made the discipline more "scientific," economics remains inward looking. Rarely do economists draw on the physical sciences. Even when discussing the economics of energy, for example, most economists ignore the physical laws governing the transformation of energy into "work."

Bioeconomics is a genuine hybrid. It is an amalgam of economic theory, evolutionary biology, and thermodynamics. The second law of thermodynamics—the entropy law—is basic to Georgescu-Roegen's system of thought. This law states that there is a continuous transformation of energy from a "free" state to a "bound" state. A lump of coal represents free or unused energy. Once burned, the energy in the lump of coal has been converted to a bound state. It can never be used again. *The entropic process is irreversible.*

Traditional economics is compartmentalized. Some contemporary theorizing is static; time isn't considered at all. This branch of theory has grown increasingly sterile in recent years. Dynamic analysis is basically the economics of growth. The equations used to describe growth models have exponential solutions. They're specified in ways that guarantee this result when the equations are solved to find a "growth equilibrium."

Bioeconomics is a *unified* way of looking at the economic process. The biological focus stresses interdependence and evolutionary change. There's no need for the simplifying assumptions of static analysis. The idea of a "general equilibrium," or ideal state in which no change would benefit anyone, is foreign to the philosophy of bioeconomics. The economic process is viewed as one of continuous change. There is no end point or ultimate equilibrium. *The economic process, because of its entropic nature, is not only cumulative, it is irreversible.*

Conventional Economic theory ignores the supply side of the economic equation. The "new" supply-side economics of the 1980s is a resurgence of the *laissez faire* ideal. It is concerned with investment incentives that are supposed to stimulate productivity. This, in turn, is supposed to result in a revival of robust economic growth. Energy and raw material supplies are assumed to be inexhaustible. There is in fact nothing "new" about this approach to economic policy.

Bioeconomics—Two of the fundamental propositions of bioeconomics is that all resources are scarce and that matter as well as energy is subject to entropic degredation. Some resources can be recycled. But even when they are used repeatedly, there is some loss—however small—each time they are used. Over a long period, pieces of metal (coins, for example) and other substances gradually wear out. The particles lost cannot be used again. There's no such thing in bioeconomics as a raw material or other usable substance that is inexhaustible.

There are other differences. Those noted, however, should make it clear that bioeconomics is not a modification of, or addition to, conventional economics. It's an entirely new way of viewing the economic process. Unfortunately it has disturbing implications. If the basic premises and principles of bioeconomics are true, economic policies as well as economic theory will be affected.

Although academic economics has become increasingly abstract, economists serve as advisers to political, business, labor, and other leaders who are responsible for, or influence, public policies. While political decisions might be more sensitive to election returns than to abstract ideas, specific policies show the imprint of economic advisers. And the advice that conventional economists give is, not surprisingly, conventional. Even when the current news is bad, conventional economists—influenced by a generation or more of exposure to the problem-solving mentality of mathematicians—feel impelled to convert present bad news to future good news. Conventional economists remain determinedly optimistic.

In the summer of 1980, the results of a three year study called *Global 2000* were made public by Secretary of State Edmund Muskie.[15] The study pointed out that: "World population growth, degradation of the earth's natural resource base, and the spread of environmental pollution, collectively threaten the welfare of mankind." It provided further grim details. The fastest population growth will be in the poorest countries. Better fertilizers and mechanization, needed to increase agricultural productivity, will require more energy. But poor countries won't be able to afford energy from alternative sources. Forests will disappear, and with them hundreds of species of birds and animals. This will threaten the ecological balance of the globe. An estimated 800 million people will go hungry.

When the report was made public, Muskie had the following to say: "*Global 2000* is not a prediction. If we begin our work now, we will say in twenty years that *Global 2000* was wrong. What a glorious achievement that would be." And how are the potential catastrophies vividly described by the authors of the report to be avoided? Simple. The nations of the world will have to get their economic houses in order. Faster growth will be the order of the day. Alternative sources of cheap energy will have to be discovered quickly. Productivity must be increased. The world can't be allowed to reach the state described by *Global 2000!*

It would have been out of character for Julian Simon to remain silent about this report. He and the late Herman Kahn edited a book intended to refute the findings of *Global 2000*.[16] Even before their book was published, Simon and Kahn circulated an executive summary of their views. The 23 contributing authors were not obligated to be in full agreement.

"If present trends continue," Simon and Kahn wrote, "the world in 2000 will be less crowded, less polluted, more stable ecologically, and less vulnerable to resource-supply disruption than the world we live in now." They also predicted "declining scarcity, lowering prices and increased wealth."[17]

Politically, *The Resourceful Earth* is in tune with the times. It advocates greater reliance on free markets. Shortages of the past are alleged to be the result of government interference with prices. In the mythical world of Simon and Kahn there's no such thing as a shortage; there is only a price.

How did Simon and Kahn reach conclusions which many must consider to be wildly optimistic in view of today's global problems? First, they extrapolate liberally. The world economy is better off now than it was a century ago, so it will have to be better off still a century hence. They also assume that the experience of industrialized societies is transferable to the LDCs. They accept without question the principle of unlimited substitutability. Finally, they rely heavily on what I have called Disney's first law: Wishing will make it so!

How does a bioeconomist respond to *Global 2000?* First, it's a welcome antidote to the blather published by sincere but misguided futurists who insist there will be a Utopia on the other side of "the transition." Wishful thinking won't solve the problems of a world in which population is the one consistent growth variable. Second, the report is a prediction, whatever its authors intended, and probably a conservative one at that.

Most "long-range" forecasts end with the year 2000. But population won't stop growing then. The standard answer to that problem is more economic growth. But in any finite environment, and the world is finite, there are limits to growth. Perpetual growth cannot be the answer to the world's economic problems. If not economic growth, what policies does bioeconomics suggest? The first is conservation and an emphasis on thrift. Not the cosmetic conservation we now practice, but a determined effort to prevent waste in all its forms. Moral suasion won't change the habits of a society spoiled by a half-century of rampant consumerism. Conservation will have to be enforced by taxation, where that will work, and by more stringent measures—including rationing—where it won't.

Let's not delude ourselves that the world can feed, house, and clothe another two or three billion persons without sacrifice on the part of the presently industrialized (and prosperous) nations. There will have to be a far more equitable distribution of wealth and income—both within the United States and among the nations of the world—if further chaos and localized catastrophe are to be minimized. Ethiopia and the Sudan aren't isolated cases. Like it or not, the Malthusian "future" has arrived.

Some of the more wasteful practices of consumerism could be eliminated with little more than psychological sacrifice. These include frequent style changes, planned obsolescence, expensive hype, and needless duplication of many consumer goods. This is not to question the psychic satisfaction engendered by product differentiation. But the time will come when a stable social order won't permit such satisfaction for an overfed, overstyled minority while billions elsewhere starve or live on the ragged edge of starvation. Serious conservation of energy and resources, moderate redistribution of wealth and income, and abolition of the worst excesses of rampant consumerism are far removed from the growth policies of conventional economics.

One major issue remains to be discussed. This is technological progress, the *deus ex machina* of conventional economics. Technological progress lies behind the principle of unlimited substitutability and the belief that growth is the answer to all economic problems. Why shouldn't technology accomplish as much in the future as it has in the past?

Bioeconomists are fully aware of the economic benefits of invention and innovation. If the world is to avoid disaster well before the year 2000, we will need all the scientific and technological progress that can be mustered. But as Edward Renshaw has pointed out, technological progress itself is subject to diminishing returns. This is undoubtedly the major cause of the decline in productivity noted by Denison.[18] That, in turn, explains declining growth rates in older industrialized nations. Those declines, furthermore, are not a temporary phenomenon to be reversed by some dramatic "technological fix" or scientific breakthrough.

Popularizers sometimes portray science as a series of finished modules built on one another. But that isn't the way science evolves. "The great body of science," Lewis Thomas has said, "built like a vast hill over the past 300 years, is a mobile, unsteady structure." The entire arrangement of scientific thought, he went on, "is something like the unpredictability and unreliability of living flesh." There is a lot of trial and error in scientific thinking. Science is not, as sometimes thought, "a way of building a solid indestructable body of immutable truths . . . it keeps changing, shifting, revising, discovering that it was wrong and then heaving itself explosively apart to redesign everything. It is a living thing, a celebration of human fallibility."

Thomas was talking about the evolution of the hard sciences: physics, chemistry, biology, and so forth. What he said applies even more to the social sciences. Unfortunately, that's not the way social sciences are taught, which is one reason we make so little progress in adapting to a constantly changing world. "We are in trouble," Thomas continued, "whenever persuaded that we know everything." The public, however, including many college or university graduates, is likely to have an exaggerated notion of how far we've progressed in understanding the complex world we live in. "The culmination of a liberal arts education ought to include," Thomas stated, "the news that we do not understand a flea much less the making of a thought."[19]

There have been changes in economic doctrine. But for the reasons Thomas has indicated, they don't come easily. In 1935, John Maynard Keynes wrote: "The difficulty lies, not in the new ideas, but in escaping from the old ones, which ramify, for those brought up as most of us have been, into every corner of our minds."[20] Those are without doubt the most prescient words written by the great British economist.

Keynes demonstrated that mature free enterprise economies are not self-equilibrating, the essence of received doctrine before his time. He argued that as an economy matured it could settle into a false equilibrium in which there can be chronic, high-level unemployment for an indefinite period. An unregulated economy will not eliminate such unemployment. Keynes concluded that government could close the gap by adopting policies that would maintain investment and consumer spending at full-employment levels. The idea of such governmental involvement was considered radical in 1935. It's the basis of monetary and fiscal policies that are accepted orthodoxy today.

Keynes didn't discuss energy and resource problems. He was concerned solely with insufficient demand, which was the problem of his time. He taught us how to solve that problem. As Georgescu-Roegen has pointed out, however, today's problems, and those of the future, are on the supply side. We could maintain demand at full-employment levels, without inflation, in a world of inexhaustible energy and material resources. Such a world exists, however, only in the pages of abstract economic treatises.

An inescapable conclusion of bioeconomics is that mankind will have to adjust to a steady diminution of energy and non-renewable resources. This is a more revolutionary notion than Keynes's pronouncement that mature economies are not self-equilibrating. It's being resisted even more vigorously than Keynes's teachings were in the late 1930s.

The idea that economic growth can't go on forever clearly lacks emotional appeal. But it's one we will have to learn to live with. Since bioeconomics is the only analysis of the economic process that is built on solid foundation of biological and thermodynamic reality, it will become the economic orthodoxy of the future. Georgescu-Roegen is a thinker far ahead of his time. His views have made more headway in western Europe than in the United States.[21] American resistance might be due to a combination of intellectual and hedonistic influences. Consumerism is not quite as unbridled in Great Britain and western Europe as it is in the United States. And the idea that thrift is a virtue, which Keynes tried to dispel, is more deeply embedded in European culture than in America. Thus the notion that economic growth can't go on forever might be less traumatic for many Europeans than for most Americans.

It would be misleading to imply that Georgescu-Roegen's ideas have had no impact on the intellectual community in the United States. He and his views have been featured in *Science* and in *Chemical Engineering News*. *The Entropy Law and the Economic Process* has been widely acclaimed as a modern classic. Half the contributors to a Festschrift in his honor are Nobel laureates in economics. It remains true, however, that while the "Economics Establishment" has honored the man and his powerful and stimulating intellect, it has resisted acceptance of the principles of bioeconomics. Those principles have not been attacked in the journals of the economics professions; they've simply been ignored.

Major differences between the principles of bioeconomics and the central tenets of conventional economics were pointed out earlier. One cannot view the economic process in mechanistic and biological-thermodynamic terms at the same time. The two approaches are mutually exclusive. It's clear which one most economists have chosen up to now. In spite of the poor performance of the world economy, they cling to the belief that technological progress and economic growth will "solve" mankind's problems.

As the gap between the promises of conventional economics and the performance of the global economy widens, the older view will lose its credibility. Then the bioeconomic paradigm, which is already gaining adherents—however slowly—will become the dominant view. This process, which has been described in scientific terms by Thomas Kuhn, will be hastened by the observations of noneconomists.[22] An early contributor to this trend is Jeremy Rifkin, who (with Ted Howard) published a volume called *Entropy: A New World View*.[23] It's a lucid, nontechnical introduction to some of the principles of bioeconomics.

"Each day we awake to a world that appears more confused and disordered than the one we left the night before," Rifkin wrote. "Nothing seems to work anymore. Our leaders are forever lamenting and apologizing. Their attempts to deal with ... problems ... create even greater problems than the ones they were meant to solve." We respond by blaming politicians. They blame one another. It's no surprise that the public is confused. The accounts of public discussion of major issues that reach the public are filtered through writers and commentators as uncomprehending of the complexity of the problems as are the politicians.

Rifkin's book was widely reviewed. On the whole the reviews were favorable, even by reviewers unwilling to agree with his conclusions. One of the first was by Michael Sheldrick, energy editor of *Business Week*. His review illustrates Keynes's dictum about the tenacity of ideas. Sheldrick's summary of the entropic process is excellent. But he is unwilling to follow the entropy law to its logical conclusion. Rifkin's "grim scenario," he said, "leads the author to a solution that, while it may be correct in the abstract, is nonsensical in practice."

Why nonsensical? Because "most economists view the economic process as activity that adds order and value to otherwise disorganized and valueless materials."[24] Isn't it possible, however, that most economists might be wrong? Before the Keynesian revolution, most economists thought that free-market economies were self-equilibrating. No one publicly subscribes to that quaint belief today.

Sheldrick went on to say that "mankind has never willingly given up the fruits of technological progress." He's right. But the key word is "willingly." There was no need to give up gains from progress in the past. But the world changes. When global energy consumption grew more slowly than population, which it did until the late 1950s, it made economic sense to use energy freely. Since then, energy consumption has grown faster than population. This unstable condition can't persist indefinitely. Frugality in the use of energy has become an imperative.

The statement that Rifkin's conclusions about entropy may be "correct in the abstract but nonsensical in practice" is illogical. Either the conclusions are correct, both in the abstract and in practice, or they are wrong in both cases. This is a classic example of the meaningless assertion that something is "correct in theory but won't work in the real world." If something won't work in the real world the theory is unsound. No one has yet suggested that the second law of thermodynamics is an unsound theory.

Some physical scientists, commenting on Rifkin's book, expressed annoyance that social scientists are "dabbling" with thermodynamics. They are evidently unaware that an eminent scientist believes that the entropy law "could create that long-sought bridge between the physical and social sciences."[25] His work on this idea won the Nobel Prize in Chemistry for Ilya Prigogine in 1977. A nontechnical description of his effort follows:

> In thermodynamics the second law appears as the evolution law of continuous disorganization, or the disappearance of structure... In biology or in sociology, the idea of evolution is, on the contrary, related to the increase of organization resulting in structures whose complexity is ever increased. Thus the classical thermodynamic point of view indicated that chaos is progressively taking over, whereas biology points in the opposite direction. Are there two different sets of physical laws that need to be involved to account for such differences in behavior? The general conclusion of Prigogine's work is that there is only one type of physical law, but different thermodynamic situations: near and far from equilibrium.[26]

This proposition has attracted little attention outside a limited scientific circle. But it could be one of the more important discoveries of modern science, as the Nobel Committee clearly believes. It reinforces the principles of bioeconomics and provides scientific support for the policies that would follow from acceptance of these principles. As Lepkowski has noted: "Prigogine and Georgescu's ideas dovetail... Prigogine in social systems, Georgescu in economic systems."[27]

When a piece of coal is transformed from available to unavailable energy in the process of performing "work," thermodynamic equilibrium has been reached. As a society progresses from the arbitrary exercise of power by a few leaders to a democratic rule of law, it becomes more orderly and stable. It is moving away from thermodynamic equilibrium. That is the essence of the "Prigogine Bridge" between the physical and social sciences. A system based on *laissez faire* would be inherently unstable. Ubiquitous competition means constant struggle, not only between buyers and sellers, but among sellers in any given market. In principle, only the "fittest" would survive. Aggressively competitive markets are chaotic; they're close to thermodynamic equilibrium.

What systems are consistent with movement away from thermodynamic equilibrium? There are two possible outcomes. One is a centrally planned, totalitarian society. The other is a system based on cooperation. The first is antithetical to democracy. Cooperation, however, is not only consistent with democracy, it represents the democratic ideal.

The idea of economic cooperation goes back at least to the days of John Stuart Mill. It has been ignored by conventional economists who insist that free-market pricing insures the optimal allocation of resources and a "fair" distribution of income. A recent study by Axelrod and Hamilton, using the methods of conventional economics, disputes this belief.[28]

Axelrod and Hamilton used game theory, an esoteric branch of mathematical economics, to analyze a problem known as "the prisoner's dilemma." The dilemma arises when one group competes with another that wants to reach a cooperative settlement. The competitors gain at the expense of the cooperators, forcing the latter to compete as well. Axelrod and Hamilton demonstrate, however, that both groups will gain if they cooperate instead of competing.

In another study, with the misleading title *Economic Games People Play,* Shlomo and Sharone Maital use the same method to extend the analysis to more than two parties. They analyze interactions among labor, management and the government.[29] They also conclude that cooperation could extricate these parties from some of the dilemmas aggressive behavior has created.

There have been few analytical studies of cooperation. Axelrod and Hamilton believe there's a need for "a formal theory of cooperation." Such a theory wouldn't be limited to economic cooperation; it would be extended to biological cooperation as well.[30]

Cooperation implies the substitution of some orderly arrangement for the "invisible hand" of the marketplace. This means, in a word, planning. But not the central planning of totalitarian societies. Planning does not have to be coercive to work. And democratic planning is entirely consistent with American economic and political institutions. It would require, however, the sort of cooperation last experienced in this country during World War II.

The leading advocate of non-coercive planning—or strategic planning, as he prefers to call it—is Wassily Leontief, who was awarded the Nobel Prize in Economic Science in 1973 for the development of input-output analysis. Only a brief sketch of strategic planning can be given here. It is, essentially, an extension to the national economy of what goes on regularly in corporate boardrooms.[31]

Strategic planning would be carried out by a council representing all major sectors of the American economy. A necessary adjunct would be a technical staff to provide the council with timely statistical information. The data would be organized in a highly detailed input-output table. This is a large two-way grid that shows how every economic activity is related to every other activity.

The input-output system would be used to explore alternative scenarios. Each would consist of a feasible "bill of goods" to be produced for consumption, capital formation, and export. It would also show material, labor, energy, and other input requirements. The scenarios prepared by the technical staff would provide the council with a range of choices. One scenario would have to be selected to establish a set of goals. No group or organization, however, would be forced to go along with the plan. Its successful implementation would depend entirely on voluntary compliance.

Democratic planning is consistent with the principles of Georgescu-Roegen's bioeconomics and also with Prigogine's social thermodynamics. We will no doubt have to experience further economic shocks before it becomes accepted policy. As Leontief has said, we will accept strategic planning "not because some wild-eyed radicals demand it, but because businessmen demand it to keep the system from sputtering to a halt."[32]

The aftermath of the "transition" won't be the utopian existence prophesied by Simon and Kahn. If we're lucky, however, we will learn to cope with energy and resource problems cooperatively. Lewis Thomas believes that: "The urge to form partnerships, to link up in collaborative arrangements, is perhaps the oldest, strongest, and most fundamental force in nature."[33] Let's hope he's right. The most likely alternative to cooperation would be destructive nihilism.

Ultimately, in the debate between conventional economists and bioeconomists, one side will be proved wrong. And the acid test of any policy is the consequences of being wrong. Make the highly improbable assumption that the U.S. and other leading nations become convinced in the near future that it is imperative to adopt bioeconomic policies. They take the steps necessary to conserve the world's dwindling stocks of energy and resources. Then assume that, after several decades, the warnings of bioeconomists are found to be false. No problem. Although the principles of bioeconomics are based on the irreversibility of the entropic and economic processes, *bioeconomic policies are completely reversible*. It would be a simple matter to switch from a regime of stringent conservation to a set of policies that would revive today's consumerism.

On the other hand, conservation works only as long as there is something to be conserved. If we continue to use energy and resources as though they are inexhaustible, and if the promises of fusion and unlimited substitutability aren't realized, the discovery is likely to come too late for anyone to do anything about it. *The ultimate consequences of conventional economics are irreversible.*

All nations, the rich and the poor, are affected by the entropic process. Again, we can only hope that as the world's stock of energy and resources is steadily transformed from useful forms to waste, the Prigogine principle will work—that mankind will adopt some form of cooperative organization. The outcome of the race between the evolution of cooperation and destructive nihilism is at best in doubt. As Carrol Pursell put it, in his review of Rifkin's *Entropy,* "we never save time by using energy—rather by using up energy we destroy time itself. It's an old message, but one that becomes increasingly important as time runs out."[34]

Notes

1. This is a summary of the key ideas in my book, *The Illusions of Conventional Economics,* Morgantown, WV: West Virginia University Press (1982). Some parts of the book have been updated in this paper.

2. *Problems Economiques* (December 7, 1977) p. 4.

3. For a summary of recent criticism see Robert Kuttner, "The Poverty of Economics," *The Atlantic Monthly* (February 1985), pp. 74-84.

4. "Conventional economics" includes not only the dominant Neoclassical school, but Monetarists, Keynesians, Neo-Keynesians, Rational Expectationists, Supply-Siders, Marxists, and others who share a common belief that economic growth is imperative. This is probably the only dogma they agree on.

5. The principle was stated in this form by H.G. Goeller and A.M. Weinberg, "The Age of Substitutability," the *American Economic Review,* Vol. 64 (December 1978), pp. 1-11.

6. See Wassily Leontief, "Theoretical Assumptions and Unobserved Facts," *The American Economic Review,* Vol. LXI (March, 1971), pp. 1-7; Nicholas Georgescu-Roegen, "Methods in Economic Science," *Journal of Economic Issues,* Vol. XII (June 1979), pp. 317-328, and his "Rejoinder," in *Idem* (March 1981); and William J. Baumol, "Economic Models and Mathematics," in Sherman Roy Krupp (ed.), *The Structure of Economic Science,* Englewood Cliffs, NJ: Prentice-Hall (1966), pp. 88-100.

7. Vol. 208 (June 27, 1980) pp. 1431-1437.

8. (June 1981), pp. 33-41.

9. See, for example, the communications in *Science,* Vol. 210 (December 19, 1980), pp. 1296-1305.
10. Ibid., p. 1305.
11. Princeton, NJ: Princeton University Press (1981).
12. For a representative sample of reviews see: R. Bruce Briggs, *The New York Times Book Review* (September 13, 1981); Garrett Hardin, *The New Republic* (October 28, 1981); Herman E. Daly, *The Bulletin of the Atomic Scientists* Vol. 39 (January 1982); Mark Perlman, *Population Studies* Vol. 36 (November 1982), pp. 490-494; a review symposium by C. Peter Timmer, Ismail Isrageldin, John Katner and Samuel H. Preston in *Population and Development Review,* Vol. 8 (March 1982), and Albert Bartlett, *American Journal of Physics* (forthcoming).
13. *The Wall Street Journal* (October 23, 1981).
14. The first complete statement of bioeconomic principles was given in *The Entropy Law and the Economic Process,* Cambridge, MA: Harvard University Press (1971). An excellent summary and additional references are given in his article, "Energy and Economic Myths," *Southern Economic Journal,* Vol. 41 (January 1975), pp. 347-381. See also, "Energy Analysis and Economic Valuation," *Idem,* Vol. 45 (April 1979), pp. 1023- 1058.
15. Council on Environmental Quality and the Department of State, *The Global 2000 Report to the President,* Washington: Government Printing Office (1980).
16. Julian L. Simon and Herman Kahn (eds.), *The Resourceful Earth: A Response to Global 2000,* Oxford and New York: Basic Blackwell (1984).
17. Constance Holden, "Simon and Kahn Versus Global 2000," *Science,* Vol. 221 (July 22, 1983), pp. 341-343.
18. See Edward F. Renshaw, *The End of Progress—Adjusting to a No Growth Economy,* North Scituate, MA: Duxbury Press (1976); Renshaw, "Productivity," *Economic Growth from 1976-1986: Prospects, Problems, and Patterns,* Vol. 1, Washington: Government Printing Office, pp. 21-56; and Edward F. Denison, *Accounting for Slower Economic Growth,* Washington: The Brookings Institution (1979).
19. Lewis Thomas, "On the Uncertainty of Science," *Harvard Magazine* (September-October 1980), p. 19.
20. John Maynard Keynes, *The General Theory of Employment, Interest and Money,* New York: Harcourt Brace and Company (1935), p. viii.
21. See, for example, Nicholas Georgescu-Roegen, *Demain la Decroissance,* with a preface and introduction by D'Ivo Rens and Jacques Grinevald, Paris and Lausanne: Editions Marcel Favre (1979), and Stefano Zamagni, *Georgescu-Roegen,* Milan: Etas Libri (1979).
22. This is the process described by the quotation from Lewis Thomas. For a more rigorous discussion, see Thomas S. Kuhn's classic *The Structure of Scientific Revolutions,* Second Edition, Chicago: The University of Chicago Press (1970).
23. New York: The Viking Press (1980).
24. *Business Week* (September 8, 1980).
25. Wil Lepkowski, "The Social Thermodynamics of Ilya Prigogine," *Chemical and Engineering News* (April 16, 1979), p. 30.
26. Itamar Procaccia and John Ross, "The 1977 Nobel Prize in Chemistry," *Science* (November 18, 1977), p. 717.
27. *Op. Cit.*

28. Robert Axelrod and William D. Hamilton, "The Evolution of Cooperation," *Science*, Vol. 211 (March 27, 1981), pp. 1390- 1396. For a more extended discussion, see Axelrod, *The Evolution of Cooperation,* New York: Basic Books (1980).
29. New York: Basic Books (1984).
30. *Op. Cit.*, p. 1391.
31. For further details see Wassily Leontief, "National Economic Planning: Methods and Problems," *Challenge,* (July- August 1976), pp. 6-11.
32. Quoted in Robert Heilbroner, "The American Plan," *The New York Times Magazine,* (January 25, 1976).
33. *Op. Cit.*, p. 21.
34. *The New York Times Book Review,* (October 26, 1980).

The Crisis of Industrial Overcapacity: Avoiding Another Great Depression

by

Frederick C. Thayer

More than a half-century ago, two U.S. presidents used similar language to describe an economic crisis and to suggest what should be done. "Destructive competition," said Herbert Hoover in 1931, had brought "demoralization" to such industries as coal, oil and lumber; the coal being produced, for example, required the services of only half the available miners. Hoover wanted to revise the antitrust laws so that industries could reduce excessive competition.[1] Two months after taking office in 1933, Franklin Roosevelt outlined the philosophy of his economic New Deal. "We have found our factories able to turn out more goods than we could possibly consume," he asserted, adding that "cutthroat" and "unfair" competition was punishing workers with "long hours and starvation wages." He promised to "encourage each industry to prevent overproduction" and to end the "disastrous overproduction" that had plunged farmers into poverty.[2] Hoover initially supported the cornerstone of the New Deal,[3] the National Industrial Recovery Act (NIRA), which permitted the firms in individual industries jointly to plan output, wages, and prices (antitrust laws were suspended). Hoover had changed his mind by the time the Supreme Court gutted the New Deal in 1935 by declaring the NIRA unconstitutional.[4] That decision ruled out industrial self-regulation as a legitimate means of protection, or recovery, from depression, but it did not affect the more direct forms of economic regulation instituted in the 1930s for such industries as banking, communications, trucks and airlines.

The Great Depression and the words of two presidents are worth recalling because many industries in this country and

---

Frederick C. Thayer is professor of Public and International Affairs at the Graduate School of Public and International Affairs, University of Pittsburgh, Pittsburgh, Pennsylvania.

others now face problems similar to those that Hoover and Roosevelt attributed to excessive competition (overcapacity), overproduction, and, in the case of banking, overspeculation. Among these industries are steel, autos, copper, textiles, chemicals, rubber, oil, and agriculture as well. The same problems appear to be affecting the industries subjected to direct regulation in the 1930s, especially banking; significantly, these industries have been substantially or wholly deregulated in recent years. Leaving aside the banks for now, the problem is quickly summarized: much more is produced, or could be produced in existing capacity, than can be sold at fair prices that bring reasonable profits—a summary that is equally valid for socialist economies. If Hoover and Roosevelt correctly (if belatedly) described the problem, then a crisis of overcapacity and overproduction now grips both the old industrial countries and the developing countries that have been rapidly adding to global industrial capacity.

The view of the earlier presidents was entirely at odds with the traditional view, dominant before the depression and since the late 1930s, that because overcapacity and overproduction are impossible, there is a constant need for more capacity and more production. As the Supreme Court declared in 1904, "the unrestrained interaction of competitive forces will yield the best allocation of our economic resources, the lowest prices, the highest quality, and the greatest material progress."[5] This paper argues that Hoover and Roosevelt were indeed correct, that their view is valid today, and that the traditional view, one endorsed by all schools of economic thought, defines the problem (overcapacity and overproduction) as the solution, and the solution (economic regulation) as the problem. Overcapacity is the recurring cause of economic depression and the inevitable outcome of unrestricted competition and free trade, even if neither has ever reached the condition economists label "perfect" competition. No industry can sustain its viability without some form of administrative machinery that regulates its capacity, output, prices, wages, or some combination thereof, and, in many cases, imports and exports. Only regulation can prevent overcapacity and overproduction, or make it possible to recover from the havoc they wreak.

Neither the arguments nor the proposals to follow are as extreme as they may appear at first glance. While even the word "regulation" leads many to visualize hordes of government officials making secret decisions on economic matters they know little about, the most important form of regulation proposed herein would closely resemble the manner in which the U.S. economy functioned in the 1950s and 1960s—that should not be frightening. Similarly, such terms as "saturated markets," "gluts," "surpluses," and even "excessive competition" are reasonably familiar, but they describe presumably temporary conditions. Addressing any such problem, economists may prescribe that government either do nothing because the problem will correct itself, stimulate demand so that the output can be sold at fair prices or, in the case of farm surpluses, buy what cannot be sold. A fourth prescription, reluctantly advanced when farm surpluses reach massive proportions, is to provide farmers incentives to produce less, and the prescriptions to follow are quite similar. Regulation of suppy, not demand, is the critical requirement, and it must be permanent, not temporary; these propositions are wholly at odds with cherished principles that virtually all economists share.

The overcapacity crisis of the 1980s must soon engulf much of the world if regulation is not installed, but it should be much easier now to discard irrelevant ideological arguments. If Marxists once could identify capitalism as the cause of depression, they cannot do so today. Some of the world's producers are capitalist firms, some are socialist enterprises, some are merged enterprises or consortia that include both capitalists and socialists, and some are in countries whose leaders deny allegiance to both nineteenth-century dogmas. The specific examples to be cited later should make it clear that because the problem has nothing to do with ideology, so must a workable solution be non-ideological.

Following this introductory section, remaining sections will attempt to present the arguments and the evidence in systematic fashion:

- Say's law of markets is the first of two economic principles that must be discarded. While some economists, notably the Keynesians, insist that the law has long since been discredited, their argument is as erroneous as the law itself. Say's law holds that because supply creates its own demand, supply cannot exceed demand for any length of time; overcapacity and overproduction, therefore, are impossible. Yet supply must greatly exceed demand in conditions of unregulated competition, and prices must then collapse. Correctly interpreted, Say's law is a prescription for depression, not equilibrium.

- If prosperity is sustained for any significant length of time, some form of economic regulation must be at work, even if the regulation is not clearly visible. The industrial overcapacity of the 1930s was corrected by an unusual form of regulation. World War II destroyed much of the capacity outside the U.S. The long period of postwar U.S. prosperity can be traced to a largely concealed form of industrial self-regulation that has now been made ineffective by the pressure of global competition. To the extent that economists and policy-makers noticed some aspects of that self-regulating system, they constantly attacked the industries involved, ignoring the likelihood that the regulation was indispensable to prosperity.

• A second economic fallacy holds that it is wasteful and inefficient to produce for any reason other than to sell the output, because only private (consumer) goods create "wealth." From that perspective, the production of such public goods as military arms and social infrastructures (water, sewer, environmental and transportation systems) create only "waste." That belief leads most economists and the policy-makers they advise to advocate virtually limitless investment for the production of private goods, but to condemn expenditures on public goods except when war threatens national survival. Taking overcapacity and overproduction into account, the traditional view mislabels waste as "wealth," and wealth as "waste," while wholly misconstruing the relative significance of the debts incurred in producing private goods and those incurred in producing public goods. Deficit spending that leads to overcapacity (corporate debt in this country, government debt in some countries) is far more dangerous than its public goods counterparts.

• The necessary agenda includes economic regulation for all important industries, one by one, perhaps on a multilateral basis that crosses ideological boundaries. Equally important are massive quality-of-life public works programs to build or rebuild the nonexistent or collapsing social infrastructures of many countries. Regulatory schemes will have to allow for new industries and technologies, but unrestricted competition is less helpful in this regard than many believe. Compatible taxing policies also are needed, and not only in this country, to discourage overinvestment in private goods and to make funds available for quality-of-life programs. Because overcapacity and overproduction can so easily lead to depression, economic imperialism and war, this agenda is as crucial as arms-control agreements to a sustainable world future.

The arguments and proposals in this paper build upon actions and trends already underway, but are based upon an expansion of the Hoover-Roosevelt rationale, not the rationale currently used to explain policy decisions to institute regulation. During the 1984 U.S. presidential campaign, for example, the incumbent conservative and his liberal opponent both acknowledged that the auto and steel industries needed immediate help. The president implied that he would continue the automobile import quotas earlier negotiated with Japan and announced that he would negotiate import quotas for steel with a number of countries. His challenger favored a more complex form of assistance for the domestic auto industry, and mandatory steel quotas. Any such quotas for the immediate future would seem to demonstrate that the combined ability of firms in the negotiating countries to manufacture autos and steel is far in excess of what can be sold, and that this situation can be described as overcapacity. Because few are yet ready to agree that overcapacity ever can be a problem, however, the candidates stated their positions in traditional language.

Both Ronald Reagan and Walter Mondale looked upon import quotas and similar measures as only temporary and reluctantly granted exceptions to the traditional principles of unrestricted competition and free trade. They argued that if temporary protection enabled firms to become profitable, as had occurred in the auto industry, the profits should be used to modernize old plants or build new ones incorporating the latest technologies, and that labor unions should restrain their wage demands. The logic was that U.S. firms could quickly reposition themselves to undersell foreign competitors. Executives seeking help, therefore, had to promise or at least imply that they would modernize, but they did not appear to believe that if all factories in the world were up-to-date and operating at peak efficiency, everything produced could be sold at fair prices. The executives were forced to accept Say's law as the basis for discussion because policy-makers so insisted. At least three additional factors have contributed to the narrow view of economic decision-making that has continued to dominate official Washington.

The problems of overcapacity come to government one industry at a time. This encourages the different congressional committees and the often different federal agencies that must deal with those problems to see them as unrelated to each other. Even the affected industrialists often see their individual problems as unique, rather than as examples of a more general problem. The effect is to turn industries and economic sectors against each other. The auto industry dislikes the higher steel prices that quotas impose; industries using copper oppose quotas (and the President rejected copper quotas); retailers condemn efforts to restrict garment imports from China; and farmers fear that quotas on industrial imports will incite other countries to buy their food elsewhere. In this environment, those seeking help are labeled "special interests" who, by definition, threaten the broader public interest. Liberals turn against traditional labor supporters, and conservatives attack business, because the problems are misidentified as declining productivity and mismanagement, not overcapacity. The second factor is that the issues and political alliances of regulation and deregulation have shifted so quickly that neither liberals nor conservatives are yet prepared to acknowledge and deal with the shift.

The Reagan administration entered office in 1981 with a commitment to relax, in some cases even remove, the *social* regulations, especially those recently instituted, that protect workers and consumers from excessive risks to their health and safety, and protect the environment from pollution and other forms of degradation. Along with many in industry, such key officials as Chief Economist Murray Weidenbaum, Secretary of Interior James Watt, Environmental Protection Agency Administrator Anne Burford, and Federal Trade Commissioner James Miller believed in 1981 that if the dollar costs imposed by social regulations could be reduced without adding undue risks, U.S. firms could recapture some of the business they had lost to foreign competitors and rehire many of the workers they had laid off. Many of the administration's liberal opponents were equally committed to maintaining and even expanding social regulation. Debates were rancorous and unceasing until three of the officials left government and the president announced that he was as interested as anyone in conservation and environmental protection. The administration and its business supporters also seemed to lose their zeal for social deregulation when it became obvious that even total deregulation would not solve the problems of U.S. industries. Relaxing pollution standards for steel mills is useless when exports from Brazil and South Korea inundate industrial countries that cannot reduce wages enough to meet such competition. Issues of social regulation, then, were not prominent in the 1984 campaign, an outcome that few would have predicted only two years earlier.

During the decade or more when liberals and conservatives heatedly debated the efficacy of social regulation, they became more and more united in favor of economic deregulation. From the mid-1970s until very recently, everyone in Washington seemed to want the credit for deregulating the regulated industries left over from the 1930s. Such unusual allies as Ralph Nader, Milton Friedman, Edward Kennedy, Gerald Ford and Jimmy Carter joined hands, even if their assumptions were not identical. Liberals hoped that consumers would benefit from lower prices and better service as competition intensified, while conservatives cheered the departure or diminished authority of bank and airline regulators, among others. Hardly anyone noticed that the growing problems of the basic industries hinted that unshackled competition might be more a problem than a solution. Because deregulation euphoria was bipartisan, neither liberals nor conservatives are ready to admit they erred, to attack the opposition for having erred, to urge re-regulation of what they so recently deregulated, or to propose even wider forms of economic regulation; yet the trends are unmistakable. Liberals and conservatives have resolved some important differences on social regulation, and they are slowly withdrawing their allegiance to unrestricted competition and free trade. The same shift soon must occur among the citizenry at large.

Only a year or two ago, many in the U.S. still were entranced with the apparently miraculous achievements of the West German and Japanese economies. Business and labor leaders were asked to study the managerial and technological improvements that seemed responsible for the miracles, especially the one in Japan, and prescriptions for copying the success stories became overnight best-sellers. Industries in those countries increasingly face the same problems as industries here, along with those in other countries affected by the overcapacity crisis, but this has occurred too quickly to attract widespread notice. Indeed, a book describing the managerial "excellence" of the "best-run companies" in the U.S. remained a runaway best- seller for most of 1984, even though its list of outstanding companies indicated that managerial knowhow might not be enough to deal with emerging crises. Among the listed firms that have since encountered substantial difficulties are Texas Instruments, General Electric, Caterpillar Tractor, and Atari;[6] the latter was a notably ironic example. After the company moved its production facilities overseas because intense competition compelled it to seek cheaper labor, little more was heard from the "Atari Democrats" who had been advocating a national industrial policy to subsidize expansion of high-tech industries.

Americans, finally, were not quite ready to consider that the seeds of depression might soon bloom, because an apparently strong recovery appeared to have ended the steepest recession since the 1930s. Presidential candidates could not be expected to predict a depression; indeed, both conspicuously said little or nothing about domestic and global banking problems that already had reached crisis proportions. The principles and practitioners of economics also lent a helping hand: those who adhere to economic principles do not even acknowledge the Great Depression. The National Bureau of Economic Research, a private nonprofit group of economists whose declarations on such matters are widely accepted as authoritative, maintains that while an economic *recession* began in 1929, it ended in March of 1933, and that the next recession did not begin until 1937, lasting until

June of 1938; there was no further downturn until 1945.[7] Historians and those who remember the 1930s might insist that a devastating slump gripped this country and others for twelve uninterrupted years, and that minor ups and downs during that period of misery were not significant at the time and are even less so in retrospect. Nonetheless, such small upturns in economic indicators as occurred between 1933 and 1937 can be interpreted as the beginning of a sustained recovery; thus, Roosevelt found little support (none from economists) for a counterattack on the Supreme Court. While economists in the 1930s "could not agree on what caused the Depression or what to do to get out of it,"[8] they spoke principally of recession, not depression, because only the former has a widely accepted technical definition. Economic principles, moreover, rule out the most likely explanation for depression.

Economic Fallacy #1:
Overcapacity and Overproduction Are Impossible

Say's law of markets is named for the French economist who asserted in 1803 that any economy generates sufficient demand to buy its own output; because supply creates demand, so to speak, supply and demand automatically move toward equilibrium. Sometimes the law is restated so as to portray supply as only another form of demand, in that the output of any producer expresses that producer's demand for whatever he will buy with the proceeds of selling. While markets may experience temporary fluctuations or cycles, these are presumed to be self-correcting. A lack of buyers quickly will bring down prices, encouraging new buyers (elasticity of demand) to "clear" a saturated market—reasoning that Marxists also accept. The most dedicated contemporary believers in the law, supply-side economists, argue that so long as government does not intervene, any cyclical fluctuation automatically returns to the supply-demand equilibrium; unlimited production, therefore, always is the preferred course of action.[9]

The law's power lies in its sweeping simplicity; because overcapacity is absolutely impossible, the question is beyond study or discussion. Even those who believe they have repealed Say's law seem unaware of the extent to which they accept the law's fundamental premise. John Kenneth Galbraith, for example, expresses the "widely accepted" Keynesian view that a temporary deficiency in demand (underconsumption) may indeed require government intervention to increase purchasing power (priming the pump).[10] Rather than repealing Say's law, however, this modification argues only that if supply does not automatically create demand, government should carry out Say's law by stimulating the demand side of the supply-demand equation; Keynesians agree that there cannot be too much supply. The dispute between traditionalists and Keynesians, then, is one of methods, not purpose, even if the dispute involves significantly different alternatives that can be frightening to the affected individuals. A traditionalist may insist that every individual must produce before being provided the wherewithal to buy. A Keynesian may suggest that because all joblessness is not voluntary, those without work should be helped until jobs again become available. All schools of economic thought believe that demand is or can be made immediately available to absorb any amount of supply. No school entertains the notion that the solution for depression is to limit the supply of private goods, not increase it. Keynes, often considered a supporter of the New Deal, strongly opposed its supply-regulating core.[11]

Three corollary assumptions further obscure the outcomes of excessive competition. The first is that any worker's wage is equal to the marginal value of his output. Even Marx believed that in a competitive market, price was determined by the amount of labor time needed to produce what was sold.[12] It is more likely that the amount of competition (duplication) determines price. Overproduction can drive wages to poverty levels; only minimum wage laws, a frequent target of economists, keep floors under wages. By the same token, only an excess supply of labor can provide sufficient competition for jobs to restrain wage inflation. Presidents routinely accept a "natural rate of unemployment."[13]

A second corollary is that a business failure demonstrates that a market is working well, in that more efficient producers have driven out the less efficient. This traditional view does not explain how a single bankruptcy can be a good sign when the alarmingly high failure rates of steep recessions and depressions cannot possibly be indicators of market success. Say's law rules out the more likely explanation of overcapacity. When too many producers are trying to sell to the same consumers, some of the former must fail, and many of the wasteful costs of business failures are borne by society as a whole.

The third corollary is that because supply cannot exceed demand, the latter is essentially infinite, in that human beings have a limitless desire to consume. The assumption becomes more attractive when it is restated in somewhat different terms: so many people suffer from too little food, clothing, and shelter that the amount of additional production needed to overcome these deficiencies is so large as to be incalculable. Marxists, along with

Keynesians, suggest that redistribution, perhaps in the form of transfer payments, could transform those needs into effective demand;[14] in principle and practice, a market recognizes only demand. While the redistribution argument has much to commend it, demand is not infinite.

Economist Robert Mundell observes that there are limits to every individual's ability to consume. An extraordinarily rich person is conditioned by a shortage of time, and all of us can eat only what our bodies can accommodate.[15] If transfer payments enabled everyone in the world to satisfy his or her needs, the principle of competition would compel sellers to produce much more than could be consumed. Unless the competitive principle is abandoned or modified by some type of supply regulation, this outcome remains inevitable. The implications of all these assumptions can be avoided only by shifting the focus of economic analysis.

Economists have long found it convenient to deal with supply and demand as aggregate functions, i.e., the sum total of all decisions made by all buyers and sellers. This has the effect of obscuring the more fundamental relationship of *one* consumer to *many* sellers. Duplication presumably benefits the "sovereign consumer" (a phrase often attributed to Keynesian Paul Samuelson) who should be "free to choose" (monetarist Milton Friedman's language) from the offerings of many producers. At the time of each decision to buy, supply must greatly exceed demand if the buyer is to have enough leverage to force down prices. Defined more accurately, aggregate supply is the response of all competing producers to the demands of all consumers. The greater the number of competitors for each sale, the greater the excess of supply over demand at the time of each purchase, and the greater the excess of aggregate supply over aggregate demand. Neither Say's law nor its Keynesian modification explains why an excess of supply for the individual consumer, one that is mandated by antitrust laws, suddenly disappears when supply and demand are treated as aggregates.

Admittedly, it is difficult to *prove* that overcapacity exists, let alone *prove* that it is the cause of depressions. In a social world where experimentation cannot be controlled to the extent necessary to meet laboratory standards, cause-effect assumptions are accepted or rejected solely on the basis of plausibility. People make decisions when they believe that one event or fact has a causal relationship with another event or fact. Economists, after all, cannot *prove* that *undercapacity* is the endless problem they claim it to be; nor can they *prove* in advance that breaking up an existing monopoly will produce more socially desirable outcomes. In this context, the decision to break up the AT&T telephone monopoly was an experimental test of the hypothesis that divestiture and long-distance competition would produce such outcomes. Perhaps the best known opponent of economic regulation is Nobel laureate George Stigler, but he is able to condemn the deficiencies of regulation only by reasserting the "known" benefits of consumer sovereignty and unrestrained competition.[16] As an assumption that has attained the status of an article of faith, a theological principle, Say's law has thus far survived the efforts of many reputable observers to unmask it by using the available evidence to make plausible assumptions that could repeal Say's law.

The Recurring Disaster of Overcapacity and Overproduction

The overbuilding of railroads in the 1880s has been labeled the cause of the steep depression of 1893. Competitors "recklessly and hastily threw up lines that were not needed, through miles and miles of uninhabited wilderness, merely to insure that another road would not claim the territory first." When the railroads began to fail, so did steel companies, 32 in the first six months of 1893. By this time, banking and the country's reserve capital had become centralized in New York, and the capital had been "freely used in speculation." Stock market and bank crashes followed, but the sequence began with overcapacity.[17] Among the recurring indicators of overcapacity and overproduction have been collapsing prices, economic imperialism, widespread corporate mergers, farm surpluses, and high industrial inventories.

The falling prices of deflation are more frightening even to think about than are the rising prices of inflation, because the purpose of unrestricted competition is to deflate prices. Many fear that as individual firms become too large and too powerful, they set "artificially high" prices, but hardly anyone worries about prices becoming too low until disaster has struck. Many in the U.S. rejoice that inflation has abated in recent years, but the cure for inflation is an excess of supply over demand, and the fabled invisible hand of the free market has been known to dispense too much of that medicine. Wholesale prices dropped 16% in 1931, but dropped 18% in Great Britain, 20% in the Netherlands, and 21% in Japan.[18] This was a boon for some consumers, but those who had no jobs or who worked for 35 cents an hour could not take advantage of the bargains.[19] The unintended consequences of free market theory and its basic principles is to create depressions, and political leaders who have been dismayed at the results of playing by free market rules have felt compelled to take extreme measures.

English economist J.A. Hobson may have been the first to mention "dumping" when he declared at the turn of the century that Western industrial countries took to imperialism because they had to find markets for domestic overproduction. At a time when 25% of the British lived in poverty, Hobson foreshadowed Keynes by suggesting that stimulating home-front demand, even if this involved only an increase in wages, would be better than selling abroad at gunpoint;[20] when the Great Depression arrived much later, Hobson again argued for wage increases.[21] The Marxist-Leninist view, of course, is that imperialism represented a search for cheaper labor and raw materials.[22] If both arguments are plausible, Hobson's seems to have a firmer grip on the sequence of overcapacity and overproduction.

This country's first wave of corporate mergers occurred at the turn of the century, and 78% of the mergers resulted in firms that produced 50% or more of the total output of their individual industries.[23] Was it only a coincidence that the mergers followed closely upon the depression of the 1890s? The merger wave intensified the fear of industrial concentration and led to the expansion of antitrust legislation and enforcement. While Roosevelt's New Deal suspended the antitrust laws, it encouraged joint planning among firms as a cartel-like substitute for mergers. By the time the Supreme Court overturned the NIRA, 557 industries had adopted "codes of fair practice" to regulate themselves.[24]

Farm surpluses have been more a constant problem than a cyclical one because agriculture resembles the mythical perfect market of innumerable producers who, because there are so many of them, cannot individually influence prices. Unless there is too little arable land, or weather intervenes, farm surpluses are inevitable; the history of farm cooperatives is one of farmers collectively seeking to keep crops from market until prices rise above costs. Assessing six decades of U.S. experience, one observer concluded in the 1950s that the endless "trials and tribulations" of farmers could be summarized in the proposition that "the supply of farm products as a whole has exceeded the demand for them at prices which cover the costs of most farm units" (emphasis in original).[25] During the 1920s, for example, farm output was stable (15% higher than from 1919 to 1921), but such new grain competitors as Canada and Argentina led to stagnation and surpluses in this country. As depression took hold, 1932 prices dropped to less than half the already low prices of 1929. The paper value of 1931 farm output actually was $1 billion higher than for 1930 because "millions of small farmers reacted to falling prices by trying (unsuccessfully) to maintain their receipts."[26] As industry also has learned, at least to some extent, increases in productivity only worsen a crisis of overcapacity and overproduction.

The first industrial indicator of the Great Depression was a "typical inventory recession" that began in mid-1929,[27] near the end of a decade in which productivity increases had been two to three times greater than the increases in real-wage purchasing power of workers.[28] As depression deepened, plausible explanations multiplied. The *New York Times* praised soft coal operators for suggesting in 1931 that the industry be regulated, arguing that a "public utility" approach might remedy "overproduction."[29] Senator David I. Walsh of Massachusetts introduced legislation in 1932 to authorize "curtailment of production."[30] When Hoover's attorney general proposed antitrust revisions, he referred to "overproduction."[31] Railroad executives met throughout 1932 to "avoid preventable and competitive waste."[32] Hoover in 1931, and Roosevelt during the 1932 campaign, asked for the removal of "duplication" and "waste" from the railroad system and also recommended regulation of the new trucking industry that largely duplicated the railroads. The *New York Times* quickly praised Roosevelt's plan as statesmanlike and thoughtful.[33] Using principles that committed them to ignore all these suggestions, economists joined together only to protest the Smoot-Hawley tariffs, an obviously clumsy approach to reducing imports. As they always have, economists generally endorsed more competition and more production. If by 1984 the world had not yet plunged into deep depression, there were similar indications that one might soon occur. A few indicators may be mentioned.

The proliferation of mergers in recent years has led many to fear the presumably undesirable effects of restricting competition, raising prices and otherwise harming consumers. Mergers, however, are wholly understandable if overcapacity is taken into account. They become superficially attractive when managers have money on hand that they cannot use to invest in new plants because there already are too many. They decide to add to retained profits with borrowed funds, and then they buy other firms whose stock prices appear to be "undervalued"; the total value of all shares appears to be less than the value of existing plants and equipment. A manager who buys another firm does not consider that a low stock price may accurately reflect the declining value of surplus plants or that, as other potential buyers make competing bids, the stock price rises until it has become *overvalued* by the time the merger is completed. This leads to unusual outcomes when mergers accomplish the needed purpose of combining firms in the same industry. When Chevron (Standard Oil of California) acquired Gulf, for example, the price of Gulf stock recently had doubled; yet the merger was designed to reduce excess capacity. Antitrust enforcers recently have become much friendlier toward mergers in the same industry (Chevron-Gulf is the largest in U.S. history), a possible acknowledgement of overcapacity. Conglomerate mergers are equally traceable to overcapacity, but conglomerate managers unwittingly make things worse.

When the antitrust enforcers were less inclined only a few years ago to approve mergers in the same business, executives who could not use their retained profits to expand their own capacity took to buying firms in other industries. They ignored the likelihood that the industries they entered were also suffering from overcapacity. While many observers worry about the sheer size of conglomerates, antitrust laws do not affect such mergers. The immediate effect of these mergers is to perpetuate or even increase the excessive competition of overcapacity by propping up firms whose assets are surplus to market demand. The longer-term effect is a bit different: U.S. Steel's acquisition of Marathon Oil and DuPont's purchase of Conoco ensured that a huge oil merger (Chevron-Gulf) would soon follow. Ironically, Chevron formerly was Standard Oil of California, and the 1911 divestiture of Standard Oil of America is an antitrust landmark. The usual argument that conglomerates improve efficiency because the "synergistic whole" of all member firms can be managed better than each firm separately can be managed is a much less plausible explanation of why conglomerates are formed. Indeed, the manager buying into another industry is unlikely to know enough about the industry to do a good job; the sorry outcomes need not be listed here.[34]

Despite their antipathy toward actions that may reduce competition, economists generally insist that whatever the problems associated with mergers, they do not adversely affect the efficient deployment of capital. This is so, according to the economists, because the shareholders of a firm that is sold immediately put their profits into new investments that will help the economy. In making this argument, economists must ignore more plausible conclusions. If there were many opportunities to build new plants in its own industry, or even in another industry, the buying firm logically might invest on its own. Because there is no way to know precisely what happens to the funds paid to the shareholders, it is likely that many of the funds are recycled through banks into other mergers. Meanwhile, the mergers have transformed hundreds of billions of dollars in old equities into new debt. Financier Felix Rohatyn has been intimately associated with many such deals, but he has increasingly come to question their effects. Using the example of the "leveraged buy-out," a scheme in which the managers of a firm use the firm as collateral for borrowing enough to buy it, he explains the workings of financial markets that have become a "huge casino":

> A public company with, say, $100 million of debt and $900 million of equity is turned into a private company with $900 million of debt and $100 million of capita... exactly the opposite of what our national investment objectives ought to be.[35]

While the relative importance of government and corporate debts will later be analyzed, it is sufficient to emphasize here what economists do not, i.e., mergers incur huge new debts that add nothing to, but may subtract from, productive capacity. If the debts are ever to be repaid, and many may not be, the money will come from consumers who pay higher prices than they should be charged, workers who are paid less than they should be, and citizens in general who pay taxes to make up for the business tax incentives that induce mergers. All this waste, or inadvertent thievery, is a byproduct of the unwillingness to recognize overcapacity.

A second example of 1984 indicators of overcapacity is that of a single major industry, although others could easily be added. When steelmakers ask government for import quotas, they must speak the language of the traditional view. When they speak off the record to journalists who promise not to reveal the names of their sources, the steelmakers say something else. Executives in Europe, Japan, and the U.S. made it known early in the year that only a comprehensive multilateral steel pact could solve the industry's acute overcapacity crisis. The pact would have to include machinery for deciding what new plants to build, where to build them, and what old plants to retire.[36] While President Reagan was considering the request for quotas, the American Iron and Steel Institute called for an international conference of steel-producing countries to consider the problem.[37] After Reagan decided to negotiate quotas, some steelmakers expressed the hope that quotas might be sufficient, but warned that further action probably would be needed.[38] While all sorts of estimates are available (one puts noncommunist overcapacity at about 40%,[39] it is enough to suggest that when those who know the most about a given industry, whether executives or union leaders, repeatedly define overcapacity as the industry's major problem, they deserve something other than ridicule from economists and policy-makers.

Hardly anyone would deny that the banking industry has increasingly been troubled in recent years. The industry is something of a special case, for at least five reasons. It is reasonable to assume, first, that the general health of this industry reflects economic conditions as a whole. Second, banks have been substantially deregulated in recent years, and it is reasonable to assume that increased competition has had some effect upon the industry. Third, the effects of increased bank competition are an unusual variation of the more general pattern usually associated with overcapacity. Fourth, the problems of banks have become global in scope. Fifth, the evidence is clear: the chairman of the U.S. Federal Deposit Insurance Corporation announced on October 19, 1984, that 797 banks were listed as "problem" banks, a new record. He affirmed that the cause of "problem" banks is "problem" loans, those on which interest and principal are not being paid or are paid late.[40] While many observers continued to cite mismanagement as the cause of each major bank collapse as it occurred, more plausible explanations are available. These include interest-rate deregulation and an unusual form of overcapacity.

Banks have been permitted in recent years to compete for depositors by offering them whatever interest rates bank managers choose to offer. While some hoped that this would stimulate savings and the new plant investment believed necessary, the effects of interest rate deregulation seem not to have been thoroughly explored in advance. Rather, bank rates were deregulated because the banks had been losing depositors to money market funds offering higher rates. Interest rates have stayed high, but the popular analysis ignores the effect of deregulation, putting the blame on federal deficits. Yet the purpose of deregulation was to increase interest rates; to argue that deregulation had no such effect is to raise the question of why the rates were deregulated. It is much more likely that deregulation is the culprit; the reason is simple, but it is much less understood than it should be. The normal effect of unrestricted competition is to drive prices down. This occurs because there is no immediate limit to the availability of the necessary resources. In principle, the materials are on hand for any number of, say, shoe manufacturers to enter that business. Money is in a different category.

The total supply of money is limited, or regulated, by the Federal Reserve Board. While critics assail the board for being too restrictive, being not restrictive enough, or making inconsistent decisions, the total supply remains limited. When the supply of any resource is limited, whatever the reason for that limit, unrestricted competition drives up its price. This would occur, for example, if a war cut off oil supplies to oil-importing countries. Rationing at government-set prices might be necessary, just as the U.S. rationed a number of commodities during World War

II. When many banks must compete for a limited supply of money, its price must go up, and deregulation has had the further effect of sharply reducing the Federal Reserve's ability to control interest rates in history (the difference between the inflation rate and interest rates). The board could bring down interest rates only by following standard economic principles; if it vastly increased the money supply, interest rates would indeed fall, but the influx of new money would bring runaway inflation. Nobody suggested that the Board should take such action and, understandably, it did not. Meanwhile, the sequential effects of deregulation have been little noticed.

When banks (even Sears now owns one) and other depository institutions compete head-to-head with fewer geographical restrictions, the effect is about the same as having many new banks enter the market. The total number of banks may not increase, or may decrease, but more banks (and "non-bank banks") chase every potential customer. To attract depositors, especially the rich, banks must offer large rewards, but they must then charge borrowers even higher rates in order to pay depositors and make profits. The entire industry has been trapped in a two-way squeeze. To compete for both depositors and borrowers, banks must keep the difference between the rates offered each group as small as possible. Managers are compelled to make quick decisions on loan requests, but they must also employ as few analysts as possible. Managers feel compelled to discourage or even forbid the opening of small accounts and to rapidly escalate their fees for miscellaneous services. The competition has been intense enough to incite false or misleading advertising, but the larger effects are much more frightening.

Soon after the 1984 failure of a major Chicago bank, the author appeared before the Committee on Banking of the U.S. House of Representatives to suggest that excessive bank competition had something to do with bank failures. When one committee member expressed the standard view that failures are attributable solely to poor management, the chairman outlined the relationship he saw:

> There were poor judgments on these loans. But perhaps one of the reasons for the poor judgment on the loans was [that] they had a lot of money on which they were paying high rates on these [Certificates of Deposit] and they had to have some place to put that money. There was competition there for placement of that money. I think that was part of it.[41]

The chairman's view remained in the minority throughout 1984, but his was the view of a longtime observer of the banking industry. Susan Kaufman Purcell has outlined how this competition works on a global scale, using the example of Mexico:

> Assuming that oil prices would continue rising, Mexico adopted an ambitious development strategy involving large-scale Government spending... to modernize industry... foreign banks repeatedly raised lending limits. Why not? As Mexico's situation deteriorated, the cost of loans increased. Bank profits soared, as did the temptation to lend more money... banks competed with one another; as long as some would lend, those refusing to do so risked exclusion from the Mexican market once the situation improved... United States banks—creditors for between $18 billion and $34 billion—apparently convinced themselves that Mexico knew what it was doing—and that if Mexico did not, Washington would bail it out.[42]

Whatever critics may say, the number of problem banks does not reach a new high solely because bank managers suddenly have forgotten how to manage. They are swept along by the unrelenting tide of two-way competition. As interest rates stay up, money floods into the banks, much of it from abroad. With much more money than sound opportunities for profitable lending in this country, managers accept the guarantees of foreign governments. Along with domestic firms and their laid-off workers, developing countries cannot repay their loans. Global overcapacity once again is the problem. If it has recurred so often, however, how was prosperity sustained in this country for so many years following World War II?

Concealed Self-Regulation And Its Demise

Wartime destruction of competing capacity was not the only cause of prosperity. While unemployment defied complete solution, a partly hidden form of industrial self-regulation stabilized the U.S. economy. While many have attacked the ability of large firms to exercise market power, few have noticed the unintended effect of antitrust laws as a stabilizing deterrent to runaway competition. The regulation was beneficial, not detrimental, but since it was a byproduct of war, it cannot be reinstated by using the methods that enabled it to thrive.

The U.S. pattern of oligopoly is familiar to those who study industry; one standard definition includes any industry in which no more than four firms account for at least 70% of total sales.[43] Using 60% as his yardstick, Galbraith observed that for many years, four firms dominated aluminum, copper, rubber, cigarettes, soap and detergents, liquor, glass, refrigerators, cellulose fibers, photographic equipment, cans, computers, sugar, and other industries as well; three firms dominated automobiles.[44] In economic jargon, this was "imperfect competition," in that each big firm was powerful enough to influence price levels. An "administered" or "target" price could be set high enough to accumulate enough profits to pay dividends, finance large advertising campaigns to maintain market shares, and provide retained earnings for new investment. Stabilized prices enabled interdependent firms and industries to make long-term contracts with each other and to reach similar agreements with workers. Many economists approved the outcomes of stability, but they overlooked its wartime origins and gave the credit to government fiscal policies because their theories condemned self-regulation. Galbraith was almost alone in pointing to the broad virtues of truly large scale organizations:

> It is the usual claim against the oligopolist that he keeps prices too high and has an undercommitment of capital and labor; it is evident that he makes effective use of capital, organization and technology because he is big and because he is big he is also an oligopolist. No one can ask him to be an oligopolist for the purposes of capital investment, organization and technology and to be small and competitive for the purposes of prices and allocative efficiency. There is a unity in social phenomena which must be respected.[45]

True to Keynesian principles, Galbraith defined the achievements of these industrial goliaths as those of demand stimulation, not the regulation of supply. In his view, the large firm spent huge sums on advertising to create the demand for whatever it produced, but a leading supply-sider plausibly argues that all such firms functioned entirely in accordance with Say's law, not its Keynesian modification. Galbraith, of course, repeatedly argued that the affluent should make do with less so that transfer payments could enable the poor to buy, but he remained an admirer of the big firms. Indeed, he cited the AT&T monopoly as the best example of big-firm effectiveness, clearly a minority view.[46] From the time the Supreme Court overturned the New Deal, rigorous antitrust enforcement remained a bipartisan policy, and the breakup of AT&T is today's most prominent example of it.

Given the prevailing view, U.S. oligopolies constantly faced attacks from many directions. When Judge Learned Hand decided that the Aluminum Corporation of America had violated the law solely by achieving too great a market share, bigness alone became a crime.[47] General Motors, an obvious target when it accounted for half of all auto sales in the country, figured in important antitrust decisions. The Supreme Court forced DuPont to relinquish in 1957 a 23% interest in GM that it had held since 1917, because DuPont supplied too much of GM's fabric, finishes, and antifreeze. GM was compelled in the 1960s to help competing bus manufacturers and to sell the plants of a subsidiary road-machinery company.[48] President John Kennedy directly attacked the steel industry; incensed over one increase in steel prices, he used all his clout to force a temporary rollback. In 1972, outlining charges that were abandoned a decade later when the charges could not be made to stick, the Federal Trade Commission accused the cereal oligopoly (Kellogg, General Mills, General Foods, Quaker Oats) of using anticompetitive practices to set artificially inflated prices, predicting that divestiture would lead to a 25% price reduction in a "competitively structured market."[49] Given such attacks, oligopolists doubtless took them into account as they made decisions.

A critic of antitrust laws has outlined a wholly plausible hypothesis. Former Solicitor General Robert Bork suggests that if "the law announced a policy of dissolution of any firm that exceeded 50% of the market, [any firm] approaching that size would have every incentive to restrict its output in order to avoid the penalties of law."[50] To Bork, any restriction is reprehensible, and he criticized antitrust enforcers for having contributed to reduced competition. It is wholly plausible to conclude that producers felt compelled to make sure they did not grow enough to attract antitrust prosecution, and that they competed less vigorously than they might have. The antitrust enforcers routinely avoided announcing precisely what share of any market would be considered too large, thereby providing even greater incentives for self-regulation. This can be shown by looking at familiar evidence in the context of overcapacity.

Executives of General Electric, Westinghouse, and some smaller manufacturers of electrical equipment were convicted of illegal conspiracy in a famous case of the late 1950s. Ultimately, the courts levied $2 million in fines, half of them paid by the two giants; a number of executives were jailed, and others were demoted or fired. They had secretly developed a plan to divide the business according to agreed market shares, at a time when government subsidies for back-up mobilization capacity had led to overcapacity. While the case stands as a widely praised example of antitrust enforcement, an equally plausible explanation is available. Had GE and Westinghouse competed as vigorously as they might have, they probably could have driven their small competitors out of business. While lower prices are the desired outcome of competition, large firms that cut prices to destroy competitors are subject to prosecution for predatory behavior. As some of the executives later explained, GE and Westinghouse found it necessary to *lose* business they otherwise might have gained.[51] There is little reason to believe the big firms had reason to stand in awe of the small ones, and yet the executives who hatched the scheme could not logically ask their chief executives for written permission to conspire.

When price fixing (which the New Deal legalized), bid rigging, and collusion occur, it is likely that firms are trying to avoid the disasters of overcapacity by engaging in illegal self-regulation. The members of oligopolies generally could regulate themselves without having their executives speak with each other; the electrical companies were an unusual exception. Smaller firms often find themselves virtually compelled to collude, especially when they are asked to submit sealed bids for government or private contracts—a contemporary example is state contracts for highway construction. Five companies, to use a hypothetical example, cannot afford to assemble the equipment and workers for a huge construction job when they know that only one of them will be selected. If all bid for many contracts, one of them may be awarded more than it can handle. When they secretly meet to divide the business and rig the bids, they may then be prosecuted. Each firm knows also that if it wants to ensure that it wins a given contract, it must consciously understate its probable costs. When overruns become necessary, critics condemn them. If overruns seem impossible, a firm may feel compelled to cheat on contract specifications by paying illegally low wages, using substandard materials or bribing inspectors. Rather than launching the largest antitrust investigation in history, as the Justice Department did only a few years ago with respect to highway construction, it should have analyzed why firms feel compelled to collude and what might be done about the effects of excessive competition.[52]

The oligopolies, of course, can no longer regulate themselves. That form of self-regulation vanished because U.S. supremacy gave way to all-out competition that crosses both national and ideological boundaries. Not only have international price wars taken center stage, but so have bribery, false invoices and other forms of smuggling, and even large-scale industrial espionage. In retrospect, the largely concealed form of self-regulation served the country well, and even illegal collusion produces better outcomes than unregulated competition. The oligopolies remain the best example. If they prospered, so did their workers who, for the first time, enjoyed stable employment at wages high enough to make them full-fledged members of the middle class. The effect was to make Marx appear a false prophet, discrediting the view that workers in capitalist societies would forever be consigned to poverty. To be sure, self-regulation was not inexpensive. To maintain market shares, competing oil companies often built four service stations at intersections where a single station could have served all customers. These costs, however, are trivial compared to those levied by overcapacity and depression.

It remains an open question whether the big firms ever fully understood, or understand even now, all the implications of self-regulation. Their behavior patterns were established before World War II intervened to help them. They have long raised capital by charging consumers higher prices and by resisting wage demands. While critics have occasionally complained that profits were too high or that executives had overpaid themselves, the critics have muted their attacks on retained earnings because of the assumed need for more capacity. As imports begin to cut into domestic sales, firms are almost compelled to compete against themselves. They know they cannot build more domestic capacity, so they build in low-wage countries hoping to undersell higher-wage competitors and knowing that their overseas plants will eliminate jobs at home.[53] They have little choice in the absence of government acceptance of permanent regulation. This reinforces the Leninist interpretation of imperialism, but greedy executives are not the problem. Rather, it is the widespread belief that funds available for the production of private goods are always put to better use than those available to produce public goods.

Economic Fallacy #2:
Industrial "Wealth" and Public "Waste"

Imagine for the moment that someone wishes to build a needed factory alongside a river that separates the site from the city that will house the factory's workers and be its transportation center. Imagine further that no bridge is near the site and that the decision to build the plant is contingent upon government's decision to build a bridge. The latter, then, is indispensable to economic development. The funds used to build and equip the new factory will be carefully calculated, and then they will be recorded and published in that portion of U.S. national income accounts labeled "investment," a widely accepted indicator of economic health. The funds that government uses to build the bridge will not be so labeled. Charles L. Schultze, who served as President Jimmy Carter's chief economic adviser, is also a leading authority on national income accounting. As he puts it:

> Part of federal, state and local government spending represents investment in productive assets (schools, highways, sewerage and water systems) which contribute to the capacity and efficiency of the economy. In the U.S. national income accounts, however ... such investment-type outlays are not included in the investment category of GNP, which is reserved for private investment.[54]

This does not immediately appear to be a problem: Schultze acknowledges that government builds "productive assets" that, in practical terms, are useful investments. Like many other economists, however, he seems unaware of the deeper economic principles that make this labeling so important to the evaluation of borrowing and spending for the production of private and public goods. An apparently insignificant bookkeeping practice is part of a larger myth that clearly separates "wealth" from "waste." This distinction creates much havoc.

When government builds a bridge, it does not plan to sell the bridge; the bridge, therefore, has no market value and, technically speaking, is worthless. If government borrows money to build the bridge, the latter cannot be collateral; government is accused of "monetizing" the debt by printing unsecured money. This has led some observers to lobby for a return to the gold standard. This would solve the assumed problem of worthless money by compelling government to buy gold before printing money to build the bridge. The more dominant view, however, is that government spending should be kept at the lowest possible level because it does nothing but deplete the nation's wealth. *Public* goods, having no market value, are "waste."

The imaginary factory and its equipment, and all other factories and their equipment, not to mention racetracks and gambling casinos, are considered to be "wealth." Any factory, according to Say's law, is always worth at least as much as was spent to build it; the factory, therefore, serves as collateral for the borrowed funds. With Say's law discarded, it is clear that when overcapacity strikes, many plants become worthless; often, they can neither be used nor sold. Similarly, overcapacity makes impossible the "ripple effects" always attributed to industrial investment. Contrary to economic belief, then, government spending will almost always stimulate other forms of economic activity, but industrial spending often may not.[55] The underlying belief that wealth (the bridge) is "waste" and that waste (overcapacity) is "wealth" leads policy-makers to worry about government debt while paying no attention at all to corporate debt.

One immediate result is both fascinating and tragic. Despite sophisticated data-gathering methods and mountains of government reports, nobody knows precisely how much debt U.S. corporations have incurred. One fact seems beyond question; corporate debt, much smaller than federal debt only thirty years ago, now greatly exceeds federal debt. In 1950, the war-induced federal debt was $217 billion, and corporations owed a relatively small $142 billion. By 1976, the last year for which the Department of Commerce collected data, federal debt had climbed to $516 billion, but corporate debt had skyrocketed to $1.4 trillion. The Federal Reserve Board has compiled the figures since and reported that corporate debt for 1981, was $1.2 trillion; recalculating from earlier years, the Federal Reserve put the 1976 corporate debt at $687 million, indicating that the Commerce Department had been off the mark by 100%. Interestingly, corporate debt is the only category of debt for which the two sets of data are in substantial disagreement, and diligent staff members of congressional committees have been unable to pry a satisfactory explanation from the data gatherers. Three factors stand out at this intersection of economic fallacy and deficit spending.

The first is that no matter whose data are used, federal debt is much less significant than it once was, and its significance has been declining for more than three decades. As a share of total credit market debt, government debt has dropped from one-third in 1950 to one-sixth in 1981; as a share of gross national product, it has dropped from two-thirds in the early 1950s to one-third today. Federal deficit spending and debt cannot possibly be responsible for all the ills attributed to them. Those who argue that federal deficits never should be permitted to exceed 2% of gross national product (contemporary deficits are around 4% to 5%) are fond of noting that even in the 1930s, deficits reached only 4.7% in 1933 and 4.2% in 1939. They mistakenly accept the view that 1939 was a year of recovery (unemployment was 17.2%), and they ignore wartime experience. According to economic principles of course, those deficits (14.9% of the GNP in 1942, 31.0% in 1943, 23.3% in 1944, and 21.9% in 1945) could not possibly have ushered in prosperity, in that the spending was for economically wasteful purposes.[57] Nor was this a purely Keynesian demand stimulation: full employment did not alone bring prosperity, but only in combination with supply regulation. A more plausible conclusion is that federal spending was much too *low* in the 1930s and is too *low* in the 1980s. Yet another conclusion is that the overcapacity crisis demonstrates that the thirty-year record of federal and corporate debt accurately reflects excessive industrial borrowing and spending.

The second factor is that because corporations and government use different accounting practices, corporate debt may be actually and relatively larger than the data imply. Albert T. Sommers, chief economist of the Conference Board, points out that if business used government reporting standards, the "fastest-growing and most potentially successful businesses" would report deficits year after year.[58] Professor Alan S. Blinder makes the same argument in reverse: if government used business practices, it would have "run a budgetary surplus during most of the past 20 years."[59] These comparisons, unfortunately, draw little attention; only the federal deficits that create "waste" are noticed, not the industrial borrowing that creates "wealth."

Third, the strength of the grip that this economic fallacy has on the minds of economists and policy-makers is, like that of Say's law, truly phenomenal. They virtually shout that relatively trivial federal borrowing "crowds out" legions of industrial entrepreneurs who, were it not for the high interest rates that federal deficits cause, would borrow every dollar they could find in order to invest in new capacity. The argument ignores the effect of interest rate deregulation, ignores such comparisons as those above, and ignores the obvious fact that firms have no difficulty in borrowing hundreds of billions of dollars to consummate mergers. When a theory is powerful enough to convince its believers to ignore important evidence or discard it as immaterial, the theory has indeed become theology. Those preaching its gospel have persuaded governments here and elsewhere to refuse to do what they should.

Setting the Agenda

The obvious solutions are economic regulation of industry and giant quality-of-life programs. Regulation is in order not only for all the major industries that are both indispensable to prosperity and the most significant victims of overcapacity depressions, but also for the recently deregulated industries, especially banking. For most of the major industries, regulation cannot be effective unless it is multilateral. Regulatory schemes will have to make careful allowances for inventions and new technologies, but unrestricted competition is less helpful for these purposes than many believe. This country and others will have to sharply revise their taxing policies to provide disincentives for overcapacity and monies for huge public works programs. Much of the agenda is less drastic than it appears to be, even if it attacks some widely held images associated with free market theology.

The word "regulation" often evokes about the same response as "committee"; both are considered evils to be avoided as much as possible. Free markets and individual choice are thought to be sacred ideals beyond question. Individualism, unfortunately, becomes authoritarianism when it is applied in a social context; if any individual has complete authority to make a decision, whether as a right or responsibility, all those affected by the decision must obey it. This has been the case for blue-collar workers who take direction from foremen and for the wives in traditional families who have been oppressed by their husbands. The philosophy of individualism, then, reflects the desire to have authority and the fear of losing it. The free-market version presumably transfers ultimate authority from producers to consumers:

the greater the number of competing producers, the greater the authority of consumers.

From this individualistic perspective, economic regulation seems an unjustified intervention by one authority (government) that diminishes the authority of consumers, producers, and perhaps workers. Social regulation of safety and health standards seems an equally bad intervention that reduces the authority of producers to make their own decisions; often, however, social regulation can be seen as a necessary intervention that prevents producers from risking the lives and health of workers and consumers. Taken together, these beliefs may account for the liberal-conservative support for the economic deregulation of some industries and for the more divided opinion on social regulation. The corporate managers who now want government to help protect their markets are at least implying that the image of the hard-driving, decisive, and brilliant executive should give way to a concept of *collective, team* or *partnership* decision-making that may even have to be global in scope. To be sure, the executives themselves, the media, and the general public seem reluctant to abandon the notion of rugged individualism. The Chrysler Corporation, for example, needed import quotas and government financial support to regain its health, but recovery was credited to a widely publicized executive who would have been helpless without government intervention. In looking at proposals for economic regulation, the list begins with the issue of authority.

1. *Designing Economic Regulation.* The fear of authority is real; the image of regulation as a prime example of how the "dead hand of bureaucracy" stifles freedom and progress must be taken into account, despite the evidence that government involvement, as in the space program, enhances progress. As industry leaders now acknowledge that government must lend a hand if their industries are to survive, so are they gradually seeking new ways of dealing with labor. Despite a long history of labor- management conflict frequently marred by violence—yet another outcome of overcapacity and depression—executives now solicit labor support for the proposals they make. Some workers, on the other hand, believe that various forms of worker ownership are necessary, but this partly reflects the Marxist notion that the technical issue of ownership is paramount. It is not. While no single regulatory design can be applicable to all industries, the basic principle of *shared* authority is paramount; all affected parties ultimately will have to be involved. Exclusion breeds only resentment, then outright opposition and perhaps even revolution; no political system is immune. If even the most dissatisfied know that the absence of regulation can bring only chaos, they may be persuaded

to continue their efforts to improve regulation.

Government's role, it follows, should be one of facilitating domestic consensus and coordinating the necessary multilateral negotiations. This would only recognize and expand decision-making processes that have been widely used for years. Lobbying, including that by consumer and environmental groups, is at least as much a function of providing indispensable expertise as of pursuing greed. Representatives of industry have long been participants in national and multinational planning processes. Unfortunately, the only widely accepted processes have been those associated with war or potential war, the ultimate expression of domination. In economic principle, shared authority simply must replace consumer sovereignty.

2. *Regulating Major Industries.* The Japanese recently demonstrated how any country, or even a group of countries, might take initial steps to alleviate overcapacity; the chemical industry was the immediate problem. The government brought together the twelve producers of ethylene and the six producers of ethylene derivatives to devise a plan for reducing capacity. The firms agreed to reorganize themselves into three consortia, each committed to a capacity reduction of 36%. They agreed to sustain surplus workers through a period of underemployment, an accepted "welfare aspect of Japanese corporations" that guarantees job security; later, the workers would be shifted to other jobs. Because the planning was only in the form of advice to government, even though the latter accepted the advice, Japanese monopoly laws were not violated.[60] The process, it may be noted, bears some resemblance to the original New Deal. Had something like the New Deal been initiated in the 1920s, or had the Japanese begun planning earlier, both overcapacity crises might have been averted. The Japanese plan also is a more open and systematic version of the largely concealed U.S. self-regulation of the post-World War II years.

Import quotas demonstrate that overcapacity is a multinational problem. When the laws associated with quotas include references to unfair trade practices, quotas act to regulate prices as well. Permanent quotas, even if subject to periodic changes, would enable many countries and industries to make long-term plans to build new capacity and retire old capacity. Ironically, many criticize U.S. firms for concentrating on short-term profits, but truly strategic planning is impossible in the absence of a regulatory scheme that includes all the firms in an industry—small wonder such planning is in decline.[61] It also should be kept in mind that there is no obvious reason to import large amounts of any commodity when cheaper labor is the only factor involved;

this is a misuse of the economic doctrine of comparative advantage. Steel is doubtless the most important example of how the U.S. may join with others in regulating steel output. When the President announced in 1984 that he would seek negotiated quotas, the bargaining promised to include at least those countries supplying steel to U.S. buyers: in addition to the European Economic Community, the list included Japan, Canada, South Korea, Brazil, Mexico, Spain, South Africa, Argentina, Taiwan, Venezuela, East Germany, Finland, Poland and Rumania.[62] If the range of political ideologies is broad, the domestic consensus should logically include the U.S. steel companies, labor unions and other groups. To avoid disjointed merger wars, steelmakers should be asked to develop a joint reorganization plan similar to the Japanese chemical plan.

When Japan concluded in 1981 that it must agree to restrict auto exports to the U.S., five other countries immediately negotiated similar agreements with Japan: Canada, West Germany, Belgium, Luxembourg and the Netherlands. Voluntary quotas among European industrial countries involve European film, tires, plates, forks, and innumerable other goods. Among U.S. industries now helped by import quotas are meat, shoes, radios, television, and, of course, textiles.[63] A good many of the agreements are bilateral, and all countries have had long experience in negotiating such agreements for, say, landing and passenger-boarding rights for international airline operations. As such agreements inevitably expand, it may become more obvious that the Soviet Union has as much interest in long-term industrial agreements as in similar guarantees of grain supplies. Ultimately, the issues become even broader: developing countries are seeking to earn foreign exchange so that they can repay their loans, but if they continually increase their exports to industrial countries, they will cause higher unemployment in those countries and diminish the ability of those countries to buy. The tough question of equity looms large, and it will not do to assume that demand is automatically infinite.

Because this paper focuses upon the major industries, no detailed schemes for re-regulation are outlined here. The direct involvement of government in regulating such industries as transportation, however, is difficult to avoid. These are public utilities; no firm can be permitted to cut off service to any community whenever the firm so decides. Joint planning which brings together government and the firms in each industry is just as necessary as in the case of Japanese chemical firms. The operating rule for transportation would reverse the wasteful rule of the regulated years; the objective is to minimize head-to-head competition on the same routes rather than maximizing duplication. While many consolidations will be needed, especially in trucking, there is no need at all for national monopolies. Once again, the banking industry is a special case.

The major question is when banking problems will be recognized as byproducts of overcapacity. When this relationship becomes clearer, it should be obvious that solutions for the banking crisis are inseparable from solutions for overcapacity in general. The latter can be systematically corrected only by acknowledging that many currently unrepayable loans never will be repaid. As many have suggested, the interest rates charged developing countries will have to be reduced; this re-regulation should logically trigger re-regulation in this country. In principle, interest rates should follow the inflation rate; what could possibly be wrong with pegging interest rates at the inflation rate so as to ensure no loss of purchasing power by depositors? While still other forms of re-regulation must emerge before the financial world is stabilized, this would be a desirable first step.

3. *New Technologies and Industries.* Unrestrained competition, innovation and continuous progress are often thought inseparable, but this belief is open to challenge. AT&T and its subsidiary, Bell Laboratories, were engines of innovation. Ideological articles of faith are often self-contradictory in even broader ways. If the U.S. truly believed that the Soviet Union cannot manage anything very well because its managers have never been subjected to free-market discipline, there would be little reason to worry about its military and space efforts. Too many Americans still believe that the Soviets never could have entered the nuclear era without deploying hordes of spies. In this country, the industrial self-regulation of the postwar period was not devoid of progress. The problems of new technologies and new industries, however, are a bit different.

Much of what is labeled "modernization" is unworthy of the name; tax laws make many technological advances appear to be more efficient than they are. A new factory may be designed to have a useful life of 40 years, but the costs of building it will be deducted from taxes in as little as 10 years. The builder of the new plant may well undersell competitors, but more because of the tax breaks than because of progress. The same tax laws make the human worker appear less efficient than he may be; his useful working life also may be 40 years, but the plant operator can deduct wages only one year at a time. It would seem ludicrous to deduct 40 years of wages in 10 years of tax returns, yet the cost of a robot that replaces the worker may be deducted in even fewer years. Because others must make up for the tax breaks of business, technological advance is often only a byproduct of extravagant and hidden subsidies. Meanwhile, the new plants compel only slightly older plants to close long before they are worn out. While economists label the process "creative destruction," it is grossly wasteful.

New inventions and industries are something else again, and the dysfunctional aspects of competition are becoming obvious. Intense price competition among small firms prevents any of them from engaging in serious research and development. There is a recognizable move toward collaborative forms of research that bring government together with oligopolistic firms. While the U.S. is moving less quickly than it might, collaborative research now justifies antitrust exemptions. Another economic contradiction may yet be exposed: competitively secret research retards progress by preventing researchers from sharing with each other what they learn, but classical economic and scientific principles hold that new information immediately spreads. Progress, therefore, is more likely to emerge from collaboration than from competition, and multilateral collaboration is preferable to national collaboration.

When an entirely new industry is involved, a tough question presents itself; examples can be used to illustrate its boundaries. Scores of auto companies sought footholds in the market of the 1920s for a revolutionary commodity, but the stability provided by three dominant firms and a smaller one here and there emerged only after a disastrous cycle of depression and war. As the U.S. entered the 1950s, on the other hand, the Columbia Broadcasting System and Radio Corporation of America presented incompatible technologies for the desirable innovation of color televisions; the CBS version would have required the attachment of a spinning three-colored disc to each television receiver. Acknowledging that standardization was necessary, government carefully studied the two systems before decreeing that the RCA system be adopted. Along with a need for standardization, there is need for an upper limit to the number of entrants in any new industry that promises to become truly important. Taken together, standardization and regulation suggest that full development and introduction of innovations into the market might better be delayed rather than accelerated as rapidly as possible, and that unrestricted entry must be prevented if the new industry is not to move overnight into an overcapacity crisis. Those who purchased video-disc players doubtless wish they had known that tapes soon would hold sway.

Computers may be the best example of all; the issues raised by progress in the industry encompass those mentioned earlier and others as well. Japan and the U.S. remain ahead in the competitive struggle for domination of the markets for "supercomputers" (the fastest at any stage of advance) and "fifth-generation computers" (based upon artificial intelligence). Because there has been no agreement to standardize up to now, many computer systems are "incompatible" with others; programs, equipment and information are not interchangeable. Incompatibility has damaged efficiency in government and elsewhere; different computer systems made a stumbling adventure of the Pennsylvania-New York Central railroad merger. The largest U.S. firm, IBM, dropped out of supercomputers years ago; while profits promised to be small, many believe that IBM feared antitrust action because it knew it could crush competitors. U.S. firms then designed machines incompatible with IBM equipment and programs, but Japanese supercomputers are fully compatible with the IBM system. U.S. buyers of supercomputers would prefer to build upon old IBM installations rather than having to begin all over again. Yet if IBM feels it must re-enter supercomputer competition, the antitrust problem will remain. There is little doubt that competition, which also includes the less advanced European and Soviet efforts, has delayed progress in basic research.[64] At the same time, either a Japanese or American "victory" will create disgruntled and economically depressed losers glutted with overcapacity. Collaboration would indeed bring new perils (involuntary sharing of state secrets, more efficient invasions of privacy), but might it be better to attack those problems than to accept the protracted economic struggles that have so often led to more violent confrontations? Stable oligopolies did not earlier come into being through orderly and naturally evolving market processes. In the future, they will have to be the byproducts of peaceful, not war-induced, regulation.

3. *Taxing and Other Industrial Policies.* Because too much, not too little, has been invested in industry, it is time to discourage, not encourage, limitless investment. Taking overcapacity into account, business tax breaks have reached the status of scandal; immediate rollbacks are in order. New depreciation schedules should accurately reflect the design life of plants and equipment. Retained profits that cannot be invested at home in the same industry should be taxed away as excess profits. Mergers within industries are needed (conglomerates should be broken up), but mergers should take the form of industry-wide reorganizations and tax revisions to eliminate the huge profits now generated by mergers that reduce capacity. One veteran merger warrior, the chairman of Seagram, argues that tax deductions should not be allowed on the money any firm borrows to buy another firm.[65]

Because stock markets are only lotteries, both dividends and capital gains reflect the luck of the winners, not their intelligence;[66] limits on the former and higher taxes on the latter are obviously desirable. Just as obviously, these proposals are out of step with most contemporary suggestions.

While those who seek tax revisions and even broader industrial policies do not agree on every detail, they often reach traditional conclusions in unusual ways. One noted economist acknowledges that investment rates were higher for some years in Japan and West Germany than in the U.S., because countries devastated by war felt they had to retard consumption in order to rebuild.[67] A second observer admits that "inadequate capital formation has not been the problem" in the U.S., the 11.7% rate for 1982 being the highest since 1928.[68] Yet the first concludes that the U.S. should "create incentives for investment . . . and accumulate the necessary funds for investment,"[69] and the second argues that "consumption taxes are necessary to encourage savings so that there is more money to invest."[70] The Bipartisan Budget Appeal—600 business leaders, economists, and university presidents formed by five former secretaries of the treasury and a former secretary of commerce—concurs; they "would prefer to place main reliance on broad-based consumption taxes, in order to avoid weakening incentives to work, save and invest."[71] Another group of business and education leaders adds that the U.S. must "meet the competitive challenge" and reverse the decline in the country's share of world export sales. They would appoint a "Presidential Advisor on Economic Competitiveness" whose task would be to help recapture the lost business.[72] Whatever the evidence, then, traditional principles dictate the recommendations. Those favoring yet more investment in new capacity seem unaware that intensified competition merely exports unemployment from country to country in ways that can be doubly self-defeating. If the U.S. uses consumption taxes to stimulate savings and investment (an idea borrowed from the countries devastated in World War II), less domestic purchasing power will be available to buy the output of the new or updated industries but, since expansion here will increase unemployment abroad, the number of overseas buyers also will decline.

The regulatory proposals outlined in this paper, on the other hand, could lead to a more openly collaborative version of the oligopolistic pattern of the postwar era. If Bork's hypothesis became an explicit norm, no U.S. firm could exceed a 50% share of the domestic market; this would allow for a reasonable amount of competition. With permanent and adjustable import quotas, multilateral collaboration could act to replace trade wars. Even as U.S. actions now reflect an almost inexorable movement toward collaboration, however, the accompanying rhetoric continues to glorify competition. Yet truly massive government-industry collaboration is inevitable in, for example, energy research and development. Indeed, multilateral collaboration would appear to be the only logical approach. These five proposals would only regularize the collaboration already underway, fleshing it out with compatible auxiliary policies. *Some* massive new investment in industry always is necessary, but regulation of private goods production also must involve other forms of investment, employment, and output.

During World War II, the unemployment rate in this country fell to 2%, indicating that citizens are ready to work when jobs are available; the experience also is a yardstick for measuring full employment. If the war brought prosperity, the same result could have been achieved years earlier by "crisscrossing the country with super-highways and building hospitals, schools and underground urban parking facilities."[73] That is a narrower approach to quality-of-life programs than this paper envisions, but it makes the point that this society and others were unable in the 1930s to fully understand the phenomenon of depression. Had much of the world discarded the dominant economic fallacies, the war could have been avoided. While Roosevelt instituted a modest effort in public works, only war seemed to justify all-out production of public goods, and even then, 25% of the labor force was in military service.

Recent assessments of infrastructure decay indicate why some observers refer to an *American in Ruins*:[74]

- 45% of 557,516 highway bridges are deficient or obsolete.
- The deterioration of a still incomplete interstate highway system already requires reconstruction of 2,000 miles per year, and there is a backlog of 8,000 miles.
- The rail system is in such a shambles that estimates of repair and renewal costs are beyond calculation.
- In 10 of 28 cities, leaking water systems lose 10% or more of what they carry, and two of the worst systems (New York, Boston) have yet to be surveyed.
- Half of the country's communities operate waste-water systems at full capacity, and many sewer systems are badly deteriorated.
- The Congressional Budget Office conservatively estimates that public works expenditures should be at least doubled.

The environment and other transportation modes also need large-scale attention. Those who criticize environmental regulations are victims of the old economic fallacies; they must try to reduce the costs of producing what they may not be able to sell. Transportation systems might usefully include giant "mega-projects" for the movement of indispensable resources (food, fuel, perhaps water); emergency food shipments to famine-stricken countries have in recent years languished at airports and seaports because there is no means of further delivery. Huge logistics networks, including offshore port complexes, might develop unbreakable linkages among the continents. Nor do possibilities end even there: instead of collecting taxes through the industrial pricing system to build unneeded factories and consummate high-cost mergers, why not put the same funds into vast improvements in all public goods? Many now attack school systems for permitting widespread deterioration; few advocate the hiring of many more teachers and a reduction in class sizes to 10 students or even less. Americans and others worry about having too many firefighters on duty; few worry about the waste associated with having too few.

Since Hoover and Franklin Roosevelt rejected economic principles in search of explanations for depression, a half-century of experience has provided striking contrasts that warrant even stronger rejection. As the "arsenal of democracy," this country produced military public goods in amounts that greatly exceeded World War II's demand for supply, wholly understandable in light of any war's unpredictable course. Even as unused output was thrown away, prosperity continued, although most recessions were followed by progressively weaker recoveries. As global competition gradually increased, liberal and conservative believers in economic theology constantly asked for more and more competition. Now that competition has reached new heights, the believers insist that only mismangement, not the overcapacity of excessive competition, is responsible for the social and economic waste of unemployed and underemployed plants and workers and for the political dangers of permanent poverty for many citizens and low wages for those who find jobs.[75] The believers even fear that any recovery that is "too fast" or "overheated" will make things worse by putting too many people to work. What the believers *prefer* appears to bring bad times; what they *dislike* appears to bring good times. One conclusion seems inescapable. If more is to be spent than is absolutely necessary, the least damaging forms of waste accompany the overproduction of public goods.

Notes

1. The *New York Times,* Dec. 9, 1931; Apr. 3, 1932.
2. Ibid., May 8, 1933.
3. Ibid., Oct. 29, 1933.
4. In May, 1935, Hoover condemned "Fascist regimentation." "The NRA," in his *Addresses Upon the American Road, 1933-1938.* New York: Charles Scribner's, 1938, pp. 45-47.
5. Approvingly quoted in Mark J. Green (ed.), *The Closed Enterprise System: Ralph Nader's Study Group Report on Antitrust Enforcement.* New York: Grossman, 1972, pp. 5-6.
6. Thomas J. Peters and Robert H. Waterman, Jr., *In Search of Excellence: Lessons From America's Best-Run Companies.* New York: Harper & Row, 1982, pp. 20-21.
7. A list of recent recessions compiled by the Bureau showed that the most recent one lasted from July, 1981 to November, 1982; beginning with 1929-33, there had been eleven recessions. The *New York Times,* July 9, 1983.
8. Lester C. Thurow, *Dangerous Currents: The State of Economics.* New York: Random House, 1983, p. xv. While Thurow adds that "Keynesianism rescued economics from that time of confusion," this article argues that it did not.
9. George Gilder, *Wealth and Poverty.* New York: Basic Books, 1981, pp. 31-35; Jude Wanniski, *The Way the World Works: How Economies Fail and Succeed.* New York: Basic Books, 1978, pp. 155-56.
10. John Kenneth Galbraith, *Economics and the Public Purpose.* Boston; Houghton Mifflin, 1973, pp. 21-22.
11. "I have no belief in the efficacy [for direct stimulus to production] of the price-and wage-raising activities" of the New Deal. Reprinted in The *New York Times,* Apr. 10, 1983. The New Deal combined price-and wage-raising with shorter working hours, hoping for an increase in production that would be gradual enough to avoid another crash. Arthur M. Schlesinger, Jr., *The Coming of the New Deal.* Boston: Houghton Mifflin, 1959, Parts I-II.
12. Karl Marx, "Wage-Labor and Capital," in his *Selected Writings, I,* quoted in Bertell Ollman, *Alienation: Marx's Conception of Man in Capitalist Society.* Cambridge: University Press, 1971, p. 100.
13. This rate presumably keeps increases in real wages at or below productivity increases, regardless of inflation. Using different language in each case, John Kennedy used a target of 4%; Lyndon Johnson, 4.5%; Gerald Ford, 5%; Jimmy Carter 6%; Reagan, 7%; Presidents, understandably, do not advertise a need for joblessness, but their economic reports so imply. Thurow, op. cit., p. 82.
14. E. K. Hunt and Howard J. Sherman, *Economics: An Introduction to Traditional and Radical Views.* New York: Harper & Row, 1972, p. 438.
15. Robert A. Mundell, *Man and Economics.* New York: McGraw-Hill, 1968, p. 7.
16. *Can Regulatory Agencies Protect Consumers?* Washington: American Enterprise Institute for Public Policy Research, 1971, Ch. 1.
17. Harold U. Faulkner, *Politics, Reform and Expansion: 1890-1900.* New York: Harper & Brothers, 1959, p. 145.
18. Goronwy Rees, *The Great Slump: Capitalism in Crisis, 1929-1933.* New York: Harper & Row, 1970, pp. 85-86.
19. Celebrating its own centennial, one newspaper quoted from its front-

page story of Aug. 9, 1930. The *Pittsburgh Press,* Oct. 9, 1984.
20. J. A. Hobson, *Imperialism: A Study.* London: George Allen & Unwin, 3rd ed., 1938, pp. 74-85.
21. Ibid., *Poverty in Plenty.* London: George Allen & Unwin, 1931, p. 65.
22. Hunt and Sherman, op. cit., p. 128.
23. J. Fred Weston, *Mergers and Economic Efficiency.* Washington: U.S. Government Printing Office, 1981, Ch. 2.
24. Ross M. Robertson, *History of the American Economy.* New York: Harcourt, Brace, 1955, p. 562.
25. Ibid., p. 390.
26. Murray R. Benedict, *Farm Policies of the United States, 1790-1950.* New York: Twentieth Century Fund, 1963, p. 277; Harry N. Scheiber, Harold G. Vatter, Harold Underwood Faulkner, *American Economic History.* New York: Harper & Row, 1976, p. 378.
27. John Kenneth Galbraith, *The Great Crash.* Boston: Houghton Mifflin, 3d ed., 1972, pp. 179-80.
28. Robertson, Op. cit., p. 558.
29. The *New York Times,* Aug. 8, 1931.
30. Ibid., Jan. 25, 1932.
31. Ibid., Dec. 8, 1932.
32. Ibid., Aug. 17, Dec. 18, 1932.
33. Ibid., Dec. 9, 1931; Sep. 18, 1932; Sep. 19, 1932.
34. Many examples could be listed. Thurow summarizes by using the hypothetical example of steel executives who "have learned via the unsuccessful conglomerate movement that they could not run a successful cosmetics firm." Lester C. Thurow, *The Zero-Sum Society: Distribution and the Possibilities for Economic Change.* New York: Penguin Books Edition, 1981, p. 175.
35. The *Wall Street Journal,* May 18, 1984.
36. Steven Greenhouse, "A World Steel Pact is Debated," The *New York Times,* Jan. 13, 1984.
37. The *Washington Post,* Mar. 17, 1984.
38. The *New York Times,* Oct. 9, 1984.
39. Demand is projected to be 467 million tons in 1995, and current capacity is 640 million tons. The chairman of the American Iron and Steel Institute would build no new capacity anywhere for at least a decade. The *New York Times,* Oct. 11, 1984.
40. Ibid., Oct. 20, 1984.
41. Statement by Representative Fernand J. St. Germain, in U.S. Congress, House of Representatives, Committee on Banking, Finance and Urban Affairs, *Financial Deregulation,* Hearings before Committee, 98th Congress, 2nd Session (Washington: Government Printing Office, Serial 98-83, 1984), p. 1105.
42. "Banking on Mexico—Badly," The *New York Times,* Aug. 24, 1982.
43. John S. McGee, *In Defense of Industrial Concentration.* New York: Praeger, 1971, Ch. 8.
44. John Kenneth Galbraith, *The New Industrial State.* Boston: Houghton Mifflin, 2d ed., 1971, p. 180.
45. Ibid., p. 184.
46. Ibid., pp. 358-60.
47. Robertson, op. cit., pp. 497-98.

48. Ed Cray, *Chrome Colossus: General Motors and Its Times*. New York: McGraw-Hill, 1980, pp. 385-94, 445-47.
49. The *New York Times*, Jan. 25, 1972.
50. Robert H. Bork, *The Antitrust Paradox: A Policy at War With Itself*. New York: Basic Books, 1979, pp. 3-4, 197.
51. John M. Blair, *Economic Concentration: Structure, Behavior and Public Policy*. New York: Harcourt, Brace, Jovanovich, 1972, pp. 576-80; John G. Fuller, *The Gentleman Conspirators: The Story of the Price-Fixers in the Electrical Industry*. New York: Grove Press, 1962; "Collusion Among Electrical Equipment Manufacturers," The *Wall Street Journal*, Jan. 10, 12, 1962, reprinted in Edwin Mansfield, *Monopoly Power and Economic Performance: The Problem of Industrial Concentration*. New York: Norton, 1968, pp. 89-95. Only the last source included the perspectives of the executives.
52. A lengthier version of the argument, including a number of examples, is in my "Regulation Is Inevitable: Legal Planning or Illegal Collusion?", The *American University Law Review* 32 (Winter 1983), 425-53.
53. Evidence indicates that in the absence of permanent import quotas, U.S. automakers will build more plants overseas. Maxwell Newton, "Auto import pact is critical," *The New York Post*, May 29, 1984. IBM soon will make personal computers in Mexico. The *New York Times*, Oct. 26, 1984.
54. Charles L. Schultze, *National Income Analysis*. Englewood Cliffs, New Jersey: Prentice-Hall, 1964, p. 28.
55. One careful study concludes that "most types of government spending generate more jobs than private spending." For 1980, each $1 billion of nondefense government spending created about 50,000 jobs; $1 billion of defense spending created 30,000 civilian jobs and 16,000 military jobs; but $1 billion in private spending created only 30,000 jobs. The author seemed surprised at how "rarely" the ripple effects of government spending are even discussed. Russell W. Rumberger, *The Employment Impact of Government Spending*. Stanford University Institute for Research on Educational Finance and Governance, 1983, pp. 9, 11, and Table 6. Economic principles, of course, dictate that such evidence should be ignored.
56. Data compiled from yearly volumes of the *Statistical Abstract of the United States*, and from Robert Ortner, "The Deficit Problem is Exaggerated," The *New York Times*, Oct. 19, 1984. A combined table is in my *Rebuilding America: The Case for Economic Regulation*. New York: Praeger, 1984, p. 128.
57. Data provided by the staff of the President's Council of Economic Advisers, who stated they never before had compiled wartime deficit percentages. Telephone calls in May, 1984.
58. Albert T. Sommers, "The Federal Deficit Should be Rebuilt From the Ground Up," *Across the Board*. New York: The Conference Board, May, 1981, p. 19.
59. Alan S. Blinder, "Vaudeville on the Potomac," *Washington Post*, Aug. 27, 1982.
60. The *New York Times*, May 18, 1983.
61. A cover story noting many failures in strategic planning generally blamed them on "ivory tower" thinkers, but case-by-case analysis indicated that overcapacity was the problem. "The New Breed of Strategic Planner: Number-Crunching Professionals Are Giving Way to Line Managers." *Business Week*, Sep. 17, 1984, 62-68.

62. "Fact Sheet," Bethlehem Steel Public Affairs Department, Oct. 3, 1984, 6 pp.
63. The *New York Times,* Oct. 15, 1984.
64. Ibid., Oct. 23, 1984. Also see note 52.
65. Edgar M. Bronfman, "End the Tax Subsidies for Corporate Mergers," Ibid., Sep. 29, 1982.
66. Thurow, *Zero-Sum Society,* p. 175.
67. Ibid., p. 79.
68. Robert B. Reich, *The Next American Frontier.* New York: Times Books, 1983, p. 120.
69. Thurow, *Zero-Sum Society,* p. 97.
70. Reich, op. cit., p. 242.
71. The *New York Times,* May 4, 1984 (emphasis in original full-page statement by the group).
72. *America's Competitive Challenge.* A Report to the President of the United States from the Business-Higher Education Forum. Washington: 1983, Foreword and Ch. 1.
73. Robertson, op. cit., pp. 565-66.
74. Pat Choate and Susan Walter, *America in Ruins: The Decaying Infrastructure.* Durham: Duke University Press, 1983. While the book advocates large-scale programs, those envisioned in this article would be much larger. Other data from The *New York Times,* Jan. 4, 1982, Jul. 18, 1982, May 9, 1983.
75. Many of the lost jobs paid middle-income wages; new jobs, including those in high-tech industries, pay much lower wages. This is the conclusion of a study by Barry Bluestone and Bennett Harrison. *Washington Post,* May 18, 1984. Some dispute the conclusions, but the concessions exacted from many unions, and the court-approved termination of labor contracts so that workers can be rehired at lower wages, are obvious trends. Indeed, many economists argue that wages have been too high.

Note: A little-noticed but important relationship is not explored here in detail. Intensive competition compels producers to violate the social regulations that protect consumers, workers, and the environment. Economic regulation, then, is a prerequisite for effective social regulation.

World Future Society Publications

Cornish, Edward, ed. *The Future: A Guide to Information Sources.* Revised 2nd edition. Washington, D.C.: World Future Society. 1979. 722 pages. Paperback. $25.00. The revised and expanded second edition of this indispensable guide to the futures field contains even more information than the highly-praised first edition.

Cornish, Edward, ed. *1999: The World of Tomorrow.* Washington, D.C.: World Future Society. 1978. 160 pages. Paperback. $4.95. This first anthology of articles from THE FUTURIST is divided into four sections: "The Future as History," "The Future as Progress," "The Future as Challenge," and "The Future as Invention."

Cornish, Edward. *The Study of the Future: An Introduction to the Art and Science of Understanding and Shaping Tomorrow's World.* Washington, D.C.: World Future Society. 1977. 320 pages. Paperback. $9.50. A general introduction to futurism and future studies. Chapters discuss the history of the futurist movement, ways to introduce future-oriented thinking into organizations, the philosophical assumptions underlying studies of the future, methods of forecasting, current thinking about what may happen as a result of the current revolutionary changes in human society, etc. The volume also includes detailed descriptions of the lives and thinking of certain prominent futurists and an annotated guide to further reading.

Didsbury, Howard F., ed. *Student Handbook for The Study of the Future.* Washington, D.C.: World Future Society. 1979. 180 pages. Paperback. $5.95. This supplement to *The Study of the Future* is designed to help students develop a basic understanding of the field of futuristics. Much of the material has been "classroom-tested" by students in futures courses at Kean College of New Jersey.

Didsbury, Howard F., ed. *Instructor's Manual for The Study of the Future.* Washington, D.C.: World Future Society. 1979. 24 pages. Paperback. $2.00. A brief complementary volume to the *Student Handbook for The Study of the Future*, containing course outlines, research suggestions, teaching aids, bibliographical additions, and more.

Feather, Frank, ed. *Through the '80s: Thinking Globally, Acting Locally.* Washington, D.C.: World Future Society. 1980. 446 pages. Paperback. $12.50. Prepared in conjunction with the First Global Conference on the Future, held in Toronto, Canada, July 20-24, 1980. Subjects covered include the inventory of resources, economics, human values, communications, education, and health.

Jennings, Lane, and Sally Cornish, eds. *Education and the Future.* Washington, D.C.: World Future Society. 1980. 120 pages. Paperback. $4.95. Contains selections from THE FUTURIST and the *World Future Society Bulletin* on the future of education. Packed with ideas for the classroom.

Kierstead, Fred, Jim Bowman, and Christopher Dede, eds. *Educational Futures Sourcebook.* Washington, D.C.: World Future Society. 1979. 254 pages. Paperback. $5.95. This book contains selected papers from the first conference of the Education Section of the World Future Society, held in Houston, Texas, in October 1978.

Marien, Michael, ed. *Future Survey Annual 1980-81: A Guide to the Recent Literature of Trends, Forecasts, and Policy Proposals.* Washington, D.C.: World Future Society. 1981. 290 pages. Paperback. $25.00. Abstracts of about 1,500 books, reports, and articles divided into 15 sections: World Futures, International Economics, World Regions and Nations, Defense and Disarmament, Energy, Food and Agriculture, Environment and Resources, General Societal Directions, The Economy, Cities, Crime and Justice, Education, Health, Science and Technology, and Government. Future Survey Annual 1979 (255 pages, $25.00) is also still available.

Martin, Marie. *Films on the Future.* Washington, D.C.: World Future Society. 1977. 70 pages. Paperback. $3.00. This is the third revised and expanded version of the film guide first produced in 1971. The films are grouped by major subject areas (Education, Technology, etc.). A brief description of each film is supplemented by information about length, source, and rental costs.

Redd, Kathleen M., and Arthur M. Harkins, eds. *Education: A Time For Decisions.* Washington, D.C.: World Future Society. 1980. 301 pages. Paperback. $6.95. Selections from the Second Annual Conference of the Education Section of the World Future Society, arranged in four sections: Policies and Plans for the Present and the Future, Issues and Challenges for the Present and the Future, Theory and Visions for the Present and the Future, and Action and Examples for the Present and the Future.

FUTURE SURVEY Saves You Time and Money

- **On Target.** FUTURE SURVEY gets right to the point, with brief, accurate, and readable abstracts that capture the essence of important new literature.

- **Breadth.** FUTURE SURVEY goes where the good ideas are, crossing the barrier between books, journals, newspapers, and reports, and between the different academic disciplines, professions, and worldviews.

- **Selects the Best Ideas.** New ideas, updated ideas, practical ideas, outrageous but interesting ideas—FUTURE SURVEY selects the most important thinking in every problem/possibility area.

- **Idea Networks.** FUTURE SURVEY arranges our intellectual wealth in clusters so you can see different views and how ideas are interconnected. FUTURE SURVEY ANNUAL (distributed as a part of each subscription) offers additional help in understanding idea connections by arranging items into an action-oriented taxonomy of 17 major categories and more than 75 sub-categories.

- **Five-Way Access.** Pick up FUTURE SURVEY and read it straight through, cover to cover. Or check the subject and author indexes in each monthly issue. Or consult the "Highlights" box on the front page, where 10 or so of the most important and/or original items are featured. Or skim the alternative headlines at the end of each abstract, which underscore key words and phrases. Or consult the ANNUAL, which provides a handy consolidation of abstracts and a comprehensive index.

- **Low Cost/High Benefit.** A subscription to FUTURE SURVEY—12 monthly issues—costs only $45 per year for individuals ($65 for institutions). Along with this, FUTURE SURVEY ANNUAL—a $25 value—is distributed to all subscribers.

- **Receive a Free Issue for Subscribing.** Sign up for a one-year subscription and receive a complimentary copy of FUTURE SURVEY. If you're not completely satisfied with the free issue, write "cancel" across your bill and return it. The issue is yours to keep, with no obligation. If you pay in advance—in cash, money order, or using your American Express, Visa, or MasterCard—you'll receive two free issues, and, if less than 100% pleased, you can receive a full refund at any time.

Send your order to:

World Future Society
4916 St. Elmo Avenue
Bethesda, Maryland 20814

THE COMPUTERIZED SOCIETY
Living and Working in an Electronic Age
Edited by Edward Cornish

New! From the FUTURIST LIBRARY

This anthology of articles selected from THE FUTURIST explores the impacts that computers will have in such areas as work and careers, education, lifestyles, business, and government. Will books become obsolete? Could computer networks produce hyperintelligence? What will it be like to live in a computerized house?

Catalog number B-969
Price $6.95 paperback

Contents

WORKING
Technology and Changing World of Work
  by Fred Best
Eight Scenarios for Work in the Future
  by Martin Morf
CAREER PLANNING
Getting Ready for the Jobs of the Future
  by Marvin J. Cetron
Emerging Careers: Occupations for a Post-Industrial Society
  by S. Norman Feingold
New Choices: Career Planning in a Changing World
  by David C. Borchard
EDUCATION
The Changing University: Survival in the Information Society
  by Samuel L. Dunn
Why Books Will Survive
  by Lane Jennings
The Future of Sex Education: Computerizing the Facts of Life
  by Parker Rossman
LIFESTYLES
A Day at Xanadu: Family Life in Tomorrow's Computerized Home
  by Roy Mason and Lane Jennings

Telecommuters: The Stay-at-Home Work Force
  by Peter Eder
Computer Chess: Can Machine Beat Man at His Own Game?
  by Lane Jennings
BUSINESS AND GOVERNMENT
Networking by Computer
  by C. Jackson Grayson, Jr.
The Electonic Investment System: Making Money with Your Computer
  by Grant J. Renier
Retooling American Democracy
  by Jim Rubens
TECHNOLOGY
Robots and the Economy
  by James S. Albus
Cellular Radio: First Step in the Personal Communications Revolution
  by Stuart J. Crump, Jr.
Maps of the Future
  by Hollis Vail
FUTURE IMPLICATIONS
A Global Information Utility
  by Robert S. Block

And more!

Take an Active Part in Building Tomorrow . . . Today
Join the World Future Society

Join the 25,000 people from all over the world who want to make sense out of today's rapidly changing world. The World Future Society is unique. Since its founding in 1966, the Society has served as a neutral clearinghouse for people at the forefront of social and technological change. Through local chapters, seminars and conferences, and its many publications, the Society reaches out to those who want to explore the alternatives for tomorrow.

As a member of the World Future Society, you will receive:

THE FUTURIST
—The Society's bimonthly magazine of forecasts, trends, and ideas about the future. The latest in technological developments, trend tidbits, interviews, and in-depth articles give members a comprehensive look into tomorrow.

NEWSLINE
—An occasional newsletter exclusively for members of the World Future Society, NEWSLINE keeps members up-to-date on Society activities and reports on other items of interest, such as regional conferences.

RESOURCE CATALOG
—A twice-yearly guide to the hundreds of books, cassette tapes, and other materials carried by the Society bookstore. Members also receive discounts on these products.

CONFERENCES
—Special rates at all assemblies and conferences. The Society sponsors and organizes meetings to bring together futurists from around the world. Some 3,000 people attended the Fifth General Assembly in Washington, D.C., in June 1984.

LOCAL CHAPTERS
—Access to your local chapter. Over 100 cities in the United States and abroad have chapters for grass-roots support for future studies.

Take a part in building tomorrow. Send your check or money order for $25 for the first year's dues. You'll receive a one-year (six bimonthly issues) subscription to THE FUTURIST, the twice-yearly RESOURCE CATALOG and discounts from the Society bookstore, the occasional NEWSLINE, and special invitations and rates for meetings sponsored by the World Future Society. You may also join the local chapter in your area.

Send your order to:
World Future Society
4916 St. Elmo Avenue
Bethesda, Maryland 20814